ALSO BY JORGE AMADO

Dona Flor and Her Two Husbands
1969

Shepherds of the Night
1967

The Two Deaths of Quincas Wateryell
1965

The Violent Land
1945; 1965

Home Is the Sailor
1964

Gabriela, Clove and Cinnamon
1962

These are Borzoi Books, published in New York
by Alfred A. Knopf

TENT OF MIRACLES

JORGE AMADO

Tent of Miracles

Translated from the Portuguese by Barbara Shelby

Alfred A. Knopf   New York   1971

WITHDRAWN

For

ZÉLIA,

rose and magic spell.

While I was writing this book
I often thought of
Professor Martiniano Eliseu do Bonfim, Ajimuda,
now deceased—wise man, babalaô, *and friend.*
Let his name be remembered here,
with those of Dulce and Miécio Táti,
Nair and Genaro de Carvalho, Waldeloir Rego
and Emanoel Araújo, axé

Thus thou art, Bahia,
and such the things that happen in thy streets.
GREGÓRIO DE MATOS

Brazil has two real claims to greatness:
the richness of its soil and the sharp wits of its mestizos.
MANUEL QUERINO
(*"The black settler's contribution to Brazilian civilization"*)

They fall back, then, on an outrageous but fashionable solution:
they make him into something he is not. They fashion of him a
big, docile, institutionalized robot. A machine which suits our
times, a perfect reflection of a system which is dead or the one
about to take its place. It will resemble Gregório de Matos but
will be far more genteel and handsome. And this simulacrum
will be given out to school children and college students, sold
at bookstores and newspaper kiosks. All the propaganda ma-
chinery of the schools and government agencies will be used to
implant this false image in the minds of children and adults
alike, with the same efficiency in selling half truth that is used
to sell any other commodity.

These clever men should bear in mind that in fact our Poet
chose neither justice nor injustice, neither fame nor anonymity;
he never retreated to a hermit's sanctuary, never took refuge in
the countryside he longed for with such nostalgia. Gregório de
Matos did not abstain from action; he did not choose the con-
templative life over one of commitment. He lived the life his
own poems taught him to live, a life of human love and free-
dom far exceeding the common measure.

And this is the image here presented in all its purity—or
impurity, if the reader wills.
JAMES AMADO
(*"The photograph forbidden for 300 years"*—
marginal notes to the editor's version of the text of the
COMPLETE WORKS OF GREGÓRIO DE MATOS)

Mulatto, indigent, native of Bahia;

always the know-it-all, wise guy,

and life of the party

(from a police report on Pedro Archanjo, in 1926)

A iaba's *a she-devil without a tail.*

CARYBÉ

(Iaba, *film script*)

TENT OF MIRACLES

In the neighborhood of Pelourinho in the heart of Bahia, the whole world teaches and learns. A vast university branches out into Tabuão, the Carmo Gates, and Santo-Antônio-Beyond-Carmo, into Shoemakers' Hollow, the markets, Maciel, Lapinha, Cathedral Square, Tororó, Barroquinha, Sete Portas, and Rio Vermelho, wherever there are men and women who work. And from the working of metal and wood, the blending of medicines from herbs and roots, and the cadence of quick-blooded rhythms, is created a fresh, original image of novel colors and sounds.

Listen to the wood and leather drums, the twanging bow, the beaded gourds and rattles, the tambourines and coconuts, the metal bells and gongs, atabaque, berimbau, ganzá, adufe, caxixí, agogô: musical instruments of the poor, rich in melody and rhythm. Music and dance were born on the common man's campus:

Camaradinho ê
Camaradinho, camará.

Next door to the Slaves' Church of Our Lady of the Rosary, on a second floor with five windows opening out into Pelourinho, Master Budião set up his Angola Capoeira Academy. His pupils begin to arrive in the late afternoon and early evening, weary from the day's *work but still ready for fun. The taut wiry twanging of the* berimbau *sets the pace for the feints and lunges, each more terrible than the last: half-moon, slash, triphammer, headstand, whiplash, leg-kick, belly-kick, clamshell, hammerchop, and the crouching trip. The young men wrestle to the twang of the* berimbaus *as these signal the mad geography of the blows: Great São Bento, Little São Bento, Santa Maria, Cavalaria, Amazonas, Angola, Double Angola, Little Angola, Pick the Orange off the Ground, Iúna, Samongo, Cinco Salomão—and more others than you can count. Angola* capoeira *has changed and developed at this college: it's a ballet now, though a battle still.*

It's unbelievable how Master Budião can skip around at his age. Was anyone ever so skillful, so nimble, so light on his feet? Watch him jump back or to the side; no adversary can touch him. All the great masters of capoeira *have demonstrated their courage and competence, proved how much they knew in this room: God Loves Him, Captain Ketch, Chico da Barra, Tony the Tide, Big Zacaria, Piroca Peixoto, Seven Ways to Die, Silk Mustache, Man of Peace from Rio Vermelho, Pretty Head of Hair, Vicente Pastinha, My Strength Is as the Strength of Twelve, Tiburcinho from Jaguaribe, Give It to Me Chico, Nô from the Factory, and Barroquinha:*

> *Who taught you that trick, kid?*
> *It was Barroquinha taught me.*
> *He hadn't grown a beard but was fast with a knife,*
> *Carved up the cops and spared a poor man's life.*

Came the choreographers and found the ballet steps there, ready-made. Came the composers—all kinds, good, bad, and indifferent—and found more than enough inspiration to go around. Here at the Pelourinho campus of our free university, the people create works of art. Far into the night the students sing:

> *Ai, ai, Aidê*
> *You got a good game going and I'd like to play*
> *Ai, ai, Aidê.*

Professors are to be found in every house, every store, every workshop. In an inner patio of the building that houses Budião's Academy, the Sirens meet to rehearse for the parade and festival of the Sons of Bahia under the direction of young Valdeloir, a cracker-jack when it comes to street plays and carnival frolics. He knows everything there is to know about capoeira, *including some inventions of his own which he added when he opened his own school in Tororó.*

The samba circle meets in the big courtyard on Saturdays and Sundays, and that's when black Ajaiy loves to show off. He has a rival for the post of Afoxé Ambassador in the person of Lídio Corró, but when it comes to samba he rules supreme as band leader and chief choreographer. He sets the rhythm and he charts the steps.

Then there are the miracle painters, artists who work in oils, or crayon, or a powdered paint mixed with thin glue. Whenever anyone makes a promise to Our Lord of Bonfim or Our Lady of Candlemas or some other saint, and his prayer is granted, he always comes to the miracle painters' shops to order a picture to hang in the church as a sign of gratitude. Some of these self-taught artists are João Duarte da Silva, Master Licídio Lopes, Master Queiroz, Agripiniano Barros, and Raimundo Fraga. Master Licídio makes woodcuts, too, and designs handbills and flyers.

Street singers, guitarists, and improvisers sell romance and poetry for a few pennies in this free territory, as do the composers of little leaflets hand-printed on Master Lídio Corró's printing press or in some other ill-equipped little shop.

These men are poets, pamphleteers, historians, chroniclers, and moralists. They report and comment on life in the city, setting to rhyme both real events and the equally astonishing stories they make up themselves: "The Virgin of Barbalho Who Stuck a Banana up Her . . ." or "Princess Maricruz and the Flying Knight." They offer protest and criticism, moral lessons and entertainment, and every so often they father a surprisingly good piece of verse.

In Agnaldo's workshop the fine hardwoods—rosewood, Brazil

wood, mahogany, peroba, putumujú, massaranduba—*are transformed into vehicles for Xangô the Thunderer, the spirits of water, the Oxuns, the sea mother Yemanjá, and the Indian spirits—Pathfinder, Triple Star, and Seven Swords, who carries the glittering blades in his powerful hands. Agnaldo's own hands are powerful even though his heart is failing, for he has been fatally stricken by Chagas's disease, which in those days did not even have a name but simply meant slow, certain death. His tireless hands form African gods and caboclo spirits that have something mysterious about them, no one quite knows what, as if Agnaldo, himself so close to death, breathed into each a kind of immortality. They are disquieting figures, reminiscent at once of legendary beings and ordinary men. Once a* pai-de-santo, *a witch doctor from Marogogipe, ordered a huge wooden statue of Oxóssi the hunter and brought the trunk of a jacktree to carve it from. It took six men to carry the tree. Agnaldo, mortally sick and gasping for breath, smiled when he saw it; he loved to work an enormous piece of wood like that. As he carved the trunk with ineffable delight, he gave Oxóssi a rifle to hold instead of a bow and arrow. It was a different kind of Oxóssi: still the king of Ketu and the lord of the forest, of course, but with a strong resemblance to Lucas da Feira, the bandit from the backlands, or a rough-and-ready* cangaceiro *like Beetle Goldencord:*

> *Just before old Beetle died*
> *He spoke right up and he said*
> *"Don't let nobody push you around, sonny boy,*
> *If you want to take after your Dad."*

That's how Agnaldo saw Oxóssi and that's the way he carved him, with a fishknife and a rifle and a cangaceiro *star on the brim of his leather hat. But the* pai-de-santo *refused to accept the profane image, and Oxóssi stayed behind to guard the shop for many months until a traveling Frenchman stopped in one day and offered good money for him. They say Oxóssi ended up in a museum in Paris, but then, they tell a lot of tales in the no man's land around Pelourinho.*

In the hands of a frail, almost white mulatto named Mário Proença, tinplate, zinc, and copper are beaten into swords for Ogun the Warrior, fans for Yemanjá, the round metal symbol of Oxun which is both fan and musical instrument, and fly whisks for Oxalá, the greatest god of all. The sign of Proença's workshop is a huge Yemanjá in copper: TENT OF THE MOTHER OF WATERS.

Dour, fierce, and pock-marked Master Manú, a man of few words and difficult temperament, forges Exú's trident, Ogun's many iron weapons, Oxóssi's taut bow, and the cobra of Oxumarê, the rainbow god. Like their emblems, the divinities—the orixás *—are born of the fire and Manú's violence.*

Sculpture is born from the creative hands of these unlettered men.

At his stand by the Carmo Gates, Master Didi works with beads and straw, horsetails and leather, to create and create again the reed flail of Omolú and all the other emblems—the ebirís, adês, eruexins, erukerês, xaxarás. *Next to him is Deodoro, a mulatto with a strident laugh who specializes in making the wooden drums of every African nation—Nagô, Gêge, Angola, Congo—and the smaller drum, the* ilu, *of the Ijexá. He makes metal instruments and beaded rattles, too, but Manú's agogô bells are the best.*

In a doorway on the Rua do Liceu, Miguel the saint-carver pours forth a stream of gay and voluble chatter as he fashions angels, arch-angels, and saints. Catholic saints and churchly devotion, the Virgin of the Conception and St. Anthony of Lisbon, Archangel Gabriel and the Baby Jesus—how is it they are found so close to Master Agnaldo's orixás? The only thing the Vatican elect and the voodoo and caboclo gods have in common is their mixed blood. If Agnaldo's Oxóssi is a backlands gunman, so is the saint-carver's St. George. His helmet looks more like a leather hat, and his dragon might be a cross between a crocodile and the fabulous monster in the Christmas pageant of the Three Kings.

Once in a while, when he has time on his hands and feels the urge, Miguel carves a nude, voluptuous Negress just for the fun of it and gives her to a friend. One of these statues was the spitting image of black Dorotéia: the high breasts, the indomitable derrière, the flowering belly, and the rounded feet. And who but Pedro Archanjo was good enough to own her? Miguel never was able to carve a statue of Rosa de Oxalá, though. He couldn't "get the feel of her," as he put it.

Gold- and silversmiths work the noble metals. Silver and copper take on an austere beauty when fashioned into fruit, fish, or amulets —the figas and balangandans; and in the Largo da Sé and the Baixa dos Sapateiros, gold turns to necklaces and bracelets at the goldsmith's touch. The most famous of these was Lúcio Reis, whose father, a Portuguese expert, had taught him well. But Lúcio neglected the Lusitanian filigrees and instead made cashew fruits, pineapples, Brazil cherries, sugar apples, and figas of all sizes. From black Predileta, his mother, he inherited a taste for inventing things; and the earrings, brooches, and rings he invented are worth fortunes in antique shops today.

In the palm-leaf sheds, cola nuts and magical ritual seeds add their strength to ordinary medicine. Dona Adelaide Tostes, with her foul mouth and infinite capacity for guzzling cachaça, knows the destructive power of each seed and leaf and the curative qualities of roots, barks, plants, and grasses: alum for the liver, verbena to calm the nerves, sticky sedge for hangover, breakstone for the kidneys, holy grass for stomach ache, goat's-beard sedge to raise the spirits and the prick. Dona Filomena is another expert: if you ask her nicely and pay her well, she will render your body immune against the evil eye, and she never fails to cure a chronic cold or chest pains with a dose of wormseed goosefoot, honey, milk, lemon, and God alone knows what else. No cough, not even the most convulsive whoop, can hold out against it. A doctor who had learned a recipe for purifying the blood from Dona Filomena moved to São Paulo and got rich curing syphilis.

The Tent of Miracles, Ladeira do Tabuão No. 60, is the main building of this popular university. There's Master Lídio Corró painting miracles, casting magic shadows, cutting rough engravings in wood; there's Pedro Archanjo, who might be called the chancellor of the university himself. Bent over the old worn-out type and temperamental printing press in the ancient, poorly furnished shop, the two men are setting type for a book about life in Bahia.

Not far away on the Terreiro de Jesus is the School of Medicine, where students learn other cures for illness and other ways to care for the sick. And they learn other things as well—bad rhetoric, and how to spout sonnets, and theories of dubious value.

Of how Fausto Pena,

a poet with a B.A.

in social science, was

entrusted with a mission

and carried it out

In the pages that follow the reader will find the results of my researches into the life and works of Pedro Archanjo. The job was entrusted to me by the great James D. Levenson, and paid for in dollars.

First of all there are a few points that ought to be cleared up, since the whole affair was a comedy of errors from beginning to end. Looking over my notes, I can hardly deny the evidence: too much of the nonsensical foolishness remains, and the whole story is confused and obscure in spite of my best efforts, which were enormous and unstinting, believe it or not.

When I speak of doubts and uncertainties, vagueness and lies, I am not referring merely to the life of our author, Pedro Archanjo of Bahia, but also to the sum total of the facts in all their complexity: from events of the distant past to contemporary incidents, including Levenson's sensational interview; from the monumental binge on Pedro Archanjo's fiftieth birthday to the closing night of the centennial. As for reconstructing Pedro Archanjo's life, that was never my intention and I was not, in fact, asked to do so by the Columbia savant, whose interest lay only in Archanjo's research methods and the kind of working conditions capable of engendering and fostering such lively, original work. All Levenson asked me to do was to collect data which would give him insight into Archanjo's character and personality, since he planned to write a few pages about him as an introduction to the English translation of his works.

It was not only minor details of Archanjo's life that eluded me but important, and in some cases vital, facts. I frequently found myself up against a blank wall, a vacuum in time and space, or face to face with unexplained events, multiple versions of the same story, absurd interpretations, a total lack of order in the material I was able to gather, contradictory information and informers. I was never able to find out, for example, whether the Negress Rosa de Oxalá was the same person as the mulatto girl Risoleta, whose ancestors came from Mali, or as Dorotéia, the woman who had a pact with the devil. There were those who thought she was personified in Rosenda Batista dos Reis from Muritiba, while others attributed her story to the comely Sabina dos Anjos, "loveliest of all the angels," in the gallant words of Master Archanjo. Confound her, I said to myself, was she only one woman or several? I gave up trying to find out, and I'm sure no one else knows any more than I do.

I must admit that I became so exasperated by that clutter of contradictory accounts that I gave up trying to bring definitive revelations to light. It always came back to "maybe so," "could be," "if it wasn't this way it must have been that way"—absolutely no consistency, no certainty. They attributed so many exploits to him, it was as if the people I talked to didn't have their feet on the ground, as if they saw the deceased not as a creature of flesh and blood but as a whole cohort of heroes and magicians. I never was able to fix the line between reality and fantasy, fact and invention.

As for his books, I read them all from beginning to end. It was not much of a task, really—only four little books, the longest of them less than two hundred pages. (A São Paulo editor has just published three of them in one volume, omitting the cookbook because its specialized nature will appeal to a larger public.) I will not venture an opinion on Archanjo's work, which is now above criticism or quibbles. No one would dare to deny its value, now that it has been consecrated by the great Levenson and translated into several languages. It seems to have been well received everywhere. Only yesterday I read a cable in the newspaper: "Archanjo published in Moscow and praised by *Pravda*."

The most I can do is add my praise to the universal chorus. I will say I found the books pleasant reading: many of the things Archanjo refers to are a part of daily life in Bahia even today. I was most amused by the next-to-the-last book (he was about to publish another when he died), the book that brought so much trouble down on his head. Now, when I hear certain acquaintances of mine bragging about their blue blood, family trees and escutcheons, noble ancestry and other such nonsense, I just ask them what their family name is and then look it up on Archanjo's list. He was so serious, so painstaking, such an ardent seeker after truth.

I have not yet explained how I made the acquaintance of the North American scholar and how he happened to honor me with this task. James D. Levenson's name speaks for itself, and the fact that he confided such a difficult task to me is a source of both pleasure and pride. My memories of the brief moments I spent in his company are pleasant ones in spite of everything that happened. Unassuming, smiling, cordial, elegant, handsome, he's a living rebuttal to all the caricatures of tiresome old scholars in mothballs.

I must take this opportunity to dot the *i*'s and cross the *t*'s on one aspect of my collaboration with the distinguished Columbia professor which has been shamefully exploited by the envious and the unsuccessful. Not content to meddle in my private life and drag my name and Ana Mercedes's through the gutter, their natural habitat, they have tried to put me in bad odor with the left by trumpeting to the four winds that I sold myself and Archanjo's memory to North American imperialism for a handful of dollars.

Now I ask you, what possible connection could there be between Levenson and the Department of State or the Pentagon? As a matter of fact, Levenson's position is considered highly unorthodox by reactionaries and conservatives because his name is linked to progressive movements and protests against the war. When he was awarded a Nobel Prize for his contributions to social science and the humanities, what the European press seized on was precisely the youth—he had barely turned forty—and the political independence of the new laureate, which made him suspect in official circles. Besides, Levenson's work is there for all to read, that immense, sweeping panorama of life among primitive and underdeveloped peoples which has been described as "a dramatic cry of protest against a wrong and unjust world."

I had nothing to do with publicizing Archanjo's books in the United States, but I consider that publicity a victory for progressive thought. After all, our fellow Bahian was also a libertarian. True, he professed no ideology, but he burned with a passionate and boundless love for his people. He was a standard-bearer in the struggle against racism, prejudice, misery, and unhappiness.

I met Levenson through Ana Mercedes, an authentic representative of our best young poets who is now devoting her considerable talents to popular Brazilian music but who at that time was working as a reporter for a local daily newspaper and had been assigned to cover the scholar's brief visit to our city. She carried out her editor's orders so conscientiously that she never left the American's side. She was his interpreter and constant companion, day and night. Her recommendation doubtless had something to do with his choosing me for the job, but a vast distance and a sea of calumny lies between that truth and the things that certain low-minded individuals have dared to say about the two of us. Levenson had ample opportunity to evaluate my qualifications before giving me the contract.

The three of us went together to the ceremonies on Yansan's feast day at the ritual ground, the *terreiro* of Alaketú, and I was able to display my specialized knowledge of Afro-Brazilian culture and show him how useful I could be. In a mixture of Portuguese and Spanish, with a smattering of English which I pooled with Ana's even slimmer smattering, I explained a little about the syncretic rituals. I told him the names of the spirits—the *orixás* —and the reasons for the different movements, gestures, and postures; about the dances and chants, the colors of the costumes worn by the devotees, and a great many other things besides—I'm a fine talker when I'm in the mood, and what I didn't know I made up. I had no intention of losing those dollars that gleamed before my eyes. Dollars, mind you, not devalued *cruzeiros*. I received half of them a little later in the hotel lobby, where I rather reluctantly told them good night.

And that's all I have to say. There's nothing else to explain, except that to my regret the great Levenson evidently paid not the slightest attention to this work of mine. As soon as it was completed I sent him a typewritten copy as I had agreed to do and attached one of the only two photographic documents I had been able to lay hands on: the faded photograph shows a light-brown mulatto, a husky young man in a dark suit, striking a pose and looking very pleased with himself—Pedro Archanjo himself, not long after he had been hired as a runner at the Bahia School of Medicine. I thought it best not to send the other picture, which showed Master Pedro, old now and decrepit, only a remnant of a human being, surrounded by women of doubtful virtue, holding up a glass and quite obviously drunk as a lord.

About two weeks later I received a letter signed by Levenson's secretary, acknowledging receipt of my MS and enclosing a check in dollars for the other half of my fee, plus enough to cover a few expenses I had incurred or might have incurred. They paid it all without haggling over pennies, and I'm sure they would have paid even more if I had not been so modest in my expectations, so unenterprising in my list of expenses.

Out of all the material I sent, Levenson used only the photograph when he published the English translation of the body of Pedro Archanjo's work as one volume of his monumental encyclopedia on life among the peoples of Africa, Asia, and Latin America (*Encyclopedia of Life in the Tropical and Underdeveloped Countries*), written in collaboration with some of the foremost

authorities of our time. In his introduction, Levenson barely ana-
lyzes our Bahian's books and gives very little space to his life—
just enough to prove to me that he did not cast so much as a
passing glance at my text. In his preface Archanjo is promoted to
"distinguished professor, a member of the teaching faculty of the
School of Medicine," under whose auspices he supposedly carried
out his research and published his books. Imagine that if you can!
Who it was who foisted off such whopping lies onto Levenson I
don't know, but if he had at least glanced through my original
notes he would never have fallen into such gross error—from
runner to professor, ah! poor Archanjo, that's all you needed!

My name is not mentioned even once, and there is no reference
to my work in James D. Levenson's book. In the circumstances
I feel completely at liberty to accept the offer I have just received
from Mr. Dmeval Chaves, the prosperous bookseller and publisher
on the Rua da Ajuda, who has offered to publish my modest effort. I have imposed only one condition: a properly made out
contract, for it is rumored that Mr. Chaves, in spite of his wealth
and visible opulence, drives a hard bargain and sometimes has
lapses of memory when it comes to paying authors' royalties. In
this he is merely following a local tradition: our friend Archanjo
was the victim of one Bonfanti, also a bookseller and publisher,
who had a bookshop in the Largo da Sé long ago, as we shall see.

Of the arrival in Brazil

of the North American scholar

James D. Levenson

and the implications and

consequences thereof

I

"Oh yummy, yummy, is he a doll! A living breathing doll!" cried Ana Mercedes, taking one step forward so that like a slender tropical palm she stood out from the mass of reporters, teachers, students, society women, men of letters, and idlers gathered in the spacious salon of the big hotel waiting for James D. Levenson to face the press.

As if she had been delegated to give the great man the keys to the city, the girl reporter from the *Morning News* smiled and shimmied her way through a jumble of radio microphones, television cameras, spotlights, photographers, movie and TV cameramen, and a liana-tangle of electric cables.

"Shimmy" is too low and vulgar a word to describe that undulating gait, that swaying of hips and bosom to samba rhythm, worthy of a flag-bearer in a carnival parade. Very, very sexy. Her mini-skirt showed off the brown columns of her thighs, her gaze was nocturnal, there was a smile on her half-parted, slightly fleshy lips and greedy white teeth, and her navel was showing. A golden girl from top to toe. No, shimmy was not the word. She was invitation and offering, dance itself.

The American stepped out of the elevator and stood still to inspect the room and to be inspected: over six feet tall, with the physique of a sportsman and the looks of an actor: blond hair, sky-blue eyes, and a pipe—who would have believed he was forty-five years old, as his curriculum vitae said? It was the full-page photographs in the Rio and São Paulo magazines that brought the women out in full force, but as soon as they saw him they unanimously agreed that Levenson in the flesh was even better than his pictures. What a man!

"Brazen thing!" hissed one pigeon-breasted woman. She meant Ana Mercedes.

The scholar gazed fascinated at the girl who was coming straight toward him with her navel showing. He had never seen such a dancing walk, such a flexible body, or a face so full of innocence and knowingness, white black *mulata*.

She came up and planted herself in front of him, and when she spoke it was in a warble:

"Hello, boy!"

"Hello!" Levenson replied expressively, taking the pipe out of his mouth to kiss her hand.

The women gave a simultaneous shiver and gasp at her effrontery. Oh! that Ana Mercedes is nothing but a cheap little tramp, calls herself a reporter, writes crap they call poetry . . . anyway, everybody knows it's Fausto Pena, the cuckold of the hour, who writes her poetry for her!

As the excellent Silvinho wrote in his column next day, "The charm, class, and culture of the ladies of Bahia were present *comme il faut* at James D.'s brilliant press conference, some of the dear little things spouting ethnology and the man-hunters gaping at him and showing off their sociology." Some of those women did indeed have other talents besides their good looks, their elegance, their chic wigs, and their competence in bed: they had diplomas for Department of Tourism or Theater School courses in "Typical Dress and Costumes," "Our City's Traditions, History, and Monuments," "Concrete Poetry," "Religion, Sex, and Psychoanalysis." But whether they were students with diplomas or simple amateurs, untamed adolescents or tenacious matrons on the eve of their second or third face-lifting job, all of them knew they were already out of the running and might as well give up: the brazen and cynical Ana Mercedes had got in ahead of them and, taking the manly scientist under her wing, had made him her exclusive private property. Possessive, insatiable—"insatiable cow, copulating star," in the verse of the lyrical, long-suffering Fausto Pena—she had no intention of sharing Levenson with anyone else and the other women knew they might as well throw in the sponge.

The poetess-reporter took the professor from Columbia University by the hand and led him to the middle of the room, where an armchair had been placed. Flash bulbs exploded and the lights looked like flowers. If someone had opened the piano and played the Wedding March, Ana Mercedes in her mini-skirt and miniblouse and James D. Levenson in his tropical blue suit would have been the couple of the year on their way to the altar. "Look at the bride and groom," hissed Silvinho.

Not until the scholar was seated did the two hands separate. However, Ana continued to stand guard by his side; she wasn't fool enough to turn him loose in that circle of greedy bitches in heat. She knew every one of those cows, every one of them readier to be laid than the next. She laughed in their faces just to rub in her triumph. The photographers went mad, climbing onto chairs, standing on tables, crawling on the ground in a hallucinatory vision of angles and postures. At a discreet signal from the Secretary of Tourism the waiters served drinks and the press conference began.

Heavy with importance, erudition, self-righteousness, and con-

ceit, Júlio Marcos, editor and literary critic of the *City News*,
set down his glass and rose to his feet. There was a silence and an
admiring little intake of breath from the feminine contingent. If
the foreign product in the person of the blond scholar was no
longer available, the arrogant Marcos, with his blue-green eyes and
lightly freckled mulatto complexion, had a certain charm. In the
name of the *City News* and enlightened intellectuals at large he
asked the first question, and it was devastating:

"I'd like to hear, in a few words, the illustrious professor's
opinion of the work of Marcuse. Isn't it true that after Marcuse,
Marx is hopelessly dated? Do you agree with that statement or
not?"

After he had spoken he swept the room with a triumphant
gaze, while the translator provided by the dean's office at the university (who had perfect pronunciation, of course) interpreted
the question in English. Vivacious Mariucha Palanga, a wretched
caricature of a nubile girl with two face jobs and a breast job,
said admiringly in a low but audible voice:

"How clever!"

Gazing tenderly at Ana Mercedes's navel, a well of deepest
mystery, a flower in a field in a dream, James D. Levenson took
a drag on his pipe and replied in guttural Spanish, with the rude-
ness that suits artists and scholars so well:

"That's an idiotic question and only a fool would venture an
opinion on Marcuse's work or discuss present-day Marxism in the
framework of a press conference. If I had time to give a speech or
a class about it that would be something else again; but I haven't
got time and I didn't come to Bahia to talk about Marcuse. I
came here to see the place where a remarkable man lived and
worked, a man of profound and generous ideals, one of the founders of modern humanism—your fellow citizen Pedro Archanjo.
That, and only that, is what brings me to Bahia."

He puffed on his pipe and smiled at his audience, relaxed, at
his ease, a love of a gringo. Without so much as a glance at poor
Marcos's corpse wrapped in the shroud of his foolhardy vanity,
he contemplated Ana Mercedes from head to foot, from her loose
black hair to her incredible toenails painted white, finding her

more and more to his measure and taste. Archanjo had written in one of his books: "The beauty of the women, the simple women of the lower classes, is an attribute of our mestizo city, of love between the races, of a bright unprejudiced morning." He looked again at that flowering navel, the navel of the world, and said in his hard, correct North American university Spanish:

"Do you know what I would compare to Pedro Archanjo's work? This young lady standing beside me. She is exactly like a page from Mr. Archanjo, *'igualita.'*"

Thus in Bahia, on that sweet April afternoon, began the apotheosis of Pedro Archanjo.

2

Fame, public recognition, applause, the admiration of learned men, glory, success—even worldly success, with write-ups in the society columns and hysterical little cries from society women—all this came to Pedro Archanjo after he was dead and none of it was any use to him, not even the women whom he had loved so fondly and so well when he was alive.

That was "the year of Pedro Archanjo," wrote a well-known journalist in his end-of-the-year round-up of cultural events. And it was true: no other intellectual had enjoyed so much publicity, no other work had received the praise heaped on his four little volumes, hastily reprinted after so many decades of neglect when they were completely unknown, not only to the mass reading public but even to the specialists, with certain honorable exceptions to be mentioned later.

It all began with the arrival in Brazil of the famous James D. Levenson, "one of the five geniuses of our century" (*Encyclo-*

paedia Britannica): philosopher, mathematician, sociologist, anthropologist, ethnologist, etc., Professor at Columbia University, winner of a Nobel Prize in science—all this and an American besides. His daring and controversial theories had revolutionized contemporary science: by looking at questions through the spectacles of other disciplines he had reached new and audacious conclusions, upsetting old theses and hypotheses long taken for granted. To conservatives he was a dangerous heretic; to his students and partisans, a god; to journalists he was manna from heaven, for James D. Levenson spoke straight from the shoulder and said just what he thought.

He had come to Rio at the invitation of the University of Brazil to give a series of five lectures at the School of Philosophy and Letters. As we all know, the seminar was a huge success: the first talk, which was scheduled to take place in the college lecture hall, had to be transferred at the last minute to the big auditorium in the main building. Even then there were listeners standing in the aisles and sitting on the steps. There was plenty to keep the reporters and photographers busy. Levenson was not only a genius, he was eminently photogenic.

His talks, followed by question periods and sometimes acid debates, led to violent student demonstrations of applause for the scholar and shouts against the dictatorship. More than once the students rose to their feet and gave him a delirious ovation for minutes at a time. Some of Levenson's phrases caught the public imagination and soon spread from one end of the country to the other: "Ten years of interminable international conferences are better than one day of warfare; and cheaper, too"; "Prisons and police are equally sordid under every regime, without exception"; "The world will not be truly civilized until uniforms are seen only in museums."

Surrounded by photographers and starlets and wearing the briefest of swimming trunks, Levenson reserved his mornings for the beach. He systematically turned down all invitations from academies, institutes, trade unions, cultural councils, and teachers' associations —he had more than enough of that sort of thing in New York and was sick of it, but when would he feel that Brazilian sun again? He played soccer on the beach and was actually photographed shooting a goal, although women were without a doubt his favorite sport. He became intimately acquainted with some of the finest local specimens, in the nightclubs and on the beach.

Since he had recently been divorced, the social columnists fell all over themselves inventing love affairs and engagements for him. One especially indiscreet gossip columnist predicted the ruin of a certain fashionable marriage, but she was wrong: the husband was only too honored to make the acquaintance of the studhorse and scholar. "Yesterday, on the terrace at the Copacabana Palace, Katy Siqueira Prado, in a bikini from Cannes, gazed tenderly at the great James D. and her husband Baby, who are inseparable friends," countered the knowledgeable Zul. One popular magazine displayed the athletic nudity of the Nobel scientist on that week's cover next to the promotional nudity of Nádia Sílvia, an actress of great talent to be revealed if and when she was given the opportunity which the stage and cinema had so far inexplicably denied her. When interviewed by a reporter, Nádia laughed and giggled, answering neither yes nor no to questions about love at first sight and engagement plans. "Levenson is the sixth worldfamous figure to lose his head over the irresistible Nádia Sílvia," deadpanned one newspaper, and gave the names of his five predecessors: John Kennedy, Richard Burton, the Aga Khan, a Swiss banker, and an English lord—and in addition a certain Italian countess with mannish tastes and a million dollars.

"Levenson the genius was out on the dance floor again at Le Bateau last night, 'in love' with the glamorous Helena von Kloster," wrote Gisa in the *Evening Chronicle*. "Now that he's learned the samba, he won't dance anything else," Robert Sabad revealed in eighteen newspapers and over as many TV stations, letting everyone in on a remark made by Branquinha do Val Burnier, a hostess of incomparable magnificence of board and bed: "If James weren't the Nobel Prize winner he is, he could earn his living as a professional dancer." Newspapers and magazines vied with one another to write about him, and the scholar never let them down.

None of this, however, was quite so sensational as his remark

about Pedro Archanjo. That bomb exploded in the airport when
he took the plane for Bahia. It was true that during his first meeting with the press when he arrived from New York, Levenson
had referred briefly to the Bahian and mentioned him by name:
"I'm in Archanjo's country and happy to be here." The reporters
had not included the phrase in their stories, either because they
did not understand it or because they attached no significance to
it. When he left for Bahia it was different, for the disconcerting
Nobel Prize winner declared that he had reserved two days of his
short stay in Brazil to go to Salvador to "make the acquaintance
of the city and people who were studied by the extraordinary
Pedro Archanjo, in whose books science reads like poetry, the
author who did so much to raise the level of Brazilian culture."
A free-for-all ensued.

"Who's this guy Pedro Archanjo? I never heard of him," the
dumfounded reporters queried one another. One of them, in the
hope of getting some sort of a lead, asked how Levenson had
learned of this Brazilian author. "By reading his books," the
scholar replied. "His imperishable books."

The question had come from Ápio Corréia, the editor of the
science, art, and literary sections of one of the morning papers
and a very shrewd operator.

He carried the bluff a little further and said he hadn't known
that Archanjo's books had been translated into English.

The terrible American informed him that he had not read the
books in English but in Portuguese, adding that he had been able
to do so, in spite of his very slight knowledge of the Brazilian
tongue, thanks to the fact that he knew Spanish and Latin. "It
was no problem," he said imperturbably, explaining that he had
discovered Archanjo's books in the Columbia library recently
while doing research on life in tropical countries. He intended to
have "the works of your great fellow countryman" translated
and published in the United States.

I'll have to act fast, thought Ápio Corréia, running to hail a
taxi to take him to the National Library.

There was a scramble among the reporters until they discovered and cornered Professor Ramos, who was eminent in several

fields and worth even more to them now, since he was familiar with Archanjo's work and had more than once proclaimed its value in articles in little magazines which unfortunately had few subscribers and even fewer readers.

"For years and years," he told them, "I trudged from one publishing house to another, asking them to republish Archanjo's books. Believe me, it was a thankless, weary job. I wrote introductions, footnotes, explications: not a single publisher was interested. I went to Professor Viana, the Dean of the School of Philosophy, to see if he would use his influence at the university to get them published, and he told me I was 'wasting time with the drivel of a drunken Negro, a subversive.' Maybe now they'll wake up and realize how great Archanjo's work really is, now that Levenson has given it the importance it deserves. Incidentally, Levenson's own work is no better known in Brazil than Archanjo's, and the people who fawn over him have not even read his most important books and haven't the faintest idea of what he's driving at; they're a bunch of phonies."

Professor Ramos spoke rather bitterly, as well he might; after all, he had sufficient reason for feeling abused, after struggling for years to get Archanjo a place in the sun, only to be turned down by publishers time and again. He had had to endure crude insults and threats from Hard-Nosed Viana, only to see a foreigner put the wheels of the press in motion with just one statement. Levenson had set the whole yawping pack of intellectuals on the trail of Archanjo's books. The intelligentsia of all stripes, colors, and ideologies, from the festive left to the pompous right, were now snuffing eagerly after the memory of the hitherto unknown Bahian; Pedro Archanjo had come into his own with a vengeance, and no one who was unfamiliar with his works and unable to quote them could expect to keep his place in the vanguard.

When it appeared three weeks later, Ápio Corréia's story, "Pedro Archanjo, ethnological poet," was a real sensation. In it was a curious, one might even say brilliant, version of the dialogue in the airport between the learned Levenson and the erudite Corréia, both of them evincing a profound knowledge of Archanjo's work. It was only natural that the critic's knowledge should be

somewhat deeper and more extensive, since he was, after all, a
Brazilian.

The excitement was even greater in Bahia, Archanjo's native
heath, the locale and subject of his study, the source of his research material, and the *raison d'être* of his work.

The name that Levenson had made famous overnight was not
so universally unknown here as in Rio and São Paulo. (It is worth
recalling that in São Paulo the reporters were hard put to it to
find even one reference to the Bahian, but when they did it was
a good one: an article that the art critic Sérgio Milliet had written in 1929 for *O Estado de São Paulo*. Commenting in a very
friendly spirit, with lavish praise, on Archanjo's book about the
culinary art of Bahia—*Bahia Cookery—Its Origins and Precepts*
—the great critic perceived that the author was a forerunner, "and
one of the greatest, the most truly authentic," of anthropophagy,
"the revolutionary and controversial movement recently
launched by the artists Tarsila do Amaral, Oswald de Andrade,
and Raul Bopp." The "delightful volume," with its quintessentially
Brazilian contents and flavorful prose, struck him as "a perfect
example of a true anthropophagic essay." Milliet concluded by
regretting his unfamiliarity with the other books by this well-
informed writer, who, though he had almost certainly never heard
of the anthropophagists of São Paulo, had stolen a march on them
nonetheless.)

In Bahia there were people who had actually known Archanjo
and talked with him, as the press soon discovered. But this first-
hand acquaintance was limited to a few people and a handful of
anecdotes. Those four little books on life in Bahia, which Pedro

Archanjo had painfully printed in tiny editions on the precarious printing press of his friend Lídio Corró in the Rua do Tabuão, that body of work whose merit had so impressed the American scholar, was as neglected and as difficult to unearth in Bahia as in the rest of Brazil.

If Archanjo had not sent copies to national and foreign institutes, universities, and libraries, none of his books would ever have been heard of again, because Levenson would not have discovered them. In Salvador only a few ethnologists and anthropologists were familiar with them, even by hearsay.

And now, all of a sudden, not only journalists but public institutions, intellectuals, the University, the Historical Institute, the Academy, the School of Medicine, the poets, the professors, the students, theater people, the numerous phalanx of ethnologists and anthropologists, the Center for the Study of Folklore, even tourist agents and other people with nothing to do, all realized at once that they had had a great and distinguished author in their midst without even knowing it, that they had not even made token use of him in public utterance but had relegated him to the most absolute anonymity. Then the commotion about Archanjo and his work began. After Levenson's interview much paper, much ink, and much column space were used to hail, analyze, study, comment on, and praise the unjustly neglected scribe. The delay must be made up for, the error corrected, the silent dust of so many years shaken off.

Now, at last, Archanjo's work had been given the place in the sun that it justly deserved. Among all the puffery of quacks and charlatans who jumped on the bandwagon with a view to gaining publicity for themselves, there was a residue of serious writing, a few pages worthy of the memory of the man who for so many years had worked steadily on, indifferent to success and profit. Some of the testimony of his contemporaries, those who had known and had dealings with Archanjo, bore the stamp of genuine feeling and revealed something of the true character of the man. Archanjo was not so distant in time as had at first been assumed: only twenty-five years ago, in 1943, he had departed this life at the age of seventy-five, and in singular circumstances, it seemed. He was found dead, sprawled in a gutter, very late at night.

There were no identifying papers in his pockets, nothing but a notebook and the stub of a pencil. He needed no documents in that poor, filthy neighborhood in the oldest part of the city, where everyone knew him and loved him.

Of the death of

Pedro Archanjo,

Ojuobá, Eyes of Xangô,

and his burial in

Quintas Cemetery

I

The old man stumbled up the hill, supporting himself by clinging to the walls of the ancient houses; you would have thought he was drunk to look at him, especially if you knew him. Total darkness, every lamp out in the streets and houses, not a single crack of light—for it was wartime, and German submarines prowled near the Brazilian coast, where peaceful freighters and passenger ships were occasionally sunk.

The old man felt the pain well up in his chest and tried to quicken his steps; if he could only make it home he would light

the oil lamp and set down the conversation, the splendid phrase
in his little notebook. His memory wasn't what it used to be; in
the old days he could remember a conversation, a gesture, an
event in all its details for months and years without taking notes.
Once he had written down that debate he could rest. This wasn't
the first time the same pain had come and gone. It had never
hurt quite so much, though. Oh, if he could only live a few
more months, only a few! Just long enough to finish his notes,
put them in order, and give them to that nice young fellow who
worked at the print shop. Just a few more months.

He clutched at the wall and tried to look around him, but his
sight was growing dim. He didn't have the money for a new
pair of spectacles; for that matter, he didn't have the money for
a shot of rum. A deeper pain drove him panting against the wall.
All he needed was just enough strength to cover those last few
blocks to his little room at the back of Ester's "castle." He could
write there by lamplight in his meticulous hand—if the pain
would only settle down and let him do it. He thought of his
compadre Corró, slumped dead over one of his miracle paintings,
a thread of blood at the corner of his mouth. They had done so
many things together, he and Lídio Corró: run up and down the
steep streets, rolled in the doorways with mulatto girls. Lídio had
been dead a long time: at least fifteen years, maybe more. How
long *had* it been, *meu bom?* Eighteen years, twenty? His memory
was beginning to fail him, but he remembered the blacksmith's
phrase word for word. Clinging to the wall he tried to repeat it
to himself. I mustn't forget it, he thought, I'll have to set it down
in my notebook the very first thing. Just a few more blocks, just
a few hundred yards. With a mighty effort he murmured the
blacksmith's final imprecation, which he had emphasized by a
blow on the table from his black hand like a hammer striking an
anvil.

He had gone one night to listen to the foreign news broad-
casts on the radio: the London BBC, Radio Moscow, the Voice of
America. His friend Maluf had bought a radio set that you could
hear the whole world on. The news that night was really good:
the Aryans were taking a beating. Everyone was berating the
"German Nazis," the "German monsters," but old Archanjo just

called them "Aryan swine," murderers of Jews, Negroes, and Arabs. He knew some very fine Germans. Mr. Guilherme Knodler, for one, had married a Negro woman and fathered eight children. One day someone made a remark about Aryanism and he pulled out his penis and said:

"If that day ever comes I'll have to cut off my prick."

When Maluf treated them to a round of *pinga* on the house to celebrate the day's victories, the argument began: if Hitler won the war, could he or couldn't he kill every single human being who was not pure white? Would he exterminate everybody else? Some said one thing, some said another, yes he can, no he can't, you bet your life he can, and finally the blacksmith shouted:

"Not even God who made the human race can kill everybody at once! He kills us one at a time, and the more He kills the more babies are born and the faster they grow up, and that's the way it's always gonna be. They're gonna go on being born and growing up and mixing and making more babies, and no son-of-a-bitch is gonna stop 'em!" When he struck his great hand on the counter he knocked over his glass, rum and all. But Maluf the Turk was a good fellow and stood them all to another round before they said good night.

The old man tried to walk a little farther up the hill, turning the blacksmith's words over in his mind: "They'll go on being born and growing up and mixing . . ." The more mixed, the better. The old man could almost smile under the pain weighing down his back like a cross. Such a heavy pain to carry. He smiled when he remembered Rosa's granddaughter, so like her grandmother and yet so different: the straight silky hair, the slender figure, the blue eyes and dark skin. It had taken many different kinds of people to make her perfect as she was. Rosa, Rosa de Oxalá, perdition in the form of woman! The old man had loved and possessed many women, but none of them could hold a candle to her. For her sake he had suffered excruciating pangs, done incredible things, played the fool, wanted to die, to commit murder.

He would give anything to see Rosa's granddaughter again, with her grandmother's laughter and verve, the dancing walk and those blue eyes . . . who had given them to her? And if only he

could see his friends one more time, visit the *terreiro* and salute
the saints, dance a few steps, sing a song, eat some chicken or fish
stew cooked in palm oil at the table in Ester's castle with Ester
and the girls. No, he didn't want to die, what on earth for? That
wasn't any way to do. What was it, exactly, that the blacksmith
had said? He had to write it down before he forgot; he was
beginning to forget it already. The book was only half-finished;
he still had to write the rest, pick out anecdotes, phrases, stories
like the one about the *iaba* who had it in for the woman-chaser
and went out of her mind over the good-looking, swaggering
Bahiano, turning to putty in his hands. He knew that remarkable
story better than anyone else. Oh, Dorotéia! Oh, Tadeu!

The pain tore him in two and burst his chest. Oh, now I
won't make it to Ester's house, the blacksmith's phrase is lost and
it was so exactly right. Oh, and Rosa's granddaughter. . . .

He dropped to the sidewalk and rolled slowly toward the gutter. And there his body remained, blanketed only in darkness
until the first streaks of dawn came and clothed it in light.

2

The saint-carver laughed as he pointed to the prone body, and
laughed again as he tried to steady himself on his legs:

"That guy's put away more of the sauce than the three of us
put together. Look, he fell on his face and threw up his guts."
Still laughing, he tried to perform a circus pirouette and tripped
clumsily in the air.

Major Damião de Souza, either because he had drunk less or
had had more experience with death (he was a popular lawyer by
trade, an habitué of the morgue, and an old acquaintance of crimes
and corpses), suspected something and going closer, noticed the

blood. He touched the old man's back in its tattered jacket with the tip of his boot and said:

"Dead as a doornail. Come give me a hand."

The saint-carver pondered the question of how much alcohol the major could handle without getting drunk, thus echoing the question asked by every sot in the world, all equally humiliated at a mystery beyond all understanding. So far the gin mills of Bahia and the Recôncavo had never been able to keep up with the demand, and according to Mané Lima the major was quite capable of exhausting the world's supply. Lucid to the very end.

Stumbling and laughing, the saint-carver and Mané Lima lent a hand, and the three men turned the body over. Even before he had seen his face the major recognized something about him, the jacket, perhaps. But Mané Lima, wholly taken by surprise, was first struck speechless and then let out a terrible cry:

"It's Pedro Archanjo!"

The major straightened up stiffly; a shadow crossed his copper face. No, there was no mistake; it was the old man, and the major, for all his forty-nine years, felt like an abandoned orphan. Yes, it was the old man, and oh, there was nothing to be done. Why couldn't it have been someone else, some stranger? So many useless bums in this world, this damned shitty world, and Archanjo had to be the one to die like this in the street, in the middle of the night, without anyone's knowing.

"Oh, God, it's the old man!" All the rum flowed down from the saint-carver's head to his legs, and he sat down abruptly on the sidewalk, mute and helpless. All he could do was lift the dead man's hand out of the mud and hold it clasped in his own.

Every Wednesday without fail, rain or shine, Archanjo would come to the saint-carver's shop and they would go out. First they would down schooners of ice-cold beer at Osmário's bar and then enjoy a hearty dish of shrimp in palm oil after the *candomblé* rites at the Casa Branca. The talk was always mild and punctuated with anecdotes, the kind of talk they were used to:

"Take off your coat, *meu bom*, and tell me what you've been up to."

"I don't have any news, Master Archanjo, don't know a thing."

"Oh, sure you do . . . *Meu bom,* things are happening every minute, lovely things, some to laugh at, others to cry about. Come on, get the knots out of your tongue, *camarado,* mouths were made to talk with."

How did he do it? What spell did he have to unlock the hearts and mouths of others? Not even the strictest, most jealous spirit guides—respectable matrons like Tia Mací, Dona Menininha, or Lady Mother of Opô Afonjá—could keep a secret from the old man. They told him everything they knew without having to be coaxed; in fact, the *orixás* had ordered them to do so. "No door is closed to Ojuobá." And now Ojuobá, Eyes of Xangô the King, was lying dead in the gutter.

How they used to down their beer—Master Archanjo could always drink three or four bottles. One week the old man stood treat, and the next time it was the saint-carver who paid the bill. Lately the old man had been going around like a peeled whistle most of the time, without a penny to his name; but it was something to see his satisfaction the week he managed to get hold of some small change. With what an air he rapped on the table to call the waiter:

"Bring us the check, *meu bom.*"

"Now, now, Master Archanjo, keep your money . . ."

"Now what did I do to offend you, *camarado?* Why are you treating me this way? When I'm broke you can pay for it; I don't mind, it isn't my fault. But if I'm the one who's rich today, why should you be the one to pay? Don't take my duty and my privilege away from me, don't cut old Archanjo down to size. Leave me the way I am, *meu bom.*"

And he would laugh with his perfect white teeth, all of them still sound because he sucked on tough sections of sugar cane and chewed equally tough jerky.

"I didn't steal this money, you know. I earned it by the sweat of my brow."

He had earned it at his last job of errand boy in a whorehouse. Seeing him so smiling and contented, no one could have imagined the privations, the penury, the distress and austerity, the infinite poverty of the last years of his life. Only the Wednesday before he had been beside himself with joy: in Ester's house he had met a student, part owner of a print shop, who was willing to print his book. The young fellow had read the others and emphatically told everyone who would listen that Archanjo was not afraid of anybody. Hadn't he unmasked that whole pack of quacks at the Medical School?

When the two old friends were on the streetcar going to Lower Rio Vermelho where the White House that used to belong to the old sugar plantation stands on the hill—stars were beginning to come out and the sea wind starting to blow fresh—Master Archanjo told the saint-carver about the new book, his little eyes gleaming with mischief. What a lot of stories he had gathered and written down for that book, that "ragbag of odds and ends," that was full of what the people had learned at their university.

"You can't imagine, *meu bom*, how much I've collected in that whorehouse, just from the prostitutes alone. For your information, *camarado*, a philosopher couldn't find a better place to live than a whorehouse."

"You really are a philosopher, Master Archanjo, the best one I ever knew. There's nobody like you for making the best of what you've got."

They were on their way to celebrate the rites of Xangô, a Wednesday obligation. Tia Mací gave Xangô his *amalá*, the sacred food, to the sound of the metal gong and the singing of the female devotees. Afterward, when they were all seated around the big table in the parlor, she served shrimp stew and bean cakes, with sometimes a dish of turtle. Master Archanjo was a hearty eater, and a healthy drinker, too. The talk would go on far into the night, lively and cordial in the warmth of friendship. Listening to Archanjo was one of the privileges of the poor.

Now it was all over. No more book, no rites, no ritual food or rum, no more trips on the streetcar, no more surprises out of Archanjo. The old man had known every nook and cranny along the way; every house and tree was as familiar to him as if he had lived with them for a hundred years, because he knew not only their present but their past, knew whose they had been and who owned them now, father and son, father's father and grandfather's father, full blood and mixed blood. He knew about the black man

brought from Africa as a slave, the Portuguese banished from the
Court, the Jewish convert fleeing from the Inquisition. Now all his
knowing, all his gaiety and laughter had come to an end, and the
eyes of the Eyes of Xangô had closed. The only place Ojuobá
had to go to now was the cemetery.

The saint-carver dissolved into tears, abandoned, lonely, and
desolate.

The major found it as impossible to weep for sorrow as to get
really drunk. The only times he ever cried—and how easily then!
—were when he was pleading before a jury or whipping up his
listeners' emotions, trying to win them over to his cause. When
real pain gnawed at his vitals, it never showed in his face.

From his post in the middle of Pelourinho, a fitting and proper
place, Mané Lima proclaimed the old man's name and his death
to the world, but in the dim hour before dawn his cries were
heard by no one but a few enormous rats and one skinny dog.

The major tore himself away from the terrible sight and set
off up the street to Ester's castle, the weight of the bad news
bowing down his shoulders. He would down the strong drink he
needed when he got there.

Suddenly the street sprang to life. From the Largo da Sé, from
Shoemakers' Hollow, from Carmo, grief-stricken men and women
came streaming. It was not the death of Pedro Archanjo, learned
author of possibly definitive studies on miscegenation, that
brought them to the scene, but the death of their father, Ojuobá,
the Eyes of Xangô. From Ester's place the news had spread by
word of mouth from door to door, from one tenement to the
next, through the side streets, up the steps, down the hill, reaching

Cathedral Square in time to ride the first streetcars and buses of the day.

Women snatched from sleep or from the arms of tardy customers awoke in tears and lamentation. Workers going to their jobs, bums with no time clock to punch, beggars and sots, inhabitants of the garrets of old houses or filthy warrens, Arab money-lenders, old men and boys, traffickers in saints and peddlers from the Terreiro de Jesus, a pushcart vendor trundling his cart. And Ester, too, with a kimono flung over her nakedness, showing all she had to anyone who cared to look. But at such a time, all anyone saw was Ester tearing her hair and beating her breast.

"Ai, Archanjo, my poor angel, why didn't you tell me you were sick? How was I to know? Oh, Ojuobá, what are we going to do now? You were our light, our eyes to see with, our mouth to talk with. You were all the courage and understanding we had. You knew what happened yesterday and what would happen tomorow, and where can we find anyone like you?"

Where, oh, where? In that dreadful hour those men and women were face to face with death in all its squalor. There it lay in the gutter, stripped of the least softening, consoling detail. Pedro Archanjo Ojuobá was not yet a memory, just a corpse and nothing more.

Doors and windows were flung open, and Ester, sobbing, embraced the sexton when he came with his lighted candle. People crowded around the dead body and a military policeman appeared, invested with arms and authority. Ester sat down beside the saint-carver, took Archanjo's head in her hands, and wiped the blood from his lips with the edge of her kimono. Turning his eyes away so as not to see her uncovered breasts at this inappropriate time—but is there any time that's not appropriate, Archanjo? You used to say there wasn't, that "any time's a good time to entertain the body"—the major addressed her:

"Let's take him to your place, Ester."

"My place?" Ester broke off in the middle of a sob and stared at the major, unable to believe her ears. "Are you out of your mind? Don't you know it wouldn't be right? It's Ojuobá who's being buried, not some whore or pimp who doesn't deserve any better than to have his funeral leave from a whorehouse . . ."

"I didn't mean the funeral should leave from your house, but we ought to change his clothes before we do anything else. He can't be buried in those dirty trousers and that patched old jacket."

"Or without a tie on. He never went to a party without a tie," put in Rosália, the oldest of the girls, who had been Archanjo's sweetheart in former days.

"He doesn't have a change of clothes."

"If that's what's worrying you, I'll give him my blue broadcloth suit. I had it made when I got married and it's just as good as new," offered João dos Prazeres, a master carpenter who lived nearby. "If that's all that's worrying you . . ." he repeated, and went off to get the clothes.

"But where are we going to take him afterward?" asked Rosália.

"Don't ask me, honey, I'm in no condition to think or make up my mind about anything, ask the major and just leave me with my old man," wailed Ester, holding Archanjo's head on her lap and enveloping him in the warmth of her flesh.

The major was taken by surprise. Where to take him? Oh, don't bother me with details; the important thing now is to get him out of the middle of the street. There'll be plenty of time afterward to think about which house would be best. But all at once the sexton of the Slaves' Church of Our Lady of the Rosary, an old drinking companion of Pedro Archanjo, remembered that the latter had once belonged to the Brotherhood. He was a member emeritus with his dues paid up, and he had the right to a wake in the church, Requiem Masses prayed over his corpse, and a perpetual grave in Quintas Cemetery.

"Let's go, then," commanded the major.

As they started to pick up the body, the soldier stuck out his chest and halted them in their tracks: no one was going to lay a finger on that corpse until the police, the doctor, and the coroner arrived. He was a young soldier, still in his teens; almost a child, he had been dressed in uniform and given weapons and drastic orders. Incarnate in him were the two worst things in the world: power and brute force.

"Don't anybody touch him!"

The major inspected the soldier and considered the situation: a recruit from the interior of the state, imbued with the mystique of discipline, not easy to get around. The major tried:

"Are you a native of these parts, young fellow? Or are you from the Sertão? Do you know who this is? If you don't, let me tell you . . ."

"I don't know and I don't care. He's not leaving until the police come and get him."

Now it was the major's turn to dig in his heels. He was not going to let Archanjo's body lie there in the middle of the street like the corpse of a common criminal with no right to a wake.

"He is leaving, and he's leaving right now."

There were many cogent reasons for Major Damião de Souza's being called the Poor Man's Attorney: with no law school diploma, he still deserved the title a thousand times over. It was the people who had given him the title of major—a major without rank, battalion, stripes, or uniform, with no one to obey his orders, a major who was nothing but one hell of a fine fellow. His voice trembling with indignation, the Lawyer of the People stepped up onto the sidewalk and began his oration:

"Will the people of Bahia consent to let the body of Pedro Archanjo of Ojuobá lie in the middle of the street, in the mud of this gutter, surrounded by filth the mayor doesn't see and never orders cleared away? Will you let him lie here until the police see fit to send a doctor? How long will you let him lie? Until noon? Until four o'clock in the afternoon? Will the people, ah! the glorious people of Bahia, who expelled the Dutch and defeated the Lusitanian sailors! will they let our father Ojuobá lie here in this muck until he rots? Ah, people of Bahia!"

The people of Bahia—thirty of them at least, not counting those who were still on their way—howled and shook their fists, and the wailing women started toward the stalwart guard. It was a moment of peril, an ugly, dangerous moment. Just as the major had foreseen, the soldier stood his ground and wouldn't yield an inch. Stiff as a ramrod, implacable because his youthful authority could not be flouted, he drew his sword. "Come one inch closer and you'll die on the spot!" Ester got to her feet, prepared to die.

The blast of a high, shrill whistle cut through all the noise. It was the quasi-civilian whistle of Everaldo Honeyfucker the night-watchman, on his way home after a night's work and a few swigs of rum. What was all this caterwauling about so early in the morning? He saw the soldier with the unsheathed saber in his hand and Ester with her boobs hanging out—just a chippies' hair-pulling, he thought; but still, he owed a lot to Ester:

"Soldier," he bawled at the recruit. "'Attention!'"

It was one authority versus another: on one side the night-watchman, lowliest of uniformed men, with his whistle that warned away thieves and his rascality, resourcefulness, and cunning; and on the other the little tin soldier with his saber, his revolver, his regulations, his violence, and his brute force.

Everaldo caught sight of the corpse lying on the ground.

"What's old Archanjo doing here? He's just drunk, ain't he?"

"Oh, if he only was—"

The major explained how they had found the body and about the soldier's stubborn refusal to let them take Archanjo to Ester's house. Everaldo, known as Honeyfucker, broke the impasse by saying, as one man in uniform to another:

"Soldier, you'd better clear out while the going's good. You've lost your head and insulted the major."

"Major? I don't see any major."

"He's standing right there: Major Damião de Souza. Haven't you ever heard of him?"

Who hadn't heard of the major? Even the young recruit had heard his name every day in the barracks in Juàzeiro.

"Is that the major? Why didn't you say so?"

Once his brittle strength—his stubbornness—was broken he became as meek as a lamb, ready to be the first to follow the major's orders. The corpse was deposited in the pushcart and they all set out for Ester's castle.

Now Master Pedro Archanjo was as happy in death as he had been in life: his funeral procession in an open cart pulled by a burro with a bell around its neck, accompanied by drunks, night owls, whores, and other friends, with Everaldo leading the cor-tège and blowing his whistle and the soldier saluting in the rear —ah! that little trip might have been an invention of Archanjo's own, one last spree to set down in his little notebook to tell about at Xangô's supper table next Wednesday.

Most of the money for the funeral expenses came from the prostitutes. It paid for the coffin, the buses, the candles, and the flowers.

Rosália, Archanjo's old sweetheart, dressed herself in widow's weeds, a black shawl over her sparse, peroxided hair, and went up and down Pelourinho collecting contributions. No one refused to give, not even Marquis, a miser who had never given a customer credit for so much as a sip of rum. He added his mite and even had a few good words to say about the deceased.

For it was not only money that Rosália was collecting. She wanted stories, interesting sayings, reminiscences of all kinds; and Pedro Archanjo's tracks were everywhere. Little Kiki, rachitic and not quite fifteen, a delicacy for barristers and judges at Dedé's establishment, opened wide her enormous eyes, showed the doll Archanjo had given her, and burst into tears.

Dedé, the pock-marked procuress, said she had known Archanjo all her life and that he had always been freedom-loving and wild. When she was a girl, a shepherdess in the Festival of the Three Kings, she had been his favorite partner in all the festivities at the end of the year: at novenas and thirteen-day prayers, at block parties and samba rehearsals, and in all sorts of carnival fun. You had to keep an eye on Archanjo; you never knew what he'd be up to next. He had deflowered a good many girls in his day, including a fair number of shepherdesses. Dedé cried and then laughed at her memories: " 'I was pretty and modern, and he was a rascal and a rogue.' "

"Was he the first? Did he do you the favor?"

The question went unanswered, Dedé would say no more, and Rosália was still in doubt when she left. She had a story of her own, and so she was able to contain herself and go about her collecting without breaking down.

"I'll give you what I've got and be glad to, and I only wish it was more," said Roque, emptying his pockets of a few *milreis*.

All five workers at the shop contributed, but it was Roque who told the story.

"It wasn't so long ago, maybe fifteen years, maybe not even that long . . . Wait a minute and I'll tell you exactly, it was in thirty-four, nine years ago; how could anybody ever forget the power strike? It started with the streetcar workers, and the derned old man had no call to get mixed up in it at all."

"Did he work for the Power Company? I never knew that."

"Just for a little while. He used to deliver light bills. He had a hard time getting that job, and he needed the money."

"He always did."

"Well, he went out on strike just the same, and they put him on the strike committee. He was lucky he wasn't thrown in jail when it was over instead of just being booted out the door. But then, he never had to pay streetcar fare again for the rest of his life. The old man always came out on top."

On the second floor next to the church, Master Budião sat all by himself on a bench in the Capoeira Academy and stared in front of him, shriveled to skin and bones, ears pricked to catch every sound. As if his blindness were not enough, at eighty-two he also suffered from dropsy; but even so, he would take up the *berimbau* and lead the singing on evenings when the room was full. Rosália delivered her message to him.

"I've already heard, and I just sent my wife to take something for the funeral. As soon as she comes back I'm going to see Pedro at the church."

"But uncle, you're in no condition to . . ."

"Hold your tongue. How could I think of not going? I'm a lot older than he is and I taught him *capoeira*, but all I know about anything else is what Pedro taught me. He was the most reliable, honorable, serious man I ever knew."

"Serious? He was so full of fun."

"When I say he was serious I mean you could always count on him to do what was right, not that he went around with a frown on his face."

Lost in his shadows, a captive of his uncertain legs, Master Budião saw young Archanjo surrounded by books and more books, studying all by himself. He had never had a teacher.

"He didn't need one; he learned things on his own hook."

As the *capoeira* teacher's wife, a stout lady in her fifties, mounted the stairs, her voice filled the room:

"He looks real nice in his new clothes, with flowers all over the place. They're taking him to the church now, and there're more people than you can shake a stick at. The funeral begins at three."

"Did you give them the money?"

"Yes, I gave it to the saint-carver, Miguel; he's taking care of things."

Rosália went on her way, from house to house, store to store, castle to castle; she crossed the Carmo Gates and went down Tabuão Street. When she came to what had once been Lídio Corró's printshop and was now a store that sold odds and ends, she stopped for a moment.

It had happened more than twenty years ago, it might even have been twenty-five or thirty. What use was it to count the years? She, too, Rosália, had been "pretty and modern," no longer a young girl but an appetizing woman in the prime of life; Archanjo was then close to fifty. They had had a wild love affair, a mad, desperate passion.

They spent part of their time in Lídio Corró's shop: the two men, with one young helper, working over the trays of type, stopping once in a while for a swig of rum to keep them going. Rosália would light the stove and they would cook special dishes they enjoyed, and in the evenings friends dropped in and brought something to drink.

A little farther on, at the corner, there had stood a two-story house that was no longer there. From the attic under the eaves they could see dawn break over the wharfs, see the ships and the fishing boats. The broken window panes let in the rain, the sea

breeze, the yellow moon, and the stars. Sighs of love died away
in the folds of the morning. Pedro Archanjo was a champion in
bed, and what a considerate, polite man he was!

Now there was no more house, no more attic, no more window overlooking the ocean; but as Rosália set out again, she no
longer felt lonely or sad. Two men came striding up the street.

"I knew one of his sons, worked with him down on the docks
until he ran away to sea."

"But Pedro never married . . ."

"Well, he made upward of twenty children anyway, he was a
studhorse if ever there was one."

The speaker laughed loudly and his companion joined in. Yes,
Pedro Archanjo had always come out on top. But where did that
other, louder laughter come from, Rosália? Only twenty? Come
on, add a few more sons, *camarado*, don't be bashful; that was a
powerful tool I had, you know; it broke in virgins, it seduced
married women, it was God's gift to whores—what with one
thing and another, and one woman and another, Pedro Archanjo
helped populate the world, *meu bom*.

The Slaves' Church shone blue in midafternoon, standing
there in Pelourinho. Was that a dazzle of sunlight or a streak of
blood on the stone pavement? So much blood had run over those
stones, so many groans of pain had risen to that sky, so many
prayers and so much blasphemy had echoed from the sky-blue
walls of the Slaves' Church of Our Lady of the Rosary!

It had been a long time since such a large crowd had gathered
in Pelourinho. It overflowed the church, the churchyard, and the
steps and spread out onto the street and sidewalks. Would two
buses be enough? What with gasoline rationing it had not been
easy to get even those; the major had had to pull some strings. A
mob at least as large was waiting at the foot of the hill. Many
people had gone to the church to gaze at the calm face of the
departed, and some of them had kissed his hand; then they had
taken the streetcar in Shoemakers' Hollow to wait at the cemetery gates for the others. A streamer of black cloth was suspended
from the roof of the carnival association headquarters.

On the steps of the church the major smoked his cheap cigar
and muttered greetings when spoken to; he was not in the mood

for polite conversation. Inside the church Pedro Archanjo was all ready for the funeral: clean, well dressed, and decent. He always did spruce up for a special occasion, whether it was a *candomblé* ceremony, a street festival, a birthday, an anniversary, a wedding, a wake, or a funeral. Only toward the end of his life he had let down a little—extreme poverty left him no choice—but one thing he never lost, and that was his good humor.

When he was a young man of thirty or so he used to come every morning for his coffee with cornmeal mush and tapioca to *Comadre* Terência's stand in the Golden Market. She was the mother of that limb of Satan, Damião. Master Archanjo ate there for nothing; who would have had the heart to ask him to pay? Early in his life he had got into the habit of not paying for certain things, or rather, of paying for them in the coin of his laughter and his talk, at once entertaining and instructive. It was not that he was stingy—he threw money away like water—but simply that people did not expect him to pay, and often because he had nothing to pay with; money never wore a hole in his pockets. What use is money if not to spend, *meu bom?*

The minute he heard the sound of Archanjo's clear laughter, young Damião would stop what he was doing, even a good fight, and sit down on the ground to wait for a story. Archanjo knew everything there was to know about the private lives of the *orixás*, and of other heroes, too: Hercules and Perseus, Achilles and Ulysses. If Archanjo hadn't taught him, Damião, who was already wild and debauched, the terror of the neighborhood, and the head of a lawless gang, would never have learned to read. No school could hold him, no beating could straighten him out; he ran away from the reformatory three times. But Archanjo's books —*Greek Mythology*, the Old Testament, *The Three Musketeers*, *Gulliver's Travels*, *Don Quixote de la Mancha*—coupled with that infectious laughter, that warm, fraternal voice saying: "Sit you down, *camaradinho*, here's a corking good yarn for you," won the young desperado over to the side of the three R's.

Archanjo knew reams of poetry by heart and could recite them well; he was a born actor. Poems by Castro Alves: ". . . it was a Dantean nightmare . . . The deck all bathed in blood, the ruddy gleam of livid light"; by Gonçalves Dias: "Weep not, child,

weep not; for life is one long struggle, and to struggle is to live."
All the street arabs listened to him open-mouthed, marveling at
what they heard.

When Terência was down in the mouth over the husband who
had run away with someone else and been swallowed up by the
world, her *compadre* would bring a smile to her lovely lips by
reciting love lyrics: ". . . her mouth was a scarlet bird where
sang a festive smile . . ." *Comadre* Terência at her food stand,
living only for her wild son Damião, would let her pensive eyes
rest on her *compadre*—and what could she do but smile and push
her sorrow away? In Miro's shack, hot-tempered Ivone would
fling down her packages in rapture at the spell of the verses: "One
evening I'll always remember . . . She languidly dozed in her
hammock . . . Her robe half open, her hair hanging loose . . ."
And Terência's eyes would grow thoughtful again.

In the Golden Market one stormy evening when the sky was
pitch-black and the wind blew strong, Pedro Archanjo came face
to face with Kirsi the Swede. The major almost thought he could
see her: a fascinating vision standing in the doorway, curious and
frightened, whipped by the rain, her dress clinging to her form.
The boy had never seen hair like that, so straight and blond, so
flaxen fair, nor such rosy skin, nor eyes of such cerulean blue, the
blue of the Slaves' Church of Our Lady of the Rosary.

Inside the church there was a loud hum and much coming and
going, with a crowd constantly around the coffin. It was not a
first-class coffin, a luxurious lined casket, because the money had
not stretched that far; but it was nothing to be ashamed of with
its festoons and gold braid, the red cloth draped over it, the metal
handles, and inside it Archanjo, wrapped in the red cloak of the
Catholic Brotherhood.

Seated around him were all the venerable mother spirit guides
in Bahia. Earlier in the day, in the little bedroom hidden away at
the back of Ester's house, Mother Pulquéria had performed the
first ritual obligations for Ojuobá's *axexê*, his seventh-day funeral
feast. The fetishists filled the church and the plaza: respected
chiefs, younger priestesses, and still younger novices. There were
blue and yellow and lavender flowers, and a red rose in Archanjo's
brown hand. A red rose was what he had wanted. The sexton and

the saint-carver went to call the major; it was five minutes to three.

The hearse and the buses, filled to the roof, set off toward Quintas Cemetery where Ojuobá, the Eyes of Xangô, had the right to lie forever in the plot of the Catholic Brotherhood. Accompanying the procession was a car containing Professor Azevedo and the poet Simões, the only two people who were there because the deceased had written four books, defended his theories against the arguments of the learned men of his time, and, denying the official scientism then in vogue, had risen to strike it down. All of the others had come to say good-bye to an old man who was very wise and very shrewd and very experienced, who gave good counsel and could talk up a storm, a drinker of quality, a woman-chaser to the last, prodigious maker of sons, favorite of *orixás*, crypt of all their secrets, an old uncle who deserved the highest respect, almost a magician—their Ojuobá.

Quintas Cemetery is on a hill, but the hearse, the buses, and the automobile did not go all the way up to the gate as was usually done. Since this was no ordinary funeral, the dead man and his companions got out at the foot of the slope.

The crowd coming from the church mingled with the even bigger crowd waiting at Quintas. The only funeral that had drawn so many people as this was Mother Aninha's four years before. No politician, no millionaire, no general, no bishop had ever gathered so many people together to tell him good-bye.

Kings and chieftains, some of them bent with old age, ancients who had made the rough crossing from Africa, picked up the coffin along with the major and the saint-carver, Miguel, lifted it high three times, and set it down three times on the earth to initiate the Nagô ritual.

The voice of the spirit guide Nezinho was raised in the funeral chant in the Yoruba tongue:

Axexê, axexê
Omorode.

The voices rose in chorus, repeating the chant of farewell: "*Axexê, axexê.*"

The funeral proceeded up the hill: three steps forward, two

steps back, dance steps made to the sound of the sacred chant, the coffin raised to the height of the priests' shoulders:

Iku lonan ta ewê xê
Iku lonan ta ewê xê
Iku lonan.

Halfway up the hill Professor Azevedo picked up a handle of the coffin. The steps were easy for him to follow; they were already there, in the mixture of his blood. The windows were full of faces, and more people came rushing up to see the unique sight. Nowhere out of Africa could such a funeral be seen but in Bahia, and only rarely there.

There goes Pedro Archanjo Ojuobá, looking very fine in his new suit and tie and red cape, dancing his last dance. The powerful song cut across the houses, pierced the city sky, interrupted business, and immobilized passers-by. The dancing filled the street, three steps forward, two steps back—the dead man, the friends who were carrying him, and all the people who followed:

Ara ara la insu
Iku ô iku ô
A insu bereré.

At last they reached the cemetery gate. The *obás* and *ogans* brought in Ojuobá's coffin, walking backward as the ritual demands. Beside the open grave, in the midst of the flowers and the weeping, the drums fell silent and the dancing and singing stopped. "We're the last to see such things," Simões the poet told Professor Azevedo, who wondered anxiously how many of those who were there had any idea of the importance of Archanjo's work. Would it be a good idea to mention it in a little speech? But shyness clamped a lock on his tongue. Everyone was dressed in white, the color of the dead.

The coffin was set down for a moment before being sealed up forever in the tomb: Pedro Archanjo was still among his own. The crowd pressed close and someone sobbed.

And then, when total silence had fallen and the gravediggers had picked up Pedro Archanjo in his coffin, there rose a solitary voice in poignant, solemn tremolo, a most tender and sorrowful farewell. It was Master Budião in his white suit of mourning, led by his wife and helped by Mané Lima to stand blind and paralytic at the verge of the grave. Father and son, inseparable brothers, together for the last time: farewell, brother, farewell, farewell forever, a loving phrase, *iku ô iku ô dabó ra jô ma boiá.*

"Be sure you put a red rose in my hand when I die." A fiery rose, a rose of copper, singing and dance, Rosa de Oxalá, *axexê axexê.*

Of our poet

and researcher as lover

and cuckold, with

a sample of his

poetry

I

Since the great Levenson needed Ana Mercedes's help to put a few notes in order that very night, and since my presence was neither useful nor desirable for the job at hand, I said goodnight in the hotel lobby. Levenson, with what struck me as a cynical air, wished me happy hunting.

I thereupon called his new collaborator aside and recommended prudence and firmness in case the gringo should decide to play the role of a cheap Don Juan and evening homework degenerate into lascivious fun and games. Arrogant and wounded in her pride, Ana Mercedes cut short my doubts and scruples with a brusque question and a terrible threat: Did I or did I not trust her loyalty and honor? Because if I had the slightest doubt, then it would be better . . . Alas for me, I did not let her finish; I assured her of my blind faith in her and obtained her forgiveness, a fleeting kiss, and an equivocal smile.

Then I went out in search of a bar where I could take up guard duty. I wanted to get loaded to the gills, to drown in rum the lingering jealousy that the American's dollars and the protestations of Ana Mercedes had not dispelled.

Yes, jealousy. I died of jealousy, only to be reborn—each morning, each moment of the day, and worst of all each night, if she wasn't with me. I was jealous of Ana Mercedes. I fought over that girl, knocked men down because of her and was knocked down in turn, suffered indescribable torments for her sake. I became a bottomless well of humiliation and rancor, a worthless rag, the laughingstock of literati and subliterati—but she was worth it all; she deserved more, far more.

Ana Mercedes, muse and mainstay of the newest generation of poets, was a member of the Hermetic Communication Movement. It had taken real genius to dream up a formula like that, and only envious people and squares would think of denying its relevance. Among the hosts of New Poets my name is applauded and admired. "Fausto Pena, author of *Burp,* one of the most significant young poets in the vanguard of the future," wrote Zino Batel (the author of *Up with Crap*) in the *City News*—and he is no less in the vanguard than I am, and no less significant. As a student of journalism in the same university where I had taken my degree in sociology two years before, Ana Mercedes hired out her scintillating intelligence for a pittance to the city room of the *Morning News.* It was as a reporter that she made Levenson's acquaintance, and as a reporter that she graciously bestowed her divine, her peerless body on this bearded, penniless poet. Ah! How can I describe God's own mulatta, pure gold from head to foot, her flesh redolent of rosemary, her crystal laughter, her voluptuous insouciance, her infinite capacity for telling lies!

When Ana Mercedes undulated through the city room like a fishing boat in a heavy sea, not one of the low scoundrels who worked at the *Morning News,* from the owners to the doormen, not to mention the reporters, managers, and linotypers, had any other thought in his mind but to shipwreck her somewhere, anywhere—onto one of the soft couches in the publisher's office in front of Jenner's portrait of the paper's esteemed founder; on one of the rickety desks in the city room; on top of the ancient press, on the reams of newsprint or the greasy, garbage-strewn floor. That filthy floor, with Ana Mercedes lying on it, would be transformed into a bed of roses, holy ground.

I don't believe she ever let any of those impudent rascals have his way with her except for the one time they told about, when to get the job, she went out with Dr. Brito, the executive director of the paper, and was seen with him in the suspicious vicinity of the "81," a luxurious "hotel" run by the efficient Madame Elza. She swore to me she was innocent; yes, she had gone to that neighborhood with her boss, but only to prove her aptitude and nose for news—a confused story that I would just as soon not dwell on further. This is not the place for it, anyway.

I accepted her far-fetched explanation. That one and many others, including the scientific explanation on the evening I committed myself to go looking for Pedro Archanjo in the streets and alleys of Bahia. All my atrocious, violent, murderous, suicidal jealousy melted into vows of eternal love every time the serpent tore off her mini-blouse and mini-skirt, opened her arms and legs, and showed me all she had. In that golden landscape, gold and copper and perfumed with rosemary, she was a high priestess of fornication. "Prostitutes have learned their art from you," I wrote in one of the innumerable poems I dedicated to her—innumerable and quite lovely, if I do say so myself.

It was literature that first brought us together, and Ana Mercedes admired the poet and his rough poetry before yielding to the wicked cobra with his beard, long hair, and blue jeans. Yes, "wicked cobra," if you'll forgive my presumption; that's what the lady poets call me, a real cobra.

Ah, that unforgettable moment when Ana Mercedes shyly, fearfully held out her student notebook with her first efforts in it for me to judge: such touching beauty, such humility, such a suppliant smile. That was the first time, and the last, that I had Ana Mercedes humbly at my feet.

Zino Batel had been given leave to run a Young Poets' Column in a quarter page of the *City News* Sunday Supplement, and he wanted me to help him with it. Since he slaved in a bank eight hours a day and worked on the copydesk at night, he had no time to collect poems and choose the best, and so I got the job. It was hard work and paid nothing, but in a way it was worth it; there was a certain amount of prestige attached to the job. I set up shop in a tiny, badly lit bar at the back of an art gallery and immediately found myself swamped by girls and boys. I had not dreamed there were so many young poets in Bahia, and so many of them bad—each more prolific and inspired than the last, all of them eager for an inch of space in our column. The candidates, who were usually rich in inspiration and poor in worldly goods, would treat me to a rum sour; a few of the more enterprising offered me scotch. I want to make it clear at this point that my judgment and choice of original poetry were never influenced by the quantity or the quality of the drink. Not even some of the more determined poetesses vanquished my well-known critical severity by opening their skinny legs; they softened it, at most.

But in a very few seconds Ana Mercedes put an end to all my impartiality and firmness of character. The moment I glanced at the verses in her notebook I had the proof that that was not what she had been born for: God in heaven, how atrocious they were! But her knees, and the hand's breadth of her thigh that I could see, were perfections of nature; and her eyes were so fearful—"Baby," I told her, "you've got talent." When she gave me a grateful smile, I added emphatically: "You bet your sweet life you've got talent!"

"Are you going to publish them?" she asked eagerly, showing the tip of her tongue between her parted lips. My God!

"I might. That depends on you," I replied in a voice full of artful insinuations and *sous-entendus*.

I must confess that at that point I was still thinking deceitfully that I might get out with profit and honor intact: that is, by tak-

ing the poetess to bed and not printing her crap. I was very much
mistaken: the very next Sunday there she was, taking up the
whole of the Young Poets' Column, with laudatory comments
from me: "Ana Mercedes, the greatest literary revelation of modern times," and I hadn't been able to get any farther than a few
kisses, an occasional feel of her breast, and promises. I should explain that the three poems published over her signature were written almost entirely by me. The only thing of Ana Mercedes's that
I used in one of them was "subilatorium," a lovely word and one
that I had never heard; it means anus. As a matter of fact, all of
Ana Mercedes's poetic output might rightfully be said to be first
mine and then Ildázio Taveira's, when the ungrateful bitch,
wearying perhaps of my jealous scenes, abandoned my bed to begin a new phase in her literary career. Later on she left Ildázio
and took up pop music as songwriter Toninho Lins's partner,
more often in bed than in words and music.

When Levenson came to Bahia my affair with Ana Mercedes
had reached its culmination of blazing passion and eternal love.
For months and months I had had no eyes, no strength for any
other woman, and if she was sometimes false to our vows of love
I never was able to prove it—could it have been that I didn't
really want to? What use would proof have been to me unless it
led to a definite break—no, never! unthinkable!—or to the bitter
loss of the last benefit of the doubt, the slightest, most infinitesimal
shred of doubt?

Full of suspicion and jealousy, longing to have her in bed with
me and thinking of her in the hotel with Levenson at that hour
of the night, crucified by my own pusillanimity but well paid in
dollars, I went to hide my head and get stoned at Where Angels
Piss, a justly unpopular hole in the wall where no one I knew ever
went.

Hardly had I settled down before my draught of straight *cachaça*, when whom did I see in intimate colloquy with a scrawny
old hag, either a prostitute or a long-time old maid, an indescrib-
ably awful rag, bone, and hank of hair, but Professor Luiz Batista,
bastion of Morality and the Family, the most pious old hymn-
singer of them all, the Paladin of Noble Causes! He trembled

when he saw me, but had no choice but to come over to my table, where he launched with forced affability into an explanation as confused as those of Ana Mercedes.

In high school I had suffered through Professor Batista's classes, his bombastic discourse, his bovine conservatism, his bad breath, his finicky grammar; we did not get along well then or later, on the rare occasions when our paths had crossed. And now, here we were in this filthy, germ-infested one-horse bar, I racked by hurt resentment and cuckold's pains and Batista caught out in a scurrilous mockery of matrimony. We were linked by a common cause, a common enemy: Levenson, the learned American scholar, and his Brazilian counterpart, the unknown Pedro Archanjo.

The eminent academician trotted out his suspicions regarding Levenson and his mission in Brazil. I said nothing about my own since they were of an intimate nature. His, on the other hand, concerned the public interest and touched on national security.

"So many famous men in Bahia, the home of geniuses and heroes since the time of the immortal Ruy Barbosa, the Eagle of the Hague. And whom does this foreigner choose to laud, as the only personage worthy of his praise? A drunken black scoundrel."

His indignation got the better of him and he rose to his feet and struck an oratorical pose, in as rapturous a religious trance as any young devotee at the Alaketú Terreiro. Turning now to me, now to the glorious hank of hair, now to the waiter picking his teeth, he said:

"If we looked into the matter closely, I'm sure we would discover that all this talk about culture is nothing more nor less than a Communist plot to undermine the regime." Now his voice sank to a conspiratorial whisper. "I know I read somewhere that this fellow Levenson was almost called up before the House Un-American Activities Committee, and I know from an unimpeachable source that his name is on the FBI's list."

He wagged a finger toward the solemn indifference of the waiter, who was used to all sorts of ridiculous inebriates:

"After all, what is this he's trying to palm off on us as the acme of scientific knowledge? Driveling nonsense in bad Portuguese about the riffraff, the ordinary common scum. Who was this fellow Archanjo, anyway? A well-known man in his field, a professor, a learned scholar, a luminary, a great statesman, a wealthy businessman at least? Not at all: a humble runner at the School of Medicine, a beggar, practically a day laborer."

The worthy man was literally foaming at the mouth with rage, and I must say I could hardly blame him. He had devoted his whole life to loud warnings against licentiousness and dissolute habits, bathing suits, Marx and Lenin, the bastardization of the Portuguese tongue ("Latium's latest flower") and what had he accomplished? Absolutely nothing. Pornography is rampant in books, movies, the theater, and daily life; dissolute habits are the norm. Girls carry the Pill next to their rosaries, bathing suits have turned into bikinis and may not stop there; and as if Marx and Lenin weren't bad enough we have Mao Tse-tung and Fidel Castro, not to speak of priests who are obviously possessed by the devil. As for books and the Portuguese language, the tomes of the illustrious academician, cast in the stately, aristocratic mold of Camões and published at the author's own expense, are languishing on dusty shelves, eternally unsought, while scribblers who scorn the rules of grammar and reduce the classical tongue to an African subdialect are turning out best-sellers by the carload.

I was almost afraid he would take a bite out of me or the waiter; but he did not. He collected his fair companion, got into his Volkswagen, and went off in search of some really discreet corner where a patriotic, upstanding man could carry out the indispensable pre-preliminaries that might lead him for once in his life to practice carnal coitus with someone other than his saintly wife without being observed during that pleasurable enterprise by individuals of low moral and literary character.

Yes, low character is the word for it. If it were otherwise, instead of pickling my doubts in *cachaça* and scribbling verses of doubtful inspiration, I would have marched into that hotel and up to their room to catch her *in flagrante delicto*, the dollars in one hand, ready to throw them in the cad's face, and in the other a loaded revolver: five bullets into the unfaithful woman, right in her dissolute, treacherous, pleasure-giving navel, and the last bullet in my own ear. Alas, my jealousy is both murderous and suicidal—and impotent.

CUCKOLD COBRA

Polluted star
foreign beds
coitus in Latin
ah polluted woman
i will take your leavings
i will eat your scraps
roses weary watchful night
this Brazilian weary of the world
will eat your sociological
leavings
smell of rosemary lavender cologne
whiskey bath soap pipesmoke
oh yes

Worthy weary deserving you
no gun no knife
no razorblade no vomit no
tears whining shouting threats
only love
i will eat what's left

King of cuckolds
cobra   king cobra   king cuckold
garden of horns

antlers fasces blades branches bristles
on forehead hands and feet
down my spine
in my subilatorium
their points will pierce you
pure polluted star
your lord and master speaks.

FAUSTO PENA
Where Angels Piss,
very late at night, 1968

Which deals with eminent

and well-bred people,

top-drawer intellectuals, some

of whom know what they

are talking about

I

Levenson's statements sufficed to engage every newspaper column, radio microphone, and television camera in memorializing the life and works of the Bahian who had been so unaccountably ignored until then. Now, suddenly, he was a celebrity, and there were news stories, interviews, pronunciamentos by the top dogs of the world of culture, articles in the literary supplements, columns, and round-table discussions on prime-time TV programs.

The object of most of the intellectuals who wrote articles or were interviewed on radio or television was to prove their long and intimate knowledge of Archanjo's work. As you can see, there was little if any difference between Bahia's home-grown intellectuals and those of Rio and São Paulo: it is remarkable how progress is eliminating the inequalities and cultural differences that formerly distinguished the metropolis from the provinces. Today we are just as advanced, every bit as competent, cultured, and in the vanguard as any of the great centers in the south, and our talented young men owe nothing to Ápio Corréia and the other intellectual giants of the bars of Ipanema and Leblon. There remains one marked difference, however: salaries and lecture fees here in Bahia are still wretchedly low—provincial, in fact.

Surprisingly enough, it was revealed that every one of our most talented figures had long proclaimed, by every medium of communication known to man, the inestimable value of the works of Master Pedro Archanjo. They even promoted him from runner at the School of Medicine to holder of a master's degree from the university, only to meet with impenetrable indifference on the part of their colleagues. Reading what these worthies wrote, one would certainly not have thought that the name and works of Archanjo had ever languished in the obscurity and anonymity from which they had been snatched by Levenson's pronouncement, but had been always in the public view, their fame trumpeted abroad in essays, classes, lectures, and debates by a whole phalanx of followers of the work and philosophy of the author of *Daily Life in Bahia*. What exciting unanimity of thought, what touching testimony! Who would have thought that Pedro Archanjo had so many disciples? Why, their name was legion. But then, Bahia has always been extremely rich in ethnologists, sociologists, anthropologists, folklorists, and other such fauna, each more studious and clever than the man next to him. Our Lord of Bonfim preserve us!

It is only fair to disentangle from this mass of erudite, burlesque reportage two or three serious and noteworthy contributions: Professor Azevedo's extensive interview for *A Tarde*, to name one example.

As head of the Department of Sociology, the professor had nothing in common with the ruthless publicity-hunger of the general run of intellectuals. He actually was familiar with Arch-

anjo's work; he had collaborated with Professor Ramos of Rio de
Janeiro on a set of notes to make it clearer and bring it up to date,
and he had done all he could to try to interest young specialists
in those little volumes; but the specialists were quite satisfied with
themselves and their knowledge as it was. Only when James D.
Levenson, Nobel Prize winner, appeared on the scene did they become enthusiastic converts and assume command of Archanjo's
tardy triumph.

Since it was not easy to lay hands on Archanjo's books, which
had been printed in very limited editions a very long time ago,
Professor Azevedo's interview was the principal fountain from
which those who signed the brilliant articles in the supplements
and reviews had to drink. The meticulous Azevedo explained,
analyzed, and described in detail the work of the author of *African Influences on the Customs of Bahia*, emphasizing his auto-
didacticism and his scientific earnestness and courageousness,
which were amazing for the times in which he lived. He quoted
titles, excerpts, research sites, names, dates, and also gave some information about the man himself, with whom he had been slightly
acquainted and to whose funeral he had gone.

More than a score of essays, articles, and columns came out of
that one interview. A few earned fulsome praise for their authors;
not one mentioned Professor Azevedo, but all of them quoted
from Levenson's writings and those of other Yankee and European authors. One writer, well in the vanguard, categorized the
"Archangian message" as a "retroactive product of Mao's
thought." Another, scrambling to catch up with the first, wrote
on *Archanjo and Sartre: Two Measures of Man*. Real prodigies,
all of them.

One curious piece of writing worth singling out in the midst
of all that claptrap was a column by Guerra, one of the few who
made no claim to being either an ethnologist or one of Archanjo's
disciples. Guerra, a man with an irreverent wagging tongue in his
head, entered the fray for just one reason: to expose the incessant
plagiarizing suffered by the only one of Archanjo's works that—
on the bookstore counters more than thirty years before—had enjoyed a modest success.

Professor Azevedo bore witness to the sacrifices the poor runner, with his tiny salary and his huge thirst, had had to make to get his books published. His friend and collaborator, Lídio Corró, miracle painter, flautist, and partygoer, had set up a small printing press in the shop on Tabuão Street. There he put out flyers and ads for neighborhood stores and the movie houses in Shoemakers' Hollow, leaflets containing street-singers' ballads, and the sensational popular stories sold in markets and fairs. (A well-researched essay on Lídio Corró written by Valadares as a contribution to Archanjo's centennial, *Corró, Archanjo, and the University of Tabuão,* is worth a careful perusal.) In that grubby printshop three of the neglected master's four volumes, all of the worst possible typographic quality, first saw the light.

One of Archanjo's books, however, was published by a real editor in an edition of one thousand copies, a large one in those days and enormous for Archanjo, whose previous works had not gone beyond three hundred. In fact, he had been able to print only 142 copies of the last one, the very important *Notes on Miscegenation in the Families of Bahia,* before running out of paper. One hundred forty-two volumes—not so very many, but more than enough to stir up scandal, terrorism, and violence. Just when Lídio had managed to get hold of some extra reams of paper and was about to start the presses rolling again, the police had arrived on the scene.

Bahian Cookery—Origins and Precepts was destined for a better fate. One Bonfanti, of dubious origin and shaky credit, set himself up in the Praça da Sé with a secondhand bookstore specializing in school supplies and the exploitation of high school and university students, from whom he bought books cheap and sold them back at a profit: anthologies, tables of logarithms, dictionaries, and treatises on medicine and law. Pedro Archanjo soon became a regular customer. He spent hours chatting with the *mafioso,* and for a time actually owed him a few cents for a secondhand but complete edition of Dumas Père's *Memoirs of a Doctor,* a proof of great esteem on the part of the bookseller, who was not in the habit of giving credit to anyone.

Bonfanti had a few trots to help backward students at the Bahia Gymnasium and the private high schools pass their exams: a translation of Plato's *Phaedrus,* which was always sure to be given on the written Latin test; solutions to algebra and geometry problems; the essentials of grammar, and an analysis of the *Lusiad*, all in convenient small volumes of a size to be carried clandestinely and consulted furtively in the examination room. To complete the education of the young people whose welfare he had so much at heart, the Italian printed and sold pornographic pamphlets, for which he could also count on a select clientele of grave gentlemen.

Tasty dishes were another bond between the Bahia mulatto and the bronze-skinned Italian. Both of them enjoyed good appetites and subtle palates, and both were lavish cooks. Archanjo was unrivaled in the preparation of certain Bahian dishes: his sting-ray stew was nothing less than sublime; while Bonfanti, grumbling all the time that the proper ingredients were unobtainable in Bahia, could prepare a *pasta-sciuta-ai-funghi-secchi* to make you lick your fingers. The idea of putting together a Bahian cookbook, a collection of recipes theretofore transmitted by word of mouth or jotted down in kitchen notebooks, grew out of those talks and Sunday dinners. — *O comgo*

The edition was not all smooth sailing. Bonfanti wanted to limit the book strictly to recipes, with an introduction half a page long at most, while Archanjo insisted on publishing the whole book just as he had written it, with no cuts at all: first the results of his research, his comments, his careful study; then the recipes. The book was finally published in its entirety, but it was years before the first edition was sold, either because "cookbooks are meant for housewives and shouldn't have science and literature in them," as Bonfanti insisted, complaining about how much he had lost and refusing to pay Archanjo any royalties, or because "the Italian crook printed a whole lot more than a thousand copies," or because the public was simply not interested. When Archanjo died Bonfanti still had a few unsold copies on hand.

Nevertheless, if at first there was lack of interest, with the passing of time, the growth of the city, the beginnings of industry, and above all with the flourishing tourist trade, the cuisine of Bahia began to enjoy the national fame and popularity it had always deserved. A number of recipe books were published in Rio and São Paulo, some in very handsome editions, graphically perfect and illustrated with colored pictures of the various dishes. A host of amateur authors—journalists, society ladies, a Frenchman who owned a restaurant in the Corredor da Vitória—and their publishers all made a pretty penny from their *Cuisine of Bahia; 100 Main Dishes and Desserts of Bahia; Palm Oil, Pepper, and Coconut; Afro-Brazilian Cookery; Os Quindins de Yayá;* etc.

It was the scrappy Guerra's opinion that all of these authors were shameless plagiarists who had copied Archanjo's little book without adding anything new or original. What was still worse, they had left out, thinking it useless and dull—"Numskulls!" the columnist exclaimed angrily—the study, comments, and conclusions, and used only the recipes. However, after a brief stay in Bahia, one Rio reporter endowed with more effrontery and even less shame than the others had plagiarized the whole book, page by page, except where he had had the audacity to rephrase Archanjo's theories, muddying and debasing them in the process. Guerra, an honest man of letters, exposed the trick, adding for the benefit of his readers: "Remember, *I'm* no ethnologist or expert on folklore."

As for the interview with Major Damião de Souza, popular hero of countless forensic battles and memorable campaigns, its consequences were so far-reaching and so unexpected that it deserves a chapter to itself.

2

A few people, but only a very few, had the right to turn the doorknob and enter the office of Dr. Zèzinho Pinto, publisher and owner of the *City News,* the office where the great man withdrew to meditate and make up his mind. He never had time to think at the bank or at the Petrochemical Corporation, much less at the headquarters of the Manufacturers' Association. But in that office that no one was allowed to enter, at two o'clock in the afternoon before the daily hullabaloo began in the newsroom and the composing room, he could find the restful quiet he needed for his lucubrations, and sometimes for a restorative little doze.

No door was closed to Major Damião de Souza. He put his bony hand on the knob, turned it, and went in.

"Dr. Zèzinho, my worthy friend, I hope you and your excellent wife are in the best of health. Everybody well at home? And yourself? Healthy and getting wealthier all the time, aren't we? That's what I like to hear and that's the way it ought to be. Well now, I came here to talk to you about Pedro Archanjo. The fellows on your paper listen to what everybody else has to say, every Tom, Dick, and Harry gets his picture in the paper; but your humble servant here, the only man in Bahia who really knows all about Archanjo, is forgotten, neglected, pushed into a corner. What's this, Dr. Zèzinho? Isn't the old major good enough for you?"

He had touched on a raw nerve: Dr. Zèzinho Pinto was just recovering from the monthly luncheon at which the three press lords of Bahia, magnates of the newspapers of Salvador, synchronized their watches. They were old friends and the lunches were always festive, with good wine and contraband whiskey. Besides trading news and analyzing the political and economic situations, they laughed and gossiped and teased one another, not forgetting the latest gaffes committed by one another's papers. That day the victim had been Dr. Zèzinho, because of the poor coverage given by the *City News* to the great story of the hour: Pedro Archanjo. So much reportorial talent, the flower of the intelligentsia, and yet the reportage on this momentous topic could not compare with *A Tarde*'s triumphs—the interview with Professor Azevedo, to give only one example—and the *Morning News*, with its special supplement, "Archanjo of Bahia"—not to mention the exclusive statement Levenson had given Ana Mercedes, which had been printed in the newspapers of Rio, São Paulo, Pôrto Alegre, and Recife.

"Oh, come on, Brito, let's be honest. If you're going to stoop to such methods . . . Who wouldn't give Ana Mercedes an exclusive interview in a hotel room? I'd give her one myself. If that isn't unfair competition I don't know what is. Do you know what the reporters call her? The golden ass."

"Is it really made of gold, Brito? You ought to know," joked Cardim.

All three men had laughed and sipped their excellent German wine, but the incident had stuck in Dr. Zèzinho's craw. He was a fierce partisan of his own paper and jealous of its reputation. After all, he paid good money to those self-satisfied young pups with their Ph.D.'s and let them print their heretical notions in his paper, precisely so that the *City News* would be the standard-bearer of culture. And now, when an important story like this came along, they let themselves be outclassed by their square competition. Today he was going to call in those responsible—after forty winks in his air-conditioned office—and warm their learned gold-plated tails for them; he was paying those guys more than they were worth. His newspaper scooped by the others! No, he wasn't going to stand for it.

"Archanjo? Were you a friend of his, Major?"

"Was I a friend of his? Who do you think taught me to read? Who found him lying there in Pelourinho? The only reason he wasn't my father was that *Sinhá* Terência, my mother, didn't meet him until after Squint-Eyed Souza vamoosed and she had to set up shop in the Golden Market. Archanjo used to have his breakfast there every morning and, believe me, he was a one-man circus. You never heard so many stories, such a lot of poems and funny sayings. To this day I'm not sure *Sinhá* Terência wasn't soft on old Archanjo, but there wasn't enough of him to go around. He was the one who raised me and taught me my ABC's and how to tell right from wrong."

And a liking for rum and a taste for women, he might have said but didn't. Dr. Zèzinho was no longer listening; he pressed the buzzer and shouted for the copy boy.

"Is there anybody in the newsroom? Who? Ari? Tell him I want to see him right away." Turning to the major, he smiled his famous smile. "Major, you're the greatest guy in the world, bar none"—and he smiled again, as if he were giving him a present. "You're the greatest."

Actually, it was true; he was. On the eve of his seventy-fifth birthday, the major's popularity was unrivaled and he was far and away the most colorful character in Bahia. Lawyer of the People, Poor Man's Attorney, God's Gift to the Unfortunate, whenever he appeared in court he beat all records for defending his clients and getting them off scot-free. For close to fifty years he defended a never-ending procession of hopeless, last-ditch cases, most of them for nothing. He was a writer with space in every newspaper. All of them published the universally read "Two Lines" of pleas and demands to the authorities, the denunciations of violence and injustice, the clamor against poverty, hunger, and illiteracy. Having once been elected to the city council (under the aegis of a small party which had also elected two thieving, power-hungry rascals, the president and the first secretary of the party, at the flood tide of its popularity), he turned the Town Hall into Liberty Hall for the poor, kept the other assemblymen on a short leash, staked his council seat on the squatters' invasions out of which whole new neighborhoods were born, and never appeared on the party ticket again. The major was an all-purpose orator, not only before juries and appellate courts but at any ceremony or party where he happened to find himself. His voice was heard on solemn civic occasions and at wedding breakfasts, anniversaries, and baptisms; at dedications of public schools and health clinics, and also whenever a new shop, grocery store, bakery, or bar opened its doors; at bigwigs' funerals and at political rallies, in the old days, when they were still allowed. According to the major, when it came to defending the interests of the people and registering a protest against poverty, unemployment, and a shortage of schools, any tabloid, any gossip sheet, would serve, any platform was good enough, and he didn't give a hoot for the consequences.

It was worth going out of one's way to listen to a speech of his. Ah! That never-failing speech he gave every July 2 in Cathedral Square, standing in front of the statues of the Caboclo Man and Woman, Labatut, Maria Quitéria, and Joana Angélica, himself a monument of baroque civic oratory. How many times the delirious masses raised him to their shoulders!

His voice, coarsened by rum and tobacco, was exactly right for the rhetorical figures and timeworn phrases that always drew ap-

plause, and the quotations from great men, compatriots and foreigners alike. Jesus Christ, Ruy Barbosa, and Clemenceau were his
favorites. Phrases and concepts attributed to famous men, whether
living, dead, or invented by himself, glittered like nuggets in the
major's speeches; when speaking before a jury he would fling
them in the prosecutor's face, and the man's jaw would drop at his
sheer audacity. On one occasion, having quoted "the immortal
jurist Bernabó, the glory of Italy and the Latin mind," in support
of some wild theory of justifiable homicide, he was challenged by
the beardless prosecutor who, burning with self-righteous zeal,
was determined to denounce the impostor, to unmask the lying
rogue on the spot:

"Excuse me, Major, but I never heard of the criminologist
Your Excellency has just quoted. Is this Bernabó a real person?"

The major piously rested his eyes on the callow and presump-
tuous youth.

"Your Excellency is still a young man and not well read and
it is only natural that you should not be familiar with Bernabó's
classic works; no one can insist that you should have read them.
If Your Excellency were my age, and almost blind, with your eyes
worn out by constant reading, why, such ignorance would be
unpardonable. . . ."

His eyesight was excellent and he had never worn glasses. At
an age when most men have one foot in the grave and are long
since retired and waiting to die, he kept himself as straight and
slim as a ramrod by "pickling himself in rum," eating blood pud-
ding at midnight in São Joaquim, the Seven Doors, or the Market
Ramp, and throwing himself on top of a woman every chance he
got. "If I go to bed without humping I can't get to sleep." A
cheap cigar in a mouth full of bad teeth, big knotty hands, a high
collar, and a white suit—a son of Oxalá, he never wore anything
but white, though the collar and cuffs were sometimes a little
grimy.

His office was theoretically the best place to find him, for the
major was never seen walking by himself. He could not set foot
on the sidewalk without three or four unfortunates clamoring for
his attention, and no sooner did he lean against the bar in some
little café for a drink (always a healthy measure against cold or

heat) than the stories, complaints, and requests began. He took
notes on scraps of paper which he stuffed into his jacket pocket.
But his official office, where he gave consultations every morning,
lay behind the door of a two-story colonial building on the Rua
do Liceu in what used to be Miguel the saint-carver's workshop.
When Miguel died a shoemaker rented the place and set out his
tools and his last. But the major's desk remained and the new arti-
san, a good-natured freckle-faced mulatto, kept him in rum and
friendship.

Early every morning an amazing assortment of clients gathered around the door: convicts' wives, often surrounded by their
broods, mothers with children old enough to go to school but
with no school to go to, unemployed men, prostitutes, vagabonds,
sick people who needed a doctor, a hospital, and money for medicine, burglars out on bail and waiting to be tried, dead men's
relatives with no way to pay for the funeral, women whose husbands had left them, girls who had lost their virginity, girls made
pregnant by seducers averse to matrimony, all kinds of people,
all hounded by the courts, the police, or the higher-ups. And
then there were the drunks who were simply drunk as usual and
hoped for a morning swig to wash out their mouths—distressed,
hungry, thirsty citizens. The major listened to them, one by one.

He had residences in Liberdade, Cosme de Faria, and Itapagipe, and in each of them an affectionate concubine waited for
him fondly, even until dawn, when it was her night with the
major.

In Liberdade lived Emerência, a fat, placid black woman in
her forties, lavishly endowed as to hips and bosom, who prepared
typical Bahian dishes for the tables of the rich and catered to a
select clientèle. She was the eldest of the major's contemporary
loves, having eloped with him twenty-five years before.

In Cosme de Faria, gentle Dalina did sewing and embroidery
for sale—twinkling fairy hands, pock-marked face, thirtyish,
blondish, delightful. She had first gone to ask the major for help
after her overbearing father, on seeing her big belly, had thrown
her out of the house. The man who had done her wrong, a married
Army corporal, wangled a speedy transfer south. The major arranged for a maternity clinic and a doctor for Dalina and then

took in her and the baby; he could hardly leave them to starve.

In Itapagipe, in a green-painted cottage with rose-colored windows, lived Mara, a lovely *cabocla* of eighteen summers and a mouth full of gold teeth who made crepe paper flowers for a notions store on Avenida Sete and sold all she could make. The owner of the store had proposed another, more advantageous arrangement, and so had the artist Floriano Coelho, a handsome, well-spoken man. Either one of them would have been delighted to look after her. But Mara was faithful to her flowers and her man. When the major arrived she would nestle in his skinny arms, smell his strong breath, and hear his hoarse nocturnal voice:

"And how's my little birdie?"

Three houses? Three mistresses? Reacting to the natural incredulity of many who learned of the three beauties—"It can't be true, it's a lie"—the major would plead for understanding and forgiveness: "You have to remember I'm getting on, and I have so much work to do I've got hardly any time to myself." When he was younger and had more time on his hands, it was not just three then; there were countless houses and women, some steady, some now and then, and some by chance, as it were.

"Archanjo always had a lot of people around him, and the girls wouldn't leave him alone," the major reminisced, as Ari, the chief reporter, recorded the information in his illegible script. Dr. Zèzinho listened curiously to the interview. It was a cavalcade of people, anecdotes, places, dates; the major's memory was a bottomless well. Tent of Miracles, Lídio Corró, Budião, Kirsi, Terência's food stand, Ivone, Rosa, Rosália, Ester, women and more women, the Festival of the Sons of Bahia, the pursuit of Procópio, "that animal" Commissioner Pedrito Gordo, the Power Company and the strike in '34 ("Better not talk about strikes with the situation the way it is; stay off that subject, Ari," Dr. Zèzinho warned the hotheaded journalist, who was quite capable of making the whole story center around the strike and getting them into hot water with the censors), the Sirens, Miguel the saint-carver. Yes, there was a wealth of material there, but the major's wagging tongue wore the publisher out: all that gab wasn't really worth much as news, and there was nothing scientific about it at all.

"He practically starved to death, didn't he?" Ari asked.

Archanjo never put on airs, but he was hardheaded and proud, and no one could tell him what to do. Any number of times the major (and not only the major, other friends too) had offered to take Archanjo to one of his houses to live after it became impossible for the old man to work any longer. "Would you have said yes? Well, neither did he. 'I can get along by myself, I don't need charity.' Damnfool old man.

"He died just twenty-five years ago. And next December, the week before Christmas, December eighteenth, it will be exactly one hundred years since he was born."

There was an exclamation from Dr. Zèzinho: he finally had what he wanted.

"What was that, Major? One hundred years ago? Would you say that again?"

"That's right: it'll be Pedro Archanjo's hundredth birthday. When he celebrated his fiftieth birthday, Dr. Zèzinho, that was a party to end all parties. It lasted for a week!"

Trembling with emotion, Dr. Zèzinho stood up and announced:

"A week? A week is nothing! Major, we're going to celebrate Archanjo's hundredth birthday for a whole year, beginning tomorrow. And we'll wind up with a great big public ceremony on December eighteenth. Ari, the *City News* will sponsor the centennial of the immortal Pedro Archanjo. Do you see now, do you get the idea? I'll have the last laugh yet. I want to see Brito's and Cardim's faces. Ari, tell Ferreirinha and Goldman we're going to have a meeting today to launch the greatest publicity campaign this town has seen in years, and we'll do it in style. We'll invite the government, the university, beginning with the School of Medicine, the Historical Institute, the Academy of Letters, the Center for the Study of Folklore, the banks, commerce and industry, and we'll set up an honorary commission and bring up some people from Rio. Oh, boy! We'll show those rags how to make news. We'll be so far out in front of them they won't see our dust."

Ari seconded the idea:

"This paper's been needing a good campaign. Circulation's been falling off ever since we had to stop attacking the government."

Dr. Zèzinho Pinto turned to the major:

"Major, you've given me an idea for the promotion campaign of the year: Pedro Archanjo's centennial. I really don't know what to say or how to thank you."

Dr. Zèzinho smiled. Surely there could be no better payment, no richer reward, than that public notable's beaming smile. But the major, ah, that Major Damião de Souza, came back at him quick as a flash:

"Why, think nothing of it, Dr. Zèzinho. Let's go over to the Cubs' Bar and you can stand me to a brandy—or let's make it two, not counting yours. I'll have one for myself and one for Archanjo: the old man was nuts about applejack. Let's go; now's as good a time as any."

It would hardly have looked well for the press magnate to be seen swilling domestic brandy at the bar of a third-class café, certainly not in the hottest part of the afternoon. However, in a burst of generosity he told the manager to give the major a chit for his rum. Everything has to be paid for nowadays; the good old days are gone.

The great Levenson was not informed of Major Damião de Souza's interview, published after the scientist had left Bahia. Several months later, a brief letter from his secretary to Dr. Zèzinho Pinto expressed his regrets at having to refuse the invitation of that esteemed organ of the press to give a lecture at the "solemn session dedicated to the memory of the immortal Pedro Archanjo" which would mark the closing ceremonies of the centennial honoring the learned Bahian. "Professor Levenson wishes to express his thanks for the news of this tribute to Pedro Archanjo and adds his own cordial best wishes. He is delighted to know that the Brazilian people are showing their appreciation and respect for the eminent author." Unfortunately he could not be there himself; he had prior commitments, which could not be postponed, in the Far East, in Japan and China. An odd postscript in the scientist's own hand and bearing his signature lent the priceless value of his autograph to the typewritten letter signed by the secretary:

"*P.S. The China referred to above is of course Continental China, the Chinese People's Republic. The other China, the island of Formosa, is nothing but an absurd and dangerous invention created by warmongers.*"

NOBEL PRIZE WINNER EXTOLS CITY NEWS INITIATIVE

read the headline over the story about the enthusiastic support of James D. Levenson, "the most famous scientist in the United States of America, to this newspaper's campaign" and the regrettable news that he would not be present. "I am happy to add my best wishes to the other tributes to Pedro Archanjo," the daily quoted from the letter, leaving out both secretary and postscript.

Dr. Zèzinho was unable to conceal his annoyance: he had been sure Levenson would come, and now he saw his promotion campaign reduced to the usual national geniuses and provincial talents. Professor Ramos had promised to come from Rio, but this was but feeble consolation for the absence of the Nobel Prize winner "coming all the way from the Giant of the North, the American colossus," as the glowing announcement had put it.

The Bahian press lord did not guess how Levenson had hesitated and almost made up his mind to say the hell with that course at the University of Tokyo and the invitation from Peking; I'll go back to Bahia, I'll see that blue-green ocean again, and the sails of the fishing boats, and the city set on its hill, and those people with their civilized good humor, and that tall girl—what was her name?—like an erect palm tree, with her unforgettable lips, breasts, hips, and belly, a true mestiza from one of Archanjo's books—that disturbing Archanjo, of whose traces he had scarcely caught a glimpse in the mystery of the town.

He had meant to stay two days and remained for three—three days and three nights—but his brief visit had left an absurd and poetic idea in his head: Archanjo was a magician, he knew that; and Archanjo had invented that girl for him, Levenson, in order to give him a living proof of everything he had written. What was her name again? Ann, yes, Ann—open-armed, intrepid Ann, with her idiotic fiancé trailing along behind her.

Pointing to the poet Fausto Pena, who dogged their every step, the learned man had asked: "Who's that sour-faced guy who follows us around everywhere we go? An admirer of yours, or a policeman, '*un policía*'?" He was familiar with the customs of underdeveloped countries and the dictatorships that ruled them. "Him?" laughed Ana saucily. "He's my fiancé. By the way, didn't you say you wanted to hire someone to dig up some information on Pedro Archanjo? He's just the right man for the job. He's a sociologist and a poet, he's smart enough, and he has plenty of free time."

"If he'll promise to start working right away and leave us alone, then he's hired."

Those three days were full ones. The intrepid Levenson roamed through the city in Ana Mercedes's company: the alleyways, the steep streets, swampy Alagados, the red-light district, the baroque churches with their gold and painted tiles. He talked with all sorts of people: Oxóssi's Cameo, Eduardo de Ijexá, Mestre Pastinha, Menininha and Mãezinha, Miguel de Santana Obá Aré. He fled from notables and managed to get out of a dinner in his honor by pleading intestinal trouble, declining to partake of the elegant menu and listen to a speech of welcome by the prominent academician Luiz Batista. Instead he went to eat *vatapá, carurú*, and *efó*—shrimps, herbs, rice, and oil, stewed soft-shell crabs, coconut candy, and pineapple—above the Model Market, in the restaurant once owned by Maria de São Pedro, now deceased, where he could see the fishing boats with unfurled sails cutting through the gulf and the brightly colored piles of fruit on the ramp overlooking the sea.

In Alaketú, at the voodoo rites presided over by Olga, a daughter of Lôko and Yansan, he recognized the *orixás* from Archanjo's books and greeted them like old friends, while turning a deaf ear to the tedious explanations of the girl's follower. Oxalá came dancing toward them, leaning on his glittering *paxorô*, and embraced him. "Your father is old Oxalá, Oxolufan," Olga said, taking him to see the *pejís*, the shrines. She was a queen, that Olga, in the long ruffled skirts and necklaces of a Bahiana, surrounded by her court of woman adepts and young female disciples. "Queens on the city streets with their trays of dishes and sweets, they are queens twice over, mothers and daughters of spirits, on the *terreiro*," Pedro Archanjo had written.

When evening fell on each of those three short Bahia nights, they had gone to bed and to love, and he could not forget the girl's long legs, her buttocks, her brown breasts, her tropical perfume, her insolent, fearless laugh:

"All right, Mr. Gringo, let's see if you're any good or if all you've got is your face," she said on the first night, tearing off what few clothes she had on. "I'll show you what a Brazilian mulatta is."

It was a feast, a celebration of laughter and sighs. A celebration, what else was there to say? The words died away and the learned Levenson, dear Dr. Zèzinho, was on the point of chucking it all, including Japan and China—Continental China, don't forget—and saying yes to your invitation to see Archanjo's city of mystery and magic again.

Ah, if Dr. Zèzinho had only known, he could have printed a different headline in his paper: "In New York, the great Levenson feels *saudades* for Bahia."

A few of Pedro Archanjo's contemporaries, diffident, humble old people whom the reporters discovered more by accident than as the result of a methodical search, could only recall a man who was a good neighbor, a bohemian who was a little bit touched in the head, who had a mania for taking notes on everything and knew just what questions to ask and how to tell a story, an attentive listener, and a talented musician. He played the guitar and the *cavaquinho,* not to mention the *berimbau* at *capoeira* matches and the ritual *atabaque* drums—instruments that held no secrets for a man who had been playing them in street festivals and voodoo rites since his childhood.

These were the timid declarations of shy witnesses made tongue-tied by the impatient questioning of reporters avid for sensational details of debauched, unhappy sex and violence for the sake of violence. These old ones remembered a time and people who held no charm for the *mondo-cane* press, a time and a people still close by the calendar but so distant in their habits, sentiments, and way of life that one reporter, Peçanha, remarked to his crowd as they sat in a cheap nightclub:

"You know what? Here I am, way down—down so long it looks like up—and here's this old colored guy who's been dead and buried for the last twenty years and doesn't know it yet, giving me all this blah blah blah that he thinks is the greatest, all about some dump called the Tent of Miracles. . . ."

Peçanha had been down so long it looked like up, and so had all the boys and girls, every last one of them farther down than the others, and anyone who wasn't down was nowhere, man.

"Me, I'm so far down I get stoned and don't feel a thing, and here's this old creep handing me this line about his cruddy tent where that dumb Archanjo used to strut around like an actor and spout poetry. Shit, man. You want to know what I think? That guy Archanjo was nothing but a clown."

In which we are told of

carnivals, street fights, and

other magical events, with Mulatas,

Negresses, and a Swedish girl

who was really Finnish

I

The people came running to see the show, clapping, shouting, jumping up and down, and dancing with wild enthusiasm. They saw the carnival from beginning to end: rhythm bands, clowns, revelers, bass drums, fancy costumes, groups of friends dressed alike, tatterdemalions, false painted heads, grimacing masks. When the *afoxé* burst on the scene in front of the Politeama Theater, it was greeted by a wave of applause and one single shout: *viva, viva, vivoooo!*

Surprise turned joy to delirium: Hadn't Dr. Francisco Antônio de Castro Loureiro, temporary Chief of Police, expressly forbidden the *afoxés* to parade anywhere in the city, under any pretext whatever, after 1904, "for ethnic and social reasons, for the sake of our families, decency, morality, and the public welfare and in order to combat crime, debauchery, and disorder"? Who had dared to disobey the law?

The Sons of Bahia had dared. Never had such a majestic carnival pageant, such a constellation of grandeur and beauty, been seen or dreamed of: such rhythmic drumming, such marvelous colors, such admirable discipline, and Zumbí, the rebel slave king, in all his glory!

They had been doubly daring in choosing such a theme, for the Republic of Palmares had been brought out into the streets armed for war, with its heroic combatants and its commander-in-chief Zumbí, greatest of warriors, who had already beaten three armies and was ready to lick a fourth, imperiling the Brazilian Empire and the Emperor himself—Zumbí triumphant on his hill of fire and freedom.

There was Zumbí standing on the peak, grasping a spear, bare-chested, with a jaguar skin concealing his private parts. His war cry was the signal for the dance of the fugitive blacks—away from the sugar plantations, the whip, the overseers and the masters, away from the condition of brutes to that of men and fighters, never more to be slaves. In one row were the half-naked warriors, in the other the mercenaries led by Domingos Jorge Velho the slavocrat, the pitiless, lawless, implacable general. "I want them taken alive, every last one of them, as slaves," he declared in his speech to the people of Bahia as they celebrated carnival. He had a long beard, a tunic and baldric, a *bandeirante's* slouched hat, and a cat-o'-nine-tails in his hand.

The people cheered for the ungovernable blacks and their brave act of defiance: Have you ever seen anything like this, Mr. Francisco Antônio de Castro Loureiro, you policeman *pro tem*, you white man with a black ass? Who ever heard of a carnival without *afoxés*? They're entertainment, theater, and ballet for the poorest of the poor. Don't you think their poverty, the scarcity of food and jobs, the diseases—smallpox, yellow fever, malaria, dysentery that carries off their children like flies—are enough for them to bear? But no. You, Mr. Francisco Antônio Coonkiller, want to make them even poorer. Up your ass, chief; boos, whistles, jeers, go fuck yourself. Applause and vivas for the dauntless revelers, *viva, viva, vivoooo!*

Everyone in the carnival crowd came to greet the Sons of Bahia and cheer the free Republic of Palmares. Not even the African Embassy *Afoxé* had garnered such applause when it appeared for the first time in 1895 portraying the mirific court of Oxalá, nor the same group three years later, when it displayed to the city the court of the last king of Dahomey, His Coal-Black Majesty Agô Li Agbô. Not even the African Merry-makers, with the West African chief Lobossi and his Angola ritual. Nor the Sons of the Village in 1898 with their *caboclo afoxé*, a dazzling novelty that roused enthusiastic applause. In the year of the prohibition, nothing could even come close to the Sons of Bahia.

Carnival whooped through the streets, with the police and the cavalry right in the middle and the people fighting back to defend their *afoxé*. Down with Shitty Chico! Down with intolerance! As the battle spread, with mounted soldiers laying about them with swords and horses' hoofs treading on people and knocking them down, the *afoxé* melted into the crowd. Shouts and groans, *"morras"* and *"vivas,"* the crowd milling about, people hurt, falls, blows, some rebels taken prisoner by the myrmidons of the police, only to be set free again by the crowd, which was spoiling for a fight and some fun.

Such was the first and final performance of the *afoxé* of the Sons of Bahia, the carnival pageant that brought Zumbí of Palmares and his invincible band out into the streets.

A policeman shouted out:

"Get that high-yellow one, he's the ringleader."

But along with two other men, Pedro Archanjo, the high-yellow ringleader, had disappeared down a precipitous alleyway. One of the others must have been Zumbí's secretary, for he had a loincloth on and was carrying a pen, a parchment scroll, and a bottle of blue ink over his shoulder. Who could the scribe be but Lídio Corró? As for the second fugitive, his uniform and the whiteness of his skin revealed him to be Domingos Jorge Velho the slaveowner, although in the heat of the battle he had lost his beard and slouched hat. In civilian life he was none other than the Galician Paco Muñoz, owner of a bar called The Flower of Carmen.

The three men sprinted off like champions. But then, all of a sudden, Pedro Archanjo, a simple Palmares warrior and the chief of the whole shebang, stopped the race, and bursting into a peal of laughter, the loud, clear, hearty laughter of a man who has disobeyed an unjust order, shouted out: "The show's just beginning! Down with despotism! Long live the people!"—peals of transparent, joyous, infinite laughter: "Bug off! Go fuck yourself! *Viva, viva, vivoooo!*"

The year of the Sons of Bahia was Pedro Archanjo's last real carnival spree: in 1918 the *afoxés* came back after fifteen years of banishment, but Archanjo did not lavish as much time and energy on them as formerly, though at Mother Aninha's request he did take part in directing the African Merrymakers when their glorious banner was borne high above the carnival again in the hands of Bibiano Cupim, *axogun* of the Gantois *candomblé*.

Every *afoxé* needs a charm, and the very first charm to be used in a carnival was put into Pedro Archanjo's hands by the awesome Mother Majé Bassan. Archanjo had gone to consult her about a decision he had made and to ask for her blessing and advice. Lídio Corró, José Aussá, Manoel de Praxedes, Budião, Sabina, and Archanjo himself, after coming to an agreement with some enthusiastic dancers from Tororó, had decided to organize a carnival *afoxé* which would honor the devotees of *candomblé* by calling itself the African Embassy, and would show the pre-

Lenten revelers a sample of the civilization that had spawned Negroes and mulattoes.

Mother Majé Bassan cast the cowrie shells to learn which divinity would preside over the Embassy and which demon spirit would protect it. It fell out that the sea siren, Yemanjá, would preside and that Exú Akssan would shoulder the responsibility for its success. And so the *iyalorixá*, the mother spirit guide, brought out the little lamb's horn set in silver, containing *axé*, the mystery, the foundation of the world. "This is your charm," she said, "and no *afoxé* should dare to go out into the streets without this or something just as good."

"This is the *axé*, the charm," she repeated, placing it in Archanjo's hands.

It was in 1895 that the African Embassy, the first *afoxé* to vie for public favor and applause in the streets, challenged the Great Societies: the mighty Red Cross, the colossal Congress of Vulcan, the Marionettes of Euterpe, the Innocents of Progress. Lídio Corró was its ambassador, master of ceremonies, and peerless choreographer. At his signal the Dancer, Valdeloir, a youth from Tororó, stopped the procession and led the singing:

> *Afoxé loni*
> *E loni*
> *Afoxé ê loni ê.*

And as the chorus began to dance again it sang:

> *E loni ô imalé xê.*

There's a spell today, they said, today there is a spell. The pageant of Oxalá and his court, the theme they had chosen, was such a success that the following year the African Merrymakers, founded and directed by some Angolans in Santo-Antônio-Beyond-Carmo, joined the Embassy; and the year after that there were five groups chanting the Negro and mulatto songs which had theretofore been hidden away at voodoo ceremonies. Now the samba belonged to everyone and took possession of the streets.

Because everyone enjoyed the Negro singing so much—enjoyed the circle samba, the dances, the rhythmic drumming, the bewitching beauty of the *afoxés*—of course they had to be forbidden.

The daily press protested "the manner in which the carnival holiday, that great feast of Christendom, has become Africanized among us." A violent and systematic campaign was waged against the *afoxés,* and the great lords of commerce, the learned doctors, and the wealthy squealed in horror as each year saw new triumphs for the "African revelers" and dismal failure for the Great Carnival Societies—Ancient Greece, Louis XV, Catherine de Medici. "The authorities must put a stop to this drumming and these voodoo rites which are spreading their shocking din and clatter through the streets. Why, we might as well be back in the jungle or down on the Old Plantation. Masked riffraff in skirts and turbans, singing those abominable sambas, are totally incompatible with our present state of civilization!" cried the *News Journal,* the powerful spokesman of the conservative classes.

Yes, the *afoxés* did spread like wildfire through the streets, corrupting and degrading everything they touched. Caught up in the swaying samba beat, the crowd no longer gazed with such admiring eyes at the floats of the Great Societies with their French court themes. The old days when "enthusiastic cries burst forth as each victorious club, passing in procession, became the cynosure of all eyes," were long gone. The *News Journal* called for radical measures: "What will become of the Carnival of 1902 if the police do not take steps to keep our streets from becoming *terreiros,* fetishism rampant, with its procession of *ogans* and its native rattles, gourds, and tambourines?" *Afoxés* reigned supreme in the streets and plazas, in front of the Politeama Theater, in Campo Grande, in the Rua Baixa, in the Praça do Teatro, each new one surpassing the one before in rich colors, lilting songs, and inventive samba rhythms. They won victory after victory: cheers, applause, and even prizes. Like wildfire they did indeed spread through the streets, an epidemic of sambas and *afoxés.* Only drastic remedies would serve.

In 1903, thirteen Negro and mulatto *afoxés* paraded in marvelous succession. ("TWO BUGLERS will announce the start of the procession, shivering the air with blasts from their instruments and wearing LOVELY TUNISIAN COSTUMES as a proof that civilization on THE BLACK CONTINENT IS REAL AND NOT UTOPIAN, as evil tongues would have it"—this is how the handbill, the mani-

Africa → *"magical"*

festo to the people, distributed by one *afoxé* began.) In 1903, when carnival was over, the editorial writer who had called for strong measures poured shame and ashes over his head: "An observer judging Bahia by its carnival could hardly help equating it with Africa. And let it be noted, to our shame, that a commission of Austrian scholars is visiting our city. No doubt the ready pens of these learned men are even now noting this unhappy fact and will divulge it in the newspapers of civilized Europe." Where were the police? What were they doing "to show that civilization does veritably exist in this fair city?" How long can our Latin heritage endure if we continue to let this scandalous African exhibition go on—the drumming, the lines of mestizas of every shade from rich creole to off-white mulatta, the mesmerizing samba beat, these charms, these spells, this sorcery? For we are Latins, as all of you should well know and remember; and if you don't, maybe a good thrashing or a knock on the head will teach you.

The police finally came to the rescue of beleaguered civilization, morals, the sanctity of the family, the social order, the régime, and the Great Societies wih their floats and pageantry for the fastidious élite: the *afoxés* were banished to outer darkness along with the drums, the samba, and the "exhibitionism of clubs whose members dressed up in African costumes." Well, it was about time! Better late than never! Now learned Austrians, Germans, Belgians, Frenchmen, or those of the race of Albion may freely disembark on our shores. Yes, now we are no longer ashamed for them to come.

But the first one who came turned out to be Kirsi, the Swedish girl. Correction: she wasn't a Swede, though everyone thought so and said so until she finally gave in and might as well have been one. She was Finnish, actually; a wheat-blonde, frightened little Finn. Filled with fear and drenched with rain there at the Gate of the Golden Market, early on Ash Wednesday, with her wry scared little face and infinitely blue eyes.

Pedro Archanjo got up from the table where he was eating yams and couscous and smiling his frank smile, went straight over to her as if he had been appointed official greeter, and held out his hand:

"Come have some breakfast."

Whether she understood the early-morning invitation or not didn't matter. She accepted it, sat down at the table by Terência's stand, and greedily devoured manioc root, yams, cassava bread, and couscous.

In Miro's store hot-tempered Ivone gnashed her teeth with jealousy and muttered choice imprecations: "Peeled cockroach!" Terência gazed sadly down at the table; were her eyes even sadder than before? When the guest had eaten her fill she said a few words in her own tongue and smiled at them all. Damião the street arab, who had hung back and not said a word, finally gave in and smiled back:

"Never saw anything so white. That's Snow White."

"She's Swedish," explained Manuel de Praxedes, coming up for some coffee and a drink. "She got off that Swedish cargo ship that's taking on wood and sugar. She came in the same lighter I did"—Manuel de Praxedes was a stevedore. "Every once in a while some crazy rich dame runs away to sea on a freighter to see the world."

Her face was not that of a rich woman nor a crazy one, not there in the shed, at least; her wet hair clung to her innocent, fragile face, a sweet child's face.

"The boat leaves at three, but she knows she has to be back on board sooner than that. I saw the skipper talking to her when she came ashore."

Touching her breast with one finger, the girl said "Kirsi" and repeated the word, pronouncing each syllable distinctly.

"Her name is Kirsi." Archanjo understood and pronounced the word: Kirsi.

The Swede clapped her hands gaily and touched Archanjo's chest, asking a question in her language. Manuel de Praxedes challenged him: "Come on, tell us what she's saying if you're so smart."

"I'll tell you, *meu bom*. My name is Pedro," he replied, turning to the girl; he had guessed her question, and following the gringa's example he repeated: "Pedro, Pedro, Pedro Archanjo, Ojuobá."

"Ojú, Ojú," she said.

It was Ash Wednesday. On Shrove Tuesday the Sons of Bahia's *Afoxé* had been broken up by saber blows and horses' hoofs in front of the Politeama Theater, but only after the triumphant parade of liberty and the samba. Damião had tumbled a cavalry officer off his horse and borne away his kepi as a trophy. He had not shown it to Terência because he was afraid she would punish him, but now he went running off to get it from the place in the dunes where his gang hid things. By the time he got back, Archanjo and the Swedish girl were gone.

He had an enthusiastic audience, though, in Manuel de Praxedes, who had played the role of Zumbí himself the night before. He was well suited to the part with his gigantic frame, six feet and then some, and his barrel chest. He had spent the evening in pageantry and battle; and before dawn he was in the lighter, on his way to work in the hold of the freighter which had anchored during the night. He had not even had time to tell Archanjo and Lídio or Valdeloir and Aussá about what had happened the night before: he had forced his way through the crowd, knocking down several clumsy policemen in the process, and then given vent to his laughter on the beach while he waited for the lighter. Manuel patted the boy on the head with his iron hand:

"You're a nervy youngster."

"I'll teach him to be nervy," threatened Terência in a low, solemn voice as she gazed off into the distance.

"Oh come on, *Sinhá* Terência, who could have stayed out of the fight yesterday? We were in the right, you know."

"He's only a boy. He's not old enough for such things."

Only a boy? Damião was the youngest warrior in Zumbí's guerrilla band; he had already been tried in battle, and there was the proof, the soldier's kepi. Manuel let out a booming laugh which made the Golden Market tremble to its foundations.

Walking off in the drizzle toward Tabuão, the Swedish girl and Archanjo laughed together in lieu of speech. For some reason there was an uncomfortable silence in the shed. Manuel de Praxedes took up the thread of the conversation:

"Didn't you see the carnival yesterday, *Sinhá* Terência?"

"What for? I have no use for carnivals and such, *Seu* Manuel."

"Why, to see us, to see the *afoxé*. I was Zumbí and Damião was all rigged out like an African warrior. Master Pedro would have been mighty pleased to see you there."

"Nobody needs me, least of all my *compadre*. He has so many women after him he doesn't even know I'm alive. And now it's a white woman off a boat. You just leave me in peace with my troubles here in my corner, *Seu* Manuel."

The breeze brought back scraps of laughter. Far off on the sand dunes, Archanjo and the Swedish girl held hands and laughed.

They understood each other's laughter and gestures easily enough as they walked along holding hands. They went to Ash Wednesday Mass in the golden Church of St. Francis, again in the stone cathedral, and then in the blue Slaves' Church of Our Lady of the Rosary. Mourning specters, pious old women bent under the weight of the pagan guilt of carnival and the sins of men, were marked with the ashes of penitence. Who deserved God's mercy most? The Swedish girl went from church to church in growing surprise, her eyes wide, her hand squeezing Archanjo's arm.

They walked down streets and up hills until they came to the Tent of Miracles, but the door was closed. Lídio Corró had emptied at least a hogshead of *cachaça* in honor of the festivities the day before and was not likely to wake up before midafternoon. Then, with the aid of many gestures and much laughter, Kirsi asked Archanjo where he lived. It was not far off; he had an attic which overlooked the sea and the moon and the stars at night. He had rented the loft under the eaves from Cervino the

Spaniard five years before and would go on living there for another thirty years.

Rats scuttled up and down the dark steep staircase. When one of them boldly jumped up onto the girl, she was so startled—or pretended to be—that she found herself in Archanjo's arms and gave him her lips that tasted of sea and salt. He picked up the fragile child and carried her up the stairs.

The room smelled of Brazil: cherry leaves and rum aged in a cask of perfumed wood. In one corner of the garret was an unusual altar, with the tools and symbols of African divinities instead of Christian saints: it was Exú's *pejí* with his fetish, his *itá*. The first drink of *cachaça* was always Exú's.

Some said that Archanjo was Ogun's child and many thought he was a son of Xangô, in whose house he held a lofty place and title. But when the shells were cast and his fortune told, the first to answer was always Exú the idler, lord of change and movement. Xangô came for his King's Eyes, and Ogun was never far away; Yemanjá came, too. But in the forefront was the formidable laughing Exú, the daredevil who loved a joke. No doubt about it, Archanjo was his man.

Kirsi paused before the *pejí* and then pointed through the window at the freighter anchored beyond the fort. A thread of smoke was coming out of the smokestack. "My ship," she said in her tongue, and he understood and looked at his watch: it was exactly noon; they could hear the ringing of the bells. At the sound she shed her clothes, naturally and simply, with no shame or exhibitionism but only a smile and a word in Finnish—a vow? a proverb? who could say? The bells were still ringing and they were together; the afternoon sailed west and they didn't know it.

The sound of the ship's bell was heard no longer, but an importunate hoot announced the ship's departure, dragging cabin boys and sailors away from the red-light district. As smoke puffed from the stack, a long toot summoned the tardy passenger. In the attic the two were one, sleeping the same dream. Archanjo had taught her tickling, soothing caresses; in her outlandish but musical language she had lulled him to sleep with a northern lullaby.

They awoke at the same time to the distressed freighter's insistent call; the watch showed 3:30. Archanjo stood up, already missing her, wild with desire. Such a little while, and it was already over! The ship, the sea, and the captain were calling her. Archanjo put on his trousers, and she laughed again.

She got up in her white nakedness and waved good-bye to the ship out the window. Her hand glided down the velvety mulatto skin of Archanjo's chest and stopped at his waist. What was this foolishness about getting dressed? The foreign girl said many things, and Archanjo knew, beyond a doubt, that she was speaking words of love.

"Gringa," he said, "let's make a mulatto together, you and I. If it's a man-child he'll be the smartest and bravest man that ever was. He'll be king of Scandinavia or president of Brazil. But oh, if it's a girl, there'll be none to match her for beauty and grace. Let's hop to it."

For a long time the ship tooted for its lost passenger; the police were notified. But finally the captain ordered the ship to weigh anchor; it was out of the question to wait for her any longer. Well, the shipowner had warned him when he saw Kirsi on deck: "That crazy girl's going to give you plenty of trouble. Please do me a favor and don't hold up the voyage when she jumps ship at the first port of call." And sure enough, she had jumped ship in Bahia, where the races were mingling.

Hurry up, gringa, not so fast, hurry up! Their words crossed in the air, and all of them were words of love.

4

The afternoon light melted into shadows; steep, almost deserted Tabuão Street had still not recovered after carnival. *Mestre* Lídio Corró bent over his paper, painting a miracle. He had begun working on it before carnival and it had to be finished today. He felt tired and lazy, but a smile creased his face.

The miracle had been a remarkable one, worthy of the vow and the gratitude to which Lídio Corró, an artist of the brush, was giving tangible form, in paints that he mixed himself. But it was not the magnitude of heaven's boon—so great that it was truly a miracle—that was making Lídio smile. His satisfaction came from the act of painting itself: the effects of light he had obtained, the colors, the difficult composition with its human figures, fleeing horses, the holy apparition, and the virgin forest. He was particularly pleased with the jaguar.

A brushstroke here, another there to accentuate the green of the forest, the lowering night sky, the pallor of the human faces; the scene was full of tragic drama and the master's work was almost done. Maybe he ought to put in one or two rays of lightning cutting through the darkness to give the scene even more dramatic force.

Lídio Corró—fortyish, short and stocky, a shrewd, keen-witted mulatto—had very reluctantly taken up his brush to add the finishing touches to the miracle. He had drunk to excess the night before; he and Budião had lost count of how many glasses they had drunk during the dancing at Sabina's house. Beyond a certain point Lídio could remember nothing at all: he had no idea how the party had ended or who had brought him home. When he finally woke up it was almost two o'clock in the afternoon and he found himself fully dressed with his boots on, lying on the platform where he slept alone or in company in a room at the back of the shop. The Tent was both shop and residence, with a kitchen, a tap where he could bathe in luxury, and a little piece of a yard where Rosa liked to plant flowers and pick them. Oh, what a garden her hands would make, if Rosa would only come to stay once and for all! Lídio heated some good strong coffee for himself. No one had seen Rosa de Oxalá during carnival.

The miracle painter's one desire was to go back to bed and sleep until dark, and then to open the door of the Tent and welcome his friends in for some talk. There was plenty to talk about: everything that had occurred the day before, augmented by a whole cloud of false rumors and nonsensical bits of gossip.

Someone had brought great news to Sabina's house: the interim head of the Police Department, Dr. Francisco Antônio de Castro Loureiro, had been taken sick suddenly when he learned that an *afoxé* of Negroes and mulattoes had disobeyed his edict and gone out to prance and shuffle in the streets.

Dr. Francisco Antônio, of noble family and illustrious lineage, was strong-willed, bad-tempered, and stubborn. When he gave an order he expected blind obedience and rapid and wholehearted execution. It had never crossed his mind that anyone would dare to ignore, much less disobey, any law imposed by himself, or that an *afoxé* could actually be organized and paraded through the streets. That defiant, insulting plot was the very last straw. Of all the brazen nerve! The feat was incredible. Organizing an *afoxé* was an arduous and complicated process. There were all sorts of angles to it; it took time, money, discipline, and the greatest secrecy. The Police Chief found it unbelievable that that canaille, that riffraff, that pack of mestizos could have conceived such a complicated scheme and actually brought it off unaided. He was sure he could discern the corrupt and cunning hand of the monarchists, or a plot of the vile opposition. But if it really had been only the mestizos, the niggers and no one else, then there was no honorable choice open to him but death, or, worse still, resignation from his post.

Such was the fame of Dr. Francisco Antônio's formidable courage and cruelty that swaggering desperadoes lost all their bluster in his presence, and the most wanted criminals, the worst public menaces, peed in their pants. And now this hero of the police, this slave-trader, had been ridiculed in the public square, made the target of whistles and name-calling, up-your-ass in the mouths of rowdies and gutter snipes. Behold him in bed, surrounded by doctors and medicine, wounded in his pride, overwhelmed with hatred and humiliation, and about to resign his job.

As he painted the prodigious miracle Lídio let his imagination run wild: who knew but what the interim police chief's family might be praying that very minute to the Lord of Bonfim to save his life and his job, and who knew but what it might fall to him, *Mestre* Corró—*afoxé* ambassador, secretary to King Zumbí, and master choreographer—to paint the doctor in bed, green with rage and impotence, his heart sick at the sound of sambas and chants in Nagô—a heart that held only vanity, arrogance, and scorn for the people. Never had a joke come off so well, never had the rules and decrees of the powerful been defied with such grace and daring. When Archanjo proposed the trick after reading in the paper that *afoxés,* sambas, and rhythm bands had been forbidden, Corró himself had said: "It can't be done." But who could resist Archanjo's golden tongue as he rattled off one plausible argument after another? In the end Lídio had borne a large share of the responsibility for what had happened. He, Budião, Valdeloir, and Aussá had been the prime movers. Not to mention Archanjo, the ringleader, of course.

Lídio had taken up his paintbrush grudgingly today. How could a self-respecting carnival reveler work in the ashes on that dead Wednesday, which ought by right to be a day of rest? But the picture had to be ready without fail on the very dot of nine on Thursday morning, because the man on whom the miracle had been bestowed, a moneyed tobacco and sugar-cane planter from the interior named Assís, had hired a priest to say an eleven o'clock Mass with sermon, music and all. Assís had made a solemn commitment to God and was going to spend a pack of money, the yield from an entire tobacco harvest, in fulfilling it. He had ordered two dozen candles, each a yard high. And the fireworks, *Seu* Corró! His entire family was spending the week in town, a whole passel of folks, and they all had to be put up at the hotel. "You're invited, don't forget; we'll have us a real party after the Mass, God willing."

"Ah, *meu prezado,* I can't possibly have it ready for you by Thursday, I really can't. There's carnival in the middle and I can't promise anything during carnival, especially this year. If you're in that much of a hurry you'd better find someone else."

But the fellow would not hear of going to anyone else; only Lídio Corró would do. Lídio's fame as a miracle painter had reached the South and even into the Backlands. Customers came to the Tent from Ilheus and Cachoeira, from Belmonte and Feira de Santana, from Lençois, and even from Aracajú and Maceió. *Seu* Assís would not take no for an answer: "You're the only one

who can do it. I've heard there's no one as good as you, and only
the best is good enough, my friend. You see, it was a first-class
miracle, *Seu* Corró. That was no wildcat we saw, believe you
me. It was a great enormous monster with flaming eyes!" If you
could believe the planter, Our Lord of Bonfim had surpassed
himself that time. Under a sinister sky of ill omen the lithe, hungry beast sprang from the matted green jungle. His black and
yellow stripes dominated heaven and earth and Lídio's painting;
beside his huge body human beings were pygmies and the trees
mere garden shrubs. The blaze of his eyes, those flaring, feline
eyes, was the only illumination, for after thinking it over *Mestre*
Corró had decided that bolts of lightning would be excessive and
had left them out. The animal's eyes were fearful enough in their
hypnotic, incandescent brilliance—they were enough to pierce
the darkness and transfix the travelers to the spot.

The roar of the jaguar had awakened the four adults and
three children where they lay asleep in a clearing. Lídio showed
them rooted to the ground with terror. The horses were bolting
off in a neighing gallop; all that could be seen of them was their
curveting hindquarters. Here was a first-class miracle, an unheard-
of prodigy, and there were too many details to fit into one picture. For that very reason—because it was difficult—it had
dragged Lídio Corró from his lethargy and engaged his enthusiasm. What was easy held no charm for him; he was an artist,
after all, and he had his pride and self-esteem. Did only Dr.
Francisco Antônio have the right to self-esteem, pride, and a
sense of dignity?

It wasn't every day that a miracle was painted with such
perfection. Lídio wrote in his careful hand at the bottom of the
picture: "Great Miracle performed by Our Lord of Bonfim on
the 15th of January, 1904, for Ramiro Assís and family when the
same was traveling from Amargosa to Morro Preto with his wife,
an unmarried sister, three children, and a nursemaid and was attacked at night by a jaguar in the clearing where they were sleeping. When they called aloud on Our Lord of Bonfim the jaguar
became gentle and docile and harmlessly went away."

Reduced to four lines, the story sounded very simple. But put
our anguish in the picture, *Mestre* Corró, our terror, our afflic-

tion, the family's despair, the mother mad with fear. And the only weapon that Ramiro Assís had at hand was a tobacco knife, for his rifle was in the runaway horse's saddlebag.

Show the jaguar slinking stealthily, treacherously toward the youngest child, still a crawling baby, who smiled innocently at the big cat. It was then that Joaquina, Assís's wife and the mother of the little ones, let out a bloodcurdling scream:

"Lord of Bonfim, save my child!"

Our Lord's response was quicker than a bolt of lightning. The beast halted only a step from the baby boy, as if a celestial hand held him back. A clamorous plea went up from the adults and children, but the baby, still a pagan, only gurgled contentedly at the animal. With one voice they cried to the omnipotent saint: "Save us, Lord of Bonfim!" and Ramiro Assís made his extravagant promise.

"Mr. Corró, you would have had to see it to believe it: that wildcat turned tail and slunk back into the woods. We all started hugging each other. Everybody says you're the most famous miracle painter in Bahia. I want you to paint me a picture with everything in it, just the way I told you."

Whoever told you about *Mestre* Corró, *Seu* Assís, was telling nothing but the truth. Miracle painters abounded in Bahia; between Tabuão Street and Pelourinho alone there were three besides Master Lídio, but there was no one to equal him anywhere. It was others who said so, not Lídio; he was never one to brag and show off. "Well, I'll do my best for the saint," he said. "He's earned it."

Master Corró painstakingly drew Christ crucified, one arm free and pointing toward the jaguar and Assís with his family. At the top of the painting, where the saint was performing the miracle, light was beginning to overcome darkness in anticipation of the dawn.

Lídio Corró turned again to his favorite figure, the formidable striped cat, gigantic and pitiless, with its flaming eyes and its mouth, oh, that fearful mouth, smiling at the baby! The artist tried his best to erase the smile and the look of affection; he gave the backlands jaguar the bearing of a tiger and the ferocity of a dragon. But he couldn't help it: the fiercer he made the jaguar,

the broader the animal's smile; between the wild beast and the
child there was a secret pact, an old familiarity, an immemorial
friendship. Lídio gave up and signed the painting. On the red
border around the picture he wrote his name and address in white
ink: *Mestre* Lídio Corró, Tent of Miracles, Rua Tabuão, 60.

There in the half-light of late afternoon, in the flaring purple
twilight, *Mestre* Corró was sincerely touched. He admired the
finished work: yes, it was a beauty. Here was one more masterpiece to come out of his workshop. The Tent of Miracles (Tent
of Rosa and the Miracles, if Rosa gave her consent), where lived
and struggled a modest artist who was good at his trade. His
talent lay not only in drawing miracles, in the art of painting
ex-votos, but in other things as well; all you had to do was ask
any passer-by who Lídio Corró was and how many things he had
invented and accomplished.

It was not only Lídio; there were two of them. Lídio Corró
and Pedro Archanjo were inseparable, and no man alive was a
match for the two of them. *Compadres*, brothers, closer than
brothers, twins. Two wild men turned loose on the town. If you
wanted to know more, you could go to the police station and ask
Dr. Francisco Antônio.

Mestre Lídio backed toward the door to take a better look at
his work. The light was failing; night had almost fallen.

"Very nice," said Archanjo's voice. "If I were a rich man,
meu bom, I'd never let a week go by without ordering at least one
miracle from you, just to have them around the house to look at
when I felt like it."

The painter turned around, smiling in the darkness, and saw
the foreigner: her translucent porcelain whiteness, her childlike
face and figure.

"This is Kirsi." Archanjo introduced her with visible satisfaction.

"Pleased to meet you," said Lídio, reaching out his hand.
"Come in and make yourself at home." Turning to Archanjo, he
added: "Why don't you ask her to sit down, and you light the
lamp?"

Showing no surprise at receiving an unexpected guest, he
placed the picture against the light and gazed at it a long time,

getting it by heart. The gringa, who was tall and slender, looked at it over his shoulder with enthusiastic approval, vehemently clapping her hands and exclaiming unintelligibly. Now the only person missing was Rosa the wanderer; and who could tell, maybe she would suddenly appear in the flesh. In the Tent of Miracles anything could happen, and did.

Customers were in and out of the Tent all day, but the movement became much brisker at night. The Tent of Miracles took on new life when the lamps were lit as a signal that the show was about to begin. After it was over only close friends and their fair companions remained, and tongues were given free rein.

Even on Ash Wednesday there were plenty of customers for the magic lantern show, the puppet theater set up in the kitchen. Had it been Lídio Corró's idea, or Pedro Archanjo's, to show those primitive movies? It's hard to say, but surely it was Corró who cut the jointed figures in profile out of stiff cardboard, and Archanjo must have been responsible for the movements and gestures, the scenarios, the salt and pepper, the running give and take.

When the lights were put out there remained only the matte brightness of the oil lamp shining on the black backcloth, which projected the enlarged shadows of the crude and ingenuous characters onto the whitewashed wall. It was all very simple and simple-minded, and it cost two pennies to see. The show attracted young and old, rich and poor, sailors, day laborers, salesclerks, and shopowners. Some women even came surreptitiously.

They saw reflected on the wall two bosom friends, Trigger and Ding-Dong, embracing and swearing eternal friendship.

Flirtatious Lilly Titty sashayed onto the scene and eternal friendship went to blazes. The two men began to exchange punches and curses over the flirt. They boxed each other on the ear, poked each other in the stomach, kicked and tripped each other up. It was a splendid fight and the audience clapped loudly.

It all ended in the grossest lewdness when Ding-Dong, with an obvious hard-on, having put Trigger *hors de combat,* threw himself on top of Lilly Titty, spread her legs and let her have it. The audience went wild at the extravaganza, the mad rhythm, the supreme moment, the emotional peak of this superproduction. But no, there was still more to come: a comic scene which in itself was worth the two-cent fee. Just when the lovers had reached the climax, behold Trigger back on the scene, restored and raring to go. Swearing vengeance and all unbeknownst to his rival, he climbed up on his back and let him have it.

When the show was over the customers would leave in gales of laughter, and soon more would come. The show went on from six in the afternoon until ten at night. For two cents it was worth it.

Sometimes it happened that when *Mestre Lídio Corró* had drawn one of his miracles with art and painstaking care, he felt an impulse to waive the fee and keep the picture for himself. He would have liked to keep a few of the prettiest, at least, to hang on the workshop wall. However, only one miracle hung on the wall in the Tent of Miracles.

It portrayed a livid, emaciated individual, a victim of galloping consumption, saved from death on a certain occasion when, as he was about to cough up blood for the last time, an aunt of his who had little faith in medicine but was devoted to the Virgin Mary, called upon Our Lady of Candlemas and on a sea of blood entrusted her nephew's fate to the Virgin.

It was the aunt herself who had come to order the painting: a corpulent lady with a captivating gift for conversation. She was even more talkative than Assís with his wildcats, and she could still swing her hips in a provocative way. Manuel de Praxedes, who happened to be in the shop, feasted his eyes on her. He was fond of plump women: "I like to feel some real meat in my hands. A dog'll make do with a bone if he has to, but just try giving him a loin of pork or a hunk of roast beef and see what happens."

The favored lady was so proud of her miracle that she couldn't help putting on airs and boasting of her good standing with the Virgin Mary. Manuel de Praxedes told her that he too was devoted to Our Lady of Candlemas—never missed that holy day, went to celebrate it every year, rain or shine. She was one of the really big saints, a sure-enough miracle worker. You could count on her every time, right as rain, never let you down.

The aunt, playing up coquettishly to the sweet-talking stevedore, insisted on paying half the cost of the picture in advance, which was fortunate since she never came back. When the sick man's hemoptysis returned, the Virgin had apparently declined to perform the miracle a second time. Heaven only knew why, but there certainly must have been an interesting reason. It was the considered opinion of Rosenda Batista dos Reis, to whom Corró related the episode, that the Virgin had taken offense at that monkey business between the stout aunt and the strapping longshoreman making up to each other under her auspices, and that she had punished them by leaving the consumptive in the lurch to cough and spit blood. Rosenda was respected for her prudent, unerring judgment, and she knew as much about miracles as she did about voodoo spells.

The picture on the wall showed a gloomy bedroom without perspective in pathetic, washed-out colors, except for the spurting blood. The dying man, skeletal and bloodless, was half-erect in his single bed: skin and bones, waxen pallor, death in his face. The aunt, both pious and sprightly in a flower-sprigged skirt with a red shawl over her bun, gazed at the image of Our Lady of Candlemas and implored her pity. Blood soaked the sheets, overflowed the bed, covered the ground, and rose up to heaven. A little to one side of the bloodletting was a china chamberpot with green, pink, and red flowers, and identical flowers covered the aunt's skirt and the bedstead. Perhaps *Mestre* Corró had wanted to relieve the sordid atmosphere of death and despair. Ah, dear lady, no saint in heaven could save that miserable wretch. All you have to do is see the picture and take one look at his face.

Because it had been false, this miracle was the only one to hang on the workshop wall between the engraving of St. George on his white horse slaying a fire-breathing dragon and a poster for the Moulin Rouge in Paris. This was a cancan scene signed by Toulouse-Lautrec—Frenchwomen lifting their skirts to display thighs, garters, stockings, and ruffles. How the devil did that come to be there?

Oh, Lídio would have dearly loved to keep a few of his best miracles, drawn with such art and such painstaking care, but how could he when he was always short of money? He needed a lot of it and needed it urgently. He had a little nest egg; whatever money he got hold of went into the hands of *Seu* Herval, a wholesale dealer downtown. Printing plants, however modest, cost more than just a few pennies; you needed piles of money just to start one.

To own a printing plant someday was Lídio's sole ambition in life and he was determined to have one. His other dream, the one that concerned Rosa de Oxalá, depended neither on money nor on hard work; it was simply an impossible dream. For that ambition to come true, Our Lord of Bonfim and Our Lady of Candlemas would have had to join forces for one supreme miracle—and even then, it might have taken a ritual sacrifice to Oxolufan, old Oxalá, the mightiest spirit of them all.

7

This is what a miracle is, my love—Rosa dancing in the full circle of her white starched skirt and seven petticoats, her arms and shoulders bare under the lace dress, with her beads, her necklaces, her bracelets, and her wild laughter. To tell you what Rosa, Rosa de Oxalá, the black rose Rosa was really like, to describe her, with her velvet slippers, her night scent, that woman smell, that perfume, that blue-black skin of silk and petals, supple power rippling from head to foot, elegance and arrogance, her silver ornaments, the languor of her Yoruba eyes—oh, my love, only a famous poet could do it, a real poet with lyre and curly locks, not the troubadours of Bahia with their seven-syllable verses. They play and sing well enough when they challenge one another to battles of wit in song, but that's not good enough for Rosa!

Once she was walking down the street in a party dress on her way to the Casa Branca. It was a Friday, and she had bought a snow-white guinea hen as an offering to her father Oxolufan. Looking out the window of an opulent two-story town house, two wealthy gentlemen, one quite old and the other quite young, saw her go by with her gift and her royal air, dressed in the height of fashion, her sandals leaving a pleasant trail of music as she walked, a rose in her hair—her hair like morning moss—her *derrière* swinging like a boat navigating a high sea, and a glimpse of her breast lighting up the sun.

The two men sighed. The younger one, a spoiled favorite son, the scion of married cousins out of pure-blooded fornication, an effeminate, stunted, rachitic, vain little milksop, crowed in a stammer: "Just look at that black girl, Colonel! Oh, Lord, if I only had her underneath and me on top!" Upon which the old landowner—who had been a sturdy oak in his time, a fierce stallion, an earthquake, a turbulent river—tore his gaze from the vision of the black girl and fixing it on the feeble, watery-blooded little bantam, retorted: "Doctor, that woman needs a lot of man. That cunt isn't for a half-assed waterpipe to pee in, or for any dried-up old prick either. She's too much for me now, and she'll always be too much for you."

Lídio Corró took up his flute and waked the stars with the sound; on his guitar Pedro Archanjo searched for the moon far off and brought it back with him—nothing is too good for Rosa, who gave birth to the samba in the Tent of Miracles. The flute moaned and sobbed with love.

Rosa always came unexpectedly like this, and disappeared in the same unpredictable way. No one would lay eyes on her for weeks or months, although she punctually fulfilled her *candomblé* obligations when she received Oxalá in the White House at the Old Plantation. Except for her presence in the circle of devotees in those great celebrations, she was completely arbitrary in all she did.

One time she came every day for a week, Monday to Saturday, arriving in the evening before anyone else and leaving at daybreak, full of song, animation, and laughter; joking and talking with Lídio Corró, leaning on his arm and resting her forehead on his shoulder, an affectionate mistress, a busy housewife, putting everything in such beautiful order that he thought she had come to stay for good to be his common-law woman or his lawful wedded wife—whatever she liked, but his. Then, just when everything seemed to be definite, Rosa went off again and there was no news of her for two whole months, an empty time with no joy in it.

When the miracle had happened more than a year before—suddenly, unpremeditatedly, with no preliminaries and no beating around the bush—Lídio, who had long coveted Rosa, wanted to make their liaison official immediately: "Go get your stuff and move in."

They had been coming back from a party together one night when Lídio offered his company on the deserted, dangerous road. She had asked him to take her to see that puppet show she had heard so much about; she had almost died laughing at Ding-Dong, had drunk a glass of fermented rice flour spirits and then given herself ardently, almost flung herself at him as if she felt the need. For three days and three nights she came and went: she straightened up the shop and the bedroom, made everything shine, and filled the house with her singing. Lídio laughed contentedly to himself. But the minute he told her to bring her bundle of rags, she turned hard and serious and her voice was a bitter warning: "Don't you ever say that again or I'll never come back. If you like me, or love me, then this is the way it's got to be, just whenever I take a notion, whenever I decide to come of my own free will. I won't ask you for a thing, except to mind your own business. Don't watch me, don't spy on me, because if you do and I hear about it, I swear you'll never see my face again." She spoke such words and in such a tone that she left him with nothing to say except: "If I can see you and have you with me, I'll eat toads and snakes if I must."

He kept his promise: he asked her no questions and would not listen to gossip. Gossip, sermons, or idle envious talk, for no one really knew anything about Rosa except that she lived in a comfortable house in Barrís that had a garden in front, curtains in the windows, and a watchdog. An impenetrable castle—nothing to be seen but a little girl, daintily dressed, playing with the big dog among the flowers; a little *mulata* fit for an altar in a church, Rosa as a child but with straight, silky hair, a little brown-skinned peach.

Only Majé Bassan knew all the particulars, the whys and wherefores, of Rosa's life, and the secret was locked in her enormous bosom. The bosom of a *mãe-de-santo* should be ample, like Majé Bassan's, to hold all the cares of her children and those of strangers and foreigners, too: a locked chest full of despair and resentment, hopes and dreams; a coffer of love and hate.

Only Majé Bassan, the sweet and terrible Mother, knew anything of Rosa's life; what the others said was only talk. "She lives with a rich white man, an old nobleman, a count or a baron, the Duke of This or That, and he's the father of her little girl." "She was married by a priest and a judge to a Portuguese merchant, and the child is his." The stories were nothing but *comadres'* gossip, busybodies' twaddle, rumor and slander for the love of it. Lídio did not want to know and he never asked.

When Rosa came she was playful and carefree, and her presence was enough for him. What did the rest matter? She talked, she laughed, she danced, she sang in her nocturnal contralto voice. Rosa was wrapped in shadows in the wavering light of the Tent where Lídio's flute moaned and pleaded. For whom did she dance? For whom were the arabesques of her limbs, the swaying of her hips, the glances of her languid eyes? For Lídio, the constant, casual lover? For someone who was absent and unknown—husband, lover, rich man, noble man, the father of her little girl? For Archanjo?

This is what a miracle is, my beloved—Rosa with her songs, like the old song full of promises and witty innuendo, rich in accent and idiom:

> *Let's go behind the church*
> *To* Sinhá *Teté's house*
> Caiumba.

Mestre Lídio Corró poured his soul into the flute, his passion visibly breaking his tormented heart. Yes, to have Rosa once in a while he was willing to eat toads and lizards and rattlesnakes. She danced and sang before both men, offering herself and retreating. Pedro Archanjo showed nothing of what he felt; no one would ever know that a fire devoured him. Lídio must never suspect, much less Rosa. His face was stony, expressionless. This enigma of Archanjo's, this riddle without an answer, would never be deciphered, not even by Majé Bassan.

The women clapped their hands, the samba circle widened, the flute quavered, the guitar throbbed more loudly. Each of those present had his own secret, his yearning, his torment. At Archanjo's feet reclined the Swedish girl, all white and blonde. But she was not alone. Beside her stood Sabina dos Anjos, fairest of the angels, Queen of Sheba, Master Pedro called her. Her belly was bulging; but pregnant and all, she had never stopped dancing the night before, and now she started in again with Rosenda Batista dos Reis from Muritiba, the sorceress, heiress to the Mandê spells. When she prostrated herself at Ojuobá's feet during Oxóssi's festival, he lifted her up and touched her firm breasts with his fingertips. Standing near the chair like a supple reed, Risoleta, flower of the Murucurumim Indian nation mixed with white blood and African Ijexá, opened her lips in a smile: she had seen Archanjo behind the church and recognized him.

The only woman who was jealous of the gringa sailor-girl; the only one of them all who had never been encircled in Archanjo's arms and whose lips he had never kissed; the only one whose heart burned with hatred and who prayed that the white woman would die, that all of those women of whatever color would die—was Rosa de Oxalá as she danced before the two men with her breasts unbound under the lacy shift and her hips unfettered under the seven petticoats. Lídio sighed and smiled; before long he would hold that high, blazing bonfire in his arms. Archanjo was locked in his enigma.

This is a miracle, my little saint, a Bonfim miracle, a Candlemas miracle, a prodigy of Oxalá—Rosa singing and dancing in the Tent of Miracles on a night of heartache and enigmas.

Archanjo had a dream of desolation, a nightmare; he found himself on the harbor beach, a desert that was cold and burning at the same time, like malarial fever. Archanjo, with his heart on his sleeve and his tool at the ready, turned into Ding-Dong and Lídio Corró was Trigger. They embraced and swore eternal friendship, and played the flute and the guitar.

Then along came Lilly Titty with no skirt, no petticoats, no

lacy dress, wearing only her necklaces, beads, and bracelets, Rosa
de Oxalá naked, completely naked, blue-black, soft-petaled rose,
her perfume; and the sound of her voice was low and velvety,
and the night was huge and frigid and the sky was far away. She
danced before the two men showing everything she had, and in a
twinkling they were adversaries, enemies, deep wells of hatred,
implacable murderers with death in their hands: flute and guitar
turned to military sabers. They fought a duel on the corner where
the warehouse stood and the body of Lídio Trigger, dead beyond
recall, plummeted into the sea. A sun rose in the night as his
brother fell and was scorched in the quicklime to the dying
strains of the flute.

Now was the moment to take possession of Rosa, to part her
legs and lie down on that soft moss. Drenched in sweat, longing,
and despair, suffocating with heat and cold and fever, Archanjo
belatedly struggled against his dream as friendship lay dying at
the feet of the temptress.

I don't care about the nobleman, I don't care about the rich
man, Rosa, not a bit. Whether he turned out to be the hidalgo of
Cachupeleta or the Portuguese grocer, I'd put horns on his head
with pleasure. But listen to me, Rosa, and don't look at me like
that: if Lídio had been born of my mother and fathered by my
father he couldn't be more my brother, and he couldn't deserve
my good faith and loyalty more.

No, it can never be—not even if I die of love, not even if my
heart breaks, or I wander from port to port, searching for your
nocturnal taste and your perfume in every woman I meet and
never deciphering your riddle in any of them.

Rosa, we aren't like the puppets: we have honor and feelings.
Rosa, we haven't degenerated into filthy promiscuity like animals,
or worse still, like criminals. Yes, Rosa, that's what they say:
"Mestizo degenerates wallowing in sordid, filthy promiscuity,"
was the way one university professor and doctor of medicine put
it. But it's a lie, Rosa, a slanderous lie written by a know-it-all
who doesn't know anything.

Archanjo broke out of his dream with a mighty effort and
opened his eyes. Day was breaking on the sea and the sailboats
were just setting out. The Swedish girl was made of jasmine and

emitted a soft morning perfume. A dark child would run about in the snow. Rosa's image, completely naked, dissolved into the distance.

The gringa will help me to forget you, Rosa, and so will Sabina, Rosenda, and Risoleta; other women will help me to forget you, and I will be free of this torment and distress. Free? Will I ever forget you, or will I search for you forever in despair, for your blackness in a field of wheat and jasmine? And in every woman, Rosa of Oxalá, for your indecipherable riddle, your eternal forbidden love.

In a doorway near the bottom of the hilly street, old Emo Corró had a steady stream of customers in his barber's chair. He also kept a medicine chest stocked with household remedies and a forceps for pulling teeth. He taught the barber's trade, as well as what he knew about medicine, to his two sons, Lídio and Lucas. Lídio soon abandoned the scissors and razor, and accepting an offer from his godfather, Cândido Maia the master printer, he went to learn what he could at the School of Arts and Trades. Since he was an apt and intelligent pupil and enthusiastic about the work, he mastered the printer's trade and soon rose from apprentice to master printer.

At the school he met a strange, solitary, taciturn man named Artur Ribeiro. Ribeiro had served a prison term and it was not easy for him to get a steady job, but Cândido Maia and some other old friends managed to find him an occasional odd job at the vocational school. He had no rival in the North at metal and wood engraving, and back in 1848 he had gone into partnership with a Lebanese and a Russian to set up a clandestine printshop. No one could tell Artur's counterfeit notes from the genuine ones printed in England for the Brazilian Government.

The business was only too successful: Ribeiro did the engraving and the Lebanese and the Russian peddled the bogus bills in a ready market. They would have gone far, no doubt, had it not been for the folly of the Lebanese. He was seized by a passion for luxury and gave himself up to riotous living: women, champagne, even a dogcart. It was too good to last, and the secret found its way to police headquarters. Ribeiro and Mahul, the Lebanese, were sent to jail, but no one ever saw the Russian again. He got away in time with a suitcase full of banknotes—real ones, printed in England.

Artur Ribeiro, close-mouthed, impassive, grim, still behind bars of shame though technically no longer in prison, took an interest in the quick-witted street boy who had a knack for drawing, and taught him how to paint miracles—another odd skill Ribeiro had picked up at the rotten end of his life—and how to carve woodcuts; not metalworking, for while he was still in prison he had sworn never to touch a copper plate again. One rare day of *cachaça* and confidences he told Lídio he had only one wish in the world: to kill that wretched Fayerman with his own hands. The Russian had known what the police were up to and had made away with the loot without having the decency to so much as tip off his pals.

The death of his brother Lucas brought Lídio back to the scissors, the razor, and the forceps. Emo's hand had lost its steadiness with years and drink, and someone had to maintain the old man and Zizinha, his bride—his third wife, an eighteen-year-old chick. His hands might be shaky, his sight might be failing, he might be growing deaf, but the thing that really mattered was still in good shape. "It's all I've got left," explained Emo when he introduced his new wife.

Lídio's apprenticeship in the streets of Bahia and the old mansion where the Vocational School of Bahia functioned had not been limited to printing, drawing miracles, and making woodcuts: he had learned dance steps and the rudiments of music, checkers, backgammon, and dominoes, and how to play the flute, which was what he did best of all. Lídio was sure and skillful at all he undertook; he was shrewd and practical, and he had his feet on the ground.

For some time he stuck to shaving beards and hair, pulling teeth, and prescribing medicine—snake venom and rattles, home-made watercress syrup (it cured hectic fever in the wink of an eye), miraculous barks from restorative trees, brushwood to raise the spirits and other things, gecko powder for asthma. Then he ran into Pedro Archanjo, who had been his classmate at the trade school. Young Pedro had as much curiosity and determination as Lídio but was eight years younger. He too had gone from one workshop to another, lingering longest in the printing plant, although his forte was not so much printing as calligraphy and reading. He had already studied grammar, arithmetic, history, and geography. His writing—both his original compositions and his handwriting—was highly praised.

One day he vanished and no one heard anything of him for years. His mother, the only relative for whose sake he had stayed in Bahia, had died. He had never known his father, a recruit who had been drafted into the war with Paraguay, leaving Noca pregnant with her first child. They had been living together only a short while. He gave up the ghost while crossing the swamps of the Chaco, without knowing of the little boy's birth.

Archanjo went off to see the world. Wherever he went he found something to learn. He was not choosy about the work he did—cabin boy, bar man, mason's helper, penner of letters to be sent to remote corners of Portugal with news and *saudades* from slow-witted immigrants. Wherever he went he was always surrounded by books and women. Why did they find him so attractive? Perhaps it was his innate delicacy and his way with words. But it was not only women who succumbed to his charm: when he was still a very young man, everyone listened in attentive silence to whatever he had to say.

When he came back from Rio he was twenty-one years old, with a foppish taste in dress and a light hand on the guitar and the *cavaquinho*. He got himself a job at the Friars' Printing Plant, and one night several months later he found Lídio Corró rehearsing the shepherdesses at the Epiphany dance festival, an enviable occupation. The two became inseparable friends, and little by little the barber shop was transformed into the Tent of Miracles.

Three years after their meeting at the Morning Star Society, the ground floor of No. 60 became vacant. Lídio rented it and carefully drew a sign, each letter in a different color, saying TENT OF MIRACLES. Their main income was to come from his miracle paintings.

Archanjo had chosen the name. He had left the printing plant to teach backward children their sums and their ABC's and was now Corró's partner, more or less, a partner at work and at play. Corró prudently set aside his slim profits to earn a little interest. Lídio's ambition was to own the Democratic Printing Plant, where Sr. Estevão das Dores printed whatever came to hand: singers' ballads, popular songs, challenges in verse, the whole vast world of popular literature. Woodcuts by Lídio adorned the covers of the leaflets. *Seu* Estevão, with his white hair, his rheumatism, and his shuffling feet, had promised that as soon as he made up his mind to retire he would sell Lídio the shop and everything in it by installment.

While they waited for the Democratic's type and its customers, the Tent of Miracles became the living heart of the neighborhood where the pulse of Bahia beats highest, from Cathedral Square and the Terreiro de Jesus to the Carmo Gates and Santo Antônio, embracing Pelourinho, Tabuão, Upper and Lower Maciel, São Miguel, Shoemakers' Lane, and the Market of Yansan (or St. Barbara, if the reader prefers).

Making woodcuts, drawing miracles, yanking teeth, selling remedies, and showing his magic lantern puppets, Lídio Corró accumulated his precious money little by little. But any number of other problems were discussed and settled in that very room. Ideas were born and grew into projects to be carried out in the streets, at parties, on the *terreiros*. Matters of consequence were debated, such as the succession of spirit guides, the ceremonial hymns, the magical properties of different leaves, *macumba* formulas and spells. Epiphany groups, carnival *afoxés*, and *capoeira* schools were formed, parties and anniversaries planned, and steps taken to insure the success of the washing of the Church of Bonfim and the offering to Yemanjá, the Mother of Waters. The Tent of Miracles was a kind of Senate, a gathering place for the notables among the poor, a numerous and important assemblage. *Iyalorixás, babalaôs*, the erudite and the superstitious, singers, dancers, *capoeira* experts, masters in every art and vocation mingled there, each bringing his own special talent.

It was at about this time that Pedro Archanjo, a boy of twenty-odd years, acquired a mania for jotting down stories, anecdotes, news items, interesting thoughts, names, dates, all kinds of trivial details, anything that had to do with the life of the people. Why he wanted to do this, no one could say. Pedro Archanjo was full of notions and odd bits of abstruse knowledge, and it was certainly no accident that he had been chosen, young as he was, to assume a high position in Xangô's house: he had been raised up and consecrated as Ojuobá, the Eyes of the King. Favored among so many, many aspirants, including wise, respectable elders, it was Archanjo who had been given the title with all its rights and duties; he was not yet thirty when the saint made known his choice. And it could not have been a better one—Xangô always has good reasons for what he does.

The story spread among the people of the *terreiros* and gained currency on the city streets that it had been the *orixá* himself who had told Archanjo to see all, learn all, and write it all down on paper. That was why he had been named Ojuobá, the Eyes of Xangô.

In 1900, when he was thirty-two years old, Pedro Archanjo was hired as a runner at the School of Medicine and assumed his post at the Terreiro. He was soon popular with the students and lost no time in teaching them the rudiments of their courses. He had been given the post thanks to the mediation of Majé Bassan, who had friends and acquaintances everywhere and was respected even by those high up in the government. Quite often, when she heard the name of some powerful figure in business or politics or even in the Church, Mother Bassan would murmur: "That's one of my boys." But of all of her boys, young, old, brand new, poor, or rich, Pedro Archanjo was the favorite, the coryphaeus.

10

Kirsi was rehearsing with the other shepherdesses. She was to be the new, the true morning star. Her predecessor, Irene, had resigned to go and live with a watchmaker in the Recôncavo. If she had not consented to go, the town of Sto. Amaro da Purificação would have had no more calendar, no hour- or minute-hand for its sugar mills and distilleries: when the watchmaker made a visit to Bahia and saw Irene dancing, he forgot what time it was.

The shepherdesses wove the steps of the African *lundu* in and out, watchful for signals from Lídio Corró, the master of the dance. Kirsi stepped out in front and caught Archanjo's approving smile and glance. Just behind her, Dedé, too, gathered a glance toward her palpitating breast. Dear little Dedé, so young and so virginal, and already longing to join in the dance:

> *Bring the little donkey in*
> *So the dew won't get it wet.*
> *The saddle's made of velvet,*
> *And the blanket's silkier yet.*

Those who came to the rehearsals saw Kirsi's radiance as the morning star, but the crowd never saw her in the parade; there wasn't time. Another ship came and she sailed away after six months in Bahia, where everyone had called her a Swede. Only a few people knew she was Finnish, but all of them loved her. She was welcomed with no questions asked, and they made her one of them.

When the freighter anchored in port, she told Archanjo in her scanty Portuguese, in an accent like a sailor's: "It's time for me to go now, I'm carrying our son in my womb. Everything good lasts only so long, and it has to end when the time comes if we want it to last forever. I'm taking this sun, your music and your blood, and wherever I am you'll be there every moment. Thank you, Ojú."

Manuel de Praxedes took her out in the lighter and the cargo ship lifted anchor in the middle of the night. Pedro Archanjo stood in the star-shadow, his face like stone. The ship's whistle blew when it crossed the bar at the sea gate. I won't tell you good-bye. A bronze child, a Bahia mestizo, will run about in the snow.

Dedé skipped on the fringe of the sea and sang Epiphany songs:

> *Oh you gal with the big basket*
> *Give me just a drop to drink.*
> *Don't you do it, Cipriana,*
> *Or you'll never be the same again.*

Far out beyond the islands, bound for snowstorms and blanched stars, a gray lugger sails toward the cold North, taking with it the morning star. Dedé wants to cheer him up, to see his tight mouth relax and his stony expression soften in a smile. Dedé will be the new star. She doesn't have that luminous, shining halo, that smoldering hair like a comet, but she has her own tropical warmth and swooning languor and a scent of lavender. Dedé, the girl with the big basket.

"You're the best people in the world, and the most civilized, you Bahia mulattoes," the Swedish girl had said when she went to the Tent of Miracles to tell Lídio, Budião, and Aussá good-bye. She had come from a faraway country and had lived with them, and she knew what she was talking about—real knowledge, without limits or doubts. Why, then, had Dr. Nilo Argolo—the head of the Department of Forensic Medicine at the university and scientific mentor of the medical association, renowned for his learning and his remarkable library—why had he written those terrible pages, those scalding words, as hot as a branding iron, about the mestizos of Bahia?

The contents of the thin pamphlet, a report presented at a scientific convention and later printed in a medical review, were revealed in the title: "The psychic and mental degeneracy of half-breeds, for example, those of Bahia." Good Lord in Heaven, where on earth had the professor dug up such categorical statements? "The principal factor in our backwardness and inferiority are the mestizos, an incompetent, subhuman race." As for Negroes, it was Professor Argolo's conviction that they had yet to attain human status: "Is there any country in the world where the blacks have been able to set up a state with a modicum of civilization?" he demanded of his colleagues at the convention.

One afternoon when the sun was clear and the breeze was gentle, Archanjo strolled with his slightly rolling gait across the Terreiro de Jesus. He had gone to take a message from the secretary at the Medical School to the prior of the Franciscans, a bearded, bald, and affable Dutch friar. When Archanjo arrived he was savoring his coffee and offered a cup to the smiling runner.

"I know you," he said in his crisp accent.

"I'm around here most every day, in the school or the plaza."

"It wasn't here, though." The friar laughed a full, hearty laugh. "Do you know where it was? At the *candomblé*. But you didn't notice me because I was hidden away in a corner, not wearing my habit, and you were sitting in a special chair next to the *mãe-de-santo*."

"You, Father? At the *candomblé?*"

"Oh, I go there once in a while, but you don't need to tell anybody. Dona Majé and I are old friends. She told me you know everything there is to know about the *macumba*. One of these days I'd like to have a talk with you, if you'll give me that pleasure. . . ." Archanjo felt all the peace in the world there in the cloister, with its luxuriant trees, its flowers, its tiles; and all the peace in the world in the company of the hospitable Franciscan.

"I'll come whenever you want me to, Father."

He was crossing the Terreiro on his way back to the university and thinking, "a priest, a friar from a monastery going to the *candomblé;* now that is a surprise, something really new," when he was surrounded by a band of students.

Pedro Archanjo enjoyed excellent relations with the medical students. Obliging, attentive, and cheerful, the runner was always ready to help the young men in their problems with roll calls missed and classes cut. He kept their books and their notes for them and did them a world of small favors. Theirs was a camaraderie based on long hours of talk. Freshmen and those about to take their M.D.'s sought him out at the Tent of Miracles or at Master Budião's Capoeira Academy, and two or three of them had even gone with him to *candomblé* ceremonies.

With students and professors alike, Archanjo was polite and solicitous but never humble or obsequious. Bahians are not usually either one. In the pride of his manhood the poorest man in the city is the equal of the most powerful magnate, and far more civilized.

The young men's liking for the modest functionary turned to gratitude when Pedro Archanjo's testimony was a key factor in saving a student from being expelled in his sixth year because of a confused and complicated affair touching on the family honor of one of the professors. When a formal investigation of the outraged professor's accusations was held, it was the testimony of Archanjo, who had been on duty in the chancery, which cleared the youth. The students had all rallied around their classmate but had no real hope, and Archanjo was new on the job and needed the work. Nevertheless, Archanjo neither took sides nor allowed himself to be swayed or intimidated, and this earned the respect of the young men and the enmity of the professor, who, incidentally, abandoned his classes halfway through the term.

When Archanjo got to the fountain in the middle of the plaza, he had a whole group around him. One of them, a good-looking fourth-year student, a fun-loving fellow who appreciated Archanjo's skillful hand on the guitar and the *cavaquinho*—he liked to strum the mandolin himself—held up a pamphlet and said: "What do you think of this, Master Pedro?" The others laughed, clearly in a mood to tease the handsome, good-natured mulatto.

Archanjo glanced through the pages and his eyes narrowed and grew red. According to Dr. Nilo Argolo, it seemed, niggers and half-breeds were a disgrace to Brazil.

"The professor skins you alive. He doesn't leave you a hole to crawl through," the fourth-year student remarked in amusement. "Thief, assassin, and worse, he calls you every name in the book. You're on the borderline between irrational animal and

Homo sapiens. And just look at this: he says mulattoes are even worse than the blacks. The Monster's gobbled your whole race up alive and you along with it, Master Pedro."

Pedro Archanjo came back from a long way off and pulled himself together.

"Am I the only one he's gobbled up, *meu bom?*" he said, looking at the boy's hair, mouth, lips, and nose. "He's gobbled us all up, every half-breed man jack of us, *meu bom.* You, and me"—he glanced quickly at the others—"not one of us in this group is safe, not a single one."

First there was a little burst of involuntary snickers, and then two or three of the boys laughed out loud. The fourth-year student good-humoredly confessed:

"Nobody can get the better of you, Master Pedro. You've just torn up all our family trees by the roots."

One lad with an aloof, superior air detached himself from the group.

"Not mine," he said, reeling off four last names and two noble particles. "My family's blood is pure. Thank God, we never mixed with blacks."

Archanjo's rage had dissolved and now he was enjoying himself. He knew absolutely and beyond any cavil that the theories of Dr. Nilo—that ignorant lunkhead, that chamberpot full of shit —were pure error and calumny, born of bigoted ignorance. He looked at the lad:

"Are you sure, *meu bom?* Your great-grandmother was already dead when you were born. Do you know what her name was? Maria Iabací. That was the name of her tribe. Your great-grandfather was an honest man and he married her."

"I'm going to punch your face for you, you impudent nigger."

"Then what are you waiting for, *meu bom?* Step right up."

"Watch out, Armando, he's good at *capoeira,*" warned one of his companions.

The others teased their fatuous classmate:

"Come on, Armando, let's see your blue-blooded courage!"

"I'm not going to waste it on an errand boy," the hidalgo flung back as he retired from the arena and the argument died down.

The fourth-year boy laughed:

"He's nothing but a paper tiger, Master Pedro, all puffed up because his grandfather was a Minister during the Empire. He's an idiot."

A boy with glasses and a straw hat joined the conversation:

"My grandmother was a mulatto and she was the best person I ever knew."

Archanjo started to leave.

"Will you lend me that pamphlet?"

"You can keep it."

Never again did a student abuse Archanjo's patience by touching on the subject of race, not even twenty years later, when Gobineau's shadow fell over the Terreiro de Jesus and Aryanism came into fashion as official doctrine at the School of Medicine. When the scandal broke out the students had changed, but they all took the runner's part against the professors.

In the Band of the Morning Star, whites, blacks, and mulattoes danced together, caring not a whit for the theories of professors. Kirsi and Dedé, it didn't matter which one was the morning star, the crowd applauded with the same enthusiasm. There is no first or second, no superior or inferior, among stars.

Now the night and the ocean had swallowed up the ship. Dedé stopped singing and lay down on the sand, obviously ready and willing. Pedro Archanjo listened to the rushing of the sea wind, the sound of waves and distance. "You're the best people in the world." In cold Suomi a bronze child made of sun and snow will play King of Sweden, holding in his right hand the *paxorô* of an African god.

In which Fausto Pena,

indefatigable parvenu,

receives a small fee,

a lesson, and a

proposition

I am sorry to have to say this, but arrogance and envy are rampant among the cream of our intelligentsia. There is no denying this melancholy truth, for I have felt its consequences in my very being. It seems I am the favorite victim of low, cunning spite, of the grossest kind of presumption. Because I was honored by the great Levenson with a (verbal) contract to do research on Pedro Archanjo, my confrères make my life impossible, say outrageous things about me and Ana Mercedes, drag me through the mud, and suffocate me with filthy calumny.

I have already had occasion to mention the political intrigues, the infamous attempts to show me up as a lackey of American cultural imperialism. They earned me the hostility of the Left, which I must admit has certain advantages at present, and barred my access to a milieu of the utmost importance to anyone who wants to make a name and a career for himself—as I did and do—and who needs people to back him up and blow his horn for him. I foiled *that* plot in time, and if I choose not to proclaim my unshakable convictions in print it's because I am, after all, a research scholar, not a madman or an adventurer spoiling for a fight and a jail sentence. I prefer to do battle with the invincible weapon of my poetry, which may be hermetic but is extremely radical just the same.

The scum did not stop with the Left; they went still further and closed the doors of the newspapers in my face. I am, after all, an old hand around the *City News* and I write for nothing, too—who would have the nerve to ask Dr. Zèzinho to pay for poems published in his paper? I and the other poets can thank our lucky stars it hasn't occurred to him to charge us for the space and for printing our fulsome praise of one another's work. My contribution never fails to appear in the good old *City News* Sunday Supplement, the hospitable home of culture. It is to the *News* that 'we owe the magnificent campaign in honor of the centenary of Pedro Archanjo's birth, and in the literary supplement of that estimable organ of the press, Zino Batel and I put out the Young Poets' Column—or rather, I do the work and we divvy up the praise and the female poets.

Not content with my habitual activities as poet, critic, and collaborator on the *City News* and my present timely efforts as a sociologist "in search of living material of international relevance" (the phrase is from Silvinho's friendly column offering me "rainbows of graphic and archangelic opals"), I hied myself over to see the editor the moment I heard about the new campaign.

Now I ask you: speaking quite impartially, who could be better qualified to take part in, if not actually to direct, this campaign than a special assistant, an agent as it were, to the genius of Columbia University, who had chosen me—me, and no one else—to investigate the immortal Bahian's life? Not only had I been entrusted with the job and put under contract, I had been paid. *PAID*—allow me to write this holy, sacred, four-letter word in capital letters and rub it in the lean and hungry faces of that frogs' chorus of envy and arrogance: when was any of them ever paid, generously and promptly, for a serious piece of work, paid by an international genius, and paid in dollars? They live off what crumbs they can get from the government or the university, they're always grumbling and talking big, but they're meek as lambs when the green stuff is being passed around. Who would seem to be the logical choice, from every conceivable point of view—who, I ask you?—to act as consultant, for a small fee and a reasonable amount of publicity, on the *City News*'s noteworthy campaign? After all, Pedro Archanjo is my native heath. I had already staked my claim to him, so to speak.

Well, would you believe it, they shilly-shallied around at the paper and put all kinds of obstacles in my way when I tried to reach an understanding with Dr. Zèzinho. I actually thought I would never get to see him at all, I made so many vain attempts and was put off with so many transparent excuses. The three prime movers and shakers—that powerful trio of rascals—heard me out impatiently, or rather, one of them heard me out and sent me away with a vague promise: "Right now we don't need a thing, old man, but when the campaign's a little further along, there might be a chance for you to do an interview or a story, or something." At least I had had the sense to keep my mouth shut about acting as consultant; I had merely offered my cooperation.

But I'm not so easily outmaneuvered as all that, and I went back again. I took some material to show them, and this time I got the whole gang together to listen to me. They offered a ridiculously small sum for the documents, and they quite obviously had no intention of giving me the slightest opportunity of jumping on their bandwagon.

I decided to give them a run for their money and try the other papers. Ana Mercedes tried to intercede in my favor at the *Morning News*, but it was no use: those press lords have public opinion sewed up and they always work as a team.

Since I was left with no alternative I went back to the *City News* to take them up on their despicable offer, the only one I had had, and sell all my best material for a mess of pottage. I knocked at Dr. Zèzinho's door with the courage born of desperation, and the big boss listened to me indulgently. But when I showed him my notes he almost had a fit. "That's exactly what I *don't* want: this lack of proper respect for a great man with a lofty mind; this mockery, this debasement of Archanjo's character. I won't have it! The only reason we're buying this string of lies and gossip is to burn it, so that it can't be used to mar Pedro Archanjo's image. My dear Fausto, think of the schoolchildren!"

I thought of the schoolchildren and sold my silence for a paltry sum indeed. Dr. Zèzinho, still nervous and shaking, railed on: "A polygamist, for heaven's sake! And he wasn't even married! My dear poet, here is a lesson for you: a great man must have moral integrity, and if he did happen to step out of line once or twice or tell a lie now and then, it is our responsibility to polish up his image. Great men are our country's patrimony, worthy examples for the younger generation to emulate: we must set them on the altar of genius and virtue and make sure they stay there."

I thanked him and retired with my lesson and my voucher to go in search of those costly consolations, whiskey and Ana Mercedes.

And so I was to have no part in Pedro Archanjo's journalistic glory. I had to be content with a little scattered publicity from friendly columnists: Silvinho and Renot, July and Matilde. I was also sought out by a nice bunch of chaps who work in the theater, members of a very avant-garde group known as "No More Scripts or Footlights"—the name speaks for itself. They want me to help them put on a play about Pedro Archanjo, or rather, a show; they don't like the word "play." I'm going to think it over, and if they let me be a directing partner I may take them up on it.

On how the consumer society

publicized Pedro Archanjo's centennial,

capitalizing on his glory

and giving it true meaning

and relevance

I

The post of secretary-general of the Executive Committee set up to direct the centennial festivities was entrusted to Professor Calazans, and there could not have been a better choice.

The name of Calazans the historian long ago crossed the borders of the state of Bahia and has become well known throughout Brazil. His genuinely original and worthwhile studies on Canudos and Antônio Conselheiro have won praise from the little old men at the National Historical Institute, and, if I am not mistaken, an award from the Brazilian Academy of Letters. If my information is false and Calazans has yet to be given his laurel wreath, let my suggestion be their cue: it is still not too late for the immortals to rectify so flagrant an omission.

Kindly and scholarly professor in several disciplines, Calazans runs from one class to another all day long, always in a good humor and supplied with an ample stock of historical anecdotes, earning his bread by the sweat of his brow. With all he has to do, he still finds the time and the inclination to wear any number of different hats and titles, some honorary but all of which involve a considerable amount of hard work and none of which, needless to say, pays him a cent. He is the secretary of the Bahia Academy of Letters, treasurer of the Historical and Geographical Institute of Bahia, president of the Center for the Study of Folklore and the House of Sergipe, not counting the condominium of the building he lives in, which he represents *ab aeterno.*

So many successful activities, so many tasks scrupulously carried out, plus his own study and research and the writing of essays and articles—and still the professor always looks cheerful, relaxed and easygoing. This running about, this hurrying and scurrying, will seem extraordinary only to those who are ignorant of the circumstance that Professor Calazans was born in the quasi-mythical state of Sergipe. For the Sergipano who is born into infinite poverty in a feudal society of landed estates where opportunity and resources are nil; for the Sergipano who survives the astronomical infant mortality, endemic diseases of every kind from malaria to smallpox, and other limitations and hardships too numerous to mention; for such a hero nothing ever seems difficult again, and he is bound to have all the time and energy in the world. With Professor Calazans keeping an eye on things, the centennial was sure to be a success.

The Grand Commission of Honor, the GCH itself, had already provided a preliminary taste of the grandeur of the celebration to follow. The GCH, under the honorary chairmanship of His Excellency the Governor of the State, was composed of the Cardinal Primate, the commanders of the Armed Forces, the Magnificent Rector of the University of Bahia, the mayor of the capital, Salvador; the presidents of Bahian banks and cultural institutions, the manager of the Bank of Brazil, the director-general of the industrial complex of Aratu, the president of the Chamber of Commerce, the publishers of the three daily newspapers, the State Commissioner of Education and Culture, and Major Damião de Souza.

Except for those whose names were perforce included because any activity that did not have their consent and approval was doomed to strangulation at birth, all of the members of the GCH had been invited to serve for good and specific reasons. Dr. Zèzinho Pinto explained as much in his office, where, flanked by his secretary and the managing editor of the *City News*, he had convened the small executive committee, "purposely small, so that it will be able to act quickly and effectively."

It was not really so small as all that. Besides Dr. Zèzinho himself, who was of course the chairman, and Secretary-General Calazans, it included the presidents of the Historical and Geographical Institute and the Academy of Letters, the deans of the Schools of Medicine and Philosophy, the secretary of the Center for the Study of Folklore, the superintendent of Tourism, and the general manager of the Bahia branch of Doping Advertising and Publicity, S.A.

The committee members showed up for their first meeting in a holiday mood. The atmosphere was festive, and a waiter—the *City News* nightwatchman—served glasses of whiskey already poured, with ice, soda water, and *guaraná*.

"It's domestic scotch," hissed the lugubrious Ferreirinha, the city editor, after taking one sip.

Greeting "the eminent personages who honor the *City News* with their presence this evening," Dr. Zèzinho outlined his publicity campaign in a brief but brilliant speech and warmly praised his fellow members of the Grand Commission of Honor, from the governor to the major. At the same time he hinted broadly as to what contribution might be expected of each. Thus, it would be a graceful gesture for the progressive Mayor of Bahia to name one of the city's new streets for Pedro Archanjo, while the secretary of Education and Culture was expected to give Archanjo's name to a school where his memory would shine forever, "revered by the little children who will be the leaders of tomorrow, the marvelous Brazil of the future." The Magnificent Rector would lend the university's indispensable intellectual and material support to the campaign, especially in the matter of the proposed seminar; the superintendent of Tourism would cover the travel and hotel expenses of guests from both north and south. From the other newspaper publishers, "not competitors but colleagues," Dr. Zèzinho expected ample news coverage and unconditional support, not only in the press but over the radio and television stations they controlled. As for the bankers, industrialists, and businessmen, they would be managed by the efficient, dynamic employees of DAP, S.A. Had he forgotten to mention any of the members? Oh, yes! Major Damião de Souza, paladin of popular causes, the allegorical symbol of our metropolis! Having been a personal friend of Pedro Archanjo, he was an authentic representative of the people on the Grand Commission of Honor: "And we mustn't forget that Archanjo came from the people, from the humble working classes, and rose to the peaks of science and letters." (Applause.)

Between the scotch and the coffee ("rotten whiskey, the cheapest brand on the market, Archanjo deserved something better, some decent *cachaça*, at least," mused illustrious old Magalhães Neto, the president of the Historical Institute, as he exchanged his glass of dishwater for a cup of coffee) the committee outlined a program for the centennial, concentrating on three basic items which would not detract from whatever other proposals might be put forward:

(a). A series of four special supplements in the *City News* on Archanjo and his work. These were to be published on the four Sundays preceding December 18, and were to be made up of outstanding contributions from the rest of Brazil as well as from Bahia. Even the ads, Doping's branch manager put in, would add glory to Archanjo's name. A tentative list of contributors, all of the first rank, was drawn up. Those responsible for the supplements would be the presidents of the Historical Institute and the Academy, the secretary of the Center for the Study of Folklore, and Professor Calazans. They could not have put together so much as a page without the professor.

(b). A study seminar at the School of Philosophy under the posthumous aegis of Pedro Archanjo himself. Its theme was to be "Brazilian Racial Democracy and Apartheid: Affirmation and

Negation of Humanism." The idea of the seminar had come from Professor Ramos of Rio de Janeiro, who had said in a letter to Dr. Zèzinho: "Pedro Archanjo is the finest possible example of the unique value of the Brazilian solution to the problem of race: fusion, mixing, crossbreeding, miscegenation—and there could be no more fitting tribute to his memory, relegated to oblivion for these many years, than to assemble a conclave of scholars to reaffirm the Brazilian thesis and denounce the crimes of apartheid, racism, and hatred among men." The deans of the Schools of Medicine and Philosophy, the superintendent of Tourism, and, of course, the energetic Sergipano Calazans, were entrusted with the responsibility of organizing the seminar.

(c). A solemn closing session, to be held on the evening of December 18 in the Great Hall of the Historical and Geographical Institute. It was surely the best possible place: the headquarters of an illustrious sodality, an august, elegant, but *small* room, since, as Dr. Zèzinho prudently pointed out, "better a small room overflowing with listeners than a huge hall full of empty seats." The superintendent of Tourism, always the optimist, proposed the spacious meeting hall of the School of Medicine. Or why not the university auditorium, which was even bigger and better? But Dr. Zèzinho objected: Were there really so many loyal citizens in Bahia willing to make the sacrifice of listening, not only to Professor Ramos from Rio, but to representatives of the School of Medicine, the Academy of Letters, the Center for the Study of Folklore, the School of Philosophy, and the host organization, the Historical Institute itself? Five long speeches, however pregnant with eloquence, beauty, and conspicuous scholarship? They would be oratorical masterpieces, to be sure—grandiloquent, lengthy, and incredibly tedious. Dr. Zèzinho, with his wide experience of life and men, did not make a cult of optimism, and in his opinion the superintendent of Tourism did not know what he was talking about. The preparations for this solemn act fell exclusively on the shoulders of Professor Calazans. If he could not fill the great hall of the Institute, with its two hundred commodious armchairs, no one could.

Minutes of this preliminary meeting were deemed unnecessary, but Dr. Zèzinho had a typed list of the three items, complete in every detail—names, subjects, speakers, theories, and all the rest, point by point. He wanted to take a good look at their plans "before releasing them to the public." Smiling his captivating smile —he might have been congratulating his interlocutor, or offering him money—he added: "We'll just publish it a little at a time, give them something new every day. That way we can build up interest and suspense."

"He's going to ask for the *nihil obstat,*" muttered lugubrious Ferreirinha to jocose Goldman, the paper's business manager, who knew one hundred different ways of saying no, there was no money in the till.

"Whose? The National Information Service or the Chief of Police?"

"Both of them, probably."

Photographers recorded the "cordial and fruitful meeting" for posterity and the front page of next morning's edition, and TV cameras filmed it for that evening's news, a spontaneous gesture of goodwill on the part of Dr. Brito, who was "not a competitor, but a cordial colleague." Dr. Zèzinho Pinto had done it again.

A time was set for the next meeting and the doughty impresario shook hands all around. "I wonder if he serves this same putrid whiskey to guests in his own house?" Dr. Magalhães was still wondering. "No, of course not. He's bound to have a stock of the real thing. But then again . . . with these millionaires, you never know."

2

His full face exuding energy and efficiency, breaking now into an affable smile, now into a four-letter word, luxuriant mustache and retreating hairline, signs of premature obesity and shirt drenched with sweat, Gastão Simas, Bahia branch manager of Doping Advertising and Publicity, S.A., addressed his assistants, a compact group of five talented men, five aces, five unbeatable experts, and told them what had transpired during the first meeting of the Pedro Archanjo Centennial Executive Committee. Now it was up to them, to those five royally paid brains, to get cracking on the other part of the campaign, the one that really mattered: the ads, the business, the campaign that would bring in the profits. Gastão Simas rolled the key word around in his mouth, under his mustache. Profits—he might have been savoring ambrosia, or caviar, or some noble wine:

"Five pages of each eight-page supplement will be reserved for ads. The fourth and final supplement will be twelve pages long and we'll get seven pages or seven-and-a-half, maybe even eight if we can fill them up. And besides, we don't need to limit ourselves to the supplements. The sky's the limit. We're free to turn our imaginations loose, be creative, be artists! So let's get with it, boys, and not waste any time. I want good hard results right away. Efficiency and quality is our watchword, don't forget."

Having said his say he went back to his office and plopped into his armchair. Gastão Simas was efficient and a man of quality, hard-working, intelligent, and imaginative. When he stopped to examine his conscience, however, he was obliged to admit that advertising was not the profession he had been born for, not the way of life to arouse all his enthusiasm. He followed it out of necessity and vanity: it was financially rewarding, and it gave him status. He would have been happier, no doubt, at his old newsstand, where he had lived hand to mouth but had never had to wear this VIP mask which fitted his amiable, open face so poorly. His real pleasures in life were a game of dominoes in the Golden Market, a few drinks at a party, and good talk with no commitments to worry about. "I'm too much of a Bahiano for this game," he confessed one day to one of his boys, young Arno, a *simpático* Carioca and a fine adman, one of the best. What can I do? Oh, come on, Gastão, don't ask stupid questions. Put a good face on it and take your medicine. Being a Doping branch manager meant a fat salary and an enviable social position. An impotent serf in his luxurious office, G.S. gazed out at the gulf, the sea fort, the green island, and the ships peacefully crossing the horizon. The room was a showcase of wealth and power—rosewood furniture, a Genaro tapestry of an insolent abstract bird, one of Mário Cravo's cruel metal insects, and a tawny secretary. Of all the arts, of all the professions, the one G.S. practiced was by all odds the most profitable, the principal art of our time.

Not even the harshest critic would be fool enough to deny the pre-eminence of the art of propaganda. None of the other arts can hold a candle to it—neither poetry, nor painting, nor the art of writing novels, nor music, nor the theater, not even the movies. As for radio and television, one can say they are an intrinsic part of advertising and have no independent life of their own.

No painter has mastered as many creative techniques as the plastic publicity artists: Picassos are as thick as fleas in every advertising agency. No writer alive is the equal of the men who write ads: no stylist in prose or verse commands the resources of imagination, the realism, the surrealism, the communicative power of the agencies where dozens of Hemingways are creating a new literature. Why try to hide the truth when it stands clearly before us in broad daylight?

Even the real Picassos and Hemingways depend on advertising, for many of them are in fact created by the press agents who make them famous overnight. For a few months, at least, the favored painter's or writer's name will be in the public eye, reaping the applause of the booboisie. After a time he will vanish from the scene, of course; after all, no one but God can create literati and artists out of thin air and keep them on the crest of the wave and in the newspaper columns forever! But the subject of the promotional campaign has had his moment, his opportunity, as long as he is able to pay for it. After that it's up to him. You have to know how to blow your own horn in this world. Go to vanity fair, take a look at the smart guys and con men who were hatched in agency incubators and whose lack of talent has been cleverly promoted. There they are living it up, making money hand over fist. You don't see them killing themselves, teaching in two schools at once—that kind of daily workout is for squares and dumbbells like Calazans, who never learned the art of social climbing and the selective stab in the back—the supreme expression of our time, of our admirable, meritorious, never-to-be-sufficiently praised consumer society.

Arno, a young fireball imported from Rio, with a pen dipped in genuine scotch, was the first of Gastão Simas's boys to dazzle the boss with the result of two or three days of hard thinking and unbridled imagination. He laid a sheet of paper on the big shot's desk. On it, in big letters, were these immortal words:

> *"Whether you say it in English, German or Russian*
> PEDRO ARCHANJO IS A SOURCE OF INCOME
> *worth millions to Brazil.*
> *What else is worth millions to Brazil?*
> THE CACAO EXPORTERS' COOPERATIVE."

"Tremendous!" Gastão applauded. "You're terrific."

Other, equally splendid presentations followed; but Arno, the fair-haired boy, the young prince of propaganda, who earned as much as half the faculty of a university department, led the pack.

It may be interesting at this point to quote a few of the more successful ads for the cultural uplift of our readers:

"Toast Archanjo's centennial with Polar draught beer."

"If Pedro Archanjo were alive today, he would write his books on a Zolimpicus electric typewriter."

"In Archanjo's centennial year, the Industrial Center is building a new Bahia."

"In 1868 two giants were born in Bahia: Pedro Archanjo and the Archote Insurance Company."

Not content with his initial triumph, Arno concocted another marvel which we transcribe here, since no adjectives could do it justice:

> *"Archanjo angel star*
> *Star stella stela*
> CASA STELA CASA STELA
> *has shod four generations*
> *of angels and archangels*
> *in five easy payments."*

Arno took this ad to the client himself, humming and content with his creation. The proprietor of the shoe firm was obviously in a bad mood when Arno arrived—he was on a diet, and nothing is worse for the disposition. A man in his fifties, with bushy eyebrows and a school ring on his finger, he looked with a jaundiced eye at the natty, self-satisfied young coxcomb, and said, shaking his head:

"I'm nothing but a feeble, burned-out old man and you're a fine, strong, handsome young fellow who reeks of whiskey and beancakes, which is quite a combination—but I hope you won't take it amiss if I tell you just one little thing: your ad is a *piece of shit!*"

He began with such an air of false humility and ended in such a roar of violence that instead of being insulted, Arno burst out laughing. The client came down to brass tacks:

"There are three Casa Stelas, my friend, not only one as anyone reading this ad would think. And you don't give an address for a single one of them. And your ad doesn't mention shoes—I'm in the shoe business, in case you didn't know it. Oh, you make one passing reference to the subject, the verb 'shoe' in the present perfect tense, 'shod,' which is easily confused with 'shoddy.' No one would guess you were talking about a shoestore. Just between the two of us, I could do better myself and it would cost me a whole lot less."

They did not come to blows, and the office workers, who were always hoping the boss would punch somebody in the mouth, were disappointed again. He and Arno rewrote the ad and went out together as the afternoon turned into dusk, with a fresh breeze blowing off the ocean and climbing the steep streets. "Are you interested in antiques?" asked the shoe man. "I like modern things better," Arno confessed. But he went along with the crusty old man to some of his favorite antique shops hidden away in alleys and cul de sacs. It was the first time Arno had been in a curiosity shop in his life. He saw ancient lanterns, silver thuribles, rings, gaudy jewelry, footstools and sofas with cane seats, crystal chandeliers, engravings of London and Amsterdam, a hand-painted prayer stool, and a wooden saint, a really old one. Arno Melo suddenly felt the touch of beauty's magic wand.

Next day at the office, as he submitted the amended layout for Gastão Simas's final approval, he said:

"You know, Gastão, you were right: Bahia's not the place for this kind of stuff, it just won't work. If I had the wherewithal I'd say good-bye to all this crap and just roam around the streets. Gastão, have you ever looked at the Church of the Third Order?"

"Christ, kid, I was born here!"

"Well, I've lived in Bahia for a year now and I must have passed by that church a thousand times without ever taking the time to really look at it. I'm an animal, Gastão, a stupid fool, a son-of-a-bitch P.R. flack!"

Gastão Simas sighed; the kid would never get anywhere with that attitude.

3

The second meeting of the Executive Committee was much smaller than the first, as was only natural: second meetings are not photographed for the front page; they get a couple of lines on an inside page, at most.

The presidents of the Academy and the Institute were represented by Professor Calazans, who was a board member of both institutions. The deans of the Schools of Medicine and Philosophy and the superintendent of Tourism had also excused themselves, pleading prior engagements and pledging their agreement to and support of any and every decision that might be made.

Only one professor from the School of Philosophy was present: Professor Azevedo had come on his own initiative, attracted by the plans for the seminar. He was enthusiastically in favor of the idea. Professor Ramos had written him from Rio to request his help in organizing the symposium: "It may turn out to be a real landmark in the history of Brazilian culture—the first really systematic, scientific debate on the problem of race, which is now more vital, more a burning issue than ever before. It is exploding violently all over the world, particularly in the United States, where black power is a new factor to be reckoned with, and in South Africa, where the legacy of Naziism appears to have aggravated the problem." Professor Azevedo planned to present a documented thesis on Archanjo's contribution to Brazil's solution of the race problem at the conference, which, as he suggested to Professor Ramos, might well take as its motto a phrase from Master Pedro's *Notes on Miscegenation in the Families of Bahia:* "If Brazil has contributed anything truly significant to world civilization, it is miscegenation—that is our gift to humanity's treasure house."

The secretary of the Center for the Study of Folklore also came to the meeting. A self-taught, venturesome explorer who had had to dig out her own research with no help from anyone, bravely fighting for a place in the sun next to all the ethnologists, anthropologists, and sociologists with graduate degrees, scholarships to foreign universities and cabarets, and battalions of students and assistants to do their work for them, she had no intention of missing an opportunity like this. Edelweiss Vieira, a strapping, hearty girl, was one of the few people in Bahia who really knew Archanjo's work, and the only member of the committee besides Professor Azevedo and Professor Calazans who took the responsibility seriously.

The manager of Doping, S.A., turned up, armed with a leather briefcase, papers, charts, layouts, and diagrams, and shut himself up in the publisher's office with the managing editor. Dr. Zèzinho sent a message to Calazans and his colleagues to "have patience for just a few minutes, please," and they sat in the newsroom talking desultorily until he was ready to see them.

The lugubrious Ferreirinha dragged the secretary-general of the committee over to a window and whispered his forebodings: things weren't going very well, "the Czar's got a face like a funeral." Well aware of the secretary's reputation as an alarmist, the Sergipano paid no attention. This was a time of irresponsible rumors, of pessimistic predictions, a melancholy, restless time; and when the office door finally opened and Gastão Simas and the managing editor emerged, Calazans noticed that Dr. Zèzinho looked worried and upset in spite of his effort to appear open and cordial. "Forgive me for making you wait. Please come in," he said.

Before they sat down, Calazans said:

"Dr. Neto couldn't come and the Senator's in Brasília" (the president of the Academy had been elected a federal senator) "but he's authorized me to represent him. The dean of the School of Medicine and the superintendent . . ."

"They called and made their excuses," interrupted the magnate. "It doesn't matter, it's better this way. We can talk better *en petit comité*, put our ideas in order, and work out all the problems connected with this grand campaign of ours. Let's sit down, friends."

Professor Azevedo took the floor and said, with an oratorical flourish:

"Allow me to congratulate you, Dr. Pinto, for your praise-worthy initiative in calling for a centennial celebration. And I must single out for special commendation the seminar on miscegenation and apartheid. That will be an event of the utmost importance and relevance for the times we live in: the most serious scientific enterprise to take place in Brazil in many years. The whole committee is to be congratulated, but you, Dr. Zèzinho, most of all."

Dr. Zèzinho acknowledged the praise with the modest air of one who was doing no more than his duty toward culture and his native land and is prepared to make any sacrifice:

"Thank you very much, Professor. Your words are very encouraging indeed. But now that you've brought up this matter of the seminar, I'd like to say a few words about that very thing. I've been giving some thought to the implications of our scheme, and I've reached certain conclusions that I should like to set before you to be examined with your usual patriotism and good sense. First of all, I want to express my admiration for Professor Ramos and the wonderful work he has done. The best proof of my esteem is the fact that it was I who requested his cooperation in honoring Pedro Archanjo. However, the conference he has proposed, while no doubt of great interest to scientists, hardly strikes me as appropriate in view of the present situation."

Professor Azevedo felt a chill run down his spine: every time he heard those fateful words, *the present situation,* something disagreeable was sure to happen. The last few years had not been easy or pleasant ones for Professor Azevedo and his colleagues at the university. For that very reason he interrupted Dr. Zèzinho before hearing the worst which was sure to come:

"On the contrary, Dr. Pinto, the moment could hardly be more propitious, now that the racial struggle in the United States has almost reached a state of civil war, now that the new African nations are beginning to play an important role in world politics, now that . . ."

"That's just it, my dear professor and friend. The very arguments that have convinced you that such a seminar would be opportune are the very ones that persuade me that it would be a risky, even a dangerous, thing."

"Dangerous?" interrupted Calazans. "I don't see why."

"Very dangerous, my dear friend. A seminar with such an explosive theme—miscegenation and apartheid—would be an extremely dangerous focus of agitation and might very well be the spark to ignite a conflagration of unforeseeable consequences. Think of the university students, think of the high school pupils. I won't deny that some of their demands are reasonable, and our newspaper has had the courage to say so. But surely you will agree that professional agitators will seize on any excuse to infiltrate the student milieu and stir up disorder and riots."

There's no hope, thought Professor Azevedo, but he fought on a little longer; Ramos's idea was worth one last try:

"But Dr. Pinto, for heaven's sake! All of the students, even the leftists, are solidly in favor of the symposium. I sounded some of them out, and they were all interested and thought we should hold it. After all, it's a purely scientific matter."

"Do you see, Professor? Everything you are saying proves I am right. That's exactly where the danger lies, in student support. It's a time bomb. Before we knew it, that scientific seminar would turn into marches and protest meetings in support of American Negroes and against the United States. If we hold that seminar, they may end up setting fire to the American consulate. You've just said yourself, Professor, that it's a leftist symposium."

"No I didn't. Science is science, it has nothing to do with left or right. I said the students . . ."

"It amounts to the same thing: you said the leftist students, the student masses, were in favor of the idea. And that, Professor, is where the danger lies."

"But in that case, couldn't we . . ." once more Calazans came to the rescue of his colleague.

Visibly annoyed, Dr. Zèzinho decided to put an end to the matter once and for all.

"Forgive me for interrupting you, Professor Calazans, but all of us are simply wasting our time. Even if you convinced me you were right—and I might not be so hard to convince—" He broke off, obviously embarrassed. "Even if you did, that seminar cannot take place." He went on with increasing reluctance. "I was . . . well . . . I had a visitor . . . and I had a chance to consider the matter from every possible angle."

"A visitor? Who?" asked the secretary of the Folklore Center, totally out of things when it was a question of political subtleties.

"Someone who had a right to visit me, dear lady. Professor Azevedo, I hope you understand my position now. In fact, I wish you would explain all this to Professor Ramos; I don't want him to think badly of me."

He gazed out the window at the bar across the way, where reporters were having their coffee and milk with buttered rolls.

"We can't always see the big picture. There may be one little detail that makes something that looks like a good idea on the face of it undesirable at a certain time. I'm going to let you in on some highly confidential information: at this very moment, our diplomats are working on an important trade agreement with South Africa. It is very much to our advantage to have closer ties with a powerful nation which has enjoyed such an extraordinary rate of growth. Even a political, anti-Communist alliance is a distinct possibility. After all, we're already allies in the UN; we defend the same points of view. An airline directly linking Rio and Johannesburg is going to be established in a few days. Do you realize what that means? How can we choose this moment to hold a meeting of Brazilian scholars to beat apartheid, or rather the South African Republic, over the head? I won't even mention the United States and our commitments to that great nation. Just now when their own blacks are giving them so much trouble, are we going to be the ones to add fuel to the fire? It's only a step from racism to Vietnam. Just one short step. These are serious arguments, my friends, and no matter how much I wanted to stick up for our plan, I couldn't hold out against them."

"You mean they won't let us hold the seminar?" insisted the secretary of the Folklore Center bluntly, falling into the popular vice of direct, simple language.

Dr. Zèzinho took a grip on himself. He raised his arms:

"Dona Edelweiss, please! No one said anything about not letting us hold the seminar. This is a democracy, after all. No one says you can't hold anything in Brazil, for heaven's sake! It's been left to our discretion. We're the ones who have decided to cancel the seminar, after discussing the matter on the basis of new information that has turned up—we, the Executive Committee, and no one else. That doesn't mean, of course, that we won't commemorate Pedro Archanjo's centennial. The special supplements are already being put together, and Gastão has brought me encouraging news: business prospects are good. The solemn closing session will lend a scientific touch along with the indispensable oratory. And besides, there's nothing to prevent our coming up with some other idea, as long as it has no subversive overtones like the symposium."

In the midst of one of those silences so characteristic of the present situation, Dr. Zèzinho rose up like a phoenix from the ashes of the disagreeable subject:

"For example, what would you think of a big contest for high school students to write compositions on patriotic, contemporary subjects? We could offer a 'Pedro Archanjo Award,' a really valuable prize that everyone would want to win: a plane trip to Portugal for a week's stay with all expenses paid for the winner and whoever he wants to take with him. What do you think? Please let me have your ideas, and thank you very much."

This time he did not even offer them Brazilian scotch.

The Society of Medical Writers, which had a main office in Bahia and branches in several other states, put out a press release announcing its support of the festivities. Although he had no medical degree, Pedro Archanjo was closely linked to the medical profession by the umbilical cord of the Bahia School of Medicine "which he served with remarkable efficiency and touching devotion."

The president of that active organization was a well-known radiologist, head of a thriving clinic, who had written biographies of other eminent doctors. Having registered as a speaker—the sixth!—for the solemn closing ceremony, he went in search of more precise and intimate details about Pedro Archanjo, something that would add the human touch to his dry scientific discourse. One informant led him to another, and at length he reached Major Damião de Souza at his night consulting room of many years' standing at the Bizarria Bar, down an unsalubrious alley off Pelourinho.

The Bizarria Bar, one of the last in Bahia still to provide its customers with tables and chairs and make it possible for them to enjoy the pleasure of conversation, had once had the best location on the Praça da Sé. It belonged to an affable Galician who had come over from Pontevedra more than half a century before. Now his sons had installed a self-service cafeteria, the Eat-on-Your-Feet, on that same desirable corner. The novel idea was a dazzling and immediate success: for a modest price the customer got the day's specialty already served on his plate and his choice of soft drinks, set his plate and bottle on a kind of shelf running around the wall, and in ten minutes he was off and running, rid of the nuisance of eating—no time wasted, time when he could be making money. The elder Galician, who was fond of his customers and a glass of good wine (not that he disdained *cachaça*, if it was a superior brand), gave up the valuable location to his eager, progressive sons, but clung to his bar with its chairs and tables and lively talk uninhibited by clocks. He set it up again in an alley frequented by prostitutes and kept the patronage of the inveterate drinkers and talkers who were his friends and customers. One of these immemorial habitués, who had a chair set aside for him every evening, was the major, who never failed to show up for an apéritif before dinner.

The elegant radiologist, a rather conventional man, felt awkward, not to say nonplused, in that archaic setting. It was as though he had gone back in time to some forbidden city: the black flagstone floor, the dim light, the walls a century old, the shadows, the Oriental smells. . . . He found he was not the only one who had gone in search of the major for reminiscences of Archanjo that evening: the famous Gastão Simas and a young twerp from his advertising agency were also there. They were downing glasses of a violent brew, famous in the long ago as "billygoat gruff," and the young dandy (whose name, he later learned, was Arno Melo), was eating beancakes—"There's nothing like them to bring out the taste of something else." The same Bahiana had been coming every night for twenty years to sit with her tray and her brazier at the door of the bar; she had moved with the Galician from the Praça da Sé. It was all very new and exciting for the president of the Society of Medical Writers: his world was circumscribed by the hospital and its interns, his consulting room in the Rua Chile and his house in Graça, and his scientifico-literary meetings, dinners, and receptions. On Sundays he permitted himself the indulgence of a traditional pork and bean *feijoada* and a swim in the ocean.

"A radiologist?" said the major, reading the doctor's card. "That's fine. I've been looking for one. Dr. Natal's on vacation and Dr. Humberto's out of town. Have a seat; this place belongs to us, so make yourself right at home. What will you have? Some of the same? I recommend it. There's nothing better to whet your appetite. Paco," he called, turning to the Spaniard, "let's

have another round of billygoat gruffs. And I want you to come
and meet Dr. Benito here who's giving us the pleasure of his
company this evening."

Out of sheer civility, Dr. Benito took the glass and fearfully
tasted the impossible concoction. Ah, it was delicious! Simas and
Arno, wending their way along Archanjo's tortuous path, were
way ahead of him, on their fourth or fifth drink at least. The
inimitable major took a draw on his fetid cigar:

"They say one time a *iaba* heard about Pedro Archanjo's
woman-chasing ways and decided to teach him a lesson by making
him look like all kinds of a fool. So she turned herself into the
cutest little colored girl in Bahia. . . ."

"What's a *iaba?*" inquired Arno.

"A she-devil with her tail tucked in."

They had dinner there in the bar: fish fried in yellow palm
oil and copious draughts of ice-cold beer to wash it down with;
when they had finished they smacked their lips. Twice while
they were eating, the major ordered a round of *cachaça*, "to show
the beer who's boss."

Dinner behind them, they stepped across the way to the second floor where Ester's castle had been. Today it belongs to
Ruth Honeypot, but you can still get a distinguished brandy of
Archanjo's vintage there. Later on, Gastão Simas sang "Star-Sprin-
kled Floor" for an appreciative and romantic audience and Arno
Melo made a speech, rather muddled ideologically but violently
outspoken against capitalism and the consumer society.

At two o'clock in the morning Dr. Benito, by a supreme effort of will, managed to tear himself away. He flung himself into
a taxi, leaving his car parked in the Plaza: he had never drunk
like that in his life, not even in his student days; and he had certainly never heard such a ridiculous string of crazy stories. "Forgive me, my dear, but I got mixed up with the most extraordinary
people! And the only thing I learned about Archanjo was that at
one time he lived in sin with the devil."

"With the devil?" commented his wife, as she mixed him a
glass of fruit salts.

When Dr. Benito went to his office next day he found the
major's first three patients, each one bearing a note: "This is to

introduce the needy bearer of this card and to say that Major Damião de Souza would be grateful if you would be so kind as to give him an X ray. God will repay you many times over."

Two X rays of lungs and one of a kidney, and these three were only the first trickle of a flood of the indigent.

Of all the institutions which paid tribute to Pedro Archanjo's centennial, the Bahia School of Medicine was among the most enthusiastic. In an interview for the *City News*, given shortly after the campaign was launched and when supporting statements were still being sought, a spokesman for the school declared: "Pedro Archanjo belongs to the Medical School. His work is a part of our sacred patrimony, the peerless patrimony which was born in the venerable Plaza of the Terreiro de Jesus in the hallowed Jesuit College and which continued to flourish under the dedicated professors of the Medical School when it was built on the foundations of that first institution of higher learning in Brazil. Pedro Archanjo's work, which today is recognized even beyond our shores, would never have been written had not its author, an administrative employee of the school, steeped himself in the spirit of the illustrious institution which, though first and foremost a fostering mother of medical science, has never failed to cultivate the sister disciplines, *belles-lettres* in particular. Some of Brazil's greatest orators have raised their voices in this venerable school; and men of letters noted for their elegance of style and purity of language have also had their say. Science and literature, medicine and rhetoric have joined hands in these courtyards and classrooms. Pedro Archanjo tempered the steel of his resolve in this atmosphere of lofty aspiration and dipped his pen in the doctrines of this time-hallowed school. It is with justifiable pride that we declare on this glorious occasion that Pedro Archanjo's work is a product of the School of Medicine of Bahia."

And in a way, the speaker was right.

In which the author tells of books,
theses, and theories, of
professors and troubadours,
of the Queen of Sheba,
the countess, and the iaba, and,
along with this medley of themes,
poses a conundrum and ventures
a rash opinion of his own

I

They say, my beloved, that once a *iaba* passed through Bahia and was outraged by the incontinence, the colossal debauchery, the ostentatious licentiousness of Pedro Archanjo, master of many women and slave to none, a male with more females than were good for him, shepherd of a docile and faithful flock. He might as well have been a West African tribal chief surrounded by his harem, for the shameless things all knew one another, visited back and forth, and were seen taking care of one another's children, all of them Archanjo's. They called one another *comadre* and sister, and sang and danced, prattled and made merry, whenever they were not clustered around the fire making good things for the despot to eat.

Pedro Archanjo visited them all, one after another, and kept them happy as if he had nothing to do in life but lie around in bed and ball. A lord, a pasha, a vainglorious cock-of-the-walk, always ready to jump into bed or sit down at the table. He led a soft, sweet life, lolling at his ease. No woman alive had ever made him suffer the agony, the martyrdom, the fear of never having her or of losing her; for the shameless, wheedling womenfolk had no pride and ran after him and hung on his neck, flattering and provocative; never in their wildest dreams would they have thought of leaving him or making jealous scenes or putting horns on his head. Such were the joys of Pedro Archanjo: his mouth and his arms were never empty.

This state of things being intolerable to the *iaba* and a humiliation to womankind, she decided to punish Master Archanjo severely, to teach him a hard and bitter lesson about the pain of love—the longing and the waiting, the imploring and the refusals, the scorn and the neglect, the betrayal and the shame, the sorrow of unrequited love. The woman-chaser, the seducer sprawled on an infinite bed, on a fluffy wool mattress or a wooden cot, on a sandbank or the forest floor, at dawn or twilight, had never suffered that pain. Well, he was going to suffer now. The *iaba* swore defiance of Archanjo's carefree insouciance: You'll be the laughingstock of Bahia and the whole world, my man, with your tool gone limp and your heart a mass of sores, your head sprouting horns, the butt of taunts and gibes—Pedro Archanjo, you don't know it yet, but you've had it!

And so the *iaba* turned into the handsomest black woman ever seen in Africa, Cuba, or Brazil in story, song, or myth: an excess of Negress, a dazzle of jet. A perfume of roses unfurled to conceal the smell of sulphur; closed sandals to hide her cloven hoofs.

As for her tail, it turned into a lively, bouncing *derrière* that jounced along by itself. To give the reader some faint notion of her beauty, I need only say that along the route between the lower town and the Tent of Miracles, six mulattoes, two Negroes, and twelve white men went crazy when they saw her go by, and a religious procession broke up when she crossed in front of it. The priest was seen tearing off his cassock and abjuring his faith, and St. Onofre turned around in his litter and smiled at her.

The *iaba* laughed happily inside her starched skirts: the insolent fool would pay dearly for his pride as a matchless studhorse, a stallion in a flowery field of women. She would make his vaunted engine run down in a hurry. She would make it go limp and withered and useless, a frazzled, bedraggled museum piece. Here lies Pedro Archanjo's prick; it was famous once, but a *iaba* did it in. And that would be only the beginning.

The she-devil was absolutely sure of her victory on one point: it is well known that *iabas* can turn into women of uncommon beauty and irresistible charm, ardent lovers with knowing caresses; it is also public knowledge that they are incapable of overflowing into pleasure—they never reach orgasm, are never satisfied, demand more and more in a frenzy of frustration. Before they can reach the gates of nectar and cross over into paradise, their partner's instrument of pleasure is exhausted and becomes a worthless, shriveled scrap of flesh. No one ever heard of an engine that could storm those walls of futile frenzy and carry a barren, accursed *iaba* to the hour of hosannas and hallelujahs.

But the *iaba*'s vengeance would not stop at impotence. Archanjo's fiasco in the sweet and violent art would not be the end of it; his heart would be wounded and broken as well. For the *iaba* intended to do just as she pleased with him, turn him into a wretched suppliant, a miserable slave, a despised beggar. Which of the two kinds of shame was the most fearful, the most vile?

The false woman walked contentedly down the street, her plans all made: after she had let him taste her cunt and watched him swoon a thousand times, when she was sure she had him caught in her net, then she would go her way indifferently without so much as a good-bye. How fine to see him crawling, and let everyone else see him too, a beggar at her feet; licking the dust of the road, kissing her footsteps, the whole man a filthy rag, scum on the outside and a complaisant cuckold within, begging the favor of one glance, one smile, one gesture of her little finger or her heel—ah, take pity on me and give me your nipple, the black, swollen grape of your nipple.

After making him the butt of scorn and gibes, the *iaba* would sink him even lower, into dishonor—offering herself to others with happy talk and promises, flirting with the neighbors before his nose. And everyone would see him gnawing the rim of the bell, the lid of the chamberpot, the very stones in the street; they would see him beside himself, with his dagger raised, his knife unsheathed: you come back or I'll kill you, damn you; if you give your flower to another man, you'll die, and then I'll kill myself.

Look at him, crawling through Bahia in broad daylight for all to see, sobbing and imploring, a cuckold without honor, stripped of the last vestiges of decency and pride, reduced to a worm in the slime and feeling at last the shame, the death, the pain of loving. Come back! And bring your lovers, bring your men, give me all the horns you want to, cover me with bile and excrement. I want you, I implore you, come back! and I'll be grateful.

Iabas cannot come to orgasm, as we already know; but neither can they love or suffer because, as has been proved, *iabas* have no heart—their breasts are hollow, irremediably empty. And so, because she was both wicked and immune, she laughed to herself as she went her way, her backside revolving voluptuously behind her and men killing themselves at the sight. Poor Archanjo.

But it happens, beloved, that when the evening star lit the night and the moon left her house in Itaparica and came to bend over the oil-smooth dark-green ocean, Pedro Archanjo was lounging in the doorway of the Tent of Miracles waiting for her. He had asked for that moon, those stars, that silent sea, and a song:

> *Thank you, lady, thank you*
> *For your courtesy;*
> *I see that you are graceful*
> *Fair, and passing strange.*

So big had his prick grown as he waited eagerly that he leaned upon it as if it were a staff; his male odor deflowered and impregnated virgins leagues away.

Love, you may well ask: How can this be? How did Archanjo learn of the *iaba*'s malicious plot? Riddle me this riddle! But it's really very simple: wasn't Pedro Archanjo the favorite son of Exú, lord of the roads and crossroads? And he was Xangô's eyes—his sight reached far and he could see into the heart of things.

It was Exú who warned him of the perversity and the evil designs of the despotic daughter of Satan with no heart in her breast. Exú warned him and told him what to do: "First take an herb bath, but not just any kind; go to Ossain, who knows plants inside out, and ask him which leaves you should use. Then press out some Brazil cherries and mix the juice with salt, honey, and pepper and bathe the father-of-the-world in it, and the twins too —both balls. It's going to hurt, but never mind that, just grit your teeth like a man and watch what happens: you'll have the world's best prick for size, length, stiffness, pleasure, beauty, and excitement. No woman's cunt, and no *iaba*'s either, will be able to tire it, much less wear it out."

To make the charm complete he gave Archanjo a *kelê* and a *xaôrô*—a slave necklace and anklet. "Fasten this *kelê* and this *xaôrô* on her when she's asleep to bind her head and foot, and she'll be your slave forever. Xangô will tell you the rest."

Xangô ordered him to sacrifice twelve white cocks and twelve black ones, with twelve painted guinea hens and a pure white dove of gently rounded breast and melodious cooing. At the end of the sacrifice Xangô performed a piece of Mandingo sorcery: he took the pigeon's bleeding, loving heart and made a pellet that was white and red. He gave it to Archanjo, saying in his voice of thunder and lightning: "Ojuobá, listen to me and learn this spell by heart: when the *iaba* is fastened hand and foot, asleep and helpless, put this pellet in her subilatorium; then wait and see what happens. Don't run away, whatever happens; stay right where you are and wait." Archanjo touched his forehead to the ground and said: *Axé*.

Then he took a bath with the leaves that Ossain had chosen

one by one. With honey and black cherry water, with salt and malagueta pepper he oiled his gun and saw it grow into a formidable pilgrim's staff. He hid the *kelê,* the *xaôrô,* and the pigeon's heart, Xangô's red and white pellet, in his pocket. Then he stood at the door of the Tent and waited for her.

They started in as soon as she had turned the corner, with no coyness and no beating about the bush. No sooner had the *iaba* appeared than Archanjo's prick went to meet her and lifted her starched skirts, exactly filling her cunt: fire against fire, honey against honey, salt against salt, pepper against hot red pepper. Who could tell the story of that battle, love, that war of two most artful rivals, the clash of mare and stallion, the shrieking of a cat in heat, the howling of a wolf, the snorting of a wild boar, the sob of a maiden as she becomes a woman, the cooing of the dove, the tossing of the waves? Who, my love, could tell it?

They rolled down the street locked together and came to a stop on the harbor sand as the night wore on. The tide went in and carried them out, and they went on with their careening gallop at the bottom of the sea.

The *iaba* had not expected to meet with so much resistance. Each time Archanjo swooned away, the godless woman thought with despair and rage: "Now he'll shrivel up and keel over!" But nothing of the sort happened: instead of curling up and dying, his penis became ever more ardent and caressing.

Nor had she dreamed of such delight: that rod of honey, pepper, salt, ecstasy of ecstasies, a circus phenomenon, a wonder of the world. Ay, moaned the *iaba* in despair, if only I could . . . She could not.

The epic clash, the supreme revel, lasted three days and nights without a pause: ten thousand times he mounted her in one long fuck. The *iaba's* arid frenzy held out just so long: suddenly the spell was broken and she broke into ecstasy as the sky breaks forth in rain. The desert ran with water, the dry spell was broken, the curse overcome, hosannah and hallelujah!

She slept at last, a female animal but not a woman yet, far from it!

In Archanjo's room with its mingled odors and shadows the

iaba lay sleeping on her stomach: preposterously beautiful, extravagantly black. When her breathing was melodious and even, Archanjo fastened the *kelê* around her neck and the *xaôrô* around her ankle and made her his captive. Then, with the delicacy of a true Bahiano, he thrust into her celestial anus the heart of the bird, Xangô's enchanted pellet.

Instantly she let out a shriek and a booming fart. Both were frightful, sinister, terrifying: the air turned to pure sulphur, a mortal stench of smoke. Lightning flashed over the sea, there was a muffled echo of thunder, the winds were loosed, and a storm swept the universe from one end to the other. A huge mushroom rose into the sky and hid the sun.

But all was soon serene and jubilant again; the rainbow unfurled its colors: Oxumarê heralding joy and peace. The stink of sulphur was succeeded by a smell of blooming roses and the *iaba* was a *iaba* no longer, but black Dorotéia. The arts of Xangô had planted in her bosom the most tender, submissive, loving heart. Black Dorotéia forever, with her fiery cunt, her insolent butt, and the heart of a turtle dove.

The problem solved, the mystery resolved, an answer found for the enigma—there, beloved, the story ends; what else is there to tell? Dorotéia chose a patron saint and became a doughty daughter of Yansan, the deity of storms. She shaved her head and was initiated; she became a priestess, and danced in Exú's ritual to initiate her ceremonial obligations. Some gossips who knew her story swore they could catch a whiff of sulphur when Dorotéia led the dancing on the ritual ground, the rank odor lingering from the time when she was a *iaba* and tried to beat Pedro Archanjo at his own game.

But the mestizo was too tough a nut to crack. Others had tried it, there at the Tent of Miracles on Tabuão Street and at the Medical School on the Terreiro de Jesus, but no one ever succeeded—unless it was Rosa. If anyone ever taught Archanjo what it was to suffer, it was Rosa de Oxalá and no one else. Not even the demonic jet-black *iaba;* not even the university professor, for all his learning and his cutaway coat.

2

The printer's devil tried to conceal the sleepiness that was getting the better of him from the two men bent over the printing press. He simply had to be there when the first pages came out; his enthusiasm had burned high for months, every bit as high as Archanjo's or Lídio's. The latter was the more excited of the two; anyone would have thought that Lídio Corró was the author of Pedro Archanjo's first book, *Daily Life in Bahia*.

The last drunks had gone to bed, the last guitar had stopped thrumming its tardy serenade. Cock crows echoed in the street; in a little while the city would come to life. The apprentice had heard the chapters being read aloud, had helped compose the pages and set the type for that first block of lines. He tried to conceal his yawns, his smarting eyes, and his drooping eyelids, but Lídio noticed and ordered him to go to bed.

"Not yet, *Mestre* Lídio, I'm not a bit sleepy."

"You're asleep on your feet. Go to bed."

"Please, godfather"—the adolescent voice was more than a plea, it was warm and full of decision—"please ask *Mestre* Lídio to let me stay until it's through. I'm not sleepy any more."

The book had to be finished that night because they would need the worn old type and printing press next morning for their routine jobs: street-singers' leaflets and prospectuses for notions shops and grocery stores. At the end of the month Lídio Corró would have to pay Estevão his installment, and that was a sacred obligation. It was a fight against time and the little hand-cranked press, which was rheumatic, stubborn, and capricious. Lídio called it "auntie" and always asked for its blessing, goodwill, and cooperation. That day it had had one of its temperamental fits and they had spent most of the night trying to fix it.

The apprentice's name was Tadeu, and he loved his work. When Estevão das Dores was finally willing to retire and sell his equipment, Lídio had taken on the street urchin Damião as his helper. Not for long, though, for ink and type held no attraction for the wild, headstrong boy. What he wanted was action and the freedom of the streets. He got himself a job at the Forum as an errand boy, trotting through the streets with writs, processes, subpoenas, and petitions, running back and forth between judges and lawyers, bailiffs and law clerks. From the very beginning of his career, Damião was shrewdness and rascality incarnate. One apprentice followed another, but none of them stayed in the overworked little shop for very long, and none of them had really been up to the job. Tadeu was the first boy to satisfy Master Lídio.

He saluted his master's consent with a shout and dashed water on his face to drive the sleep away. He had followed Archanjo's work day after day, page after page, and never guessed how useful he had been to the man he called godfather; how much encouragement he had given Archanjo in that new and difficult task, the art of precision and nuances, of assertions and subtleties and truth set down on paper, the craft of words and their meanings.

Pedro Archanjo had written for those two and because of them: for his lifelong friend, companion, and partner—his twin brother—and for the thin, lively, studious boy with eyes like coals; for Dorotéia's boy. Now it was finished at last, and Lídio had got some paper on credit.

The original idea had come from Valdeloir, the *capoeirista* and carnival dancer from Tororó; but various other hints and suggestions came at almost the same time, and Pedro Archanjo was induced to take up his pen. He had always loved to read any book that fell into his hands and to note down interesting facts, tales, and happenings—everything that had to do with the habits and customs of the people of Bahia; but he had never thought of aspiring to be an author. More than once, though, it had occurred to him that those notes of his might make a crushing reply to theories held by certain professors at the university—fashionable theories which he had heard repeated in the classrooms, court-yards, and corridors of the Medical School.

The idea came one night when *cachaça* was flowing freely. A large, attentive circle was listening to Archanjo tell one story after another, each of them lovelier and more suggestive than the last, while Lídio Corró and Tadeu were tying bundles of a leaflet in which João Caldas, "poet and servant of the people," narrated in doggerel of seven-syllable lines the story of the sacristan's wife who gave herself to a priest and turned into a headless mule who ever after galloped headlong down the lanes and through the forests at night, spewing fire through her neck and terrifying the neighborhood. On the cover was a woodcut by Lídio. Spare yet rich in expression, it showed the headless mule, the terror of the highway, and all the people scattering in fright, while her head, cut off but still alive, kissed the sacrilegious lips of the priest. As Manuel de Praxedes remarked, they were having themselves a high old time.

"Master Pedro, now, he could write a heap of stories like that and give them to *Mestre* Lídio to print. He knows a powerful lot of tall tales and he sure knows how to tell them, too," reflected Valdeloir, *afoxé* dancer, sambista, *capoeira* wrestler, and an avid reader of all kinds of stories and verse.

They were talking in a sort of lean-to that Lídio had built in the yard, with a zinc roof and wooden walls. Since the printing press took up all the room in the shop, the talk and the puppet shows had had to move out into the yard.

Lídio worked day and night setting up type and running the press, drawing miracles, making woodblocks for the covers of leaflets, and occasionally pulling a tooth. He owed Estevão for the printing apparatus, and that would be a heavy monthly com-mitment for two more years. He had had to put up a lean-to because the puppet shows brought in money, and also because Archanjo would never have agreed to stop reciting the poems of Castro Alves, Casimiro de Abreu, and Gonçalves Dias, the love sonnets and protests against slavery, or dancing the samba in a circle and admiring Lídio's and Valdeloir's fancy steps, Risoleta's warm voice, and Rosa de Oxalá's dancing. And he wouldn't have given up the puppet shows even if they had been free: the poster over the door of the Tent of Miracles still said SHOW TODAY every Thursday.

It had been raining almost incessantly for a week; it was a month of storms and south wind. That wind was wet and biting; it stung like needles and fell with a funereal drizzling sound. Two fishing boats had capsized and the bodies of three of the seven men who had drowned were never recovered; they were left to swim in an endless search for the golden coast of Aioká at the end of the world. The other corpses were washed up on the beach several days later, and they were a ghastly sight, already eyeless and full of crabs. Friends knocked at the door of the Tent, shivering and sopping wet, in need of a comforting drink. It is at such times of misfortune that *cachaça* proves its true worth. That night, after Valdeloir had made his suggestion, Manuel de Praxedes took the floor and proposed an amendment:

"That's right, Master Archanjo knows plenty. He's got a whole mess of plots in his head or written down on those scraps of paper of his. But the things he knows are too good to waste on throwaways you can buy for a penny. His stuff really has some meat to it, and there ain't too many people who know about those things. What he ought to do is go to the university and tell some professor, one of those bigwigs who knows how to write —the place is full of crackerjacks, you all know that—and let the guy put it all down on paper so people can read it and be educated. I bet *that* would liven things up around here."

With calm, meditative eyes Master Pedro Archanjo stared at Manuel de Praxedes, the good-natured giant, remembering—oh, any number of things that had happened lately, there in Tabuão, in his own neighborhood, and in the Terreiro de Jesus. Little by little the placid smile returned to his face, softening the unaccustomed sharpness of his expression, and the smile broadened as his eyes, shifting from one member of the circle to another, met those of his *comadre* Terência, Damião's mother and such a pretty woman:

"Why ask a professor to do it, *meu bom?* I'll write it myself. Or do you think, Manuel, that just because we're poor we don't

know how to do anything worth doing? That we can't write anything but broken-backed verse? Well, I'll show you a thing or
two, *meu bom, meu camarado*. I'll write it myself."

"It's not that I don't think you can do it, Pedro my friend;
you go right ahead. It's just that if you got a professor to do it
you'd know it was done just right. Those people who read all
the time know everything from A to Z."

Is there anyone who twists and warps things worse than those
people who read all the time? Is there anyone who has more to
learn than those half-baked know-it-alls? Manuel de Praxedes has
no way of knowing that; you have to work around the university
to learn as you listen. In the eyes of some of those professors,
Manuel, mulatto and criminal are synonyms. How's that again,
Pedro, old pal? I don't know what a synonym is, but whatever it
is it's a bloody lie.

Tadeu the printer's devil could not keep quiet; he greeted the
sally with a laugh and clapped his hands.

"My godfather knows plenty he can teach those professors
and anyone who doesn't know that is pretty dumb!"

But would he really write the book—would he keep the
promise he had made that night when a storm was raging and
cachaça had flowed—or would he forget it in all that festive
life of parties and women, the rehearsals for street pageants,
Budião's *capoeira* school, and his *terreiro* obligations? He might,
indeed, have forgotten all about it had he not received an urgent
summons from Mother Majé Bassan a few days later.

Seated in her armchair before the shrine, a flimsy throne which
did not detract one iota from her awesomeness, Majé Bassan
handed Archanjo the bell to play and chanted a song for the saint.
Then, toying with the cowrie shells but not questioning them, as
if there were no necessity for games, she said:

"I heard tell you were going to write a book, but I know you
ain't started yet. Your doing's all in your mouth. You think about
it and talk about it, and that's enough for you. You spend all your
time asking questions and sticking your nose into everybody's
business and you write it all down, but what for? You want to
be an errand boy for the doctors all your life? Is that all you
want to do? You work so you can eat and won't want for nothing,

but it ain't to keep you quiet and it ain't all you got to do. That ain't why you're Ojuobá."

And so Pedro Archanjo took up his pen and wrote.

Lídio's help in choosing the material was invaluable, and also in making suggestions that were almost invariably good ones, for he was an astute man and a careful listener. If he had not shepherded the work along by digging up money to buy ink, getting paper on credit, giving his friend an encouraging push now and then, especially in the beginning when the going was hardest, Archanjo might have given up halfway through the book or at least taken much longer to finish, for he was still tied to intentions and circumstance, still overcareful not to commit grammatical errors. He sometimes found it hard to give up a dance in the suburbs, a Sunday spree, or a new and appetizing woman. The discipline was Lídio's, the enthusiasm the apprentice's, and the learning Master Archanjo's, who, thus aided, managed in good time to finish the task imposed by Majé Bassan.

When he began the book, an image of certain priggish professors and echoes of theories of racial superiority were ever present in his mind and they influenced his words and sentences, molding them and setting bounds on their strength and freedom. But as pages grew into chapters, Pedro Archanjo forgot both theories and professors. No longer interested in contradicting them in a polemical battle for which he was in any case not prepared, he concentrated on telling how ordinary people lived in Bahia, the miseries and marvels of that daily life of poverty and faith; in showing how the much oppressed and persecuted folk of Bahia had determined to prevail in spite of everything, by cherishing and clinging to the patrimony of dance and song, of metal, iron, and wood, benefits of culture and freedom preserved in the slave cabins and the hiding places of fugitive slaves.

Once he reached this point he wrote with an indescribable pleasure that was almost sensual, hoarding his time and devoting every free moment to the work. He no longer gave a thought to the dry, brusque professor Nilo Argolo with his hostile eyes, nor to the outgoing Dr. Fontes, who was urbane, even jocose, but for all that perhaps an even more aggressive proponent of theories of discrimination. Professors and their disciples, whether erudite or ignorant, no longer gnawed at his mind. Love for his own people guided Archanjo's hand; his passion served to give his writing a touch of fire and poetry. For that very reason the document that flowed from his pen was unanswerable.

That was a night of insomnia in the shop, a night of perspiring arms moving up and down, of the slow printing press groaning over the paper and the type. Tadeu was startled out of his weariness when he saw the first pages of paper covered with printed letters and smelled the fresh ink. The two *compadres* lifted the sheet of paper and Pedro Archanjo read—did he read it, or did he already know it by heart?—the very first sentence, his martial buglecall to arms, his truth, the sum of his knowledge: "The face of the Brazilian people is a mestizo face, and its culture is mestizo."

Lídio Corró, a sentimental man, felt a tightness in his chest and thought: I'll die of excitement one of these days. Pedro Archanjo was serious for a moment: distant, grave, almost solemn. Then suddenly his face was transformed as he burst into a loud, clear, happy laugh, that infinitely free laughter of his; he thought of Professor Argolo's face, and Dr. Fontes's, those two leading lights of the Medical School, those two know-it-alls who knew nothing about life. "Our faces are mestizo faces, and so are yours; our culture is mestizo but yours is imported. It's nothing but powdered shit." Let them die of apoplexy. His laughter lit up the dawn and illuminated the city of Bahia.

One night months before, when the celebration at the *terreiro* was at its height and the *orixás* were dancing with their children to the sound of *atabaque* drums and clapping, Dorotéia appeared holding a boy by the hand, a youth of about fourteen. Yansan tried to mount her before she had even crossed the threshold, but she excused herself and went to kneel before Majé Bassan, asking her blessing for herself and the boy. Then she brought him to Ojuobá and ordered:

"Ask him to bless you."

Archanjo saw a thin but sturdy boy with a swarthy complexion, a fine-featured, frank, open face, straight, gleaming black hair, dancing eyes, long-fingered hands, and a sensual mouth—a handsome, charming boy. Oxóssi's *ogan* José Aussá, who was standing beside him, compared the two with a fleeting, curious smile.

"What relation is he to me?" asked the youth.

Dorotéia smiled, too, an enigmatic half smile like Aussá's.

"He's your godfather."

"Godfather, please give me your blessing."

"Sit down here next to me, *camaradinho*."

Before yielding to Yansan, who was calling for her impatiently, Dorotéia said in her soft, peremptory voice:

"He says he wants to study, that's all he talks about. He doesn't amount to much so far, he won't ever be a good carpenter or bricklayer. All he can do is his sums. He knows the multiplication tables better than most teachers or books. But what good will he be to me that way? It just costs me money to keep him, and there ain't a thing I can do about it. I can't cheat the fate he inherited from the blood that ain't mine. I can't make him hoe a row that ain't his. I can't do that, because I'm his mother, not his stepmother. I have to be mother and father both, and it's too much for me when I have to keep us both off what I can sell in the streets with my charcoal stove and my pans of food. I brought him here to give to you, Ojuobá. You make a future for him. Show him the road he ought to take."

She took her son's hand and kissed it. Then she kissed Archanjo's hand and gazed at the two for a long moment. Finally she yielded to Yansan, letting out her cry that terrified the dead. Taking up the *eruexim* and the scimitar, she began the ritual dance. Man and boy saluted her at once: *"Eparrei!"*

In the shop, in Archanjo and his books, Tadeu found what he had been looking for. Master Pedro saw himself reflected in his godchild: the same irrepressible eagerness, the same curiosity and impulsiveness. The only difference was that the adolescent had already charted his course. He saw a path before him; he did not study haphazardly, for the pure pleasure of learning. He learned with a determined end in view; he wanted to be somebody. From whom had he inherited his ambition, from what remote greatgrandfather? His stubbornness and will power were his mother's, the she-devil's gift.

"My qualifying exams for the university are coming up, Godfather," he told Archanjo one Sunday, refusing an invitation to go along on an outing. "I've got an awful lot of studying to do. But I think I can manage, if you'll help me with Portuguese and geography. I don't need to take arithmetic, and I've got someone to teach me Brazilian history."

"You mean you're taking four exams this year? All four at once?"

"I can do it if you'll help me, Godfather."

"Then let's begin right now, *meu bom.*"

The outing was to have been to Ribeira. Budião had gone ahead with the provisions and the girls. One of them, Durvalina by name, had a figure like a statue! Pedro Archanjo had promised to serenade her on the guitar and the *cavaquinho*, and when the party was at its height to carry her off to Plataforma on a boat. I'm sorry, Durvalina, don't get mad, we'll do it some other time.

4

Popular poets, especially Lídio Corró's customers, never missed a chance to comment on the dispute between the professors and Master Archanjo. It was a first-rate theme:

> There've been some changes made
> At the Terreiro de Jesus.

As the years went by, the subject furnished food for at least six or seven pamphlets. All of them took Archanjo's part. His first book earned him the verses and applause of Florisvaldo Matos, an improviser with a loyal audience at every anniversary party, christening, and wedding:

> I'd like to introduce my readers
> To a book that makes you think.
> It tells about life in Bahia
> And the author's Master Archanjo
> His talented pen wrote the words
> And his courage provided the ink.

When the police raided Procópio's *candomblé*, Pedro Archanjo became the hero of three booklets full of laudatory ballads. All were greedily fought over by their readers, the poor people from the markets and alleys, the shops and the stores. Cardozinho Bemteví, the "romantic crooner," abandoned the love lyrics which were his forte to write *Commissioner Pedrito's Encounter with Pedro Archanjo at Procópio's Terreiro*, a ballad with a long, alluring title. On the cover of Lucindo Formiga's pamphlet *Pedrito Gordo's Defeat at the Hands of Pedro Archanjo*,

Commissioner Pedrito was shown retreating in disarray: his horse-whip lay behind him on the ground and Pedro Archanjo stood erect and unarmed before him. However, the greatest success of all belonged to Durval Pimenta and his sensational epic poem *Pedro Archanjo Challenges the Wild Beast from the Police Department*.

As for references to the debate over race, the greatest hits were João Caldas's and Caetano Gil's. The former, a singer who then had eight children who in time became fourteen and then branched out into a multiplicity of grandchildren, offered his public a masterpiece entitled *The Runner Who Taught the Professors a Lesson.*

> *When the profs had no leg left to stand on*
> *They said that Pedro Archanjo*
> *Was wicked Old Nick himself.*

When the dispute had just about worn itself out, Pedro Archanjo's *Notes* were published and young Caetano Gil, a brave rebel of a balladeer, entered the lists. He paid little attention to established rules but drew verses and music out of his guitar itself, sambas and modinhas that sang of love, life, and hope:

> *Master Archanjo he spoke up and said*
> *That mulattoes can read and write*
> *Did you ever hear such a thing?*
>
> *The professor he jumped up and said*
> *"Who ever heard of a writer who's black?*
> *Who ever heard of a doctor who's brown?"*
>
> *Officer, do your duty*
> *Did you hear what that rascal said?*
> *Did you ever hear such a thing?*
>
> *The professor he jumped up and yelled*
> *"Nigger, you're going to jail!"*
>
> *But Master Archanjo replied*
> *"This nigger knows how to read"*
> *Did you ever hear such a thing?*

In 1904 Professor Nilo Argolo, of the Department of Forensic Medicine at the Medical School of Bahia, presented at a scientific congress in Rio de Janeiro, and later published separately, a report entitled *The Psychic and Mental Degeneracy of Mestizos; for example, those of Bahia.* In 1928, Pedro Archanjo wrote a little volume called *Notes on Miscegenation in the Families of Bahia,* of which 142 copies were printed. About fifty of these were sent by Lídio Corró to libraries, universities, and schools, both in Brazil and abroad, and to scholars, professors, and other learned men. Throughout those two decades a bitter dispute raged behind the scenes at the School of Medicine concerning the race problem in the world as a whole and Brazil in particular. Writers, department heads, and scientific and political authorities were all involved in the polemic. Books, reports, articles, and pamphlets were published, and the subject was widely reported in the press, acrimonious crusades being mounted on the basis of certain aspects of life in Bahia and its consequent state of culture and religion.

Archanjo's first three books were directly linked to that debate, and therefore a categorical proposition can be advanced: in the first quarter of this century there took place in Bahia a war of ideas and principles between certain professors at the School of Medicine, ensconced in their departments of legal medicine and psychiatry, and the teachers of the living university of Pelourinho, many of whom did not learn what was going on—and even then only in part—until the police were called upon to intervene, and did so.

At the turn of the century, the School of Medicine was peculiarly vulnerable to the shock of racist theories. Little by little it had ceased to be the powerful center of medical study founded by Dom João VI, the original source of scientific knowledge in Brazil, the hospitable home of doctors in life as well as in medicine, and was becoming a hotbed of the most blatant, rhetorical, windy, pedantic, reactionary subliterature imaginable. The banners of prejudice and hatred were unfurled over the once-great university.

It was a sorry era, in which medical writers were more interested in the rules of grammar than the laws of science, better at placing pronouns correctly than at handling scalpels and microbes. Instead of fighting disease they did battle against French idioms, and instead of investigating and combatting the causes of endemic illness they invented neologisms: henceforward people would be obliged to wear *anhydropodotecas* instead of galoshes. Their prose was pure, precise, and classical; their science was false, inferior, and regressive.

It is hardly too much to say that it was Pedro Archanjo who, through his virtually anonymous books and his struggle against official scientism, put an end to this melancholy phase in the life of the famous school. The debate on the race question shocked the Medical School out of its cheap rhetoric and shaky theories and restored its original interest in science, in honest and original research, in real facts and problems.

But the polemic was marked by some odd characteristics.

In the first place, there are no records of it at all. Nothing in the archives, no information of any kind, even though the arguments led to violence and student demonstrations. Only the police records still have Pedro Archanjo's dossier on file, dating from 1928: "a notorious provocateur who contradicts distinguished professors." The distinguished professors who took part in the polemic would never admit to having so much as crossed words, much less having entered into a real debate, with a runner at the university. Never once, in any article, essay, study, report, or thesis, do the egregious professors refer to Pedro Archanjo's work, either to quote it, discuss it, or refute it. And only in the *Notes* did Archanjo launch a frontal attack against the books and pamphlets in which Professors Nilo Argolo and Oswaldo Fontes refuted some articles by Professor Fraga, a young doctor who had recently returned from a stay in Germany and the only faculty member to question any of his eminent colleagues' statements. In his previous books Archanjo had not quoted from the works of the two Bahian theoreticians on race. Instead of replying to them directly, he preferred to give the lie to their theories of Aryan superiority with his incontrovertible mass of facts, with his passionate defense of the mingling of the races.

In the second place, although the quarrel's repercussions eventually spread to every student and faculty member at the university, and even to the police, it never really aroused public opnion. The intellectuals all ignored it, and so it was restricted to the School of Medicine: there is only one reference to an epigram by Lulu Parola, a journalist who enjoyed enormous prestige at the time. His daily column in verse appeared in one of the evening papers, and in it he commented with elegance and mordant humor on the events of the day. A copy of the *Notes* had reached his hands, and he derived much satirical play from unmasking the "blue-bloods" and the boasting of the "dark mulattoes" (dark because they concealed the fact that they were mestizos) and praising the "light mulattoes" (because they shed the light of day on their condition as mestizos and were proud of it). So Archanjo had the poetic muse on his side: popular verse, rondels in cheap leaflets, and that of the fashionable bard of the tabloids and salons.

As for the common people, they never heard much about it. They were indignant at Ojuobá's having been sent to jail, but then, they were used to the absurdities of the police. Of all the pranks, brawls, rows, and melées in which Pedro Archanjo was involved, the most important was, perhaps, the one that contributed least to his legend.

Archanjo found himself simultaneously involved in the debate over miscegenation and in a fight between Police Commissioner Pedrito Gordo and the *candomblé* fetishists. Even today in the *terreiros,* the docks, the markets, the byways and alleys of the city, you can hear many different versions, all heroic, of the clash between Pedrito and Archanjo, when that bilious representative of authority invaded Procópio's *terreiro.* They all tell how he stood up to the police bully whose look was enough to make hardened criminals shake in their shoes. The persecution of the *candomblé* celebrants was a natural corollary of the racist preaching that began in the School of Medicine and was taken up by certain newspapers. Pedrito Gordo did nothing more than put the theory into practice. He was a logical product of Nilo Argolo and Oswaldo Fontes, a predictable consequence of their reasoning.

And so the argument was relegated to oblivion; but one might say that it represented a decisive turning point. It buried racism in the rubble of anti-science and made it a vile synonym for charlatanism and reaction, a weapon turned against the implacable march of events by classes and castes that were already doomed. Pedro Archanjo may not have finished off the racists—every era and every society will always have its fools and knaves—but he branded them with a red-hot iron and pointed them out in the street: "There go the anti-Brazilians, folks," as he proclaimed the greatness of the mestizo race.

Did you ever hear such a thing?

6

"Oh no, my dear fellow, I wouldn't say it was completely lacking in interest," Professor Nilo Argolo said thoughtfully. "It would be folly, of course, to expect any work of real substance to come from the pen of a mulatto. You can simply ignore his outrageous defense of miscegenation, since it's laughable nonsense. It's as natural that a mestizo should reason in that way as it would be inexcusable for white men who have access to scientific sources to do so. Ignore the ridiculous side of it, ignore his conclusions, and concentrate on the profusion of odd information about local customs. I must confess I had never heard of some of the practices described by that gossip."

"Well, I may read it after all, then, but I confess I have little stomach for it, and my time is very limited. Here he comes, and I have a class to meet," said Professor Oswaldo Fontes, disappearing through the door. Even though he was Professor Argolo's friend and intellectual heir and protegé, he was rather afraid of him. Nilo Argolo de Araújo was not only a theoretician, he was a leader and a prophet.

They had been talking about Pedro Archanjo's book, and Professor Argolo had astounded his co-religionist by saying:

"Point the darkey out to me if you see him. I don't pay much attention to a servant's face unless he's my own. The only runners I know by sight are those in my own department; all the others look exactly alike to me, and they all have the same smell. Dona Augusta, my wife, sees to it that our servants bathe every day."

When he heard the name of the excellent Dona Augusta Cavalcanti dos Mendes Argolo de Araújo, "Dona Augusta, my wife," Professor Fontes saluted in absentia the highborn, truculent wife of his illustrious confrère by a deferential nod of the head. A grandame of the old school reeking with nobility, Dona Augusta, head held high, ferule in her hand, intimidated not only servants; the most arrogant politicians trembled before her. Professor Fontes was a dyed-in-the-wool racist by conviction; he thought mulattoes a despicable subhuman breed, and only grudgingly conceded that Negroes were monkeys who somehow had the gift of speech; but despite his convictions he did feel sorry for the servants in the Argolo household. Taken individually, either of the spouses would have been a severe trial to any mortal, but with both of them together in the same house—!

On this sunwashed day Pedro Archanjo was coming contentedly through the hall toward the outside door, swaying slightly to a samba tune that he was whistling under his breath in deference to his august surroundings. An imperious voice stopped him near the door just as he was letting the whistle get a little louder, the plaza being free for music or any kind of racket.

"Boy!"

Reluctantly breaking off his tune, Archanjo turned and recognized the professor. Tall, erect, all in black, with a spare, dry frame and forbidding voice and bearing, Professor Nilo Argolo,

professor emeritus of Forensic Medicine and the pride of the
Medical School, resembled some fierce medieval inquisitor.
The cruel yellow light in his narrow eyes revealed the mystic and
fanatic.

"Come over here."

Archanjo slowly came forward with the rolling gait of a
capoeira wrestler. What did the professor want with him? Could
he have read his book?

Prodigal Lídio Corró had sent copies to some of the professors
at the university. Paper and ink cost money, and in order to
meet expenses other copies were sold in bookstores at a small
profit or passed from hand to hand. But Master Corró became
apoplectic when Archanjo reminded him of the cost and criticized his wastefulness. "*Compadre*, we've got to show those par-
rots in hard high collars, those puffed-up stuffed shirts, what a
Bahia mulatto can do." To Lídio, *Life in Bahia*, written by his
compadre Pedro Archanjo, that prince of good fellows, and
printed on his own printing press, was quite simply the most important book in the world. He had made huge sacrifices in order
to print it, but turning a profit from it was the last thing in his
mind. What he did want to do was rub it in the faces of "all those
grammar-crapping ass-holes" who thought mulattoes and Negroes were inferior beings occupying a place somewhere between
men and animals. Unbeknownst to Archanjo he had sent copies
to the National Library in Rio, to the State Public Library, to
authors and reporters in the South, and to some institutions
abroad. The only problem had been getting hold of the addresses.

"*Compadre*, guess where I sent our book today! To the
United States—to Columbia University in New York City. I
found the address in a magazine." (He had already sent copies to
the Sorbonne and the University of Coimbra.)

It was Archanjo himself, however, who had left copies of his
book at the university for Professors Nilo Argolo and Oswaldo
Fontes. Now, as he came through the hall, he wondered if "the
monster" could have read the grubby little volume, so unimpres-
sive in appearance. He hoped that he had, for it was at least partly
thanks to the professor that he had made up his mind to write it.
Reading Nilo Argolo's work, he had steeped himself in rage.

"Monster" was the students' name for Professor Argolo, in reference to his reputation for brilliance—"He's a monster, he reads and speaks seven languages"—as well as his malignity, and the dreary aridity of his temperament. He was an enemy of laughter, gayety, and liberty, and he knew no mercy at exam time— "The monster has an orgasm every time he gives somebody a zero." The quiet that reigned in his classroom was the envy of the professors, most of whom were incapable of keeping their students in order half as well as he did. A hypnotic lecturer, he brooked no interruptions, much less disagreement with his visionary statements, which were worthy of a prophet in trance.

Younger professors, imbued with anarchical European ideas, debated with their students, listening to objections and admitting doubts. "Intolerable license," Professor Argolo de Araújo called it. He was not going to let his classroom be turned into "a public house full of heretics and roisterers, a bordello where any folly was permitted." When one Ju, a brilliant student with highest honors in every subject, but "spoiled by the pernicious example of other teachers," accused Dr. Argolo of reactionary ideas, the latter demanded an investigation and the suspension of the lad who had dared to interrupt his class with the frightful roar of:

"Professor Nilo Argolo, you're Savonarola himself come back from the Inquisition, alive and well and living in the School of Medicine!"

Prevented by his two colleagues on the examining committee from failing the boy at the end of the year, Professor Argolo had to be satisfied with spoiling Ju's perfect record by giving him only a passing grade. But the student's outburst of rebellion at the discrimination expressed by Argolo passed into the school's stock of stories about eccentric professors and was not only repeated by the students but noised about the city. Although not the subject of such a rich store of hilarious anecdotes as Professor Montenegro, the protagonist of endless jokes because of his meticulous use of pronouns, verb forms, archaisms, and comical neologisms, the dour professor of Forensic Medicine had furnished material for an abundant flow of amusing *bons mots* and acerbic criticism (not always in the best of taste) pertaining to the anachronistic rigidity of his methods and his prejudices.

One anecdote, a true one as a matter of fact, had it that one evening it occurred to the professor to call on his old friend Marcos Andrade, a district judge in the capital, as had been his monthly habit for more than ten years. After dinner in the bosom of his family, the magistrate had made himself comfortable: that is, since the night was sultry and suffocatingly humid, while keeping on his striped trousers, his vest, his hard high collar and neckcloth, he had taken off his frock coat.

When the maid informed him that his illustrious friend was waiting for him in the sitting room, the magistrate rushed out to greet him. In his haste to welcome Professor Argolo and enjoy the pleasure of his learned conversation, he forgot to put on his frock coat. Seeing him in this shameless, immodest dishabille, this negligent attire fit only for the bedroom, Professor Argolo rose to his feet:

"Until today I had always thought that I enjoyed Your Excellency's esteem. I see I was mistaken." And without another word he walked out the front door. Refusing to accept His Honor's explanations and excuses, he withdrew his affection from him and cut him dead from that day forth.

Another story, told in verse to the accompaniment of snickers around the Terreiro de Jesus, was rude, off-color, and undoubtedly apocryphal. It was a mean act of vengeance on the part of Mundinho Carvalho, one of the students whom the monster had failed:

> *To avoid black rhymes*
> *I'll sing in blank verse*
> *A thing that happened one day:*
> *Dr. Nilo Argolo*
> *Our noble professor*
> *Can't stand darkies, you know,*
> *So he made Countess Dona Augusta*
> *Shave off all her pubic hair;*
> *It was lovely, but oh, so black.*

As he approached, Pedro Archanjo noticed that Nilo Argolo placed his hands behind his back to forestall any attempt at a handshake. A wave of blood rose to his face.

The professor studied the features and bearing of the runner with the insolent detachment of a man examining an insect or an inanimate object. He made no attempt to conceal the surprise on his hostile face at the cleanliness and distinction of the mulatto's garb and person. Of certain mestizos the professor sometimes thought and even, on rare occasions, said: "That fellow deserves to be white; his African blood is his misfortune."

"Was it you who wrote a brochure called *Daily Life* . . ."

". . . *in Bahia*." Archanjo had recovered from his initial humiliation and was willing to strike up a conversation. "I left a copy for you in the office."

"Call me 'professor,'" the illustrious lecturer corrected sharply. "Not just 'sir' but 'professor,' and don't you forget it. I earned that title in fair competition, I have the right to use it, and I demand to be so addressed. Do you understand?"

"'Yes, Professor," replied Pedro Archanjo in a frigid, distant tone. All he wanted now was to go his way.

"Tell me: those different notes about customs, traditional holidays, and the fetishist rites you call obligations: are they accurate?"

"Yes, Professor."

"The part about those rituals called *cucumbís*, for example. Is all that really true?"

"Yes, Professor."

"You didn't make it up?'

"No, Professor."

"I read your brochure, and bearing in mind who wrote it"— he examined Archanjo again with hostile yellow eyes—"I won't deny that it has merit, limited, of course, to some of the descriptive observations. It lacks any true scientific value, needless to say, and your conclusions about miscegenation are dangerous lunacy. But still the book is worthy of attention as a repository of facts. I found it interesting reading."

Pedro Archanjo made a new attempt to jump over the wall dividing him from the professor and took up the dialogue again:

"Don't you think, Professor, that those very facts speak in favor of my conclusions?"

The thin line of Professor Argolo's lips was infrequently broken by a smile. Real laughter was an even greater rarity, and was almost always provoked by the folly or imbecility of others.

"Please don't make me laugh. Your tissue of nonsense does not contain a single quotation from a thesis, book, or report by anyone else; it is not supported by the opinion of any national or foreign authority. How dare you call it scientific? On what do you base your defense of miscegenation and hold it up as the ideal solution to the race problem in Brazil? How dare you call our Latin culture mulatto? That is a subversive, monstrous statement."

"It's based on fact, Professor."

"Nonsense. What do facts signify, unless they are examined in the light of philosophy and science? Did it ever occur to you that it might be a good idea to read something about the subject you were discussing?" He laughed again mockingly. "I advise you to read Gobineau. He was a French diplomat and savant who lived in Brazil, and he is the definitive authority on questions of race. You can find his books in our library here at the school."

"The only books I read were some of yours and Professor Fontes's."

"And they failed to convince you? You confuse the horrid sounds of sambas and *batuque* drumming with music; abominable fetishistic figures carved without the least respect for the laws of esthetics are singled out by you as examples of art; to you, savage rituals are a form of culture. I tremble for this country if we ever assimilate such barbarisms, if we do not react in time against this avalanche of horrors. Listen to me: we must cleanse our country's life and culture of this mud of Africa which is befouling us. Even if it becomes necessary to resort to violence in order to do so."

"Violence has been used, Professor."

"Not enough, perhaps, and perhaps not the right kind." Argolo's habitually dry voice took on a harder timbre; the tawny light of pitiless fanaticism kindled in his accusing, hostile eyes. "We are dealing with a cancer, and we must extirpate it root and branch. Surgery may appear to be a cruel way of practicing medicine, but is actually beneficent and sometimes indispensable."

"Well, Professor, maybe if you killed all of us, one by one . . ."

Was the scoundrel daring to be ironic? The pride of the Medical School fixed his threatening, suspicious eyes on the runner, but all he saw was a composed face and correct posture without a sign of disrespect. His gaze softened and became almost dreamy. He saluted Archanjo's proposal with a laugh that was almost cordial.

"Exterminate you? Leave a world of Aryans and nothing else?"

Oh brave new world! Oh grand, impossible dream! Where was the genius dauntless enough to put this breathtaking idea into practice? Who could tell? Perhaps one day some invincible god of war would execute that supreme mission. The visionary Professor Argolo scanned the future and foresaw the hero leading his Aryan cohorts. The effulgent image, the glorious moment, lasted but an instant; he came down to earth and wretched reality.

"Oh, I hardly think it will be necessary to go quite as far as that. It will be sufficient to pass laws prohibiting miscegenation and regulating marriages: white will marry white, black will mate with black or mulatto, and anyone who does not obey the law will go to prison."

"It might be hard to separate and classify everyone, Professor."

Again the professor thought he sensed a flash of mockery in the runner's soft voice and excellent pronunciation. Ah! If only he could catch him in the act!

"Hard? I see no reason why it should be." He decided to bring the conversation to a close with a command. "Go back to your work; you've wasted enough time already. I will say this: with all the absurdities in your book, there are a few things in it worth reading." His tone, while not precisely amiable, was condescending. He held out his fingertips to the mestizo.

Now it was Pedro Archanjo's turn to ignore the proffered bony hand and limit himself to a nod, exactly like the one with which Professor Nilo Argolo de Araújo had greeted him at the beginning of their talk, except that it was slightly—ever so slightly —smaller. "Scum," snarled the professor, turning white.

Pedro Archanjo was in a pensive mood as he walked toward
Tabuão Street and crossed the alley full of racing boys. He had
more than enough food for worry and bemusement. First there
was that malignant preaching in the School of Medicine. Closer to
home, in Misericórdia, Dorotéia's head had been turned and she
was beside herself. The Evil One had ordered her to give up her
home in Bahia, her freedom, and her son, and to go away with
him. For many years there had been no pledge between Archanjo
and Dorotéia, and if on occasion something good happened when
they chanced to meet, it was purely by happenstance, a reminder
of the storm and its calm aftermath. But there was Tadeu to consider, the apple of Archanjo's eye. At the Tent of Miracles, financial problems had multiplied with the printing of his book and
things had never been so difficult for Lídio Corró.

Estevão das Dores, with his cornstalk cigarette, his walking
stick, and his rheumatism, never failed to turn up at the shop on
the first of every month when his payment fell due. He would
sit in a chair near the door the whole afternoon, chatting peacefully. If he saw that Lídio and Tadeu had more work than they
could handle he would sometimes lean his cane against the wall,
stand up with his hands on his hips "to hold the old bones together," and walk over to the trays of type. Sickly and doddering
as he was, he was a master at his trade; the work passed quickly
through his nicotine-stained hands, and even the ancient printing
press seemed less capricious and slow when he was operating it.
Although he never said a word about debts and payments ("I just
stay at home, I ain't no use to anybody. Ain't nothing tuckers a
body out like not having enough to do. That's why I like to come

and chew the fat with my friends."), the sight of his waiting
creditor always made Lídio nervous.

"I'm expecting a lot of money I'm owed to be paid back any
day. And as soon as somebody pays me, the first of it's for you,
Seu Estevão."

"Now let's not talk about that, I didn't come here to dun you
. . . But you listen to me, Mr. Corró, you give too much credit,
and that's a fact."

It was a fact: the street singers printed their leaflets on credit,
paying for the work little by little as they were sold. Lídio had
practically become the patron of popular balladeers. But how on
earth could he refuse credit to his friend João Caldas, the father
of eight, whose inspiration was his only source of income?
Or to Isidro Pororoca, who was blind in both eyes but a natural
artist in portraying the life of the people in song?

"The secret of printing is good, quick service and cash on the
barrelhead. And I'm giving you that piece of advice for free."

As soon as he was paid and had counted his money twice,
Estevão would amble off with his advice, his cornhusk cigarettes,
his rheumatism, and the walking stick that threw the apprentice
into fits of envy; he was determined to have one like it some day.
It was a fearful weapon, with a knife blade concealed in the flexible cane.

"I can just see him opening that cane and sticking the knife
into me," said Lídio, clinging to his sense of humor in the midst
of all his problems.

The solution to their financial difficulties was to put on more
shows. Some weeks they gave as many as three, with the help of
Budião and his students, Valdeloir, Aussá, and a sailor called Mané
Lima. Lima, who had been put off a Lloyd ship for unruly be-
havior and fighting with knives, was already an expert dancer of
the *maxixe* and the *lundu* and had learned the Argentine tango,
gaucho steps, and the pasodoble in other ports of call. He called
himself an "international artist" and took on Fat Fernanda as a
partner. She was very fat and very light on her feet, a feather in
the sailor's arms, and the duo soon became famous. They left the
Tent of Miracles for cabarets and years later were applauded at
the Monte Carlo Pension, the Pension Elegante, and the Tabaris.

Except for rapid tours of the northern capitals—Aracajú, Maceió, and Recife—Mané Lima, the Waltzing Sailor, never left Bahia again.

Pedro Archanjo was the only one who did not show the same enthusiasm for these performances, now that they were held more often. He never seemed to have enough time for his reading and study.

"Why do you do all that reading, Master Pedro, when you already know so much?"

"Why, *meu bom*, I read so I can understand what I see and the things people tell me."

The womenfolk sensed a subtle, almost imperceptible change in him: he was still an assiduous, faithful, gentle lover, going gladly and punctually from one woman to another, but no longer the carefree youth who had had no other occupation but that. Heretofore his life had been a round of carnival revels, samba circles, *afoxés, capoeira, candomblé* obligations, and the pleasures of good talk, hearing and telling stories, and above all the merry, diligent, idle work of bedding women. Now it was more than curiosity that led him to *candomblés, afoxés,* dancing and singing societies, *capoeira* schools, and the houses of old people who had been slaves or prostitutes, with whom he carried on interminable conversations. It was a qualitative change, though a barely noticeable one, as if, only now that he had reached the age of forty, Archanjo had become fully conscious of life and the world.

One day when he passed the house where Sabina dos Anjos lived, a little urchin ran out begging "Your blessing, Godfather." Archanjo picked the child up in his arms. He had inherited the beauty of his mother Sabina, the queen of the dance, with her firm, muscular body of mature and lusty juices: the Queen of Sheba. Sheba, I am King Solomon and I have come to visit you in the kingdom of your bedroom. He recited Biblical psalms to her as she lay redolent of jasmine, a balm for restless hearts.

"Give me some money, Godfather"—just like Sabina, always after money. He took a coin from his pocket and the boy's face broke into a smile: whose free, mischievous laughter had he inherited?

Sabina came to the door when her son called her, holding
Archanjo by the hand. The *mulata* laughed at the unexpected encounter.

"You here? I didn't think you'd come today."

Her voice was breezy, languorous, lazy.

"I'm just passing by. Got a lot of things to do."

"Since when do you have things to do, Pedro?"

"I don't understand it myself, Sheba. This obligation's getting
mighty heavy."

"Obligation to a saint? Or to Exú? Or some work at the Medical School?"

"Neither one. It's an obligation to myself."

"Nobody understands you when you talk like that."

She leaned against the door, her body tense, her bosom erect,
her mouth eager, temptation in the afternoon. Archanjo felt that
call in every fiber of his being as he gazed at the lovely woman
and drew nearer to feel her breath. He reached in his pocket and
took out an envelope with pretty foreign stamps on it. It had
come from the end of the world, from the North Pole where
there is only ice and night lasts forever.

"Does Kirsi live in the snow?"

"Yes, in a town called Helsinki, in Finland."

"I know, Kirsi's Swedish. She's so sweet. Did she send you
that letter?"

He drew the child's picture from the envelope. There was no
letter with it, only a few sentences in French with an occasional
word in Portuguese. Sabina took the photograph. What an adorable little creature! So delicate and sweet with his curly head and
Kirsi's eyes. What comeliness, what splendid and disturbing
beauty. Sabina lifted her eyes from the picture to her boy running
in the street.

"He's good-looking, too . . ." Which of the two did she
mean? "It's funny, they're different and alike at the same time.
How come you only make boys, Pedro?"

Archanjo smiled in the doorway, close to Sabina's eager mouth.

"Come on in." Her voice was warm and heavy.

"I've got an awful lot to do."

"Since when can't you take a little time to make a baby?"—twining her arm around his neck. "I took a bath just now, I'm still wet."

Pedro Archanjo lost sight of his destiny in the scent of her bosom and her soft flesh—what time would he show up at the Tent of Miracles, where Lídio and Tadeu were waiting for him? Sabina dos Anjos, fairest of angels, Queen of Sheba in the empire of her bed. Each in her turn, and sometimes out of turn. There had been a time when he was free as air, with love's labor his only task. But no longer.

"Tell me, my friend, how much will it cost me? I'm poorer than poor, I'm ruined. Do you know what that means? For a long time I spent my money like water; now I have to count every penny. Make a good price for me; don't take advantage of a poor, decrepit old woman."

Lídio's work did not come cheap. No one could compare with him in painting miracles. He made the saints and the customers happy; no one ever complained, and he was a favorite of Our Lord of Bonfim. He had more orders than he could handle, and there were months when his ex-votos brought in more money than the printing press. He had customers from Recife and Rio, and one time an Englishman ordered four paintings all at once.

"Which saint was it and what was the miracle?"

"You can put in all the saints you like and all the miracles you have a mind to."

The gringo had been no dottier than this funny old lady who was shaking her parasol at him, her white hair like cotton, her wrinkled face, her lean and skinny frame, and all her sixty years showing. But was she sixty, or thirty? Pert, talkative, determined, with an iron will and a story of a libertine tomcat with a disgusting crop of mange:

"I'm a ruined old woman, but I can't complain."

Once she had been the fabulously wealthy Princess of the Recôncavo, surrounded by pomp and luxury, mistress of sugar plantations and mills, of slaves, of town houses in Santo Amaro, Cachoeira, and Salvador. Gallant gentlemen sighed for her, and an officer slew the petted darling's lawyer fiancé in a duel. Bankers and barons ruined themselves pursuing her. She led a life full of vicissitudes and numerous love affairs; she traveled all over the world and had titles, offices, and fortunes at her feet. But she never gave herself for money, and those who tried to win her favors by lavishing jewels, mansions, and carriages on her gained nothing unless she took at least a fleeting fancy to them. An insatiable *amoureuse*, she was capricious and had a fickle heart.

When the wrinkles, white hair, and false teeth came, she dissipated her fortune by bestowing kingly presents on gigolos as nonchalantly as she had herself received them when she was a girl. Life's revels began to cost her absurdly dear, but she paid the price without flinching: it was worth it. Then at last, stripped to the bone physically and financially, she returned to Bahia with her big tomcat and the memory of those past debaucheries, so few and so ephemeral. Why had she been so parsimonious, why had she not done more?

And now she had come to settle the price, time, and conditions for the painting of a miracle. The lusty feline, Argolo de Araújo by name, had caught an abominable dose of mange on some rooftop. Several days later his hair had begun to fall out, that blue-black velvet into which the old woman loved to sink her fingers, remembering past amours. She had even consulted doctors ("There isn't a single veterinarian in this place"); she had spent good money at the drugstore for pomades and potions, all useless. He had been cured at last, thanks to St. Francis of Assisi, to whom she was devoted—in Venice, between kisses, a poet had taught her to love God's beggar; as they lay in bed he recited the sermon to the birds, and when he went away he took her purse, the *poverello*!

Mestre Lídio, confused by so many words and so much laughter, named a price for his work. The old thing was more like a vaudeville actress than anything else, haggling and arguing without the least ceremony. Still mistress of an indefinable charm, at certain moments her old age disappeared and there was a flash of her youthful seductiveness: the proud Princess of the Recôncavo turned charming and familiar, a retired madam with an elegant air. The bargaining took some time, for the old lady had sat down to haggle better and as she did so, she was startled to see the poster of the Moulin Rouge on the wall.

"Oh mon Dieu, c'est le Moulin!"

The loose tongue wagged furiously, telling how much she had crowded into her life and about the world she had lived in, what marvels she had seen and possessed. She recalled tunes, plays, exhibits, excursions, parties, cheeses, wines, and lovers, and gave herself up to the joy of reminiscence. It was a double pleasure, for she had once been wild and wealthy. In her enthusiasm she spoke in a mixture of French and Portuguese, punctuated with exclamations in Spanish, English, and Italian.

Pedro Archanjo returned from Sheba's kingdom at the moment when the decrepit old sailor woman was setting off on her circumnavigation, and he set sail with her amid a gale of delighted laughter. They lifted anchor in Montmartre, stopping off at cabarets, theaters, restaurants, and art galleries in Paris and its suburbs —or rather, the rest of the world. For you know, my friends, there is Paris, and then there is the rest of the world; and the rest, *oh la la! c'est la banlieue.*

She was happy to have a chance to tell the whole story: her great-nephews were too impatient to listen to her for long on their infrequent, hasty visits to her hovel, a little broken-down house near the Lapa Convent, where she subsisted with her cat and a crazy female servant. The full name of the impetuous old woman was Senhora Dona Isabel Tereza Gonçalves Martins de Araújo e Pinho, Countess of Água Brusca by right. To her intimate friends, Zabela.

Pedro Archanjo asked her if she had been to Helsinki. No, she had not. She had visited Petrograd, Stockholm, Oslo, and Copenhagen, but never Finland. But my friend, why do you speak so familiarly of Helsinki? Were you there as a sailor? But no, you don't look like a seafaring man, you have more the air of a professor or a college graduate.

Archanjo laughed his cordial laugh. Neither student nor teacher—those things aren't for me, *Madama!*—and no sailor either; I just run errands in the Medical School and I like to read —out of sheer curiosity. A love affair was what linked him to Finland. He showed her the picture and the countess scrutinized it closely and admired the boy's face. What charm! A work of art! In her cultivated handwriting, Kirsi's few emotion-filled words in Portuguese bridged the distance across time and the ocean: *amor, saudade, Bahia.* One sentence was entirely in French. Isabel Tereza translated it, but she would not have had to, for Archanjo knew it by heart: our son is growing beautiful and strong, his name is Ojú, like his father's, Ojú Kekkonen; he orders the other boys around and all the girls are in love with him; he's a little sorcerer.

"Is your name Ojú?"

"My Christian name is Pedro Archanjo, but I'm called Ojuobá in Nagô."

"I'd love to go to a *macumba*. I've never seen one."

"Whenever you want to go I'll be happy to take you."

"Happy nothing. Don't be a liar. Who wants the company of an old woman on her last legs?" She laughed mischievously, taking the measure of that strong handsome mulatto, the lover of the Finnish girl. "The boy looks exactly like you."

"But he looks like Kirsi, too. He's going to be the King of Sweden." Archanjo laughed merrily and the Princess of the Recôncavo (Zabela to her friends) delightedly joined in.

"Ask *Seu* Lídio to give me a discount. I can't afford to pay what he's asking, though I know it's worth even more." She was as courteous as Corró and Archanjo, as courteous as any working-class citizen of Bahia.

Lídio immediately rose to the occasion.

"Please set the price yourself, ma'am."

"No, I won't do that either."

"Never mind, then. I'll draw the miracle for you, and when it's ready you just pay me whatever you like."

"Not whatever I like; whatever I can."

Just then Tadeu came in with his books and notebooks. Zabela noticed his resemblance to Archanjo and smiled discreetly. The apprentice had grown up to be a strapping, graceful-limbed adolescent; he was irresistible when he smiled.

"My godson, Tadeu Canhoto."

"Canhoto? Left-handed? Limb of Satan? Is that his real name or a nickname?"

"It's the name his mother gave him when he was born."

Tadeu withdrew to a backroom.

"Is he a student?"

"Yes. He works here in the shop with *Compadre* Lídio and studies in his free time. Last year he took four preparatory exams. He got an eight, two nines, and one ten with highest honors." Pride throbbed in Archanjo's voice. "This year he's taking four more, and next year he'll be through. He wants to enter the university."

"What is he going to study?"

"He'd like to take engineering. I hope we can manage to send him. It's not easy for a poor boy to get through college, *Madama*. It takes a lot of money."

Tadeu came back into the room, opened his books out on the table, and as he did so caught sight of the photograph.

"Can I see the picture? Who is it, Godfather?"

"A relative of mine . . . a distant relative, very distant. He lives on the other side of the world."

"That's the best-looking kid I ever saw." He picked up his notebook; he had homework to do.

The Countess of Água Brusca, Senhora Dona Isabel Tereza Gonçalves Martins de Araújo e Pinho, turned more and more into Zabela. She helped Tadeu with his French verbs and taught him some words of argot. She sipped their homemade cordial—*crème de cacao*, a sublime nectar concocted by Rosa de Oxalá—as if she were tasting the finest champagne. When she left they hated to see her go.

"The best thing, *Seu* Lídio," she said as she was leaving, "would be for you to come to my house some day to meet Argolo de Araújo. Then you'll be able to do him justice when you paint him. He's the finest cat in Bahia. And he has the worst character."

"With pleasure, ma'am. I'll go tomorrow."

"Is the cat named Argolo de Araújo? That's funny . . . the same name as the professor," said Archanjo, puzzled.

"Are you referring to Nilo d'Ávila Argolo de Araújo? I know that microbe only too well. We're cousins on the Araújo side. I was engaged to his Uncle Ernesto, but when he passes me in the street he pretends not to see me. He sets a pretty high price on himself, he oozes aristocracy from every pore, but only when I'm not around. I know the skeletons in the family closet too well—all their shameless affairs and how much they've stolen, oh! *mon cher, quelle famille!* I'll tell you all about it some day if you want to hear."

"If I want to hear, *Madama!* Today's my lucky day: Wednesday, Xangô's day, and I am Ojuobá, his wide-open eyes that see all and know all. Poor people's affairs, from choice, but rich people's too, when I have to."

"Take me to a *macumba* and I'll tell you all about the Bahia nobility."

Tadeu helped her down the two front steps.

"An old woman's no use to anybody, but I don't want to die yet, even so"—she chucked the boy under the chin with her manicured hand. "It was a handsome, dark young man like you who made my grandmother Virgínia Martins fall head over heels in love and add some flavor to the family blood."

She opened her gaudy parasol and steadied herself on the steep slope of Tabuão Street. She was walking the streets of Paris in her *belle époque* walk, parading on the Boulevard des Capucines.

One thing is certain even if the rest is humbug: Zabela was present at Ogun's festival the night the spell was cast. The story varies depending on who is telling it. The altercation was witnessed by them all, with the eyes that the earth will swallow up one day, but each witness interprets it in his own way. The most positive, of course, are those who weren't there and didn't see a thing: they know more about what happened than anyone else, they are the chief witnesses.

But whether they were there or not, all of them agree on one thing:

"If you won't take my word for it, ask that rich old lady in Lapa, the one covered with jewels. She's a real aristocrat, she was there, and she saw it."

Without a doubt she was an aristocrat by birth and breeding, and also without a doubt she had been rich, in days gone by. But all her glittering jewelry was paste, ropes and strands of imitation stones. Only the *mãe-de-santo* wore as many necklaces and bracelets as Zabela. When she took her leave at the end of the first of many visits, the Countess of Água Brusca took off one of her necklaces in a characteristic gesture and offered it to Majé Bassan:

"It's of no value, but please keep it anyway."

Sitting erect in the armchair reserved for guests of honor, Zabela followed the ceremony intently. She stood up so that she could see better and made nervous gestures, placing her hand on her heart and exclaiming in French: *Nom de Dieu! Zut, alors!* at the moment when the *orixás* descended to the summons of the fast drumbeats, at the clashing of the swords of the Oguns, and at the dance of Oxumarê, a cobra wriggling stomach to the ground, half male, half female.

"What happened to that pretty girl who came up to speak to you and then danced for a while so vivaciously? She was standing in the doorway and then she disappeared. What became of her, why isn't she dancing any more?"

If Pedro Archanjo had the key to the riddle he did not let the old gossip know it. "I didn't notice, *Madama*."

"Don't try to make a fool of me. I saw a man standing near her behind the fire, a haughty-looking white man who was nervous and impatient. Come on, tell me where she is."

"She's gone." And he would say no more.

All those who testify apparently agree that Dorotéia was seen in the circle of devotees whirling in the tent and rivaling even Rosa de Oxalá in her beauty and the intricacy of her steps. Stela de Oxóssi, Paula de Euá, and other outstanding female dancers were present, too.

Oxóssi came with his horsetail *erukerê* and mounted Stela. Euá entered Paula like a breeze from the lagoon or water from a fountain. Rosa shuddered convulsively and became Oxolufan, old Oxalá. Three Omolús, two Oxumarês, two Yemanjás, one Ossain, and one Xangô appeared, and then six Oguns at the same time, for it was June 13, St. Anthony's Day, and in Bahia Ogun and St. Anthony are one. The people rose to their feet and shouted joyously: *Ogunyê!*

When Yansan gave her the signal, a long whistle like the whistle of a train or a ship, Dorotéia, troubled, went over to kiss Archanjo's hand.

"Why didn't you bring my boy?"

"He had a lot of studying to do."

"Pedro, I'm going away now, tonight."

"Is he coming for you? Are you leaving for good?"

"I'm going with him, and I'm leaving for good. Don't tell Tadeu. Smear your mouth with honey and tell him I'm dead. It's better that way: just one hurt and then it's over."

She knelt down and bowed her head to the earth. Archanjo touched the crisp curly head and lifted black Dorotéia to her full height. She was hardly steady on her feet when Yansan took possession of her with a cry that woke the dead. There are witnesses who say that the wail of the *eguns*, the dead ancestors, raised gooseflesh as it rose from the murky depths of the *terreiro*.

Very few of those inside the tent had noticed the scene that preceded the coming of Yansan. Zabela, however, had followed it closely from beginning to end. All of it was new and exciting to her. The watching attendants led those in trance to the dressing rooms where they changed their clothes before dancing to the ritual chants. And Yansan, surrounded by her six Oguns, danced more than any of the others. It was a farewell, though no one knew it.

While the dancers were changing costumes a royal banquet in honor of Ogun was served in another room. Zabela tasted a little of each dish, for she loved palm-oil cooking, bad as it was for her liver. When the rockets went off to announce the *orixás'* return, the old lady almost ran out of the dining room, anxious not to miss the least detail of the *macumba* rites.

The lordly procession of those possessed by the gods approached, Epifânia's Ogun in the lead. There was a riffle of the drums, and people stood up and clapped. Flashing rockets, bombs, and firecrackers lit up in the air—the month of June in Bahia is the month of corn and fireworks. Amid the bursting of rockets and the glare of lights the *orixás* entered the tent one by one, each with his emblems, arms, or ritual tools. Mother Majé Bassan began the singing and Oxóssi led the dance.

But where was Yansan; why didn't she reappear inside the tent? All that was heard of her was the echo of a distant sound, a whistle. A train? No, it was a ship. Then all saw Dorotéia in the doorway for the last time. She was not wearing Yansan's garments, although there are many who say she was and swear they may be struck blind if she was not; nor did she have on the starched skirt and lace overdress of a Bahiana. No, she was dressed like a fashionable lady in aristocratic garb: a dress of the finest stuff, with a long train and a ruffled jabot. Her breast was heaving and her eyes burned like coals.

Everyone has something to say about the man standing behind Dorotéia and all agree that he had little horns like a devil, though they cannot agree on anything else. Some saw a tail like a walking cane with the curved end crooked over his arm; others speak of his cloven hooves; most of them describe him as coal-black. Evandro Café, a highly respectable old man and a former slave, has it that the Left-Handed One was red, a brilliant crimson, in fact. To Zabela's curious and attentive eyes he was fair and blond, with two bunches of curls on his forehead, a handsome specimen of a man. The countess and the former slave, equally old and experienced, are equally reliable as witnesses.

It happened in the full glare of fireworks and the blaze of the bonfire. Amid all that blinding light and flame, in the glare of that false dawn, lit with tongues of fire, thunder, and lightning, Dorotéia melted into thin air before you could say abracadabra. One minute she was standing in the doorway and the next she was gone: there was only the empty door and a smell of sulphur, a flash of lightning, and an explosion. Was it a bombshell, a sky-rocket? Those who heard it know that it was not.

Dorotéia was never seen again, nor was Beelzebub. There was the loud noise, and to Zabela it was galloping hoofbeats, lovers fleeing to a faraway land; to Evandro Café it was the sound of cloven hooves clattering off, the Evil One come for his *iaba*. But whichever it was, Dorotéia had vanished.

For days there was no one at the stand on Misericórdia Street, where customers with a taste for beancakes with or without pepper, coconut candy, and nigger-foot molasses pralines had for years and years come to buy from black Dorotéia in her Yansan necklace with the one red and white bead that was Xangô's. Finally white, placid Miquelina, with her blue-green eyes and tray of fancy sweetmeats, came to take her place.

Hunched over his books in the Tent of Miracles, an adolescent boy wept for a mother who was dead to him. To others she was a woman bewitched who had gone back where she had come from. Every one of us has his destiny. If Archanjo had the key to the riddle, he never told anyone what it was.

In which Fausto Pena

recounts his experiences

as a playwright

and other misfortunes

My experience in the theater was a total disaster. I'm not exaggerating. It was disastrous, fatal, tragic. From whatever angle I look at the thing, the results were negative: disappointment, disillusionment, pain. Real pain, cuckold's pain.

And yet, I never even got to step out from behind the scenes, I never reached the stage. The thrill of footlights, audiences, applause, and reviews was not for me, though in the days of my feverish enthusiasm I dreamed of all that and much more. I saw my name on the arcade of the Castro Alves Theater, in neon lights on theaters in Rio and São Paulo, and beside it the name of Ana Mercedes, the triumphant leading lady, the one and only unique and sovereign Ana Mercedes, a nova bursting into the heaven of female stars. I saw packed halls, delirious audiences, enthusiastic critics, money from ticket sales and royalties rolling in—in short, the start of a new author's triumphant career.

The truth is quite another story: no money, no flattering reviews, no names in lights. My name is registered with the police, I hear, and I'm definitely under a cloud. I spent my last nickel, and lost the only thing of value I possessed.

I learned a lesson, no doubt, and I bear my companions in misfortune no ill will: not even Ildásio Taveira is my enemy. Just between the reader and myself, I confess I can't stand the sight of him and am just waiting for a chance to pay him back: all things come to him who waits, and I'm not in any hurry. Just now it would be out of the question to break off with the Judas: the National Book Institute wants him to edit an *Anthology of Young Bahian Poets* and he has promised to include some of my poems —more than one, he didn't say how many. If I cut him dead he might leave me out of the collection entirely and there I'd be, high and dry, out of the literary mainstream. So I save my best smiles for him and praise his verses assiduously and enthusiastically. You have to know when to swallow your pride if you want a place in the literary sun.

Four of us were supposed to be co-authors of the play. My three partners are all first-class intellectuals: geniuses, at the very least. Ildásio Taveira, with his thick sideburns and flashy shirts, was the most famous of the four; he had had poems published in Rio, São Paulo, and even Lisbon, and now he was making his debut as a playwright. The other two were law students. Toninho Lins, a composer, was in his third year at the university. One of his sambas had been recorded and several others were still to be published; he was hoping that the next popular music festival would make him famous.

Estácio Maia, a perennial college freshman, was a different sort: an aggressive, radical *cachaça*-drinker with a touch of charisma and an uncle, a general, whom he liked to insult when drinking among intimate friends. An advanced young man of literary gifts and boundless ability but unstable, unpredictable, and riddled with all kinds of complexes, he never stopped role playing: now he was an implacable terrorist, now a mystic begging forgiveness for his sins. He was a miserable actor and no good at all as a romantic lead. Ana Mercedes could tell his role for the day as soon as she saw him coming: "Today he's a guerrilla fighter." The day before he might have been a Dostoyevsky hero, a paperback edition of Raskolnikov. He was a character in every sense of the word.

Our first step was to reserve the Castro Alves Theater for our forthcoming production. This task was assigned to Estácio Maia, who found it useful to be his uncle's nephew on such occasions. Then began the interminable arguments about the play, with shouts, curses, threats of physical violence, and much *cachaça*.

We disagreed on both the contents of the play and the character of Pedro Archanjo. Estácio Maia, declaring himself to be an uncompromising partisan of black power, wanted to make Pedro Archanjo a Black Panther and have him come out on the stage reciting speeches and slogans à la Stokely Carmichael, advocating separatism and undying hatred between the races. A kind of Professor Nilo Argolo turned inside out: blacks on one side, whites on the other, frozen in mortal enmity, no mixing or fraternizing allowed! I never was able to find out how our violent advocate of negritude, Brazilian style, would have disposed of the mulattoes.

I don't remember whether I have mentioned that Maia was a white boy with blond hair and blue eyes and that the charms of black women and *mulatas* left him cold. I ought to be grateful to him for that, at least. There were nineteen men in the show—director, actors, electricians, stage designers, costumers, etc., not counting the eight authentic queers—and of those nineteen, Estácio Maia was the only one who didn't try to make Ana Mercedes.

Ildásio refused to go along with his notions, and so did Toninho Lins. The latter, a serious fellow who enjoyed a certain prestige among his fellow students, insisted on portraying Pedro Archanjo as a striker *par excellence*. He wanted to show him fighting against the bosses, the trusts, and the police; to make the class struggle the central theme of the play. "The race problem, comrades, is a consequence of the class problem," he explained, quoting his favorite authorities without ever losing his equanimity. "In Brazil, comrades, Negroes and mulattoes are discriminated against because of their proletarian condition: a poor white is a dirty nigger, a rich mulatto is lily-white." "Folklore and the class struggle" was his prescription for a play that would be both militantly progressive and popular. His compositions were based on folk themes, and of all the work that we put into the show, the only thing that was salvaged was the beautiful song Toninho Lins wrote for Pedro Archanjo's funeral. He later entered it in the University Festival in Rio and won second prize, but a popular vote would have given him first place.

As for Ildásio, I must admit that his position seemed to me to be closest to the real Archanjo, that is, if there is one "archangelic" truth (to use a word that's "in" this year) out of all the Archanjos who have turned up during the Centennial. We even see him on the city walls announcing Coca-Coco: "The only custom we didn't have in Bahia in my day was drinking Coca-Coco."

Ildásio Taveira agreed with Toninho that the class question must take precedence over the race question and conceded that Estácio Maia was right when he claimed that color prejudice and racists abounded in Brazil; so he proposed a nonsectarian Archanjo who was conscious of his strength and that of his people and therefore insisted that there was only one solution for the problem in Brazil: miscegenation, mixtures, mestizos, *mulatas*. All his arguments began and ended in Ana Mercedes, whom he propositioned in dark corners of the theater, the rat.

We argued in bars and nightclubs or, as a last resort, Where Angels Piss. I had helped Ildásio choose passages from Pedro Archanjo's books on which to base the dialogue, but Estácio Maia would not accept them: "The guy's a reactionary!" He put terrible speeches into Archanjo's mouth, ominous threats of destruction for the white race and the West: "We blacks will liquidate Russians and Americans alike. You're all white assassins." Toninho Lins and I finally had to intervene. The emotions of the debaters had risen to such a pitch of excitement that we were afraid the discussion would end in murderous hand-to-hand combat. Ildásio, who had a low sense of humor, dubbed the blond Maia "Carmichael's Bedbug," and they were at it again.

After the insults they would make up with abrazos and protestations of friendship, and the debate would start up again—more curses, more drinks, more abrazos. This went on for a month; they drank whole bars down to the dregs.

As for me, I struggled to conciliate opposing dogmas, obsessions, factions, ideologies, and powers into speeches and dialogue. All I wanted was to get on with the play and see my name in lights next to Ana Mercedes's—author and diva. Oh, what a glorious opening night that would be! Ana Mercedes was to be Rosa de Oxalá—there was no argument about that, at least. At that point in the debates I cared very little for Pedro Archanjo's posthumous theatrical fate: labor leader on strike, racist Black Panther denouncing miscegenation and preaching holy war against the whites, civilization-creating mulatto Bahiano, it was all the same to me. All I wanted was to get that show on the road.

By dint of infinite patience I managed to patch together a contradictory, anarchical script and get it off to the censors. Anyway, it was the authoritative, avant-garde opinion of Álvaro Orlando, who had been invited to direct the play, that scripts are only secondary in the theater—virtually useless, in fact, and therefore the contradictions were of no importance. Estácio Maia got some promises of backing and suggested that the university sponsor the opening night performance for the students. Estácio Maia, as I have said, wore his nephew-uniform on such occasions.

We decided to start rehearsing without waiting for a verdict from the censors. As luck would have it, the students were restless that week. Having discovered that government provocateurs had infiltrated the Law School, the students went on strike and were immediately supported by other professional schools. The first protest march was orderly, but the second was broken up by the police with tear gas and bullets. There were mass jailings, students were hurt, the Benedictine Monastery was invaded, shops had to close down, there were brutal and violent incidents—in short, the demonstration was a fiasco.

Toninho Lins was arrested in the Rua Chile, where he fended off the cops with his placard as long as he could. He was in jail for a week but he came through it like a man. Estácio Maia dropped out of circulation as long as it was dangerous to be around. Protest parades, street fights, and prison held few attractions for him; he was a theorist. However, his name was on a list of agitators published in the newspapers, and he disappeared completely, just dropped out of sight. Later we heard that he had got himself and his credits transferred to the university in Aracajú. He's still in Sergipe, and loonier than ever; he's back on his mysticism kick again.

The censors vetoed our play, and I am told they sent the authors' names to the police. To what depths had I sunk! Since we had already reserved the theater, Ildásio hastily wrote a play for children and invited Ana Mercedes to be the Twinkling Butterfly. I was firmly opposed to the idea and said so in no uncertain terms. To make up to her for this lost opportunity, I took her to Rio and São Paulo, spending the last of the great Levenson's dollars on this tardy honeymoon.

The dollars melted away by handfuls, in boutiques in Copacabana and São Paulo's Rua Augusta, in restaurants and nightclubs, and in treating the local literati. Precious costly friendships they proved to be. The publicity market is simply impossible these days: a piddling mention of a provincial poet's name in a literary column has to be paid for with lunch at the Museum of Modern Art or rounds of scotch in a bar in Ipanema.

I came back with empty pockets, and the sacrifice was useless. Ana Mercedes, outfitted in expensive creations by Lais, turned impatient and evasive. One Sunday morning I opened the literary supplement of the *Morning News* and what did I see but two poems signed with her name. And she had not given them to me to go over first. I read the verses. I know something about poetry, and in the very first stanza I recognized Ildásio Taveira's style. I put my hand to my forehead and found it burning with fever and horns.

I suffered and suffer still; I dream of her at night and bite my pillow, where her rosemary fragrance still perfumes the bed. But when I ran into the two of them in the street one day with their arms around each other's waists, I gave no sign of the cuckold's pain that was gnawing my entrails. Ildásio mentioned the anthology and asked me to hurry up and give him my poems; he was about to submit the manuscript to the institute. The strumpet looked at me with the most glacial indifference.

Not even *cachaça* could comfort me that day: at the end of the night, numb but still lucid, I perpetrated a farewell sonnet for Ana Mercedes. Some sorrows can only be cured by suicide or a sonnet. In the style of Camões.

In which Pedro Archanjo

becomes a prize and the subject

of a prize, with poets,

press agents, lady schoolteachers,

and the Crocodile Clown

I

"No! For God's sake!" Professor Calazans was on the verge of losing his customary good humor and ready to explode. "Not Fernando Pessoa! Anything but that!"

They were meeting in Gastão Simas's office at Doping Advertising and Publicity to choose a theme for the Pedro Archanjo Award. After the Centennial was over and his rage and disappointment had subsided into a fund of jolly anecdotes, Professor Calazans was able to regard with tolerance, as a sign of the times, the fact that the most important cultural event of the year should have been discussed and settled in the head office of an advertising agency. His comic account of the proceedings was a treat to hear.

"But Fernando Pessoa is a very interesting subject, and Pedro Archanjo was a poet himself, in a way," argued Almir Hipólito, an erstwhile emigré poet who had migrated to the ranks of advertising. He rested his deepset, romantic eyes on the husky Sergipano. "Didn't you read Ápio Corréia's article 'Pedro Archanjo, poet of science' in the *Morning News?* It was terrific."

"So what? What did your terrific scribe discover that Archanjo and Pessoa had in common?" Professor Calazans was irritated by excessive use of the adjective "terrific." He heard it all the time from his daughter and her friends; it seemed to refer to anything and everything, but especially to their boy friends. "Pedro Archanjo was fond of a nip of *cachaça* now and then, but I don't suppose we're going to give out a Sirí Award or a Crocodile Prize for the best composition on those brands of rum."

"Say, that's a good idea!" chuckled Gastão Simas. "Professor, if you'd only come to work for us you'd be an advertising wonder. You've got some terrific ideas. I'll bet the Spaniard who owns Crocodile would snap up that suggestion of yours."

"Aren't you satisfied with that shameful Coca-Coco ad? Pedro Archanjo as a flack for soft drinks. It's too much!"

According to Professor Calazans's wife Dona Lúcia, her husband lost his temper twice a year at the most. But in 1968 he lost it at least twice a day because of the Pedro Archanjo Centennial: he shouted, he got hot under the collar, he argued over trivialities. But were they trivialities? No, some of them were gross outrages. Using Archanjo's name in ads struck him as disgusting profanation, but it was even worse to use his work and misrepresent it in order to extol certain aspects of colonialism, as a certain well-remunerated writer of essays and articles had done. Yes, that really was the depth of degradation.

The Sergipano was sorely tempted to tell them all to go to blazes. The only reason he did not was that once he had undertaken a commitment he stuck it out to the bitter end. And then, if he washed his hands of the affair, who would defend Pedro Archanjo, who would keep his work from being reduced to a piece of quaint folklore, stripped of precisely what made it vital and significant? Archanjo's descriptions of folkways and customs were important, but still more important were his arguments against racism, his declaration of racial democracy.

Calazans had grown extremely attached to that poor, self-taught man of no resources and limited education, who had overcome every obstacle to learning and had undertaken and carried out an original, profound, and generous piece of work. He could be an inspiring example to young people of integrity and courage even under the most adverse conditions. It was out of love for Pedro Archanjo that the professor stuck to his post on the firing line.

"It's a funny thing," he remarked confidentially to his friend and colleague Professor Azevedo. "Here's all this commotion, all these people running around, all this fuss being made over Archanjo's Centennial, and yet they're distorting his work and his personality beyond belief. They're building him a monument, all right, but the Archanjo they're building it to isn't our Archanjo but another, far prettier, man."

"That's true enough," agreed Professor Azevedo. "For years they neglected the man and his books. Then Levenson showed up and yanked them out of their comfortable apathy. So they've dusted Archanjo off, reduced him to their own dimensions by dressing him up in new clothes and trying to drag him up to a higher social level where he'll be more useful to them. But Calazans, all that is only secondary: Archanjo is much too tough to be disfigured. And besides, all this brouhaha may have its good side. It will make the name of our Tabuão Street author a household word."

"Sometimes I get so fed up with all this I fly off the handle."

"You shouldn't. Some really bright young men are doing research on Archanjo's work and using it to establish new parameters for the evolution of Brazilian society. Professor Ramos's book is monumental; that's the only word for it. *There's* a real monument to Archanjo, if you like. And it was a result of the seminar they wouldn't let us hold."

And then there was Professor Azevedo's own book, which was coming along well. *Pedro Archanjo, Bahiano,* had also come out of the congress that had not been convened. The forbidden meeting had borne ample fruit in the form of books and research.

"Oh, you're right, of course. Even that prize for the students alone is worth all the headaches."

It was precisely the choice of subject for the Pedro Archanjo Prize that had made the professor lose his temper on another occasion in Gastão Simas's office:

"Not Fernando Pessoa, that *would* be the last straw! Be reasonable! If we're going to choose a poet as the theme, why not Castro Alves? He was an abolitionist, and at least he was Brazilian!"

Almir Hipólito waved his limp wrists in a graceful gesture of indignation. His inflamed protests were adorable:

"Oh! For goodness' sake don't make such a comparison! When you speak of poetry, please don't mention that mediocre poetaster Castro Alves, and *don't* ever compare him to my Fernando, the greatest poet who ever wrote in the Portuguese language!"— Castro Alves, the inveterate woman-chaser, made him sick to his stomach.

Swallowing several violent words, Professor Calazans managed to speak with restraint:

"The greatest? Poor Camões! And even if he were, he would not be an appropriate subject for our prize."

"He might be useful," reflected Goldman, the manager of the *City News*. "He might help us get a little more money out of the Portuguese colony."

"Make up your minds: Are we here to honor Pedro Archanjo or to squeeze money out of the Portuguese? All you people think about is money."

"Pedro Archanjo is the key," said Arno, who had been silent until then. "The key to the strongbox."

Gastão Simas intervened:

"Professor Calazans is right. Hipólito's got a terrific idea there, but we ought to save it for the next time we want to promote something in the Portuguese colony—the anniversary of Cabral's discovery of Brazil or the Gago Coutinho centennial. How about this: 'From Camões to Fernando Pessoa, from Cabral to Gago Coutinho,' how do you like that?" He preened himself for a moment. "But we can talk about that some other time. Now let's get this damned prize out of the way. We should have announced it already; there's not a minute to lose. Please, Professor, can't you come up with a specific suggestion?"

Professor Calazans pulled a sheaf of papers from his pocket and spread them out on the table. At length he found the rules for the Pedro Archanjo Prize drawn up by himself and Edelweiss Vieira of the Folklore Center. Arno Melo was touched by the disorderly mass of papers: no leather briefcase, no 007 attaché case? How does the poor guy get any work done that way? Bundles of notes on scraps of paper stretching his coat pockets all out of shape, a typical manifestation of underdevelopment. Buy yourself an 007, Professor, and let it give you a new personality —daring, decisive, managerial, ready to come up with an idea at the drop of a hat and to make your opinions stick.

The professor had his own ideas already and needed no leather briefcase or 007 attaché case to make his opinions stick: either they approved the subject, rules, and judges for the prize, just as he had written them down, or they could do it on their own hook and turn Archanjo into a skeleton key to unlock whatever damned strongbox they pleased.

2

Gastão Simas owed his position as Bahia manager for Doping S.A. primarily to his ability as a reconciliator, a trouble-shooter, a man who reaped smiles and harmony where others had sown frowns and discord. "He's a genius, the old smoothie," as Arno, his ad-mirer, summed it up. When some client was annoyed because one of the boys had goofed, or furious because of repeated mistakes made in ads already paid for and was threatening to cancel his account, it was then that G.S. grew in stature and really showed what he was worth.

Now he soothed the professor, saying: "We'll do anything you tell us, sir," and at last the plan for the Pedro Archanjo Prize was complete. The excellent Dr. Zèzinho Pinto's initial proposal suffered two or three minor alterations. The spectrum of eligible candidates was made broader, to include secondary school as well as university students. Instead of a simple composition, the rules called for an essay of at least ten typewritten pages on some aspect of Bahian folklore. The contestant could take his choice: *capoeira, candomblé,* fishing for *xaréu,* circle sambas, *afoxés,* the shepherds' tableau, the Navigators' Procession, the New Year's offerings for Yemanjá, the ABC's of Lucas da Feira, Besouro, the most famous *capoeira* wrestler of them all, the painter Carybé, Our Lord of Bonfim and the washing of his church, or the feasts of Conceição da Praia and St. Barbara. The first prize would still be a trip—not to Portugal but to the United States, since an American airline had offered two tickets. Gastão Simas planned to save the trip to Portugal for that future publicity campaign honoring Pedro Álvares Cabral and Gago Countinho which was already in the works and which he was getting television stations, a Portuguese airline, and a tourist agency to sponsor.

Additional prizes were offered: a trip to Rio de Janeiro, television sets, tape recorders, radios, the *Juvenile Encyclopedia* in seven volumes, and a dictionary. Feeling himself to some extent rewarded for running himself ragged and being forced to listen to so much twaddle, Professor Calazans declared in an interview for the *City News* that "the Pedro Archanjo Award will encourage our young people to do their own research and awaken in them an appreciation of folklore and an interest in the roots of Brazilian culture."

The professor had finished reading his interview on the front page of the paper and was smiling with satisfaction when the phone rang: Gastão Simas wondered if he could find time to come to the Doping office for a few minutes. He should come over as soon as he could; there was good news.

Cutting short his brief rest period, the Sergipano rushed

over to the agency. Gastão Simas and his staff radiated content-
ment, the joy of those whose ability has passed the test.

"My dear Professor! Or rather, allow me to address you as
fellow Doping collaborator! After all, the original idea was
yours."

"What idea?" asked Calazans suspiciously as he took a step
backward. Those unbeatable experts, so daring and unscrupulous
when it came to publicity, propaganda, and profits, made him
uneasy.

"Do you remember last Wednesday's meeting, when we settled the details about the Pedro Archanjo Award?"

"Well, of course I remember."

"Do you recall making a reference to certain brands of rum?"

"Gastão, surely you didn't bring me here to tell me you plan
to have Pedro Archanjo peddling *cachaça*. That vile Coca-Coco
ad is bad enough!"

"Let's not waste our valuable time on an insignificant detail,
Professor. As for Archanjo peddling *cachaça*, you don't have to
worry. Crocodile wouldn't buy that idea because Coca-Coco had
already used it. *But* they're willing to offer a prize for public
school children in the primary grades. We haven't given them
anything in honor of Pedro Archanjo's Centennial yet. What do
you say to that?"

"What kind of a prize will it be?"

"Oh there's nothing to it: they'll ask each child to write a
couple of paragraphs about Pedro Archanjo, the kids' teachers
will pick out the best ones, and then a committee of educators
and writers will choose the five winners of the Crocodile Rum
Prize."

"Crocodile Rum Prize! My God!"

"Do you know what that prize will be, Professor? Scholarships
to a good high school. Full tuition paid until the five winners get
through high school. Crocodile's paying for all of it."

Calazans's heart melted: five poor children would have a
chance to go to high school.

"Well, at least the *cachaça* company's behaving a little more
handsomely than the soft drink firm. They're exploiting Archanjo's name but at least they offer something in return. That's

more than the Coco people did. But I don't see where I come in."

"You come in with a little résumé for us to give the teachers
so they can tell the kids about Archanjo. Half a page, a page at
the most; just a few brief facts about our hero for the teachers to
study so they'll have some idea who Archanjo was and can pass
the info on to the kids. Then the kids can interpret it, each in his
own way. Won't it be terrific? That's why we're asking you to
write the résumé, or rather, contracting it out to you to write."

"It won't be easy."

"We know that, Professor; that's why we came to you. Besides, it was your idea in the first place, you know. You were the
one who mentioned *cachaça*. And speaking of *cachaça*, can I offer
you a drink of scotch? It's genuine, nothing like the stuff our
friend Dr. Zèzinho gives his guests."

"It won't be easy," said the Sergipano again. "This is exam
week. How can I possibly find the time to do it?"

"Only half a page, Professor. A few pithy sentences, just the
bare facts. And by the way, I'd like to make it clear that this is a
contract: the agency will pay for the résumé."

Professor Calazans was rather offended; his voice rose.

"Certainly not! I'm in on this because I respect Pedro Archanjo's memory, not for the money. Don't talk to me about
money."

Arno Melo shook his head; the guy was impossible, there was
no hope for him. Why the hell did he like him so much? Gastão
Simas apologized:

"Forget what I said about paying you, Professor. I apologize.
May I send someone to pick up the résumé tomorow morning,
then?"

"I won't have time to do it, Gastão. I have all my exams to correct today, and tomorrow I'll be at the university from eight until
noon. How on earth do you think I'll find time to write you a
résumé?"

"Give us some notes, at least, Professor, just a few little facts
to get us started. We'll finish writing it here."

"Facts? Notes? Well, maybe I could manage that. I'll leave it
with Lúcia and you can send a messenger to my house tomorrow."

The tawny secretary brought glasses and ice cubes. So quiet, so mute—but then, why waste a mouth made for smiles and promises on mere words? Why tire herself out when she was meant to be seen and enjoyed?

BIOGRAPHICAL DATA SUBMITTED TO DOPING S.A. BY PROFESSOR CALAZANS.

Name:
Pedro Archanjo.

Date and place of birth:
December 18, 1868, Salvador, Bahia, Brazil.

Parents:
Son of Antônio Archanjo and Noêmia Doe, better known as Noca de Longunedê. All that is known of his father is that he was drafted into the war with Paraguay and died crossing the Chaco, leaving his common-law wife pregnant with Pedro, his first and only child.

Education:
Taught himself to read and attended the School of Arts and Trades, where he acquired the rudiments of several subjects, including the printer's trade. He was an outstanding student of Portuguese and became very fond of reading while still a boy. In his maturity he made a conscientious study of anthropology, ethnology, and sociology and learned French, English, and Spanish in order to do so. His knowledge of the life and customs of his people was practically boundless.

Publications:

He published four books—*Daily Life in Bahia* (1907); *The African Influence on the Customs of Bahia* (1918); *Notes on Miscegenation among the Families of Bahia* (1928); and *Bahian Cookery: Origins and Precepts* (1930)—which today are considered basic to the study of our folklore and our knowledge of life in Brazil toward the end of the last century and the beginnings of this, and above all to an understanding of the problem of race in Brazil. An ardent defender of miscegenation, of the mingling of the races, Pedro Archanjo was, according to the North American scholar and Nobel Prize winner James D. Levenson, "one of the founders of modern ethnology." His complete works have just been reissued in two volumes by the Editôra Martins of São Paulo in their "Teachers of Brazil" series, with notes and comments by Professor Arthur Ramos of the School of Arts and Sciences of the University of Brazil. Archanjo's first three books were printed in a single volume under the general title of *Brazil, Mestizo Country* (the title bestowed on it by Professor Ramos), while the cookbook was published separately. Pedro Archanjo's work, unjustly neglected for so many years, is now becoming internationally known and admired. It has been published in English in the United States as part of the notable *Encyclopedia on Life in the Underdeveloped Countries* published under the auspices of Columbia University. Much has been written on Pedro Archanjo in this year of 1968, as we commemorate the hundredth anniversary of his birth. We might single out Professor Ramos's work and the preface written by Dr. Levenson for the North American translation of his books: "Pedro Archanjo, founder of a new science."

Miscellaneous:

Poor, mulatto, autodidact. Shipped as a cabin boy on a freighter while still a young lad. Lived for some years in Rio de Janeiro. On his return to Bahia he worked as a typesetter and taught children to read and write before being employed by the School of Medicine. He lost that job, after nearly thirty years of faithful service, because of unfavorable repercussions from one of his books. An amateur musician, he played the guitar and the *cava-*

quinho. He participated intensely in the life of the people. He remained a bachelor but was said to have had many love affairs, including one with a lovely Scandinavian girl, a Swede or a Finn, no one seems to know which.

Date of death:
Pedro Archanjo died in 1943 at the age of seventy-five. An immense number of people attended his funeral, including Professor Azevedo and the poet Hélio Simões.

By the example of his own life Pedro Archanjo has shown us how a man who was born into poverty, fatherless, in an unpromising environment, was able, while carrying out the humblest tasks, to overcome all obstacles and rise to the peaks of knowledge, where he equaled, and even surpassed, the most distinguished scholars of his time.

RÉSUMÉ PREPARED BY THE TOP TALENTS AT DOPING ADVERTISING AND PUBLICITY, S.A. AND DISTRIBUTED TO ALL ELEMENTARY SCHOOL TEACHERS IN THE CITY OF SALVADOR.

The immortal writer and ethnologist Pedro Archanjo, not only the pride and glory of Bahia and Brazil but internationally famous as well, whose centennial we are celebrating this year under the auspices of the *City News* and Crocodile Rum, was born in Salvador on December 18, 1868, orphaned son of a hero in the War with Paraguay. Answering the call of duty, his father, Antônio Archanjo, bade his pregnant wife farewell and went off to die in the faraway Chaco, in an unequal struggle against a treacherous enemy.

A worthy heir to the glorious tradition of his father, Pedro

Archanjo early in life began his struggle to rise above the limitations of the disadvantaged environment into which he was born. He began to study literature and music, and his unmistakable literary vocation soon distinguished him among his classmates. He quickly mastered several languages, including English, French, and Spanish.

In his youth he heeded the call of adventure, ran away to sea as a stowaway, and traveled all over the world. In Stockholm he met the beauteous Scandinavian girl who was to be the great love of his life.

Returning to Bahia, he entered the School of Medicine, and there, for more than thirty years, he found the surroundings propitious to the studies and writings that made him famous as a writer and scientist.

He was the author of several books in which he examined the folklore and customs of Bahia and analyzed the problem of race. These were translated into several languages and made him worldfamous, particularly in the United States. There his works were adopted by Columbia University in New York at the suggestion of the illustrious professor James D. Levenson, holder of a Nobel Prize, who admits to being a disciple of Pedro Archanjo.

Archanjo died in Salvador in 1943 at the age of seventy-five, admired by the learned and respected by all. Public notables, university professors, writers, and poets attended his funeral.

The glory of Bahia and all Brazil, whose name he exalted in other lands, Pedro Archanjo teaches us through his example how a man born into poverty and an environment hostile to any sort of culture can rise to the pinnacles of learning and occupy a distinguished position in society.

As we celebrate the centennial of this magnificent paladin of science and letters, all Bahians join in honoring his glorious memory, heeding the clarion call of the *City News*, which is thus carrying out one more of its memorable patriotic promotion campaigns.

Crocodile Rum could not stand aloof from this grand celebration, since it is an integral part of that folklore of Bahia to the study of which our national genius devoted his life. Is not this famous rum the creator of the Crocodile Clown who makes little children laugh with delight at his radio and television ads, true creator of modern folklore with his merry tunes and jingles?

The Crocodile Clown is sponsoring a contest in the primary schools of Salvador: our beloved teachers will tell the story of Pedro Archanjo in their classrooms, and every child from the first grade to the fifth can write his own impressions and compete for one of the five scholarships which will cover tuition for the entire high school course. These tuition grants, which can be used by the winners in any of the private secondary schools in our capital city, are being offered as a public service by Crocodile Rum.

The Crocodile Clown, joined by all the little folk in the Salvador Public School System, sings out loud and clear: "Long live the immortal Pedro Archanjo!"

5

LECTURE BY MISS DIDA QUEIROZ TO HER THIRD GRADE STUDENTS, MORNING CLASS, IN PUBLIC SCHOOL GIOVANNI GUIMARÃES, JOURNALIST, IN RIO VERMELHO.

Pedro Archanjo is one of the glories of Bahia, Brazil, and the World. He was born a hundred years ago and that's why the *City News* and Crocodile Rum are celebrating his hundredth anniversary by holding a contest for students and giving out valuable prizes like trips to the United States and Rio de Janeiro, television sets and radios, books and other things. For you children in elementary school they've set aside five scholarships for the whole high school course in any school in our capital. With the tuition rates the schools are charging these days, that's a prize and then some.

Pedro Archanjo's father was a general in the Paraguayan War, who died fighting against the tyrant Solano López when he attacked our country. Little Pedro was a poor orphan, but he didn't give up. Since he couldn't go to school he went to sea in a freighter and managed to learn foreign languages. He was a polyglot, that is, a person who can speak other languages besides Portuguese. He passed his entrance examination to the School of Medicine, and after he graduated he taught there as a professor for more than thirty years.

He wrote a lot of books based on folklore—that means books that tell stories about animals and people—but they aren't for children to read. They're very serious, important books and they're studied by wise men and professors.

He traveled quite a bit and went to Europe and the United States. I think travel must be the nicest thing in the world. In Europe he met a pretty Scandinavian girl and they got married and lived happily ever after.

In the United States he taught at Columbia University in New York, that's the greatest city in the world. He taught all of his classes in English. One of his pupils was an American doctor named Levenson, who learned so much from him that afterward he won the Nobel Prize. That's a really big prize. If you get one of those they have to put you in the history books.

He was a very old man when he died in 1943. They gave him a great big funeral and invited the governor, the mayor, and the university professors.

Pedro Archanjo's example shows us how a poor boy, if he applies himself and studies hard, can get into high society, teach at the university, earn a lot of money, travel all over the world and be an ornament to Brazil. All you need to do is have willpower and not talk back to the teacher. And now you can all write down what you think of Pedro Archanjo, but first let's all sing along with the Crocodile Clown, who's giving the scholarships: "Long live the immortal Pedro Archanjo!"

Composition by Rai, nine years old, third grade pupil at the above-mentioned Public School Giovanni Guimarães, Journalist.

Pedro Archanjo was a very poor orphan who ran away to sea with a gringa like my Uncle Zuca and went to the United States because there's heaps of money there but he said I'm Brazilian and came back to Bahia to tell stories about animals and people and he knew so much he didn't give lessons to children just to doctors and professors and when he died he was an ornament to Brazil and he got a prize from the newspaper and it was a bag full of bottles of rum. Hooray for Pedro Archanjo and the Crocodile Clown!

Of Pedro Archanjo

Ojuobá's civic battle

and how the people

occupied the square

I

"Nestor Souza speaks perfect, impeccable French," declared Professor Aristides Caires de Castro, referring to the Dean of the Law School, an eminent jurist and a member of several international associations. He repeated the name in a transport of admiration:

"Nestor Souza! What an intellect!"

Professor Fonseca, head of the Anatomy Department, put in his bit:

"No doubt about it, Nestor's pronunciation is excellent. However, I'm not sure he's the equal of Zinho de Carvalho when it comes to handling the language. French has no secrets for Zinho. He knows pages and pages of Chateaubriand's *Génie du Christianisme* by heart, and poems by Victor Hugo, and whole scenes from Rostand's *Cyrano de Bergerac*"—he pronounced them "Hugô" and "Cyranô" to show off his own ability—"Have you ever heard him recite?"

"Yes, I have, and I heartily second your praise. Let me ask you this, though: Would Zinho be able to improvise an entire speech in French, like Nestor Souza? I'm sure you all remember the banquet in honor of Maitre Daix, the lawyer from Paris who visited the school last year. Nestor greeted him extemporaneously, in French! And he made a really fine speeh. *Magnifique!* When I heard him I felt proud to be a Bahian."

"Extemporaneous? Nothing of the sort," scoffed the lean Isaías Luna, a notorious slanderer who was popular with the students because of his outrageous opinions and the generous marks he gave. "Why, I know for a fact that he memorizes his lectures the night before and practices his gestures in front of the mirror."

"Don't say that, don't repeat envious insults."

"Well, that's what they say. It's the voice of the people, you know. *Vox populi, vox Dei!*"

"Zinho . . ." Professor Fonseca dragged his own candidate back into the lists.

Those conversations between classes brought the Medical School professors together—each more haughty, each more illustrious, each more jealous of his privileges than the next. While they sipped fresh coffee brought to them by the runners, they took a break from classes and students and relaxed by talking idly of the day's affairs, from problems of scientific research to their colleagues' foibles. Once in a while they would all shake with laughter as one of them related an anecdote in a low voice. "Our kaffeeklatsches are the best thing about this school," asserted Professor Aristides Caires, who never missed one. It was he who had brought up that morning's topic: the mastery of spoken French.

A knowledge of the French tongue was essential to anyone

who aspired to the privileges of an intellectual, and it was, indeed, indispensable as a tool of higher learning. At that time there were no translations into Portuguese of the basic texts and treatises necessary to the study of the curriculum of any of the professional schools. The bibliography assigned by most professors was exclusively French; some of them were also familiar with English, and a very few spoke German. To be able to speak fluent, grammatical French with a fair pronunciation was a source of personal pride and prestige.

In the argument that followed, the names of other adepts were brought up: Professor Bernard of the Polytechnical School, whose father was French and who had graduated from Grenoble; Henrique Damásio, a journalist who had traveled to Europe several times and graduated with honors from every cabaret in Paris ("No, not him, his French is only fit for the boudoir"); the painter Florêncio Valença, with his twelve years of *vie de bohème* in the Latin Quarter, and Father Cabral, from the Jesuit College ("No, you can't count him either, he's Portuguese and we're talking about Brazilians"). Which of them all had the best pronunciation? Which was the most chic, the most truly Parisian? Who had the most meticulous r's and s's?

"Well, friends, you've named a great many people, but you're forgetting that we have four or five of the brightest stars right here on our own campus," opined Professor Aires.

There was a general sigh of relief: that strange omission of the eminent lights of their own purlieus was beginning to make them slightly uncomfortable. There was no more prestigious title in Bahia in those days than that of *catedrático* at the School of Medicine. It meant not only lifetime tenure, a good salary, an important position and deference from all; it also guaranteed a lucrative clientèle, a consulting room full of wealthy patients. Many of these came from far back in the interior, attracted by ads in the newspapers: "Professor Dr. Such-and-Such, *catedrático* at the Bahia School of Medicine, who completed his internship in Paris hospitals." The illustrious title was an open sesame to all sorts of doors: literature, politics, even plantation life. Those privileged professors became members of academies, got themselves elected state or federal deputies, or invested in ranches, cattle, and landed estates.

Each competition for a vacant teaching post had national repercussions: doctors from Rio and São Paulo came flocking to dispute with the Bahians for the post and its perquisites. High society turned out *en masse* to hear the candidates argue, defend their theses, and lecture to classes. Questions and answers were followed with close attention and witty phrases and instances of bad manners were commented upon. Everyone took sides; opinions were divided. Whatever the outcome, it was sure to lead to polemics and protests. There had been cases of dead-serious threats of retaliation and physical violence. That being the case, how could the names of the grandees of the School of Medicine be absent from the roll of experts in the art of speaking French? It would have been an absurdity, almost a scandal.

It was all the more scandalous because sitting there all the time, listening silently and no doubt expectantly, was Professor Nilo Argolo, "the seven-tongued monster," a polyglot who had mastered a number of languages. He not only spoke and understood French well; he could actually write letters and dissertations in that language. Only a few days before, he had sent an important piece of work to a congress in Brussels: *"La paranoia chez les nègres et métis."*

"He wrote it all in French, line for line and word for word!" said Professor Oswaldo Fontes emphatically, claiming first place for his mentor and friend.

As he slowly savored his coffee, the eminent Professor Silva Virajá, who had done research on schistosomiasis and had an honestly earned reputation in the world of medical science, followed with amusement the changes of expression on the face of his colleague Nilo d'Ávila Argolo de Araújo, before and after the remarks of Aires and Fontes: serious, impassive, restless, brightening suddenly, then suffused with false modesty, but conceited at all times. The professor had learned to suffer fools, but he was annoyed by priggish self-conceit.

After the chorus of universal acclamation had subsided, Professor Nilo conceded magnanimously:

"Professor Nestor Souza also excels in the language of Corneille." As for the others who had been mentioned, he did not deign to consider them as rivals.

At this display of naked arrogance, Dr. Silva Virajá set down his coffee cup and said:

"I know all the people you have mentioned, and I've heard them all speak French. But I make bold to say that in all of Bahia there is no one who handles the French language more correctly and with a purer accent than Pedro Archanjo, one of the runners in my department."

Professor Nilo Argolo started up, his face on fire, as if his colleague had boxed his ears. If anyone else had made that statement, the professor of Forensic Medicine would have reacted violently at hearing himself compared to a runner, and a mulatto at that. However, there was no one in the School of Medicine, or for that matter in the state of Bahia, who dared to raise his voice in the presence of Dr. Silva Virajá.

"Are you referring, by any chance, to that melanoderm who wrote a little brochure about popular customs several years ago?"

"Yes, Professor, I am referring to that very man. He has been my assistant for almost ten years now. I asked for his services after I had read his 'little brochure,' as you call it. Little in length, yes, but rich in observations and ideas. He's about to publish another book, not so little and even richer than the first: a work of real ethnological interest. He showed me a few chapters, and I read them with admiration."

"That . . . that . . . runner speaks French?"

"He does indeed. It's a joy to hear him. And his English is just as admirable. He knows Spanish and Italian very well, too; and if I had time to teach him, his German would undoubtedly be better than mine. As a matter of fact, my opinion is shared by your cousin and my good friend, Countess Isabel Tereza, whose own French, by the way, is delightful."

The mention of his embarrassing relative deepened the angry flush on the face of the offended teacher.

"Your well-known generosity, Professor Virajá, leads you to overestimate your inferiors. The darkey has memorized a few

French phrases, no doubt; and you, my kindhearted colleague, are all ready to certify him as a teacher of languages."

The learned man responded with a child's ready laugh:

"Why, thank you for the kind words, but I don't deserve them. I'm not as generous as all that. Of course, it's true that I'd rather overestimate other people than underestimate them, because those who underestimate others are usually judging them by their own measure. In this case, however, I am not exaggerating at all."

"A mere runner! I simply cannot bring myself to believe it."

Self-conceit annoyed Dr. Silva Virajá, but only overbearing treatment of the humble really had the power to anger him. "Those who fawn on the powerful and tread the helpless under foot are to be distrusted and avoided," he counseled the young. "They are false and petty and lack nobility of character."

"That runner has more scientific knowledge than certain professors of my acquaintance."

The professor of Forensic Medicine left the room breathing fire and lashing his tail, followed by the ever-faithful Oswaldo Fontes. Dr. Silva Virajá laughed like a child delighted with his own mischief, a glint of malice in his eyes, a note of astonishment in his voice:

"Talent has nothing to do with pigmentation or title or social class. That's all humbug. Good God, how can there be anyone left in the world who hasn't learned that yet?"

As he stood up to go he shrugged to rid himself of Nilo d'Ávila Argolo de Araújo, that sack full of prejudice, that monster of vanity, so full of himself and so empty. He went up to the second floor where black Evaristo was waiting for him with fresh cadavers from the morgue. Alas, poor Nilo! When will you learn that only science has meaning and endures, in whatever language it is explained, whatever titles are appended to the human being who experiments and creates? In the laboratory the students, slides already in their microscopes, crowded around Dr. Silva Virajá.

Between 1907 and 1918, during the more than a decade that passed between the publication of *Daily Life in Bahia* and his second book, *The African Influence on the Customs of Bahia*, Pedro Archanjo bent all his will power and perseverance to orderly, methodical study. He had to know more, and so he learned. He read all there was to read on problems of race; he devoured treatises, books, dissertations, articles, scientific papers; he pored over collections of magazines and newspapers; turned into a bookworm and haunted libraries and archives.

Not that he stopped living passionately and intensely, plunging as ardently as ever into the daily life of the city and its people. The only difference was that now he learned from books as well, branching off from the central theme of his research into multiple byways of knowledge and making them his own. All his undertakings in those years had an object, intention, and consequences.

Lídio Corró egged him on. It made Lídio indignant to read provocations and threats in the daily press under heavy black headlines: "How long will we let Bahia be one huge, degraded slave cabin?"

"It looks like you've broken your pen in two and corked up your inkwell, *compadre*. Where's that other book? You do a lot of talking about it but I don't see you writing it."

"*Meu bom,* don't rush me, I'm not ready yet."

To prod him into action, Lídio read aloud those news stories and articles telling of *candomblé* rites broken up, *pais-de-santo* dragged off to jail, festivals forbidden, presents for Yemanjá confiscated, *capoeiristas* prodded to police headquarters at knife point.

"They're giving it to us hot and heavy, and they're getting

away with it. You don't have to read all those books to know what's going on"—he pointed to the pamphlets, the medical reviews, and the books heaped on the table. "All you need to do is take a look at any newspaper: they're all full of protests against samba circles, *capoeira, candomblé.* All the news is bad. If we don't look sharp they'll finish us off."

"You're right, *meu bom.* They do want to finish us off."

"Well, what are you going to do about it, if you know so much?"

"*Camarado,* all of this fuss started with those professors and their theories. You have to get at the cause, *meu bom.* Writing letters to the editors to complain helps a little, but it won't ever solve the problem."

"I couldn't agree more. Why don't you write the book, then?"

"I'm getting ready to do it. Listen, *compadre:* when I got into this business I was as ignorant as a block of wood. Try to understand that, *meu bom.* I thought I knew a lot but I didn't know anything."

"Didn't you? Well, I think the kind of knowing we have here in Tabuão in the Tent of Miracles, is worth a whole lot more than all the learning at your fine School of Medicine, *Compadre* Pedro."

"It isn't my School of Medicine and I'm not denying the value of folk wisdom, *meu bom.* But I've learned that that kind by itself isn't enough. Let me try and explain, *camarado.*"

Tadeu, surrounded by books and exercises, did not miss a word.

"My good *compadre,*" Archanjo began, "I owe a debt of gratitude to that Professor Argolo who'd castrate all Negroes and mulattoes if he had his way, the very same one who sics the police against the *candomblés,* Monster Argolo de Araújo. One day, in order to humiliate me—and he did humiliate me—he showed me just how ignorant I really was. At first I was mad as hell. But then I got to thinking: he's right, I might as well be illiterate. I used to see things, *meu bom,* but I didn't recognize them for what they were. I knew about all sorts of things, but I didn't know how to know."

"Now you're talking worse than a professor, *compadre.* 'I didn't know how to know.' What's that, a charade or a riddle?"

"When a child eats a piece of fruit he knows what the fruit

tastes like, but he doesn't know what makes it taste that way. I
know things, but I still have to learn the whys and wherefores,
and that's what I'm trying to learn. And I'm going to do it, *camarado*, just you wait and see."

While he was learning he wrote letters to the editors, protesting against the ominous campaigns and the growing police brutality. The reader willing to take the trouble to read the few letters by Archanjo that were printed—some under his own name,
others signed by "An Indignant Reader," "A Descendant of
Zumbí," "A He-Man," or "A Brazilian Mulatto"—can easily follow the evolution of his thought over a period of years. His
arguments, bolstered with quotations from Brazilian and foreign
writers, became more forceful, more convincing, and finally unanswerable. Master Archanjo tempered the steel of his mind by
writing letters to the editors and so learned to use clear, precise
language without ever losing the touch of poetry that was present
in everything he wrote.

Almost alone he did unequal battle against virtually the entire
weight of the press of Bahia. After writing a letter he would read
it to his friends in the Tent of Miracles before sending it off.
Manuel de Praxedes enthusiastically proposed "bashing the grease-
shitters' heads in." Budião nodded his head in approbation as each
point was made, Valdeloir clapped his hands, Lídio Corró smiled
proudly, and Tadeu delivered the letter. A few of the dozens of
letters Archanjo wrote were printed, in part or *in toto*, in the
newspaper columns. Most were thrown into the wastebasket. Two
received special treatment.

The first letter was a long one, almost an essay, which Pedro
Archanjo had sent to one of the papers which most consistently
and virulently attacked the *candomblés*. His objective and well-
documented letter analyzed the subject of animistic religions in
Brazil and demanded that they be guaranteed "the same freedom,
respect, and privileges granted to the Catholic and Protestant religions, since the Afro-Brazilian cults are the faith, the belief, and
the spiritual sustenance of thousands of citizens who deserve just
as much respect as any others."

Several days later the paper printed a three-column article on
the front page in the most hysterical language under a headline in

bold black type: *MONSTROUS CLAIM*. Archanjo's arguments
were neither published nor refuted, only referred to in order to
apprise "the public authorities, the clergy, and society at large of
the monstrous claim of the fetishists who demand, *DEMAND!* in
a letter to the editors of this paper, that their base voodoo rites be
accorded the same respect and privileges as though they were on a
spiritual plane with the sublime Catholic religion—the universal
Church of Christ—or the various Protestant sects, whose heresies
we deplore without, however, denying that Calvinists and Luther-
ans also worship Christ." The editors concluded this jeremiad by
reaffirming their promise to Bahian society to wage unremitting
war, "war without quarter, on the abominable idolatry and bar-
baric drumbeats of the *macumbas*, which wound Bahian ears and
sensibilities."

The other letter proved useful to a new tabloid of liberal pretensions which was seeking readers and popularity. Archanjo had
composed an answer to an acid critique by Professor Oswaldo
Fontes which had appeared in the pages of the conservative paper
under the headline A CRY OF WARNING. The psychology
professor called the attention of the public and all the authorities
to a fact which in his opinion constituted the gravest possible
threat to the future of the country: the schools of higher education in the state of Bahia were beginning to feel the disastrous consequences of "an invasion of mestizos. Colored youths in greater
and greater numbers are occupying the places which ought by
right to be reserved for young men from good families of pure
blood." Drastic measures were called for: "the prohibition, pure
and simple, of the entrance of these deleterious elements into the
universities." He held up as examples the Brazilian Navy, where
blacks and mestizos could not aspire to become officers, and
heaped praise on the Foreign Office, Itamaraty, which, politely but
firmly, "has impeded the spread of the stain of degradation into
the cultivated ranks of diplomacy."

Pedro Archanjo's riposte took the form of a letter signed *Brazilian Mulatto and Proud to Be One*. He set forth weighty arguments supported by quotations from well-known anthropologists,
all affirming the intellectual capacity of Negroes and mulattoes,
listed distinguished mestizos, "including Brazilian ambassadors to

foreign courts," and described Professor Fontes in irreverent terms.

"Professor Fontes demands that all university graduates be of pure blood. Now surely we all know that the term 'pure-blooded' usually refers to race horses. When the students see the good professor crossing the Terreiro de Jesus on his way to the School of Medicine, they say that when he was given the title of professor of Psychiatry, thanks to the prestige and maneuvers of a certain professor of Forensic Medicine, Dr. Fontes was reenacting a celebrated historical event: Emperor Caligula rewarded his horse Incitatus with a chair in the Roman Senate; Professor Argolo de Araújo rewarded Oswaldo Fontes with a chair in the School of Medicine. Perhaps it is here that we can find the explanation for the professor's insistence on pedigrees in the school. A thoroughbred is a horse, a pure and noble beast. Is the professor a thoroughbred?"

To Archanjo's astonishment, the whole first part of his letter was printed in the guise of a feature article in the new tabloid. Arguments, quotations, phrases, sentences, whole paragraphs were incorporated just as he had written them. The editor had quoted only sparingly from his references to Professor Oswaldo Fontes, reducing the play on words about pedigrees and horses to one brief comment: "The distinguished professor, whose educational background is irreproachable, is the target of jokes among the students because of the anachronistic viewpoints he upholds." There was no mention of the "Brazilian Mulatto and Proud to Be One." The article caused something of a stir, and the paper received all the credit.

That day Archanjo had the satisfaction of seeing some medical students tacking the pages of the tabloid up on a wall of the Medical School. Professor Fontes sent his own runner to tear them down and burn them. He was in a passion. For once he lost the phlegmatic demeanor, the urbanity, and the facetious air with which he customarily parried the young men's japes.

Following the example of Professor Silva Virajá, Pedro Archanjo learned to sift and analyze opinions, formulas, and human character as if he were peering at them through a microscope in order to know them inside out. He knew Gobineau's life and works by heart—his monstrous theory, and every moment of his tour with the French Embassy in Brazil. It took complete knowledge, a knowing that left no room for doubt, to transmute his blind hatred into disgust and scorn.

And so, following the day-by-day footsteps of the French Ambassador to the Imperial Court of Brazil, he found that Monsieur Joseph Arthur, Count, or rather Comte de Gobineau, was strolling in the palace gardens of São Cristóvão discussing the state of science and the arts with His Majesty Dom Pedro II at the precise instant when Noca de Logunedê felt the onset of labor pains and sent a street boy in search of Rita Apara-Jegue, a famous and competent midwife.

In 1868, when Pedro Archanjo was born, Gobineau was fifty-two years old and had published his *Essai sur l'inégalité des races humaines* fifteen years before. He discoursed with the Brazilian monarch under the shade trees in the palace grounds while Noca, in the midst of her moans and labor, was mentally crossing forests, rivers, and mountains, her thoughts turning to the desolate landscape of Paraguay where they had taken her man, turning him from a stonemason into a soldier who would kill and die in that interminable war from which she had no hope of seeing him return alive. He had wanted the baby so much, and now he wasn't there to see it born.

Noca did not know then that Corporal Antônio Archanjo had

died crossing the Chaco. A master stonemason with a growing
reputation, he was raising the walls of a school when the military
patrol swooped down on him and snatched him up. A volunteer
recruited by the flat edge of a saber, he was not even given permission to go home and say good-bye. Noca waved farewell to
him on the morning the troops embarked. He marched dispiritedly
in the Bahian Zouave Battalion, a grieving mason without his
trowel and plumbline, but to her eyes he was jaunty and handsome in his soldier's uniform, carrying the tools of his new vocation
of war and murder.

Two or three weeks before, when Noca had told him she was
expecting a baby, he had almost gone wild with joy. He immediately spoke of marriage and could not pamper her enough:
"You're not going to work while you're in the family way, I won't
let you." Noca washed and ironed clothes until the hour she was
delivered. The baby's coming, Antônio, it's tearing me to pieces
inside. Why doesn't Rita come? Where's my Antônio, why isn't he
here with me? Oh, Antônio, darling, throw it all away, throw
away your gun and uniform and come back as fast as you can.
Now there are two of us waiting for you, all alone and miserable.

Dragged off to war by main force and seeing there was no
hope of escape, Private Antônio obeyed his orders to kill so in-
telligently and bravely that he earned a corporal's stripes. "He was
always chosen for reconnaissance missions, always in the vanguard
of the troops with whom he served," Pedro Archanjo read of his
father in the military annals when he measured the different kinds
of blood—leucoderm, melanoderm, faioderm—shed for Brazil in
that war. Who had given most in life and death?

Corporal Antônio Archanjo, now a rotting corpse and a feast for
buzzards, would never see the son who had got off to such a good
start in life by being born all alone with no help from the mid-wife,
at the very moment when Monsieur le Comte de Gobineau and His
Imperial Majesty, the theorist of racism and the determined son-
neteer, walked in the cool shady park and chatted in their witty,
refined way. Perhaps we should more properly call them *raffinés*.

When Rita Apara-Jegue arrived at Noca de Logunedê's house,
the newborn infant was already showing off the lusty power of
his lungs. The stout little woman held her sides and shouted with

laughter: "That one's an Exú, God love and protect us, only the Devil's own brood are born without waiting for the midwife. He'll be a handful, mark my words; and he'll be famous."

From the stonemason/corporal Pedro Archanjo inherited the intelligence and bravery cited in the war bulletins, and from Noca, his gentle features and his stubbornness. Stubbornly she reared her child, saw that he had a home and enough to eat, and put him through school, all without a man's support or help. She would never have anyone else, never again indulged in even a passing affair, although there was no lack of followers who hung around her doorstep coaxing her and making offers. From that hard, meager life with his mother, the child learned to endure and never to give up, but to keep right on going.

Archanjo often thought of her during that fruitful decade of hard work. She had died still young, when the seeds of yellow fever planted in the manure of the city streets grew and put forth deadly blossoms. It was a good year for yellow fever: the disease reaped an abundant harvest, taking corpses even from the houses of the rich, and Noca de Logunedê was carried off with the first batch. Not even Omolú could save her. Noca's strength melted into sores, her youthful grace rotted in the alley among pools of pus. Whenever Archanjo's strength flagged he would think of his mother, laboring to exhaustion from morning to night, locked in a circle of longing, unyielding in her determination to wear mourning forever and to earn the keep of her child with the strength of her own fragile arms.

He had learned the rest of what he knew by himself, although he was never alone and never lacked friends to encourage him.

He had Noca's memory, Tadeu's presence, Lídio's insistence, Majé Bassan's vigilance, the help of Professor Silva Virajá, the encouragement of Frei Timóteo the Franciscan monk, and the aid of his good friend Zabela.

During those years Tadeu was Archanjo's pupil, fellow student, and teacher. Tadeu Canhoto is still remembered at the Polytechnical School for his famous test done entirely in decasyllabic verse; his vocation for mathematics, which made him a favorite of Professor Bernard, and the innate capacity for leadership which placed him at the head of the class during his five-year course at the university and found him heading rallies in favor of the Allies during World War I and leading the claque as it hooted or stamped at the São João and Politeama Theaters.

Archanjo owed his mastery of foreign tongues to Zabela. In that highborn lady's company, the French, English, Spanish, and Italian that he had studied in solitude were transformed into living languages, almost as familiar to him as his own. Having the gift of a musical ear, he soon spoke French like a count and English like a lord.

"Master Pedro, you're a born linguist. I never saw anyone who could learn as fast as you!" the Princess of the Recôncavo exclaimed in delight.

She never had to correct an error in Archanjo's grammar or pronunciation twice: once he was told, he never repeated the mistake. Sitting in her Austrian rocking chair, the old woman would close her eyes while Master Pedro read aloud poems by Baudelaire, Verlaine, Rimbaud—Zabela's poets. The richly bound volumes recalled her salad days; the rhymes brought back old love affairs. Zabela sighed nostalgically, lulled by Archanjo's soft voice and precise enunciation:

"Let me tell you a lovely story, Master Pedro. You'll like this one. . . ."

The impoverished aristocrat, the old lady who was such an embarrassment to her family, had found a second family in the two *compadres* and their godson, and so she was not totally bereft when her cat Argolo de Araújo died of old age and was buried in the garden.

When Professor Silva Virajá advised Pedro Archanjo to study

German, Frei Timóteo, the prior of São Francisco and the friend
of Majé Bassan, offered to give him lessons. The good friar had
often obliged him by translating chapters of books or whole articles into Portuguese and had developed an interest in the race
question in Brazil himself, although his specialty was the study of
religious syncretism. However many hours they spent together,
it never seemed long enough; there were so many urgent ideas to
discuss that Archanjo did not make much progress with his German.

Pedro Archanjo owed a great deal to Professor Silva Virajá,
who had taken him out of the chancery, where the work never
gave him a moment's free time, and had him transferred to his
own department after reading *Daily Life in Bahia.* The professor
was already well served by black Evaristo, who had been his devoted assistant for many years, and could afford to give Archanjo
time to study in the university and state libraries, to consult the
municipal archives, and to work on his own books and documents.
But he gave him more than time: he guided his reading and
recommended new authors, keeping him abreast of what was
new in the fields of anthropology and ethnology. Frei Timóteo,
too, lent him many books, some of which were unknown in Bahia
even to professors of those subjects. Through the friar he learned
of Franz Boas, for instance, and it is likely that he was the first
Brazilian to study his work.

And what of Lídio Corró? *Compadre,* twin, more to him than
a brother—how many times had Lídio pulled in his belt a notch
to lend—but why employ that silly euphemism—to give him the
money he needed to order books from Rio and even from Europe? The new trays of type, a complete and expensive over-
hauling of the old printing press—what did he need them for?
Everything took a back seat to Pedro Archanjo's books.

"Do you want to know everything in the world, *compadre?*
Don't you know enough already? Don't you have enough to write
the book now?"

Pedro Archanjo laughed at his *compadre's* impatience.

"I still don't know very much. It looks as if the more I read,
the more there is to read and study."

All during that long decade, Pedro Archanjo read everything

on anthropology, ethnology, and sociology that he could lay hands on in Bahia or obtain from the outside world by scraping together his own pennies and those of his friends. On one occasion Majé Bassan opened Xangô's strongbox and added enough to buy *Reise in Brasilien* by Spix and Martius from a bookseller who had just set up shop in the Praça da Sé, an Italian named Bonfanti.

Even a partial list of the books and authors studied by Master Archanjo would be long and tedious, but it is worth noting a few of them as we accompany our author on his pilgrimage from indignation to derisive amusement.

At first he had to grit his teeth to read through the works of confessed racists or, what was worse, of those who were racists but too hypocritical to admit it. He clenched his fists; those theories and asseverations had the ring of insults, they were hard blows and cracks of the whip. More than once he felt his eyes burn and tasted tears of humiliation as he read page after page by Gobineau, Madison Grant, Otto Ammon, and Houston Chamberlain. But as time passed he could even stomach the lucubrations of the lights of the Italian anthropological school of criminology—Lombroso, Ferri, Garofalo—with a roar of laughter. By then Archanjo had amassed enough knowledge to fortify him with unshakable aplomb and assurance. He now recognized as nonsense what he would formerly have felt as insults and personal attacks.

He read the books of friends and enemies, Frenchmen and Englishmen, Germans, Italians, and Boas, the American. He discovered the laughter of the world in Voltaire and reveled in it. He read Brazilians and Bahians, from Alberto Torres to Evaristo de Morais, from Manuel Bernardo Calmon du Pin e Almeida and João Batista de Sá Oliveira to Aurelino Leal. He read many more besides, books beyond counting.

He never forgot the joy of living in the joy of books, nor the study of mankind in the study of writers. He found time for reading, research, gayety, parties, and love, all the fountains of his knowledge. He was Pedro Archanjo and Ojuobá at one and the same time. He did not divide himself in two, with scheduled times allotted to the scholar and the man. He refused to climb the little ladder of success even a single step above the ground where he had been born, the solid ground with streets in it, and stores, and workshops, and ritual *terreiros*, and ordinary folk. He did not want to go up at all but to go forward, and go forward he did. He was Master Archanjo Ojuobá, complete and whole.

On the last day of his life he was still learning from the people, still making notes in his little notebook. Just before he died he arranged with a student named Oliva, who was a partner in a printing concern, to publish a book for him; and when he rolled down Pelourinho he was repeating a phrase which was surely an odd one to hear from a blacksmith: not even God can kill everybody. But by then he had lost almost all his precious library, gathered so painfully one book at a time with the help of so many rude, illiterate workmen, rum swillers every man jack of them. Most of the books were destroyed when the workshop was broken into; others vanished in one way or another in all the movings and runnings about, or were sold to Bonfanti in hours of desperate need. He kept only a few, those that had built the foundation of his apprenticeship. Even though he no longer read them, he liked to have them close at hand so he could thumb through the pages, rest his worn-out eyes on a paragraph, repeat a phrase, an idea, a word long since learned by heart. Found among the books he stored in a kerosene drum in the tiny back room in Ester's castle were an old edition of Gobineau's essay and Professor Nilo Argolo de Araújo's first booklet. Pedro Archanjo's search for knowledge had been rooted in hatred.

In 1918 he bought a pair of glasses on a doctor's advice and published his second book. Except for his tired eyesight, he had never felt in such good health or so brimfull of self-confidence and high spirits, nor, except for Tadeu's absence, so perfectly happy. The first volumes of *The African Influence on the Customs of Bahia* came out just before his fiftieth birthday, a feast which was celebrated for one whole noisy week. *Cachaça* ran in waterfalls, the gourds shook with sambas, the shepherdesses trotted out all their dances, the *afoxés* returned to the streets, Master Budião's *capoeira* school was draped with festive flags, the *orixás* alighted on the *terreiros* to drumming and dancing, and Rosália laughed, unfurled on the attic cot.

That's what a miracle is, beloved: two grandmothers dancing in
the Tent of Miracles on Tadeu's graduation night, grandmothers
related not by blood but by sheer affection: Mother Majé Bassan
and Countess Isabel Tereza Gonçalves Martins de Araújo e Pinho,
Zabela to her friends.

Seated in the armchair reserved for guests of honor under
the painting of the aborted miracle, Tadeu was the center of all
the attention, all the honors. He had on striped trousers and a
tweed jacket, a shirt with a turn-down collar, patent-leather
shoes, and a college ring with a blue stone, sapphire-blue for engineers. There was deep emotion in his happy face, and a longing to
hug all of them at once. Tears and laughter mingled on his copper
cheeks and in his bashful eyes; with his jet-black, flowing hair,
Engineer Tadeu Canhoto was like a portrait of some romantic ir-
redentist. This was the night of nights. It had begun in the Polytechnical School auditorium when he received his ring and
diploma, and it was to end in the graduation ball in the salons of
the Cruz Vermelha, the rich men's club. Between the ceremony
and the ball there was the friendly warmth of the Tent of Miracles, where the two grandmothers danced.

The boy owed a debt of gratitude to everyone in the room.
During the course of years they had all contributed in one way
or another to that dazzling night, and this not counting the new
suit, the ring, the patent leather shoes, the historic graduation photograph, all paid for by pennies each had donated. He was now a
professional engineer, with a degree in sacrifice, savings, and
mutual help. Not a word was said about that, it was not something
to be talked about; but when Tadeu looked at the worn faces and

callused hands he knew how much the ten years' journey had cost them and what a high price they had paid for that hour of joy. They had no doubt at all that it was worth it, and they were there to celebrate with drums and guitars.

First the drums: Pedro Archanjo on the *rum*, Lídio Corró on the *rumpi*, Valdeloir on the *lé*. Their hands beat loosely and gracefully, and Majé Bassan's old voice grew young again as she sang the chant of thanksgiving to the *orixás*.

The women formed a circle: the old black aunts, the ladies of compact beauty cultivated by experience, and the *iaôs*, the novices, new to the divine rites and to the sweet life of the flesh. The most beautiful of all, matchless, beyond compare, was Rosa de Oxalá. Time had only added distinction to her beauty. The men raised their voices in the ritual song.

As Majé Bassan stood up the others rose to their feet and clasped their hands together to salute the beloved daughter of Yemanjá, mistress of the sea. To do her honor they repeated the greeting to the Mother of all devotees: *Odoia Iyá olo oyon oruba!* Hail, Mother with streaming breasts!

Smiling and gathering her skirts around her, she slowly crossed the room amid the acclamations: *odoia odoia Iyá!* She bowed before Tadeu, offering up the ritual in his honor. The drums throbbed and Majé Bassan began the ceremonial dance and song, her feet indefatigable, her voice lifted in praise.

She was the Mother, *Iyá*, ancient, elemental, chthonic woman, come from Aioká, flying over storms, unbridled winds, doldrums, shipwrecks, and dead sailors she had loved, to honor her beloved son, the benjamin, the grandson, the great-grandson, the great-great-grandson, her descendant returned in triumph from battle. Hail Tadeu Canhoto, who has triumphed over threats, handicaps, and all vicissitudes to earn his degree. *Odoia!*

Ageless Majé Bassan, tender and terrible mother, had so precisely mastered the elegant, intricate steps that she was as quick and light and youthful when she danced as any novice. Her dance symbolized the beginning of the world: fear and the unknown, danger, combat, triumph, the lives of the gods. A dance weaving a tale of sorcery, of man braving unknown powers and struggling on to victory. That was the dance that Mother Majé Bassan danced for Tadeu in the Tent of Miracles—the grandmother dancing for her grandson, the fledging engineer.

In a gesture that was solemn and simple, majestic and intimate, she lifted both hands, stood face to face with Tadeu, and opened her arms to him. She gathered to her huge bosom the boy's thoughts, emotions, impulses, doubts, ambitions, pride, bitterness, love; good and evil, every fiber of that young heart, Tadeu's fate, in a word: there was room in that maternal breast for all the joys and heartaches of the world. The old woman and the boy embraced—the one who had remained within the circle of primitive mysteries, and the other who was setting sail in the bark of knowledge, exulting in the freedom he had earned.

One by one the others came up to dance, women and men by turns. Lídio Corró felt his heart pound against Tadeu's chest: I'm so happy, I'll die of excitement one of these days. For years on end, Tia Terência had let Tadeu eat his fill of bread and coffee, free lunches and suppers. Damião had graduated into the school of life before Tadeu; he was already a jailhouse and police station lawyer. Rosenda Batista dos Reis—give me your blessing, my aunt who weaves spells; if I'm here today with a ring on my finger and no malaria, it must be thanks to your care, your herbs and remedies. At Master Budião's *capoeira* school I learned modesty and discipline and contempt for arrogance and presumption. And here is a tremulous embrace from Dé, with her almond eyes and fluttering breast: won't you drink me down tonight like a glass of wine, won't you deflower me, the flower of your night of nights? Manuel de Praxedes, giant among stevedores, had taught him the lore of the sea and ships. Rosa de Oxalá, the aunt of mystery, mistress of the Tent of Miracles though only a guest, a fleeting bird of passage, the most important aunt of all.

All these came and others too: Valdeloir and his ingenious rhythms, Aussá and his songs, and the rich, booming laughter of Mané Lima. Each of them danced a few steps and gathered to his breast the happiness of the new engineer who only yesterday had been an impudent youngster.

The last to approach was Pedro Archanjo. Once again all stood to salute Ojuobá, the palms of their hands turned toward him. His face was enigmatic, open in its gentle smile yet closed in thought.

Images and memories crowded his heart: Dorotéia on that last night, and the boy hunched over his books. Ojuobá, Eyes of Xangô, understood the eagerness and excitement on Tadeu's face. He still saw that girl's face, intense and passionate in its halo of gold ringlets.

Who held the key to that riddle? His dance was the epitome of a lifetime. Finally came the moment when Yansan's cry reverberated in the room. There is one right answer to every question, but many wrong ones. Pedro Archanjo held Tadeu to his heart; he would not have him for long.

Now there was no one else left and it was Tadeu's turn to give thanks, swallow his tears, and dance for the *orixás* who had had him in their keeping and the friends who had made this moment possible: his parents, brothers, aunts, and cousins, his whole big family.

At that moment the Countess of Água Brusca, Grandmother Zabela, emerged from the shadows—or perhaps she stepped out of the poster of the Moulin Rouge—and entered the circle to dance for Tadeu. Not the ritual dances, they were not her style.

Lifting the hem of her skirt to reveal high shoes, petticoats, and ruffled pantalettes, she danced the Parisian cancan in the Tent of Miracles, an ageless old woman as young as the nubile Dé. Toulouse-Lautrec's picture came to life: French *mulatas* invaded Tabuão as the women in the circle began to imitate the amusing step, trying out the unfamiliar rhythm of the funny foreign dance. The men stood and lifted their hands palms upward in salute to Countess Isabel Tereza, with the gestures, the reverence, and the Yoruba words reserved for *mães-de-santo*. *Ora Yeyêo!* they cried, for her coquettish charm made it plain that Zabela was a true daughter of the temptress Oxun.

So (in her nephew's honor) Zabela danced the French cancan in the Tent of Miracles, and then kissed him on both cheeks.

There's a real miracle for you, my love: two grandmothers, each dancing her own dance for her grandson, the engineer.

"Here they come!" Valdeloir called out.

Aussá, Mané Lima, and Budião brought the fireworks and the master *capoeira* wrestler lit them with his cigar. An arrow tore the sky and opened into a shower of light above the little cortège. A compact group of half a dozen men dressed in their Sunday clothes came slowly down the hill, pacing themselves to the hesitant rhythm of Countess Isabel Tereza's *belle époque* walk. The old woman had given Tadeu her arm and the two of them led the procession, white grandmother and dark grandson.

The group of friends in the doorway set off skyrockets and sparklers, spirals of stars, colored pistol shots and showers of silver to light the way for Engineer Tadeu Canhoto, who had just received his diploma in the Polytechnical School auditorium. That night of miracles was bright as day.

Leaning on her walking stick but refusing other help, Mother Majé Bassan left the group and went to meet the procession. About two years before, the doctors had examined her and told her not to exert herself. Go home and rest, Mother Majé, they said. The strain of being a *mãe-de-santo* is too much at your age and in your state of health; give the bells and ceremonial razor to a younger woman. Don't leave your house, don't even go as far as the corner; don't lead the singing any more. One more dance— just one, mind you—could be the death of you; that dilated heart of yours may give out any minute, it's worn out already. Stay home and rest, just sit in a comfortable chair and talk, if you want to go on living. Don't tire yourself out and don't fret. She said yes, of course, Doctor, well, of course, for goodness' sake. I'll do whatever the doctor tells me to, how could I do anything else?

And as soon as the doctors turned their backs Majé Bassan took up her old obligations—the razor, the bells, the cowries, the initiation boat of the *iaôs,* the circle of the adepts, the preparing of the sacred food, the spells for Exú. She did, however, use the doctors' injunction not to leave the house as a good excuse for not accepting a great many unwelcome invitations, and she had not set foot outside the *terreiro* for a long time. When she announced her decision to lead the singing and dancing at Tadeu's party, the women tried to stop her: What about the doctors' warnings, what about her swollen heart? I'm going anyway; I'll sing and dance and nothing's going to happen. And here she was, the other grandmother, leaning on her cane and walking alone toward the young man.

Tadeu offered her his free arm, and so he walked between the two old women to the shop, as firecrackers and rockets exploded in the air.

A lucky few had received invitations to the graduation itself. They saw the ceremony, they heard the speeches, and each reacted according to his nature. Pedro Archanjo, looking very handsome and distinguished in his new clothes, was happy and serene. Lídio Corró shouted "Bravo!" when the orators, a professor and one of the graduating engineers, spoke out against prejudice and backwardness. He couldn't take his eyes off Tadeu, he was so excited to see the boy who had grown up in the Tent of Miracles and whose studies he had virtually financed sitting among the new engineers. Damião de Souza the budding lawyer, in his white linen suit, thought to himself that if he were the one making that speech he would really raise the roof! Manuel de Praxedes was stuffed into a dress suit that was too small for his gigantic body and far too small to contain his excitement. The only woman among Tadeu's friends to come was Zabela, dressed in rococo, démodé elegance, Paris rags, jewels and perfume and dancing eyes. The professors, the rich men, and the authorities came over to kiss her hand:

"Is someone in your family graduating tonight, Countess?"

"That one over there, do you see him? That fine-looking boy, the handsomest one of all."

"Which one? That . . . that dark one?" they said wonderingly. "Is he a relative of yours?"

"A very close relative. He's my grandson"—and she laughed so infectiously that where Zabela was, the party began ahead of time.

To the surprise of many and the scandalized consternation of some, when it was time for Tadeu to receive his diploma he crossed the room on Zabela's arm ("That she-devil hasn't a spark of shame or decency," muttered Dona Augusta dos Mendes Argolo de Araújo), and since Tadeu had no mother or sweetheart it was the old Countess who placed the graduation ring, the engineer's sapphire, on his finger.

Pedro Archanjo, maintaining his calm in spite of his rising excitement, followed Tadeu with his eyes and saw him furtively pick up the carnation and put it in his lapel, then lift his head and smile triumphantly. Had the flower fallen by accident from the girl's hands or had she dropped it in the young engineer's path by design? She had fair ringlets, the biggest eyes in Bahia, and an opalescent skin, so white it had a bluish cast. Pedro Archanjo examined her curiously. She rose from her chair and clapped her hands with their long, slender fingers; she looked nervous, her face was tense, her mouth was firmly set. Tadeu, an engineer at last, stood smiling by Zabela's side while the Dean of the Medical School handed him his diploma, the longed-for scroll, and the Governor of the State shook his hand. His eyes sought the girl's in an ardent glance before resting on the group from the Tent of Miracles.

Good Lord! My boy, who's still such a child! Pedro Archanjo clapped thoughtfully, his joy no longer quite so serene. Now it was tempered with foreboding. Well, Tadeu, you have my whole-hearted approval, anyhow. Whatever happens, whatever the price, don't give up; pay it like a man. We come from strong stock, and our mixed blood is good in a fight. We never back down and we always stick up for our rights; we were born to make use of them.

A little later the class sponsor, Professor Tarquínio, stepped to the rostrum and wished the new graduates success in their future lives and careers. There was Brazil to be built and educated, freed from backwardness and prejudice, from routine and petty politicking; and there was a war-weary world to be healed of its wounds. This grand and noble task would be the responsibility of the young, the engineers above all, for we are living in the age of machines, of industry, of technology, science, and engineering.

Astério Gomes, valedictorian, picked up the generous gauntlet. Yes, we will build a new world on the ruins of war and lift Brazil from the moral apathy in which she is stagnating. The world of the future will be one of progress and freedom, free of weakness, prejudice, oppression, and injustice. Ours will be a Brazil linked by highways, factories, and machines, a wide-awake Brazil on the march, a world of opportunity for everyone under the sign of technology. Even now the workers in mysterious Russia are overthrowing the bastions of tyranny.

Amid the applause the audience in the Polytechnical School auditorium heard the word socialism and the strange name of Vladimir Ilyich Lenin pronounced by the wealthy young engineer, son of great landholders. The October Revolution had just divided the world into past and future for all time, but only a few comprehended the change and they were not yet afraid: Lenin was a vague and distant leader and socialism an inconsequential word. The speaker himself had no idea of the importance of what he had said.

For a moment Pedro Archanjo saw Tadeu and the girl side by side, when she ran up to her brother after his speech and gave him a kiss. His classmates, too, came up to congratulate him. They were side by side, the girl's diaphanous beauty and the dark, spirited beauty of the young man.

In the Tent of Miracles, after the ritual dance of greeting, the drums fell silent and bottles were opened. On the table where the type was composed was a quantity of food, all kinds and all of it delicious: stewed and fried fish, chicken with manioc flour, beancakes, *vatapá* and *carurú* and *efó* baked in leaves. Many were the friendly, competent hands that had mixed the coconut and palm oil and measured out the salt, pepper, and ginger. Early that morning, in the *terreiros* of several African nations, goats, lambs, roosters, hens, and turtles had been sacrificed for the feast. Majé Bassan had thrown the cowries and three times they had answered: work, travel, and the pangs of love.

The skyrockets burst over the rooftops and broadcast the news: there's a doctor with a mortarboard and tassel on Tabuão

Hill, the first one in the neighborhood to graduate from college. Lídio Corró hung the class picture on the wall of the shop between his own miracle painting and the poster by Toulouse-Lautrec: there was Tadeu in his cap and gown, sitting with his classmates. Never before had there been so many people in the Tent of Miracles at once.

Damião de Souza rose, glass of *cachaça* in hand, ahemed, and asked for silence: he was going to make a toast. Wait! ordered the Countess. For Zabela, a toast at any party worthy of the name called for champagne, French champagne if possible—the only drink worthy of a toast to the health of a true friend. Professor Silva Virajá had sent her three bottles of the best champagne for Christmas, and Zabela had saved one for Tadeu's party.

Majé Bassan, always courteous, moistened her lips in the aristocratic liquid. Lídio and Archanjo did the same: Zabela never had been able to win them over to fine wines, the two *compadres* were incorrigibly faithful to their beer and *cachaça*. Damião de Souza, at the climax of an impetuous torrent of oratory and inflamed figures of speech, drained his glass at a gulp. What insipid stuff! The giver drank most of the bottle in the end. Tadeu and Damião embraced. They had grown up together in the streets and on the beach and now they were parting, each to fulfill his destiny.

Ojuobá's eyes recognized those paths and followed them: the two were very different. Damião was an open book without secrets. His doctor's degree was conferred on him by the people, not by a university. Wherever his fate might take him he would always be the same, planted right where he had grown up. But Tadeu had begun to climb the ladder while he was still in college, bent on outstripping his classmates. He had made up his mind to climb all the way up and fight for a place at the top. "I'm going to be somebody, Godfather," he had said that morning, one burning flame of ambition. How much longer would they have him with them in the Tent of Miracles?

Lídio Corró picked up the flute and held out the guitar to Pedro Archanjo, and the dancers gathered in a circle. But where were Kirsi and Dorotéia, Risoleta and Dedé? Sabina dos Anjos had moved to Rio de Janeiro; her son was a sailor. Ivone had married the captain of a fishing boat and gone to live in Curitiba. It was all in vain that the novices devoured young Tadeu, in his graduate garb, with their eyes.

The party went on all night, but early in the evening the guest of honor, the *raison d'être*, the object of all the honors, Dr. Tadeu Canhoto, civil engineer, mechanic, geographer, architect, astronomer, builder of bridges and canals, of railroads and highways, polytechnician, asked for permission to leave. In the ballrooms of that élite club the Cruz Vermelha, the rich and distinguished Professor Tarquínio, the class sponsor, was treating the young engineers to a graduation ball.

"Godfather, I'll have to go now. The dance started hours ago."

"It's still early, isn't it? Why don't you stay a little while longer? Everyone here loves you, and they came because they wanted to see you"—Archanjo knew he shouldn't say it, but he said it anyway.

"I know, and I'd love to stay. But . . ."

Zabela tapped Archanjo's arm with her fan.

"Let the boy go, don't be an old spoilsport."

Confounded old woman, how much did she know about Tadeu's secret? Was she by any chance a relative of those greasy loud-mouthed Gomeses?

"Master Pedro, you're a debauché, a libertine. You don't know one thing about love, all you know about is women." The former Princess of the Recôncavo, the former Queen of the Cancan sighed: "Just like me: I know a lot about men, but what do I know about love?"

She was silent for a moment as she watched Tadeu leave.

"His name was Ernesto Argolo de Araújo and he was my cousin. I was very young and foolish and I loved him too much. So much, so much that I sent him to his death at the hands of a duelist, just to make him jealous and find out how much he really loved me."

Tadeu vanished into the darkness, his patent leather shoes echoing against the paving stones. No one could stop him from going his own way, and I won't try, Zabela. Why should I? He's going to climb up the ladder one step at a time, and he's in a hurry. Good-bye, Tadeu Conhoto, this was a farewell party and we didn't even know it.

Judge Santos Cruz, whose learning and sense of humor were as frequently and justly praised as his intelligence and integrity, was seriously annoyed: a clerk had just come to his office, where he was waiting for the jury to assemble, to report the absence (again!) of the lawyer appointed by the court. The counsel for the defense had scrawled a hasty excuse.

"Sick! . . . a cold! . . . He's drunk in some bar, more likely. You never see him anywhere else. I simply cannot let this disgraceful farce continue. How many times has that poor devil been brought here and then taken back to his cell? They won't let him have any rest even in jail."

The clerk stood before the judge's desk, waiting for orders. His Honor asked:

"What lawyers are hanging around the corridors?"

"I didn't see any when I came. That is, I saw Dr. Arthur Sampaio, but he was just leaving."

"Any students?"

"Just Costinha, that fourth-year man."

"No, not him; the accused would be better off without any defense at all. Costinha would manage to lose the case for the Mother of God if he had to defend her. Isn't there anyone around who can take care of this wretched case? Am I going to have to put off the trial again? This is intolerable!"

Who should enter the judge's office at that moment but young

Damião de Souza, wearing a white suit and a shirt with the collar turned down. He was the best-known man around the Forum, a sort of adjutant general at the service of judges, lawyers, clerks, and bailiffs. He had held two or three jobs with law firms but never stayed with them for long because he hankered after the inexhaustible variety of the odd jobs he could do at the Palace of Justice. He learned all there was to know about crimes and criminals, trials and lawsuits, petitions and solicitations, in corridors and the offices of public notaries, in jury sessions, at prison gates and police headquarters. At nineteen the precocious lad was the salvation of many young lawyers who were still wet behind the ears, intoxicated with theories but innocent of all practical knowledge. Damião had more work than he could handle.

When he saw him walk in smiling with a sheet of paper in his hand and the inquiry: "Dr. Santos Cruz, could you take care of this petition for Dr. Marino?" the judge remembered a conversation he had had once with the boy when he had invited him to his house for a St. John's Eve party.

"Leave it here, I'll have a look at it later. Tell me, Damião: how old are you?"

"I've just passed my nineteenth birthday, sir."

"Are you still thinking of applying for a certificate to practice law?"

"Just as sure as one and one are two, with the help of Our Lord of Bonfim."

"Do you think you could stand up before the bench and defend an accused criminal?"

"Could I do it, Your Honor? Don't think I'm showing lack of respect if I say I could defend a criminal better than any of those law students who send poor men to jail while they're practicing. And what's more, I could do it better than a lot of attorneys with law degrees."

"Have you seen the brief for the crime scheduled to be tried in today's session? Do you know anything about the case?"

"To tell you the truth, Your Honor, I haven't even looked at the docket. I've heard about the crime, though, and if you want me to defend the man, put your seal on it, Your Honor, give me half an hour to glance through the documents and talk to the man, and I swear I'll get him off. If you don't believe it, just give me a chance."

On an impulse the judge turned to the clerk.

"Teixeira, draw up Damião's appointment to defend the accused *ex officio,* since he lacks any other counsel. Give Damião the records so he'll have some idea of what the case is about, and summon the jury in exactly an hour. In the meantime I'll clear up some other work here. And bring some fresh coffee. If you do a good job, Damião, I'll see that you get your lawyer's certificate."

Inácia's Zé had committed a gory crime and the first jury had condemned him to thirty years in jail for murder in cold blood. The court had recognized no extenuating circumstances, nor had it taken his lack of a police record into account.

Carrying the pack of a Syrian peddler uphill and down in exchange for a few coins that were barely enough to feed Caçula, his long-time companion, Zé da Inácia invariably drank himself blind every Sunday and fell through the door when he staggered home. On Monday he would pick up his pack again and follow Ibrahim from customer to customer, quiet, peaceable, incapable of an argument or a demand, in rain or under the broiling sun.

On a Sunday no different from any other he fell in with a certain Foul-Mouth Afonso in a corner tavern, and between the two of them they despatched a bottle of white rum. Then they went to drink a second bottle at Zé's house with Caçula. Cordial and friendly at first, Foul-Mouth soon showed his true quarrelsome, insolent nature, and before Zé da Inácia knew what was happening he was caught up in an argument punctuated with vile oaths and threats—you want me to belt you one?—and mothers' names profaned. When the police asked him how the fight had begun, Zé da Inácia was not able to tell them. Whatever it was they had been arguing about had been drowned in *cachaça;* and the first thing he knew he had a knife in his hand, a worn-down, wickedly sharp old kitchen knife. Foul-Mouth was brandishing a hatchet in his face and threatening: "I'm gonna split you right down the middle, you fucking billy goat!" Pierced through by the knife, Foul-Mouth fell on the ground, stone dead, and Zé da

Inácia fell opposite him, knocked senseless by rum and the blow he had sustained. When he came to he found himself a murderer caught *in flagrante delicto*, and at the police station he was given a lively beating to get things off to a good start.

When the jury was called the first time, after Zé had waited more than a year in jail, the prosecutor, showing off his Lombroso, had discoursed on his congenital perversity. "Observe, gentlemen of the jury, the head of the accused: the typical cranium of a murderer. We will pass over his dark pigmentation, though the most up-to-date theories, those held by Dr. Nilo Argolo, an undisputed authority on the subject, a distinguished professor of Forensic Medicine in our own venerable School of Medicine, point out the high crime rate among half-breeds. Here in the prisoner's dock is telling proof of those theories."

He described the victim, Afonso da Conceição, "a poor workingman liked by his neighbors, incapable of harming anyone. Going unsuspectingly to the house of the accused for a friendly chat, he became the object of the murderous rage of the fiend sitting before you. Observe his face: not a trace of remorse." The prosecutor asked for the maximum penalty.

Zé da Inácia had no money to pay a lawyer. In jail he had been making horn combs and spatulas to earn a few coppers, but this was hardly enough to keep him in cigarettes. Caçula had managed to find work at the house of some nieces of the deceased Major Pestana, on whose fazenda she had been born. To her the major symbolized kindness and greatness of soul: "I never wanted for a thing while the major was alive. Oh, what a good man he was!" Inácia's Zé must have had some good in him, too, for Caçula did not abandon him but went to visit him in prison every Sunday to bring him cheer and comfort: "When the jury meets they're sure to let you off, God willing." And where was he going to get the money to pay a lawyer? "The judge told me he'd give you one, don't you worry about it none."

Dr. Alberto Alves, the court-appointed lawyer, bit his nails in the jury room: he had not even read the brief, and he had had to leave his wife, naughty Odete, whispering and giggling with that scoundrel Félix Bordalo. By this time they were probably kissing and hugging and here he was, powerless to do a thing to keep the

two of them from planting horns on him. He was chained to the
spot by his duty to defend the criminal in the dock. All you had
to do was look at his face and measure his skull to know the
prosecutor was right: it would be a danger to society to turn the
beast loose. But had Odete—? Well, this was not the first time,
of course; there had been that affair with a certain Dilton. Odete's
vows of faithfulness were worth about as much as the vows of
innocence of that confessed culprit, that hangdog criminal over
there. They were backsliders by nature, both of them. What a
shitty world!

He put forward a defense so empty that it was beneath criticism. Dr. Alves denied nothing, replied to no challenge, but
merely asked the jury to temper justice with mercy. He might
as well have been the prosecutor's assistant, thought Judge Lobato
when the sentence was read: thirty years in prison; the jury had
asked for the maximum penalty.

"Won't the counsel for the defense appeal the sentence?" he
asked, indignant at the lawyer's indifference. "I think you ought
to."

"Appeal? Oh, certainly." Had it not been for the judge's rep-
rimand, Alberto Alves would not have remembered that such a
thing as an appeal existed. "I wish to appeal the sentence to the
appellate court."

Now Zé da Inácia was back for his second trial, which had
been put off three times because the court-appointed lawyer had
failed to show up. Damião de Souza took the stand for the defense.

This time there was a different prosecutor, and young lawyer
Augusto Leivas, like Dr. Alberto Alves at the first trial, was thinking about a woman—not, however, from a cuckold's point of view
but as a happy lover. Marília had finally given in and all the world
was rosy. He saw no fatal propensity for crime in Zé's color, nor
did he take the measure of his cranium as Lombroso would have
done. He carried out his task mechanically, with his mind far
away on Marília's charms: how adorably shameless she had looked,
sitting up in bed with no clothes on.

Fretting at his own impulsive designation of a lawyer on such short notice, the judge breathed more freely as he followed the weak arguments for the prosecution and felt confident that the penalty would be lowered to eighteen years, or twelve, maybe even to six, no matter how inept young Damião's defense.

As it happened, however, Damião de Souza's debut in court turned into the biggest sensation of the season. It was long discussed in the Palace of Justice and was news for the press the very next day. From that time on, Damião would always be news.

As Manuel de Praxedes was walking past the Forum he saw the bustle and stir, asked why there were so many people, and was told that a new attorney was making his debut. He was only a boy, but what a speaker, a colossus at the bench! Manuel went in just as Damião's defense had reached its climax. The good-natured giant could not restrain himself: he clapped and shouted for an encore and had to be expelled from the room.

That was not the only time the judge was obliged to ring his bell for silence and threaten to empty out the courtroom, but as he did so he smiled. It had been a long time since there had been so much noise and excitement at a trial.

Damião's defense was an epic, full of romantic interest, Greek tragedy, penny novels, the Bible, and a reference at just the proper psychological moment to a famous remark of "His Honor, the noble Master of Law, Dr. Santos Cruz." To sum it all up, poor innocent Zé da Inácia had been forced to commit a crime to save his own life and the honor of his home, both of which were threatened by the vile traitor Foul-Mouth Afonso. The culprit sitting before them was a victim of fate: that loving husband, that dedicated workman trudging under the burning sun with peddler's pack on his back, earning in the sweat of his brow—and not his brow alone, gentlemen of the jury, but his whole body, because that Turk's pack weighs a ton!—the wherewithal to support his dearly beloved wife. One day this generous, upright citizen clasped a serpent to his bosom: Foul-Mouth Afonso—the name says it all, gentlemen of the jury, foul mouth, fouler heart! A mad hyena, a violent, contumacious drunk and libertine, he had tried to rob Zé da Inácia of his wife's affection and stain the honor of his home. Picture this Greek tragedy, gentlemen, if you

can! Zé da Inácia trudges home, tired out from his day's work—
and what do his eyes behold but a scene that is truly Dantesque:
poor Caçula struggling with the infamous wretch who has seized
the kitchen knife and is trying to take her by force since the innocent creature has indignantly repulsed his infamous proposals.
Zé da Inácia runs to the succor of his wife. A struggle ensues,
and then Inácia's Zé, that peaceable laborer, in defense of life and
honor, crushes the head of the unspeakable serpent.

Damião flung his arms wide and addressed the jury: "Gentlemen, you who are husbands and fathers, you who are men of
honor, tell me this: which of you would remain impassive if you
came home and saw your wife struggling with a blackguard?
None of you, I am sure."

He pointed to Caçula among the spectators: "There she is,
gentlemen of the jury, the chief victim!" Tears came easily to
Caçula and she had swallowed two glasses of rum before leaving
home so that she would be able to listen in silence while her man
was insulted. That first time had been awful. "Behold her, gentlemen of the jury. It is that poor, saintly wife bathed in tears who
demands justice for her husband. Considering the history of the
case, gentlemen, all I ask is that my client be acquitted."

Manuel de Praxedes had asked for an encore, and he got one.
Wounded in his vanity and seeing his hard-won fame already en-
dangered, the prosecutor asked the clerk for the brief and made
a rejoinder. Armed with precedents, authors, quotations, and doc-
umentary proof, he finally made a serious accusatory statement.
He could not let himself be defeated by a kid who hadn't even
studied law at a university. Why, Damião de Souza was nothing
but a bailiffs' errand boy, a nobody who accepted tips from clerks.
He tried to demolish the absurd fable of the defense, but it was
too little and too late. In his answering statement Damião wound
the jurors tightly around his little finger. Filomeno Jacob the
pharmacist was sobbing aloud. The courtroom was "a sea of
tears," as a reporter wrote in *A Tarde.*

The verdict of acquittal was unanimous. It was up to Judge
Santos Cruz to read the sentence, and he ordered that Zé da Inácia
be set free. "I almost broke down and cried myself, I never saw
anything like it in all my born days," said His Honor to the prose-

cutor, who was beside himself. "I'm going to make sure he gets his lawyer's certificate; that way there'll always be a lawyer to defend the poor."

And that was Damião's graduation. A graduation with no ring, no scroll, no photograph in cap and gown, no dance, no class sponsor, no class—just Damião and no one else. When the show was over, poor Caçula, who was fond of her man, after all, and had lost hope of ever seeing him go free, went over to the beardless young man and thanked him:

"God will repay you, *Seu* Major!"

Why Major? Only she could say; it had something to do with her past. At any rate, he was Major Damião de Souza from that day forward.

8

When he heard the boy's voice at the attic door saying "Can I come in, Godfather?" Pedro Archanjo hid the proofs of his manuscript under some books.

"Is that you, Tadeu? Come in."

It was raining, a fine, persistent, dreary rain.

"What a surprise to see you here! What's happened?"

Soon after his graduation Tadeu had found a job as assistant engineer on the construction of the Jaguaquara-Jequié Railroad. The salary was modest and the working conditions were bad, but the boy preferred that hard but useful experience in the interior of the state to moldering away in some engineering firm, twiddling his thumbs in the capital, a candidate for a government sinecure: "That wasn't why I worked so hard to get my degree."

"I've got to talk to you, Godfather."

The sound of Rosália's quiet breathing came from the bed.

Archanjo got up and threw a bedspread over the girl's opulent nudity. She had gone to sleep smiling in the warmth of sweet tender words, so longed for and so good to hear. More than ten years before when she was only seventeen, indolent Roberto, Colonel Loureiro's son, had held her chin and said: Little girl, it's time for you to go to bed. After the son it was the father's turn. The colonel gave her a dress and a little cash and Rosália went to work in Alagoinhas, in Adri Vaselina's house. She had come to Bahia with a traveling salesman and Pedro Archanjo saw her buying oranges in the Terreiro de Jesus. Only then did Rosália come to believe that she was indeed a human being and not a thing, or a rag, or nothing but a whore.

"I've got to talk to you, Godfather," Tadeu said again. "I need your advice."

"Let's take a walk." Archanjo felt a weight on his heart. He recalled the throw of the cowries on the morning of the graduation: work, travel, pangs of love, the shells had said.

They walked slowly up the street, glancing into the Tent as they passed at Lídio Corró setting type with an apprentice at his side. Tadeu talked and Archanjo listened with bent head. Advice? What advice could he give, when Tadeu had already settled his affairs and even reserved a stateroom on the boat?

"You didn't come here to listen to me, and I'm not going to give you any advice. But I think you're right. I'm going to miss you"—he repeated it—"I'm going to miss you more than you know. But I can't keep you here."

Tadeu had made up his mind to leave his job on the railroad and go to Rio de Janeiro, where he would be a member of the engineering team which was transforming the capital into a modern city under the leadership of Paulo de Frontin. He owed the opportunity to Professor Bernard, a friend of Frontin's. On a trip to Rio the professor had spoken of his young protégé's talent, of how hard-working, ambitious, and capable he was, and had suggested that he would be a fine acquisition for the great engineer's construction team. "Send the boy along, then. I need young and willing hands."

"This is my chance, Godfather. In Rio the field is wide open. If I stay here the only thing I can look forward to is being an employee of the Transportation Bureau. I didn't work for a degree just to end up as a bureaucrat chained to a briefcase, earning a miserable salary and having to wait for promotions. In the South I can have a career, especially with the man I'll be working for. Not many people have that kind of luck. Professor Bernard has turned out to be a real friend."

Is that all you wanted to tell me, Tadeu? Isn't there something else you'd like to discuss? Master Archanjo knew that the really important thing had not been said. Tadeu groped for the best way to say it.

"Tell me what's bothering you, son."

Archanjo almost always called Tadeu by his name, sometimes by his full name, Tadeu Canhoto. On rare occasions he called him *"meu bom"* or *"camarado,"* his habitual forms of address. On a few, a very few, occasions he called him "my son."

"Godfather, I'm in love with the sister of one of my classmates. You know him, Astério. I introduced him to you one time, he was our class valedictorian, remember? Now he's in the United States, he'll be there two years doing graduate work. The family's very rich."

"Blond curls, transparent milky skin, and great big eyes."

"Do you know her, Godfather?"

"And what does that rich white family of hers have to say about this?"

"They don't know anything about it, Godfather, just me and her and now you. I mean . . ."

"Zabela . . ."

"Did she tell you?"

"No, she didn't say a word about it, don't be upset. Is the girl related to Zabela?"

"No, they aren't relatives, just acquaintances. That is, Lu's grandmother—her name is Luíza but everybody calls her Lu— was a friend of Zabela's when they were young, and sometimes she goes to see her to talk about old times. That's how Lu met Zabela, and she goes to visit her sometimes. But no one in her family knows and I don't want them to. Not yet, anyway."

"Why not? Are you afraid her parents won't give their consent?"

"You mean because I'm a mulatto? They're all kinds in Lu's family, I don't know just how they'll react when we tell them. So far they've always been very kind to me, but I have no idea how they'll behave later on. Her mother gives herself noble airs, and the less said about her grandmother, Zabela's friend, the better. It's funny sometimes when Lu's mother, Dona Emília, calls one of the maids 'dirty nigger' when she's scolding her. Then she remembers me and looks embarrassed, as if she were going to apologize. But Godfather, that's not the reason I want to keep it a secret; you've taught me to be proud of my color. But I don't want to go to that rich mansion with empty hands to ask for their daughter in marriage. If they say no because I'm a mulatto, then I'll know how to handle it. But if I let them say no because I can't support a family, what right would I have to complain? Don't you understand?"

"Yes, you're right."

"I'll go to Rio and really work hard, Godfather. I'm no fool and I know I can be a real professional. I'm going to be working on the best engineering team in the country. I think I'll be in a very good situation in two or three years at the most, and then I can come back and ring the doorbell of Lu's house because I'll have something to offer. And that will be just about the time Astério will be coming back from the United States, and he could be a useful ally. His support might make all the difference. Do you remember when I used to go to his house to study? He said himself that he never would have graduated without my help. He's my friend; I can count on him."

"How old is the girl?"

"Nearly eighteen. I met Astério when we were freshmen, and the first time he took me home with him Lu was only twelve years old, just imagine! We've been in love for a long time, but it wasn't until last year that we looked in each other's eyes and made a vow."

"A vow?"

"Yes, Godfather! Lu and I are going to be married some day. That's certain!" he said, gritting his teeth almost fiercely.

"What makes you think she'll wait for you?"

"Because she loves me, and she's stubborn. When those people

want something, they really want it. Lu's like her father. Once
she's made up her mind she never gives in. Do you know who
Colonel Gomes reminds me of? You, godfather. You're different
in lots of ways, but you're alike in some. You'll meet him some
day."

"Are you prepared to face whatever comes? It may be a hard
and terrible trial, Tadeu Canhoto."

"Weren't you the one who taught me how to face things?
You and Uncle Lídio?"

"When do you sail?"

"Why, today. There's a ship leaving this afternoon and I've
reserved a stateroom."

Late that afternoon Pedro Archanjo and Lídio Corró accompanied Tadeu to the boat. The boy had gone to tell the Gomeses
good-bye and had stayed for lunch. Then he had dashed all
around Bahia to see his friends one last time. Majé Bassan gave
him a necklace of sacred beads in a leather bag, a talisman from
Xangô's shrine. Zabela, rheumatic and almost lame as she was,
insisted she wanted to see him off. But Tadeu would not hear of it;
he told her to stay in bed and read her poets. Zabela made a face
at him: this was a sad end for someone who had been the toast of
Paris. Manuel de Praxedes and Mané Lima showed up at the last
minute, having only just heard the news. The ship's whistle blew
for the second time, hurrying the visitors ashore.

The farewells were solemn; the distance was enormous and
difficult to cross. Rio de Janeiro was a long way off. Archanjo
could not hold out; he opened the strongbox and took out his
secret:

"I wasn't going to tell you, I wanted it to be a surprise. But
the book is almost ready; only a few pages still have to be
printed."

The boy's restless face broke out into the happy excitement
of the apprentice of ten years before, and the shadows disappeared. "Oh, Godfather, that's great news! Be sure to send it to
me just as soon as it's ready. Send me several copies and I'll see
that it gets to the right people in Rio."

The third whistle blew and the steward rang his bell: visitors
ashore, passengers aboard, the ship's weighing anchor. The time

had come for tears and embraces and handkerchiefs waving good-bye. The four friends went down to the dock, standing in a little group among the winches. Suddenly they saw Tadeu running down the gangplank. The fair-haired girl was desperately trying to recognize someone on the deck, but how could she see him when her big eyes were misted over with tears and there were so many people? Tadeu! she wailed desperately, but her voice was drowned out in the noisy farewells. Suddenly he was at her side, panting and out of breath. For one brief infinite second they gazed at each other mutely, self-contained in the curious crowd. Then he kissed her hand and started back to the ship. Tadeu! she called pathetically, forgetting all sense of propriety and holding out her arms and her lips. Tadeu tore himself away from that kiss, started up the gangplank, and then it was good-bye.

At the entrance to the harbor the ship said farewell with one last whistle, smoke billowing from the funnel. One last wave of the handkerchief. Good-bye, my love, don't forget me. Slowly the wharf emptied of people, and only Archanjo and Lu were left in the twilight.

"Pedro Archanjo?" The girl proffered her fine hand, with its blue veins and slender fingers. "My name is Lu. I'm Tadeu's fiancée."

"Fiancée?" Archanjo smiled.

"Just between the two of us. You know all about it; he told me you did."

"You're so young."

"Mamãe offers me a new fiancé every day; she says it's high time I was married." She was a bundle of nerves, an unsubdued flame, and her laughter was as clear and limpid as water rolling over a bed of stones: "When I introduce my fiancé to Mother she's going to have the worst fit of hysterics she's ever had in her life." Opening her great eyes even wider, she looked Archanjo straight in the eye. "Don't think I don't know how hard it's going to be. I'm the one who ought to know, I know my own family, but it doesn't matter. Don't be afraid."

"I've never been afraid of things like that."

"Don't be afraid for me, is what I meant."

It was Archanjo's turn to look her in the eye:

"I won't be afraid for either of you," he smiled with his whole face. "No, I won't be afraid, my dear."

"I'm going to the fazenda tomorrow. May I see you when I come back?"

"Whenever you want to. Just tell Zabela."

"So you know that, too? I already knew you were a wizard, a *babalaô*, isn't that right? Tadeu has told me so much about you, wonderful things. Good-bye, don't think badly of me."

She went up to him and kissed him on the cheek. The twilight was glittering gold and copper on the horizon. It's going to be a terrible trial, my girl, so be prepared for it. She was all nerves, and a bonfire in flame.

As he passed the two bookstores in the Praça da Sé, Don León Esteban's Livraria Espanhola and the Livraria Dante Alighieri, as Giuseppe Bonfanti called his secondhand hole in the wall, Pedro Archanjo glanced out of the corner of his eye at the copies of *African Influence on the Customs of Bahia* among the latest national and foreign publications imported by Don León. The book was almost two hundred pages long and the title in blue ink looked luxurious in the middle of the cover with the author's name above it in type that imitated handwriting, "beautiful italics," as Lídio Corró described it. His vanity dissolved into thought and Pedro Archanjo meditated as he crossed the plaza: that book had cost him ten years of hard work and discipline and he had had to change in order to write it; he was no longer the same man.

Don León had thrown away hard cash on five copies. He had placed two of them in the window ("the thing they want most is to see the book in the showcase") and sent one to Spain as a present to a friend who was interested in anthropology. Only as a curiosity, of course, not for the scientific value which it most certainly did not possess; it was only a book by a runner at the university who had been bitten by the scientific bug. That particular form of madness was much more common than was generally supposed; the city of Bahia teemed with poets and philosophers, and Don León had a vast experience of that breed of author. They turned up in his bookstore every day of the week, wan, belligerent, vacant-eyed, needing a shave, holding their manuscripts under their armpits: poems and sonnets, short stories and novels, philosophical treatises on man's fate and the existence of God.

Once in a great while one of those geniuses got his hands on a little money, published his immortal opus, and went straight to Don León to sell him some copies. Between the carriers of the literary bacillus and those infected by the scientific virus, Don León preferred the dreamy poets, who were generally meek as lambs, to the easily inflamed philosophers with their bounden determination to save the world and everyone in it through some original, irrefutable panacea of their own. Archanjo's brain had been addled by the company of too many doctors and so he had turned to anthropology and ethnology, but he had the ways of a poet and was one of the most appealing of that strange fauna. Poor devil, he deserved a better fate.

Don León, a well-informed and well-read gentleman of discreet and pleasing manner, recommended authors to students and to men of letters. He had made Blasco Ibáñez popular in Bahia as well as Vargas Vila, the Argentine Ingenieros, and the Uruguayan José Enrique Rodó. Ingenieros and Rodó were for the professors, Vargas Vila was very popular with the students, and Blasco Ibáñez was the favorite of distinguished families. Don León's clientele was varied and eclectic.

Judges, university professors, the better class of journalists, all the most important figures in the intellectual life of the city frequented his bookstore and learned from him; Don León received catalogs from Argentina, the United States, and most of Europe. He took orders, too, for books that were unobtainable in Brazil. Pedro Archanjo was one of those who had used Don León's good offices to order books from France, England, Italy, and Argentina. On more than one occasion the order had come in when, as so often happened, he was short of money; but his credit with the Spaniard was good. "Keep the books and pay me when it suits you." "Don't worry, Don León, I'll pay you by Saturday without fail." Don León appreciated the mulatto's scrupulousness, both in paying his debts and in his dress; he always looked as if he had stepped out of a bath, and his good breeding distinguished him from most of the other philosophers, who were inclined to be rude, excitable, unkempt, dirty, and inveterate spongers.

Yes, he spoke softly and was a delightful fellow, but he was a crackpot with a mania for science nevertheless. He spent money, great sums of money! on foreign publications, some of which not even the professors at the Medical School had read, thought Don León when Pedro Archanjo came with his book. *Muy bien, mis felicitaciones.* In an excess of generosity he bought five copies and put two of them in the show window, but it never crossed his mind to leaf through the unprepossessing brochure. He had neither the leisure nor the sense of humor for such compendiums of lunacy.

In contrast to the Livraria Espanhola, with its volumes neatly arranged on shelves by subject, language, and author, its wicker chairs in back where distinguished customers could sit and converse, and its clerk with his correct tie and collar, Bonfanti's place was a jumble shop with stacks of books on the floor, a counter filled to overflowing, and too little space to hold Bonfanti's vast clientèle of rackety students, picturesque subliterati, and old men in search of dirty books. Two scrawny, impudent urchins waited on the customers amid much rude banter. At the cash register sat Bonfanti, wearing the same shiny, threadbare blue suit he had put on when he set up shop seven years before, buying and selling in his shrill voice:

"Ten *tostões*, take it or leave it."

"But *Seu* Bonfanti, I bought that geometry book last Monday right in this store and paid five whole *milreis* for it," the student protested.

"You bought a new book and you're selling a used one."

"Used? I haven't even opened it! It's brand new, just like it was when I bought it. Give me two *milreis* for it, anyway."

"Once a book leaves the bookstore it's a secondhand book. Ten *tostões*, not a penny more."

Bonfanti had not paid cash for his copies of *African Influence;* his friendship for the author did not go quite so far as that. He had been given twenty on consignment and had spread five copies or so out fanwise in the smaller showcase, the one for new books. He kept the big one for the secondhand volumes which were the backbone of his thriving trade. He was Archanjo's crony; they traded recipes during Sunday lunches at the Tent or at meals in Bonfanti's house in Itapagipe presided over by Dona Assunta, the stout and garrulous pasta queen. When it came to food Bonfanti was a different person, a gracious, generous host; eating was his passion.

The sweet vanity of a new author, who lingers in front of bookstore windows to see his work displayed, did not last long. Pedro Archanjo was soon caught up in the celebration of his fiftieth birthday. There was an uninterrupted succession of *ca-rurú* banquets ("Dona Fernanda and Mr. Mané Lima request the honor of your company at the *carurú* they're having next Sunday for *Seu* Archanjo"), Afro-Brazilian *batucadas*, samba circles, meetings, parties, eating and drinking jags—everyone wanted to help him celebrate. Master Archanjo plunged with unflagging enthusiasm headfirst into that sea of *cachaça*, dancing, and women with open arms. It was as if he wanted to make up in one gulp for all those years of study when he was preparing to write the book. Hungry and thirsty for life, he squandered his energy, was seen everywhere, turned up in places he had not been back to since his youth, revisited old haunts and followed itineraries long forgotten. An idle vagabond again, talking and laughing his easy laugh, always ready for a drink, surrounded by a circle of women, discussing every subject under the sun, and all the time taking notes in his little black notebook with the stub of a pencil, Pedro Archanjo was greedy, hasty, avid, impatient.

That second book had not cost him merely ten years of discipline and self-control; he had paid a high price in opinions, points of view, precepts, ways of seeing and behaving; he had been one person before, and now he was another. Before he knew it he had been turned inside out and now he measured things by a new set of values.

"*Compadre* Pedro, you look like a gentleman these days," said Lídio Corró, watching him set off for the Medical School with a book in his hand.

"Gentleman, *meu bom?* When was I ever a gentleman, *camarado?*"

But this observation from his *compadre*, his "twin," put him on the alert. Lídio Corró was afraid that he would leave. Not on a trip, not for a change or for fun, but simply pack up and go, and leave them all. Lídio was perhaps the only one to perceive the inner changes, the new man who had grown up inside the old Pedro Archanjo who had been brave, rash, impulsive and rather irresponsible, freedom-loving but inconsequential, daring, no doubt, but of limited vision. For the ordinary people of Tabuão and Pelourinho, when it came to pastoral plays and *gafieira* samba, or singing and dancing, or *capoeira* and *candomblé*, he was still the same Master Pedro, wrapped in the mantle of their esteem and affection. There's nobody like him, he even writes books, he knows more than real doctors, but he's still one of us. Your blessing, Ojuobá, said the adepts, your blessing! Had Majé Bassan noticed any change? If she had no one knew about it, not even Archanjo.

At fifty years of age Pedro Archanjo plunged into life with all the intemperance of an adolescent. Besides all the rest that we have told, wasn't Tadeu's absence in itself reason enough?

Unshakable in his faith and devotion, Lídio Corró busied himself with the book; in his eyes his *compadre's* books were a sort of latter-day Testament. The miracle painter knew they were important because he felt in his own flesh and blood the truth expressed in their pages: in persecution and strife, in truth and in falsehood, in evil and in good. He spared no effort to publicize the books and sell more of them. He sent copies off to critics, professors, newspapers, individual journalists, and universities, north and south; and he put two packages in the mail for Tadeu to distribute in Rio.

The *Bahia Daily News* announced the publication of the book, calling Pedro Archanjo "a distinguished author"; and *A Tarde* dubbed the little volume "a depository of our folk traditions." Lídio was thrilled by that phrase and showed the paper to everybody and his wife. Two or three critics ventured to appraise the work, but only briefly. Valuing only Greece and France, these last of the Hellenes and devoted followers of Anatole France felt little attraction for the "curious and primitive customs of Bahia" and less enthusiasm still for Pedro Archanjo's "daring and controversial asseverations about the races" and his praise of miscegenation; that was an explosive topic.

However, some significant facts should be pointed out. First of all, a few copies—not many, to be sure—were actually sold in the bookstores, not only in Bahia but in Rio as well. A young Carioca bookseller who was just starting out in the trade ordered five copies through Tadeu and offered to take fifty on consignment to be distributed to bookstores in Rio if "the editor would be willing to give him a discount of fifty per cent." Lídio Corró, in a transport of enthusiasm at being promoted to editor, was so carried away that he sent the bookseller one hundred copies, twice as many as he had asked for, and gave him exclusive selling rights in the South. Lídio never knew how many were sold since no accounting was ever made. On the other hand, the young bookseller became a close friend of Tadeu's and was frequently mentioned in the boy's rare letters to Archanjo: "I often see Carlos Ribeiro, that bookseller friend of mine who's always praising your book."

The publication of the book did not go unheeded at the School of Medicine. Not counting those students who were friends of Pedro Archanjo, on whom Lídio pressed copies at prices which varied according to the customer's means (he had to sell them to pay for the paper they were printed on), the book stirred up a debate among the professors during their morning kaffeeklatsch. Arlindo, the other runner in the Department of Parasitology, told Archanjo about the fearful argument that had taken place between Professor Argolo and the irrepressible Isaías Luna. They had very nearly come to blows.

With a feigned expression of concern on his face, Professor Luna asked the professor of Forensic Medicine if he had heard what the students were saying around the Terreiro. Students' talk? What about? Silly nonsense, no doubt. Nilo Argolo had no time for such foolishness. What were they saying?

They were saying that Runner Archanjo had proved, in a book that had gone on sale only a few days before, that the cult of the serpent still lingered in the *candomblé terreiros* of the Gêge nation—the cult of the serpent-god, the *orixá* Danh-gbi, or simply Dan. Professor Argolo, in a previous work, had categorically denied that any such cult had survived in Bahia: there was no proof of it, no trace at all. Now that uppity high-yellow Archanjo, totally lacking in proper respect for his betters, had dared to make a show of the nonexistent *orixá*, the Cobra, the Serpent, Danh-gbi, Dan, with its shrine, obligations, vestments, symbols, holy day and troop of adepts dancing on the Terreiro of Bongó. And what about those *cucumbís?* That was an old story, the students said. In his first book the mestizo had replied to Argolo's denials, and now he had hammered the nail in with so many proofs that . . .

However, when it came to theories about the races, he, Isaías Luna, a white Bahian, would rather not go into the matter too deeply. He wouldn't put his hand in that wasps' nest, he wasn't totally lacking in sense. Still, from what they say, *Seu* Argolo, the runner's arguments are based on good solid authority, and good reasoning, too. . . .

Apoplectic by this time, Professor Nilo Argolo lost his temper and castigated the serpent before him in plain and vehement Portuguese: *"Fuão, fuinha, futrica!* Nobody, talebearer, white trash! Self-confessed, dissolute lecher!" He was referring to Professor Luna's notorious predilection for black women, "Ardent and affectionate, incomparable, *Seu* Argolo, I assure you!"

As for the skeptical Don León, he had two surprises in rapid succession. The first came shortly after he had put on display in his window the book by that runner with the delusions of grandeur. His most distinguished customer, Professor Silva Virajá, stopped in one day on his way back to the School of Medicine, as he was in the habit of doing, and asked whether "friend León has anything new." When he caught sight of the copies of *African Influence* on the shelf he picked one up:

"Don León, here is a book that is destined to be an anthropological classic. Future lecturers will quote from it and its fame will spread far and wide."

"What book do you mean, *Maestro?*"

"I mean this book by Pedro Archanjo, a runner in my department and a very learned man."

"Learned? Surely you're joking."

"Just listen, Don León!" He opened the book and read: "A mestizo culture is taking shape, so powerful and innate in every Brazilian that in time it will become the true national consciousness, and even the children of immigrant fathers and mothers, first-generation Brazilians, will be cultural mestizos by the time they are grown."

Some weeks later Don León received the clinching argument, a letter from his countryman the amateur anthropologist. In it he thanked León for Archanjo's book: "A magnificent work. It opens new horizons to scholars and works fascinating themes in that virgin soil. What an inspiring city your Bahia must be! I could see its vivid colors and smell its perfume on every page." He asked Don León to send him the same author's previous work, the name of which appeared on the title page of *African Influence.* Don León had not even known there had been a previous work.

The bookseller was an honorable man. He rushed out excitedly in search of Archanjo, but it was late afternoon and the runner had left the School. Don León walked down Pelourinho to find him, waving the letter in his hand and losing his way in alleys and twisting lanes. He asked at one place after another, and everywhere he could feel the presence of the mulatto, a sort of good shepherd and patriarch. Why, he was not a poor crazy devil with philosophical delusions at all; how could he have been so mistaken? The streetlamps went on and for the first time in many years, Don León missed the 6:10 P.M. streetcar to the suburb of Barrís.

When he finally stumbled on Aussá's house in a dirty labyrinth where he had never had the courage to venture before, the moon had risen on a sumptuous dinner of *carurú* washed down with *cachaça,* beer, and rice wine. Hesitating in the doorway with the scent of palm-oil cooking in his nostrils, Don León looked into the poorly furnished room and saw his colleague Bonfanti with his mouth full and his mustaches yellow with *dendê* oil. Sitting between Rosália and Rosa de Oxalá, a peaceful expression on his kindly face, Pedro Archanjo was eating with his fingers—the best way to eat, after all.

"Welcome, Don León. Come and sit down at the table."

Aussá brought him a glass of beer and a luscious brunette served him a plate heaped with *carurú*, cornmeal and rice cakes, and crab stew.

10

Wearing the suit he had had made for Tadeu's graduation two years before, Pedro Archanjo waited for her for several minutes at the door of the church as he tried to master his emotion: the thoughts and memories of a lifetime. At last she appeared coming from the Praça da Sé, surrounded by eyes, calls, and a halo of desire. It had been almost twenty years, seventeen exactly. Archanjo added them up in his mind. And every year had added something to the beauty of Rosa de Oxalá. She had been a dark mystery, tormenting temptation, an irresistible call. Now she was a woman whom no adjective could describe: Rosa de Oxalá.

She was not dressed as a Bahiana in ruffled skirt, shift, and petticoats of spotless white, the sacred color of the devotee of Oxalá. When she gave Archanjo her arm at the door of the cathedral, he saw that she wore a society lady's dress, cut and stitched by the most exclusive couturier in Bahia, and priceless jewels, gold and silver slave ornaments which she wore with the innate elegance of one who was born a queen. She had adorned herself as carefully as if she were going to occupy the place to which she had a right, next to the father of the bride at the priest's left hand.

"Did I keep you waiting long? Miminha wasn't ready until now. I just left her aunts' house; she's going to start from there. Oh, Pedro, my daughter looks so pretty!"

They crossed the semidarkness of the church, lit only by two trembling candle flames. Twilight shadows hovered in the air and sank to the height of the flowers—lilies, delphiniums, chrysanthemums, dahlias, filling the nave from end to end. There was a red carpet from the main altar to the door for the bride, on her father's arm, to walk on in her dress and train, her bridal veil, her wreath, her fear, her joy.

As they moved through the silent penumbra, Rosa murmured almost sadly:

"I wish they could have been married in the Church of the Bonfim, but this is one wedding I didn't open my mouth to say boo about. It's all for my daughter's good, so I didn't say a word."

As she knelt to recite an Our Father, Pedro Archanjo went in search of Anísio, the cathedral sacristan and friend of many years' standing. He was no partner in *cachaça* and guitar-playing like Jonas at the Slaves' Church of Our Lady of the Rosary; but when Archanjo had consulted him the week before he had raised no objections, observing only, in a doleful voice:

"Who ever heard of such a thing? I wonder she stands for it."

The sacristan leading the way, Pedro Archanjo and Rosa slipped behind the altar, climbed the stairs, and seated themselves on a little bench in a dark corner behind the choir. From there they could see everything that went on in the cathedral. Before leaving to turn on the lights, Anísio, a light mulatto with a nasal voice, could not forbear making one cruel comment:

"What surprises me isn't so much that the mother agreed as that the daughter did."

A triumphant smile appeared on Rosa's lips:

"Well, that's where you're wrong. It took a lot of persuading to get her to agree to not having me with her. She wanted me right by her the whole time. She even threatened to break off the marriage."

"Why aren't you, then?"

"I'll tell you just one thing and that's enough. Thanks to you,

I can sit up here in this rathole and watch my daughter be married. But she'll enter this church on her father's arm. He's recognized her legally and adopted her as his own daughter, just like his legitimate daughters, the ones his wife gave him. Now just tell me if you think I'm paying too high a price, because I'm her mother and I don't think so."

"Everyone knows best about his own affairs, ma'am. You'll pardon me, I hope."

"No, I want to thank you. You've been mighty good to let us come."

The sacristan left them. For a moment Rosa held back the sobs with her little lace handkerchief. Pedro Archanjo, lips firmly closed, stared straight ahead and saw shadows form between the images and altars.

"Don't you understand either?" Rosa asked when she was able to speak. "You know I had to make up my mind. One day he told me: 'Miminha's the daughter I love best of all, and I want her to be just as much my daughter and heiress as the other two. I've already told them so at home. I've even told Maria Amélia'— that's his wife's name—'and I've had a notary make all the arrangements. There's just one condition . . .' I didn't even ask what the condition was; all I wanted to know was what his wife had said. He spoke right up: 'She said she doesn't have anything against Miminha, that Miminha's innocent and it isn't her fault, you're the only one she's angry with.' And while I was still laughing because that spiteful woman was mad, he told me the worst: 'My condition for making Miminha legitimate is for her to be brought up by her aunts instead of in your house.' 'But won't I ever see my little girl any more?' I asked him. 'Oh yes, whenever you want to; but my sisters will bring her up and she'll live in their house and only come here once in a while. Do you agree, or don't you want what's best for your daughter?' That was when I made a pact with him. It wasn't a written contract, and he's kept his part of the bargain; how could I not keep mine? Just because I'm black doesn't mean I can't keep my word. Now do you see? It was for Miminha's own good! You don't see, I know you don't. You wanted me to fight for my rights. You think I don't know that?"

The sacristan began lighting the lamps below them as the first guests entered the cathedral in a splendor of flowers and light. Pedro Archanjo said nothing but:

"How do you know what I think?"

"I know everything about you, Pedro, more than I know about myself; I know all your thoughts. Who do you think I danced for all my life? Go on, say it! Only for two people: my father Oxalá and you; and you didn't want me."

"What about Miminha's father and *Compadre* Lídio?"

"Why do you speak to me that way? What did I do wrong? Jerônimo took me out of a bad life. When he took me away with him, I was just a prostitute passed around from one man to another, I had no say about it. He gave me food, and a house to live in, and good clothes, and even love. He was good to me, Pedro. Everybody's afraid of him—women, I mean, even his own wife. Well, he always acted right with me. He took me out of that life, he was a comfort to me, and he never raised a hand against me. He registered Miminha's name in the notary's book, just like he was telling everybody: 'She's my own daughter, the same as the other two.' "

"Except that she has no mother." Archanjo's voice came from the last remaining shadows: the lamps' brilliance covered the bitter words.

"What use would her mother have been? A low-down kept woman who used to be a whore, a black samba dancer who lifted her skirts every time she heard the drums? When he took Miminha away, I said: 'I won't give up my saint. Don't count on me when it's a day of obligation.' And wasn't that true as long as I've lived? Tell me! Wasn't it?"

"Yes, it was. On days of obligation and in the Tent with Lídio."

"That's right. He took my daughter away to live with his old maid sisters and he would only let me see her once a week. It was for Miminha's own good and I agreed to it, but I was eating my heart out because I was only good enough to go to bed with but not good enough to raise my own daughter. When they took my baby away I almost went crazy, Pedro. My eyes went blind and

my mind went dark. I ran to the Terreiro then, to get it out of
my system and try to find some comfort. And I ran into
Lídio . . ."

Her voice was such a low and broken murmur that it did not
reach the nave but was born and died in the dark corner behind
the choir grill. Archanjo could scarcely hear her.

"Lídio! He's the best man I ever met. Next to him you're just
a no-count nigger, Pedro. But one thing came out all wrong. Instead of meeting up with Lídio that night I should have met up
with you. Who do you think I danced for all those years? Just
for Oxalá and you, my own Pedro, I swear it. You know it's true
and if that dance never went any further it's because that's the
way you wanted it."

"If it had been anyone else but Lídio . . . You just told me
the reason yourself."

The guests were beginning to fill the cathedral. The women,
dressed to the teeth for this chic wedding, the most talked about of
the season, sat down in a rustle of laughter and spreading skirts.
The men gathered at the back of the nave to talk. A few people
—godparents, close relatives of the bride and groom, city and
state authorities—occupied the two ranks of chairs nearest the
main altar which were usually reserved for ecclesiastical dignitaries. Every so often Rosa recognized someone and pointed him
out:

"Look, Altamiro's father and mother! Now they're my relatives, Pedro. I've got lots of rich white relatives." She laughed, but
the laugh was a wry one.

The boy's mother waddled in, a stout lady with a kind face.
The father, a cacao colonel, was thin, blond, and nervous; all he
lacked was a horse and whip. He walked with his head held high
and a proud smile on his lips under a honey-colored mustache—
a foreigner.

"A gringo?" Archanjo asked.

"He's not, but his father was French, I think; his surname is
Lavigne. That man's got good sense, Pedro. A gringo like that
and rich as can be—well, he came to see me and brought his wife,
and he said: 'Dona Rosa, your daughter's going to be my son's

wife, my daughter-in-law. My house is yours; we're relatives
from now on.' If it was up to him I'd be right up there at the
altar. Him and the boy both."

"The groom?"

"Yes, Altamiro. They're good people, Pedro. But if I had
insisted on my rights, Miminha's father's family wouldn't have
come, and those aunts who were like a mother and father to her.
Don't you think I was right not to make a fuss? I can see from
here, Pedro."

A contented hum rose from the church; the party was warm-
ing up. Pedro Archanjo recognized Professor Nilo Argolo with
Dona Augusta on his arm. That was the only time he smiled during the ceremony. Rosa, growing more and more tense, squeezed
his arm nervously.

"There are the aunts! They're coming in: that means Miminha's here."

Two tall, proud old ladies with grizzled hair took their places
near the altar, directly in front of the groom's parents. The choir
was full; someone tried out the organ.

"There's Altamiro with his godmother, the senator's wife."

Pedro Archanjo liked the boy's looks: his blond hair and
coloring were like his father's, and he had inherited his mother's
slightly ingenuous air.

Salvador society had turned out *en masse*, and people had even
come from Ilheus and Itabuna. The Lavignes harvested thousands
of bushels of cacao a year, and as if all that money weren't enough
for him, the boy was a lawyer besides. The bride's father, a
tobacco planter and exporter, was explosive, noble, violent, and
dissolute; he had won, lost, and recovered fortunes. The mother,
the women whispered, was a Negress covered with gold and
precious stones; his concubine, a voodoo sorceress who had kept
him under her spell for more than twenty years; what can you
do when you're under a *macumba* spell? They say he was the
worst woman-chaser you ever saw, but the only one he really
loved, all his life long, was that Negress, the girl's mother. The
girl is precious, just adorable, the prettiest thing you ever
saw. . . .

The rumble of the organ turned to music, the hubbub rose in

the nave, and the choir broke into the Wedding March. Rosa de Oxalá pressed Archanjo's arm; her breast was heaving and her eyes were wet.

Miminha in her white lace dress, daughter of the most beautiful Negress in Bahia and the last hot-headed lord of the Recôncavo, walked down the red carpet on her father's arm. When he took his other two daughters to the altar the father had walked that identical way twice before over the same carpet, with the same lights and flowers, to the sound of that same music. But never before had he crossed the nave with such pride. The first two girls were dear to him because they were his flesh and blood. But this one, the dearly beloved, had been born of his flesh and blood and love.

Dr. Jerônimo de Alcântara Pacheco had possessed many women: had countless passionate love affairs with prostitutes and married women, virgins to be abducted and deflowered, and marriage to a wife of noble lineage. But real love had touched him only once, for black Rosa. Even when their daughter was the only bond remaining between them and Rosa, mortally wounded in her pride, had demanded her freedom, he would sometimes come to her at night like a man possessed in search of her unforgettable body, ready to kill to have it. Rosa never turned him away, and as long as he lived she considered him master of a part of her being.

She bit the lace handkerchief, tore it with her teeth, fought down her sobs, and finally rested her head on Archanjo's bosom: Oh, my daughter! The priest prayed, raised his voice in a sermon, spoke of the groom's talent and the bride's loveliness, the nobility of the two families united at that moment by the indissoluble bonds of holy matrimony. For Rosa de Oxalá the moment had arrived to accept a new commitment.

The cathedral emptied little by little. Miminha left on her husband's arm, followed by her aunts, the groom's parents, the godparents, the guests, and the haughty Alcântara. The music stopped and all was quiet again. The sacristan put out the lights, first the candles and then the lamps. The shadows grew thick; only two candles lit the darkness and the solitude of the saints.

"Did Lídio tell you?"

"What?"

"I'm never going back to the Tent, not to sleep, not even to visit. Not ever again, Pedro, that's finished."

He asked why, though he guessed the reason.

"Pedro, now I'm the mother of a married woman, Dr. Altamiro's wife, and I'm related to the Lavignes. I want the right to see my daughter, Pedro, to go to her house, to be accepted by her people. I want to be able to raise my grandchildren, Pedro."

Her firm, resolute voice echoed in the stillness:

"One time when Miminha was a baby, I let them take her away from me. Then I was all alone in the world and free to do what I did. But that's finished now. Rosa de Oxalá is gone." She took Pedro Archanjo's hand and held it between her own.

"What about your saint?"

"I made it right; Mother Majé let me. She got up out of bed to do what had to be done." She looked at the man standing with bowed head, his gaze lost in the darkness: "You wouldn't have me, in spite of all the times I offered myself. And now it's too late."

They heard the sacristan's steps on the ladder; it was time to go. They were in each other's arms for one long kiss, the first and last. It's too late, Master Pedro, it's too late now, it's no use. Rosa de Oxalá vanished among the shadows of the church. She left as she had come. A lifetime, a second.

I I

When Pedro Archanjo finally got there, *ogans* and *iaôs* ran to meet him with tears and lamentations:

"Hurry, hurry, she keeps calling for you. That's all she says: 'Ojuobá, where's Ojuobá?' "

Majé Bassan's eyes opened when she heard his echoing footsteps:

"Is it you, son?"

Her hand, a dry, fragile leaf, pointed to a chair. Archanjo sat down, took her hand, and kissed it. The old woman concentrated every bit of strength left in her dying body and began her story in a voice that was a whisper. In a mixture of Portuguese and Yoruba words and phrases, she taught the last lesson:

"*Umbé oxirê fun ipakô tô Ijenan*, there was a festival in Ijenan's *terreiro*. It was a big festival for Ogun, and many people came to see Ogun dance. Ogun Aiaká danced a fine dance to gladden the eyes of the people, who were tired of suffering so much. When he came to the best part of the dance, *sarapebé*, the messenger, came and said the soldiers were coming with loaded guns to stop Ogun's feast and ruin Ijenan's *terreiro*. They came galloping up on horseback; they couldn't wait to get there and start hitting people. Ogun heard what the messenger said, the warning Oxóssi had sent, and he went into the jungle and whistled up two cobras, each longer and more full of poison than the other. He placed them in the center of the floor, those two hanks of poison all coiled up with their heads sticking up and their poison tongues darting out, and their eyes fixed on the door. Ogun didn't turn a hair, he danced right in front of the door and waited for the soldiers. It didn't take them long to get there. They jumped down off their horses and without a by-your-leave pulled out their guns to club people with. Ogun said to the soldiers: All who come in peace can enter the Terreiro and dance at my feast. My heart is honey and flowers to my friends but bane to the enemy. For them my heart is a well of poison. He pointed to the two cobras coiled up in their venom and the soldiers were afraid, but orders are orders, and orders from the barracks and the police have no room for mercy, no appeal, and no recall. So the soldiers started after Ogun, their weapons raised. *Ogun kapê dan meji, dan pelú oniban.* Ogun called the cobras and the cobras rose up before the soldiers. Ogun warned them one more time: if you want a fight you'll have one, if you want war you'll have war, the cobras will bite you and kill you, and there won't be a single soldier left. The cobras darted out their poison tongues and the soldiers cried help and jumped onto their horses and ran away, they ran away as fast as they could go, because while he danced without ever stopping Ogun had called the two cobras, *Ogun kapê dan meji, dan pelú oniban.*"

Pedro Archanjo repeated: *Ogun kapê dan meji, dan pelú oniban,* the immemorial curse, the terrible threat of all the evil in the world, of eternal misfortune, spell and imprecation, Iyá's parting gift. Pedrito Gordo had unleashed his terrible wolf pack on Bahia, had given his minions a free hand to invade *terreiros,* destroy shrines, strike *babalaôs* and *pais-de-santo,* arrest adepts and *iaôs, iyakêkêrês,* and *iyalorixás.* I'm going to clean up all this filth! He gave strict orders to the police, organized his corps of thugs, and launched a holy war.

Majé Bassan, the sweet and terrible, the wise and prudent, closed her eyes. Yansan's shout was heard far away at the head of the *eguns,* the host of the dead. Xangô danced on the *terreiro* and Pedro Archanjo locked the pain inside his chest: "Our Mother is dead."

1 2

From the doorway Pedrito could see the fear on the faces of his secret police, four members of the "gangster bodyguard," as an opposition newspaper described them: "A gang of thugs promoted to police agents by the state government tries to destroy our presses."

With his suit of English broadcloth and his Panama hat, his manicured fingernails, closely shaved beard, pearl stickpin and long cigarette holder, law school graduate Pedrito Gordo, the feared and hated assistant chief of police, looked like nothing but a dandy—stoutish, middle-aged, and, one would have said, futile and inconsequential. He threw away the stub of his cigarette and cleaned the holder: his miserable curs were afraid.

Enéas Pombo, erstwhile king of the animal game and master of the city, now in disgrace and on the losing side, repeated, revolver steady in his hand:

"Whoever comes one step closer's a dead man."

The secret agents eyed one another: Candinho the Boaster, Samuel Coralsnake, Zacarias da Gomeia, and Mirandolino, the wild beast of Lençois. A long and bloody chronicle, part fact, part fiction, but all proclaiming the brave feats of Enéas Pombo, populator of whole cemeteries who never missed his man, held them back.

"You're a bunch of chickenhearted cowards!" said Pedrito.

As he spoke the words he thrust them aside; all he had in his hand was his slim, flexible cane. Raising his gun, Pombo measured the police chief with his eyes:

"Don't come any closer, Dr. Pedrito, or I'll shoot you dead!"

The cane whistled in the air like a whip or a razor blade and slashed the gambler's face, one, two cracks of the cane, and two bloody marks. Desperately Pombo, blinded with pain, fired without taking aim; but the police chief was faster. Short and squat as he was, no one would have imagined he could move so quickly. At the sight of the blood the secret agents revived and rushed at Pombo, intrepid champions once more.

"Take him away!" Pedrito ordered.

Sam Coralsnake went over to the drawer where the pool tickets and the money were, while the other three men shoved the gambler toward the door. The police chief, withering scorn in his voice, told them exactly what he thought of them:

"Cowards. Queers. Assholes."

When he stepped outside the curious crowd made way for him. With a wink at the girl in the café across the street, Pedrito Gordo got into his car and was off like a shot—he was said to be the best driver in Bahia.

The four heroes of the evening's raid strutted into the antechamber at Police Headquarters, where they found several companions in arms of the same noble lineage as themselves: Goody Ferreira, Mother's Milk, Inocêncio Seven Deaths, Ricardo Cutlass, and Bighearted Zé. They told them about Pombo's arrest and the downfall of a king. The empty throne was being auctioned off in the palace. Who would make the best offer?

The four bullies were worried, all the same. Dr. Pedrito had made himself very plain. He had gotten the better of blustering Enéas Pombo, armed only with a cane; he had brushed aside the assassin's sinister reputation, ignoring his revolver and his infallible aim, while they—the chickens, the assholes—had just stood there and watched.

"Chickens!" Bighearted Zé spit out the word before leaving on an errand: a guard had told him he was to go to the palace right away to escort Dr. Pedrito and the governor—"Assholes!"

Heads lowered, they heard him out in silence; they would rather have faced Enéas Pombo with a gun than Bighearted Zé without one. Zé never disputed the chief's orders or hesitated to carry them out. No *caboclo* waving a gun in the air would have stopped him from doing what Pedrito said. Shooting and killing were normal, everyday routine to him. As for dying, he'd die when his number was up. Bighearted Zé, a black man the size of a two-story house, was Pedrito's right-hand man, and he didn't know the color of fear.

Shamed by the chief's epithets and their colleague's jeers, the four men asked one another what they could do to get back in their boss's good graces. Pedrito Gordo didn't fool around. When he lost confidence in one of his followers, he despatched him in a hurry and for good: he retired him to a nice shallow grave; gangsters don't deserve any better. How many men had he sent to a better world so far? Izaltino, Justo de Seabra, Crispim da Bóia, and Fulgêncio Knife-Sticker, just to name the most notorious. One day they were giving orders and counterorders, swaggering through town, guzzling free booze, taking money from the Spaniards, dishing out beatings and arrests for any reason or none; and the next they were lying in the morgue, "killed in the line of duty," according to the police bulletin and the official gazette. Somehow or other they had lost their standing with the all-powerful assistant chief of police, and that was that.

They would have to find a job to do right away, anything to restore the prestige which Enéas Pombo and his revolver had brought so low. Preferably something spectacular. But what?

"What if we went out and busted up some *candomblés?*" suggested Candinho Faroleiro.

"You've hit it right on the nose. Dr. Pedrito's gonna like that," seconded Mirandolino.

"Today's Xangô's day, a lot of *terreiros*'ll be busy tonight"— the tip could be trusted; it came from Zacarias da Gomeia, who was in the know. The fellow was sure it was a *macumba* spell that had given him smallpox and ruined his face, a black voodoo spell ordered straight from Exú by a hooker in the Zone. In addition to the assistant police chief's ideological, erudite reasons, Zacarias da Gomeia clearly had reasons of his own for throwing himself into a war without quarter against the *candomblé*.

On a small bookshelf in Pedrito Gordo's office was an array of books and pamphlets, some of which he had kept from his student days. Others he had read later and marked with red pencil, while still others were only recently published. *The Three Schools of Penology: Classical, Anthropological, and Critical*, by Antônio Moniz Sodré de Aragão, an expert of the Italian school; *Degenerates and Criminals*, by Manuel Bernardo Calmon du Pin e Almeida; *Comparative Craniometry of Human Specimens of Bahia from the Evolutionist and Medico-Legal Point of View*, by João Batista de Sá Oliveira; *Seeds of Crime*, by Aurelino Leal. As a student Pedrito Gordo had learned from these books and the works of Nina Rodrigues and Oscar Freire, in what little free time he did not spend in bawdy houses, that Negroes and mestizos had a natural tendency toward crime which was aggravated by the barbarous practices of *candomblé*, samba circles, and *capoeira*, schools for criminals which put the finishing touches to those born murderers, thieves, and scoundrels. Himself a white Bahian, half blond and half freckle-faced, redheaded *sarará*, Chief Pedrito thought the display of these customs a threat to all decent families, a mockery of culture and the Latinity in which intellectuals, politicians, tradesmen, landowners, and the élite in general took so much pride.

The new volumes added since his school days were principally works by Professors Nilo Argolo and Oswaldo Fontes: *Crime Among the Blacks; Miscegenation, Degeneracy, and Crime; Psy-*

*chic and Mental Degeneracy Among the Mestizos in Tropical
Countries; The Races of Man and Penal Responsibility in Brazil;
Pathological Anthropology: The Mestizos.* When certain dema-
gogues sought support among the rabble, the plebs, the common
folk, by speaking out against the suppression of popular customs
and the violent methods used by the police to silence all drums,
rattles, bells, *berimbaus,* and gourds and to put a stop to the dancing of devotees and to *capoeira* wrestling, Assistant Police Chief
Pedrito Gordo would show off the anthropological and juridical
culture contained on his bookshelf: "These are the authorities who
affirm that no black can be trusted. It's science that has declared
war on their antisocial practices, not me." With a gesture of humility he would add: "All I'm trying to do is pull the evil up by
the roots to keep it from propagating. The day we put a stop to
all this dirty business, the crime rate in Salvador will go down
enormously, and at long last we will be able to say that we live
in a civilized country."

If the opposition papers accused him of color prejudice and of
instigating race hatred, Pedrito pointed out articles in which those
same tabloids, on other occasions, had called for forceful police
action against *candomblés* and *afoxés, capoeiras* and festivals in
honor of Yemanjá. Now in the opposition, they were attacking
the government and the police: "The pasquinaders with short
memories are conniving with a mob of actual or potential criminals."

In an interview in the government press *à propos* of the police
campaign, Professor Nilo Argolo described it as righteous and
praiseworthy: "A holy war, a holy crusade to recover the citadels
of civilization in this besmirched city of ours." He enthusiastically
compared Pedrito Gordo to Richard Coeur de Lion.

A holy war! The crusaders set out that night of Xangô to
strike down the infidel. Besides the four intrepid warriors of the
police raid on the gambler's stronghold, there were two other
noble cavaliers in the Latin hosts of civilization: Mother's Milk, so
called because he had a habit of beating his mother, and Goody
Ferreira, a specialist in beating prisoners with the flat of his saber.
Both were authentic representatives of the culture the assistant
chief of police was defending with fire and sword.

They sallied out in the early evening, each armed with his club, a cudgel fit to raise welts on the toughest hide, the lance of these latter-day crusaders. And they made a good job of it. The first three houses they invaded were easy: small *axés*, modest *terreiros*, celebrations just beginning. They laid about them with their cudgels. Soft strains of music and cries of pain from old men and women only spurred the warriors on in the execution of their civilizing mission. When there was no one left to hit they amused themselves by destroying the drums, the shrines, and the dressing rooms.

News of their errand began to run before them, silencing orchestras, causing circles of adepts and *iaôs* to melt away, dousing lights, putting an end to feasts and obligations. Heads bowed, men and women withdrew to their homes while the *orixás* returned to the mountains, forests, and oceans from which they had come to dance and sing on the *terreiros*.

The crusaders suddenly found themselves without anyone left to beat and were obliged to interrupt their amusing game. Pleased with the victories they had won, confident of regaining favor in the eyes of their terrible chief, they went from bar to bar demanding, not only free drinks, but exact information. Where are they holding a *candomblé?* Come on, hurry up, give us names and addresses! Keep your trap shut and you'll get hit over the head; sing out and you can count on us when you need us. And that was how they learned of the special celebration in Sabají's Terreiro on the outskirts of town.

In the tent, upward of ten devotees showed off their rich garments as they took part in the dance. In the center Xangô was mounted on a mettlesome steed, the mulatto Felipe Mulexê. It did one's heart good to watch that dance; the fame of Mulexê's Xangô had spread far and wide.

Manuel de Praxedes, who was protector of the room and responsible for the good order of the feast and the well-being of the guests, was attentive to every detail. When he saw them coming, full of oaths and laughter, he recognized the pack of criminals at once. The sinister face of Zacarias da Gomeia, eaten by the black pox—without eyebrows, without a nose—broke into a shout at the threshold.

"Now it's Zacarias da Gomeia's turn to dance the dance of the singing club!"

A bit unsteady on his feet from the rum he had drunk, Sam Coralsnake tried to enter the tent, but Manuel de Praxedes, mindful of his duty, demanded respect for the saints. "Go fuck yourself," retorted Coralsnake, and tried to push his way in. With one blow Manuel de Praxedes flung him back against his pock-marked colleague and the truncheon changed owners. In the stevedore's hands it became a terrible weapon, a mighty sword. All hell broke loose.

Peace-loving men and happy *orixás* who had met to celebrate on the *terreiro* found themselves interrupted and threatened. A few of the bravest joined Manuel de Praxedes in resisting. Stories are told of that fight to this very day: how Xangô gave the secret police invisible lashes with his whip and the giant Praxedes grew so tall he looked like Oxóssi, lord of the jungle; how the cudgel turned into St. George's lance killing dragons. Then Zacarias da Gomeia pulled out his revolver and fired the first shot from where he was lying on the ground.

Though wounded in the shoulder and bleeding copiously, Felipe Mulexê, Xangô's steed, went on dancing as fearlessly as ever. Following Zacarias's example, the other crusaders drew their revolvers. They had to shoot their way in.

Emptied of everyone else, the room held only Xangô bleeding as he danced and Manuel de Praxedes swinging his cudgel in the middle of empty space. The policemen rushed him in a body: let's get that son-of-a-bitch and take him to the police station and teach him what's what. At the head of the six heroes was Sam Coralsnake, wild for revenge. When we get him down to headquarters I'll skin him alive. The nerve of him. So you like to fight and play voodoo, do you? I'm going to hit you so hard, you son-of-a-bitch, there won't be enough left of you to make a dwarf, much less a giant.

In one enormous leap—a miracle of Xangô, people said— Manuel de Praxedes jumped out the window. Not, however, before giving Sam Coralsnake a smack in the mouth which relieved him of three front teeth, one of them a gold one which was the secret agent's pet and pride.

Xangô disappeared into the jungle, his shoulder bleeding from the dance of the whips. The gangsters spread out in search of the fugitives. Oh, if they could only get Felipe Mulexê and his damned Xangô! Oh, if they could only lay their hands on Manuel de Praxedes, what fun they'd have! But there was not a trace of them in the dark woods, only the hooting of owls.

Destroying the ritual objects was not enough to calm the crusaders' fury and hate. They set fire to the tent, and flames consumed Sabají's Terreiro—to set an example.

The holy war, the civilizing crusade, went on for years. As long as the reign of Pedrito Gordo lasted, that dandy and police chief, that law graduate who had read books and learned theories, there was daily violence, without appeal or amnesty. Dr. Pedrito had promised to put an end to witchcraft, sambas, and all the nigger business. "I'm going to clean up the city of Bahia."

When Manuel de Praxedes left his house in Baronesses' Alley after lunch a few days later, he took the whole charge of Sam Coralsnake's revolver in his back. One shot after another, six in all. He fell on his face without so much as a groan.

People came running from every direction. The murderer told them:

"That'll teach him. Let me get through."

The crowd did not let him through. Shouting for vengeance they surrounded the murderer, and their fury was so great that the killer's strutting turned to piss. He was afraid he would be lynched right there in the street. He threw away his gun and fell on his knees, begging for mercy. The police arrived, pushed their way through the crowd, and took away the prisoner. Some of the people followed the patrolmen to Police Headquarters.

When the criminal and his weapon had been turned over to the proper authorities, the people were dismissed. The manager of a movie house in Shoemakers' Hollow repeated to the assistant chief of police:

"He was caught in the act of murder."

"Don't worry, leave him to us."

The same afternoon at about six o'clock, Sam Coralsnake, secret agent of the auxiliary police chief, a murderer caught *in flagrante* and handed over to the police for justice to be done, was seen in the company of Bighearted Zé, Inocêncio Seven Deaths, Mirandolino, Zacarias da Gomeia, and Ricardo Cutlass in Baronesses' Alley, taunting and threatening the friends and neighbors who were holding a wake over the body of Manuel de Praxedes.

Assistant Police Chief Pedrito Gordo had wanted to know exactly what had occurred.

"A voodooist attacked me in the street. He called your mother names, Chief, and wanted to belt me one, so I shot him. I wasn't about to take any lip from a witch doctor."

All's fair in war, said the auxiliary chief. The band of agents swaggered up and down the street and then went to roost in a nearby bar, where they drank and did not pay. All's fair in war, and soldiers in a holy war have their privileges.

14

Zabela, lame with rheumatism, exploded in pain and indignation:

"Tadeu's a civilized human being and those Gomeses are a bunch of backwoods yokels from the Sertão. Why won't they have him? Because they're rich?"

"Because they're white."

"White? Master Pedro, don't talk to me about whiteness in Bahia. Don't make me laugh, it hurts too much. How many times do I have to tell you that when you talk about white blood in Bahia it's just like talking about white sugar from our mills: all of it's brown. If that's true in the Recôncavo, imagine the Sertão. Those Gomeses don't deserve a boy like Tadeu. If it weren't for that darling Lu, who comes here to see me and talks to me for hours . . . If it weren't for her, my advice to Tadeu would be to look for a better family. Those Gomeses, honestly . . . I know them very well indeed, especially the grandmother, *mon cher*, old Eufrásia. She's always in church these days, but in the old days she used to kick up her heels, believe you me."

Pedro Archanjo did not hide his resentment:

"All of those people are just alike. Some of them come right out and say what they think: that the place for Negroes and mulattoes is the slave cabins. Others call themselves liberals, egalitarians, and you'd never know they were prejudiced until somebody starts talking about marriage. You couldn't have imagined anyone friendlier and more open than that family was with Tadeu. When he was a student, Tadeu was hardly out of their house. He had lunch and dinner there, and lots of times he slept in Astério's room. They treated him just like a son. But once he mentioned marriage things changed in a hurry. Zabela, be honest now, tell me one thing: If you had a daughter, would you let her marry a Negro or a mulatto? Tell me the truth, now."

Overcoming her pain ("I'm being eaten alive by a pack of dogs, they're gnawing me all over"), the old woman sat straight up in her chair:

"Pedro Archanjo, I won't have it! If I had lived all my life in Santo Amaro or Cachoeira or right here with the Argolos, the Ávilas, and the Gonçalveses, maybe you would have the right to ask me that question. But are you forgetting I've lived most of my life in Paris? If I had a daughter, Master Pedro, I'd let her marry anyone she liked—white, black, Chinese, a Syrian peddler, a Jew from a synagogue, absolutely anyone she wanted to. And if she didn't want to get married at all, then she wouldn't have to"—she groaned in pain and dropped back into her chair. "Do you want to know a secret, Master Pedro? There's nobody like a black man in bed, that's what my grandmother Virgínia used to say"—she winked a round, malicious eye. "My grandmother Virgínia Argolo, who married Colonel Fortunato Araújo, Black Araújo. She always said just what she thought, and she used to rub Fortunato in the noses of all those brown-sugar baronesses: 'I wouldn't trade one of my black man's eggs for two dozen of your white ones!' " Indignant again, the old woman came back to the original subject: "Refuse Tadeu, a civilized human being! What nonsense!"

"I haven't refused Tadeu, I'm going to marry him, God willing!" answered Lu's voice from the hall.

There were pitying exclamations from Zabela: "*Ma chérie, ma pauvre fille, ma petite,*" and a smile lightened the cloud on Archanjo's face.

"Is it you, Lu?"

"Good morning, Zabela. Please give me your blessing, Father."

Father: Lu had been calling him that for some time. Under the protection of Archanjo, Lídio, and Frei Timóteo, she had gone for a lark to the *candomblé* with a group of her girl friends. There she had seen adepts, young *iaôs,* and even men, some of them white-haired, kiss Archanjo's hand and say: Give me your blessing, Father. "Why do they call him Father?" she had asked Lídio Corró. "Because of the respect they bear Ojuobá. All those people and many more are Pedro Archanjo's children." From then on she called him "Father" and always asked his blessing, half in jest, half in earnest.

When she told Tadeu good-bye on the wharf Lu had compared the two faces, her sweetheart's and Archanjo's. What a striking resemblance! They're only godfather and godson, but they look like father and son, as God is my witness.

Tadeu, always reticent about his family, never alluded to his father; he had never known that mysterious Canhoto from whom he had sprung. As for his mother, all he remembered of her was her beauty. "My father died when I was a little boy and I don't even remember him; my mother was very good-looking. When she realized I wanted to study, she turned me over to Godfather Archanjo. She died not long after that, while I was still studying for my college entrance exams."

Lu was curious and tried to penetrate more of the Canhoto riddle, but did not persist long, for she soon realized how touchy Tadeu was on the subject.

"Darling, is it me or my parents you're going to marry?"

Lu never again mentioned the subject, but perhaps, in the beginning, her "Father" had carried a touch of sarcasm or innuendo. Archanjo pretended to notice nothing and smilingly consented to being addressed in that way. He would give her his blessing, and responding in a jesting tone mingled with affection and respect just like the girl's, he called her "my little daughter, *axé!*" as if she had been a *iaô* in the *terreiro*.

As she knelt at Zabela's feet, Lu explained:

"The atmosphere still isn't very pleasant at home. I waited until Daddy went out and came running here to get a breath of fresh air. Now that Tadeu's gone back to Rio and Mamma's not quite so afraid I'll run off and marry him, she's loosened the string a little."

"If you did run off it would be your right. And his."

"The best thing is to wait. It's only eight more months and they'll be over soon; after all, I've already waited three years. The day I'm twenty-one, there'll be no one who can stop me."

Whose idea had it been that it was best to wait, Lu's or Tadeu's? Pedro Archanjo would have loved to know. Or would he, really?

"Maybe things will change at home in the meantime. Tadeu thinks they might. After all, it would be better to have the family's consent and not start our married life with a quarrel."

Such sensible ideas! Whose were they? The girl's, or the engineer's? Oh my, Tadeu Canhoto, you're climbing the ladder fast, but you're awfully prudent about it!

Already successful at the start of his career, Tadeu was earning good money, respected by everyone, and highly regarded by his chief and his colleagues. He had taken his first vacation in three years and gone to Bahia, bearing a letter from Paulo de Frontin to Colonel Gomes: "Dear sir, I have learned of Dr. Tadeu Canhoto's intention of asking for your esteemed daughter's hand in marriage, and I hasten to congratulate you in advance. Her suitor has worked with me for the past three years. He is one of the most talented and efficient of the engineers who are busy transforming the old city of Rio de Janeiro into a great modern capital." He went on to praise the boy's "unblemished morals, sterling character, and brilliant talent." The road to success was open before him. He congratulated the Gomes family again on the happy occasion of the betrothal, sure that the colonel and his excellent wife could not wish for a better son-in-law.

But the distinguished personage's letter of praise was of no avail. Tadeu was received with demonstrations of joy—"Well, look who's here, Tadeu, the prodigal son!"—but felt the atmosphere change abruptly when, having asked to speak to the colonel in private, he handed him his boss's letter and asked for Lu's hand.

The *fazendeiro's* initial surprise was so great that he read the letter through to the end and listened to the engineer's brief explanation without interrupting him:

". . . to ask for the hand of your daughter Lu."

Only then did the smile vanish from the colonel's lips.

"You say you want to marry Lu?" The rancher's puzzled voice held nothing but surprise.

"Yes, Colonel. We love each other and we want to get married."

"You . . ." Suddenly the change was complete and the voice took on a hard edge of anger. "You mean that Lu is aware of your ridiculous intention?"

"I would not have asked to speak with you, Colonel, if she had not authorized me to do so, and we don't consider our"—he emphasized the possessive pronoun—"intention ridiculous."

Colonel Gomes's shout, the roar of a gored and dangerous animal, resounded through the house.

"Emília, come here quick! And bring Lu! At once!"

Hostile eyes stared at Tadeu as if they had never seen him before. Dona Emília came in wiping her hands on her apron; she had been directing the cook in the confection of a dessert that Tadeu especially liked, sure that their son's best friend would be staying to dinner. Lu appeared at almost the same moment, smiling, nervous, and tense. The *fazendeiro* turned to her:

"Lu, this gentleman here has surprised me with an absurd request and he says he has done it with your approval. That's a lie, isn't it?"

"If you mean that Tadeu came here to ask for my hand, Father, everything he told you is true. I love Tadeu and I want to marry him."

The colonel made a visible effort to keep himself from rushing at the girl and slapping her. A good whipping was what she deserved.

"Leave the room! I'll speak to you later."

Lu smiled encouragingly at Tadeu and left the room. When she heard the frightful news, Dona Emília emitted a sort of muffled groan: *Ai, Senhor!*

"Did you know anything about this, Emília? Were you keeping it from me?"

"I knew nothing about it, no more than you did. I couldn't be more surprised. She never gave the slightest sign."

The colonel did not ask for her opinion, perhaps because he imagined he knew what it was or perhaps because, to his way of thinking, a wife's job was to look after the house, not to interfere in serious matters. He turned to Tadeu:

"You have abused the trust we placed in you. Because you were my son's classmate we welcomed you here without holding your color or your parentage against you. I understand you're intelligent. Why, then, didn't you realize that we didn't bring our daughter up to marry a Negro? Now get out and never come back to this house again or we'll throw you out."

"I'm glad the only thing you have against me is my color."

"Out! Get out of this house!"

Tadeu withdrew, walking at a normal pace, while Dona Emília sank in a faint. The shouts of the furious colonel could be heard from the sidewalk. Lu would have to face the wild animals, thought Tadeu, but she was strong and she knew what to expect. In Zabela's house the day before they had examined every aspect of the problem, foreseen all the possibilities, and searched for a solution to each one. Tadeu Canhoto loved mathematical calculations and drawing straight lines, and his decisions were based on study and analysis.

In spite of having expected it, Pedro Archanjo was beside himself when he heard of the rebuff. He raved and lost his head, in a way that was very rare with him. "I only lose my head over women," he was in the habit of saying.

"Hypocrites! That bunch of hypocrites and white trash!"

It was Tadeu who restrained him.

"What's this, Godfather? Calm down, don't insult my relatives. They're just a family of rich landowners like any other and they have the same prejudices as all the rest. The colonel thinks it would be a disgrace to let his daughter marry a mulatto; he'd rather see her live and die a hysterical old maid. But they're not bad people, and deep down I think their prejudice is superficial and won't last."

"Are you making excuses for them? Are you defending them? Now it's my turn to be surprised, Tadeu Canhoto!"

"No, of course I'm not defending them or excusing them, Godfather. To my way of thinking there's nothing worse than color prejudice and nothing better than a mixture of races. I learned that from you and your books. That's why I don't want to make the Gomeses out to be some kind of monsters. They're decent people. I'm sure Astério will back us up. I didn't write him anything about it because I wanted to surprise him, but in his letters to me he's always criticizing North American racism, 'unacceptable to a Brazilian,' he calls it."

" 'Unacceptable to a Brazilian!' But when it comes to letting their sister or daughter marry a mulatto or a Negro, they act just like the North American racists."

"Godfather, now it's my turn to be surprised again. Weren't you the one who always said the race problem and its solution were completely different, in fact quite opposite, in Brazil and the United States? That the tendency here, in spite of all obstacles, was the mingling and mixing of races? And now, just because we've come up against one of those obstacles, is that enough to make you change your mind?"

"The truth is it made me mad, Tadeu, madder than I thought it would. What do you intend to do now?"

"Marry Lu, of course."

That was enough to channel Pedro Archanjo's anger:

"I can work out plans for an elopement in a jiffy."

"Elopement? I don't know about that."

"I've done much harder things than that."

He saw himself as initiator of a romantic deed of derring do: *capoeira* wrestlers guarding the street, Lu escaping from her house at dawn, wrapped in fear and a black cloak, a fishing boat with bellying sails carrying the lovers to a safe hiding place in the. Recôncavo, the secret marriage, the Gomeses' rage. It was not for nothing that Pedro Archanjo had interlarded his scientific reading with romances by Alexandre Dumas: "He was a mulatto, you know, the son of a French father and a black mother, and that's a good combination!"

"No, Godfather. There won't be any elopement. Lu and I have already made up our minds what to do. In eight months Lu will be twenty-one. Then she'll be of age and able to settle her own future. If her parents haven't given in by then—and I'm counting on Astério to make them do it—she'll leave home on her birthday and become my wife. It'll be better that way."

"You think so?"

"We both think so, Lu and I. Even if the colonel doesn't give his consent, the fact that we waited for Lu to come of age will make things easier later on. There'll be certain advantages for me, too. I'll go back to Rio tomorrow and come back in eight months."

Pedro Archanjo didn't say yea or nay. Actually, no one had asked for his opinion. At the Tent of Miracles Lídio Corró was dazzling their friends with accounts of Tadeu's success in the capital: Paulo de Frontin consulted him about every slightest detail of the great urbanization plans and made him responsible for the most difficult tasks. As Lídio had it, Tadeu was practically building the new Rio de Janeiro singlehanded.

At Zabela's house Pedro Archanjo heard the girl repeat what Tadeu had said:

"I may be able to persuade them in these next few months."

"Do you think you can do it?"

"Well, what would you think if I told you that Mamma's already halfway won over? Just yesterday she told me she knew Tadeu was a nice boy, if only he weren't so . . ."

"Black."

"Well, you know, when she talks about Tadeu she doesn't call him black any more. She says: 'If he didn't have such a dark complexion . . .'"

Pedro Archanjo was finally able to laugh about it. After all, it was not his business to sit in judgment on the world. Lu and Tadeu would manage things in their own way, and whatever they decided was all right with him. This legalistic, long-drawn-out solution wasn't his way of doing things, and it wasn't the way of Alexandre Dumas, Père, the mulatto son of General Napoléon and the beautiful Negress from Martinique (or was it Guadeloupe? He couldn't remember); if *they* had had anything to say about it, they would stoutheartedly have opted for an immediate elopement.

Now that she had an audience, Zabela launched into stories about the Argolo de Araújo family. "Just listen to me. Fortunato de Araújo, a colonel in the wars of independence, a hero in the battles of Cabrito and Pirajá, known as Black Araújo, entered the noble Argolo family through Grandma Virgínia Gonçalves Argolo's bedroom; and when he did, he took over and gave the orders. He was a fine-looking mulatto, and I was his favorite grandchild. He used to lift me up on the pommel of his saddle and off we'd gallop over hill and dale. He was the one who gave me the nickname, Princess of the Recôncavo. Master Pedro, you're so clever at solving riddles. Can you tell me why the distinguished professor Nilo d'Ávila Argolo de Araújo, that microbe, *le grand con* who's always bragging about his noble ancestors, says so very little about the honorable name of Araújo? Why doesn't he tell about the feats of Colonel Fortunato in the struggle of 1823, why doesn't he tell about how Black Araújo was wounded three times in the fight for Brazilian independence? There never was a braver man in the history of our illustrious family. We have him to thank for whatever we have, including these few wretched pennies I live on. Grandma Virgínia was right to be so proud of him and to say to all those baronesses, countesses, white missies and *toutes les autres garces:* one of my Black Fortunato's eggs is worth ten times as much as *toute cette bande de cocus,* your husbands and lovers, *les imbéciles.*"

It was through Zabela's stories that Pedro Archanjo first became acquainted with the genealogy of the best families of Bahia, and in the course of time he came to know as much about the Ávilas and Argolos, the Cavalcântis and Guimarães, the whole pack of lords with their titles of aristocracy, as he knew about the family ties of those who had come off the slave ships. He knew the grandfathers on both sides, and exactly when the two bloods had mingled.

In the years following his fiftieth birthday celebration, Archanjo pursued his studies, both in the volumes read in his attic or at the Tent, where he kept most of his books in the back room that had been Tadeu's, and in life lived with passion. He had kept himself young; no one would have thought he was fifty-five years old. He still wrestled *capoeira*, still stayed up all night; he was still a good drinker, still crazy about women. After Rosália, or at about the same time, he had installed Quelé, a seventeen-year-old girl, in a house of her own and she had borne him a child. It was a son, of course. Archanjo never had any daughters, except for the "little daughters" in Xangô's *terreiro*.

Women sought him out in the Tent of Miracles, though no more shows or parties were held there after Rosa de Oxalá left. Lídio could not resign himself to that parting; he was incurably heartsick. He made a slow recovery, but was never quite the same again. They had been lovers for more than fifteen years, and the painter of miracles never found a substitute who could erase Rosa's image from his still suffering memory.

In his bedroom was the wooden statuette carved by Damião's friend, Miguel the saint-carver, but it was not very much like

Rosa. Naked it was, with high breasts and traveling buttocks. If
Lídio, the only one to see her with her clothes off, in bed, in his
arms, was never able to capture that splendid vision on canvas,
how could the saint-carver have had the nerve to imagine he could
carve her likeness in *jacaranda* wood? Where was the mouth
hungry for kisses, that fiery belly? When he couldn't sleep at
night Rosa came out of the canvas and the wood and danced for
him in the bedroom.

In the Tent and in the street, in "castles" and "pensions," at
dances and pageants, samba *gafieiras* and novenas, laughing and
singing with whores and maidens, wherever the two *compadres*
went with flute, *cavaquinho*, and guitar, Rosa's absence went with
them. No matter how women tried to please him, Lídio was never
satisfied: no man who had had Rosa could ever forget her, and no
one could take her place. And what of Pedro Archanjo? For him
the pain of loving had begun long before. You'll never know,
compadre Lídio, *meu bom*, what a high price I've paid for your
friendship.

Much had changed at the Tent of Miracles. The printing press
had taken over the big front room and the old lean-to. There was
so much work now that *Mestre* Lídio did not even have time to
draw miracles. When he did agree to do one he had to paint it
on Sunday; the week was too short for all the work he had to do.

The Tent was still the center of neighborhood life, a noisy
place of assembly full of talk, ideas, and projected undertakings.
Persecuted spirit fathers and mothers found refuge there for
themselves and the treasures of the *axés*, and Father Procópio
convalesced there after a beating at the police station that tore
his back to ribbons. But there was no longer a poster on the door
announcing recitals and exhibitions of the samba and the maxixe.
Mané Lima and Fat Fernanda showed off their skill in other halls.
As for the puppet show, it had been retired many years before.
Only once had Trigger and Ding-Dong traded blows over Lilly
Titty, and that was when Zabela had asked to see that famous
"moralistic drama on the snares of friendship."

"*Quelle horreur!* What swine you two are, *des sales cochons!*"
cried the old lady, convulsed with laughter at the gross humor
and low depravity of the performance.

"We lived off those shameless puppets for years," Archanjo explained. "They were our bread and butter."

"You really did come up from the bottom," observed the countess.

"Do you think it's any better on top? Any cleaner?"

Zabela shrugged her shoulders: he was right, there was dirt everywhere, and friendship was sold for a nickel.

But not for a nickel and not for the priceless coin of Rosa de Oxalá's love had Pedro Archanjo sold his friend. This is where I started, and this is where I'll stay. If I've changed at all, and of course I have, if old values have been lost and others taken their place, if a part of my old self has died, that is no reason for me to deny or renounce anything I've ever been. Not even the dirty peepshow. My breast contains mixtures and multitudes. Listen! Lídio, Tadeu, Zabela, Budião, Valdeloir, Damião de Souza, Major of the People and my little boy, listen to me! I want one thing only: to live, to understand what life is, to love my neighbors and all men.

The years had passed and he had one or two white hairs, but not a single wrinkle in his smooth face. Pedro Archanjo, handsome in his well-cared-for clothes, crossed Pelourinho with his usual rolling gait, on his way to the Terreiro de Jesus. Professor Silva Virajá, working in the parasitology lab at the School of Medicine, had become world-famous by analyzing and describing schistosomiasis. In that room the scientist added to our knowledge of dysentery, tugumentary leishmaniosis, Chagas's disease, mycosis, tropical diseases of all sorts. Pedro Archanjo had one more favor to ask: Would Dr. Silva Virajá be one of the sponsors at Tadeu's wedding, along with Professor Bernard of the Polytechnic Institute?

Lu's twenty-first birthday was drawing near. For two months the girl had been in exile on the fazenda with her mother, and now they had brought her back in hopes of interesting her in some worthy suitor. In the course of long conferences with Archanjo, Lídio, and Zabela, Lu examined every feature of their plan.

"Since they won't back down, there's no alternative. Actually, Dad is the one who's dead set against it. If it were only

Mamma, I could persuade her without any trouble, but she thinks through Daddy's head, and Colonel Gomes will never admit he's in the wrong." Her voice betrayed how much she loved and admired her father. "He almost took away Astério's allowance just because he sided with us."

Astério had written to his father expressing his approval of the marriage and praising Tadeu, "to whom I send my fraternal best wishes." "Who asked you?" demanded the colonel in a violent letter. "My daughter will marry the son-in-law I'm pleased to choose for her."

He had already chosen one, to judge by his frequent invitations to Dr. Rui Passarinho for lunches and dinners. An attorney with powerful clients among the big business firms, a man of good connections and high prestige, Dr. Passarinho, at thirty-six, had had no time for flirtations. Early on he had shut himself up in his office and entered the lists of justice; there were some who already considered him a confirmed bachelor. At Mass in São Francisco he had seen Lu's big eyes and blond curls, however, and her image had disturbed his dreams. He went back two or three times to see her again, and at home he told his widowed mother about the lovely young girl. The Gomes girl? Yes, she's a pretty girl, but she's not so very young, she must be more than twenty; it's almost too late for her to find a husband. But then . . . they're a good family with plenty of money, endless land, thousands of head of cattle, whole streets of rented houses in Canela, Barbalho, and Lapinha—yes, now that she thought about it, the Gomes girl might be a perfect match for her bachelor son.

It was Dr. Rui Passarinho's mother who first told Dona Emília of her son's interest, and they concocted the idea of a dinner party. A dinner, a luncheon, another dinner, another luncheon, and almost without his being aware of it the attorney was wafted gently by the two good ladies up to the gates of matrimony. As for Lu, she was very sweet and very polite, and that was all. To amuse Zabela she imitated the lawyer's confusion when he tried to find an opening for declaring his intentions; he did not know how to act or what to think. Poor man, what a rude awakening he was going to have!

As they waited for Tadeu that last week, they ironed out

details and tightened loose screws. Pedro Archanjo had passed on the invitation to Professor Bernard and had had a long talk with Frei Timóteo in the monastery cloister. The friar's beard had grown white, but his laugh was still that of a young man. Through Damião—Major Damião de Souza—Pedro Archanjo received an invitation to visit Judge Santos Cruz at his house, and they talked together for some time. Now the only one left to be consulted was Silva Virajá.

Checking the fine points of the law and going to the offices of notary publics and to sacristies for birth and baptismal certificates, and from friend to friend with invitations and much talk, Pedro Archanjo saw to all the arrangements for the marriage. It was a marriage contrary to the wishes of the family, but it was entirely legal. Alas! it had none of the romantic allure of an elopement by cloaked figures at dawn, with fishing boats and galloping horses, pursuit and combat, but it would suffice to give them a little fun and teach the arrogant a good lesson. Pedro Archanjo closeted himself with Budião and Valdeloir and they selected certain absolutely reliable men, *capoeira* wrestlers whose names made even the secret police tremble. Just in case. You never could tell what might happen.

16

When Archanjo found Professor Silva Virajá, he was in the company of a man of about thirty, thin, with a red mustache and goatee, an open face, nervous twitching hands, and gimlet eyes.

"Good morning, Pedro Archanjo. Let me introduce Dr. Fraga Neto, who is going to take over my classes when I leave. He's just come from Germany and that's where I'm going. Well, that's life!" He turned to his colleague: "This is Pedro Archanjo, whom I've already told you so much about, one of my very favorite people. Officially he's a runner here in the Parasitology Department, but he's really a highly competent anthropologist. He knows more about the folkways of Bahia than anyone. But you've already read his books."

Pedro Archanjo mumbled some modest phrases: "The professor's too kind, I'm only an amateur."

"I did read your books, and I enjoyed them very much. Especially the second. We think the same way about a lot of things. I'm sure we'll be friends."

"It'll be an honor and a pleasure, Dr. Fraga. But when are you leaving, Professor?"

"In about two months. First I'm going to São Paulo, and then to Germany."

"Will you be there long, Professor?"

"I'm going to stay, Archanjo. Not in Germany; I'll only be there long enough to equip the lab I'm going to set up and direct in São Paulo, where I'll be staying for good. They've made me an exceptionally good offer: enough to go on with my research. I can't do it here. The budget we have isn't big enough to buy even the most indispensable equipment. Out of pure patriotism Dr. Fraga has been good enough to accept my invitation and leave a splendid post in Germany to try for a professorship here in Bahia and ensure that our work goes on. I'm sure he can count on the cooperation of employees like you and Arlindo, as well as the students."

"I can if I pass the exam, that is."

The scientist laughed. "You'll pass even if it means knocking a few heads together, old fellow."

Since the examination for professors without tenure did not take the form of a public disputation among several candidates, it was usually a much less exciting and important event than the competition for a full professorial chair. Nevertheless, Dr. Fraga Neto's examination filled the Great Hall of the Medical School to capacity and ended in a riot: indignation, applause, boos, insults, tumult, disorder, and hand-to-hand combat.

The young doctor and research scientist had come from

Europe preceded by his reputation. It had been Professor Silva Virajá himself, with all the weight of his influence, who had invited him to try for the post as his successor. The only son of wealthy parents, Fraga Neto had gone to Europe soon after his graduation. He had lived for several months in Paris and London and then gone to Germany and settled down. His research had followed the same pattern as Silva Virajá's—"I'm just one of the master's disciples," he used to say.

Sparks were struck and the examination caught fire; it had been a long time since there had been such an aggressive and heretical candidate, holding such startling views and theories, for the examining bench to contend with. The only one who was not scandalized was Professor Silva Virajá himself. He rubbed his hands, almost chortling while the bellicose candidate demolished deep-rooted convictions, sacred ideas, whole structures of social convention. His arrogant red goatee cocked skyward, Fraga Neto looked like some mischievous demon.

The cause of all the uproar was not the debate on *materia medica*—Fraga Neto's thesis had to do with tropical diseases—but rather his propositions of a sociological and political nature. Many and terrible were the declarations flung in the faces of the bench and the congregation by the pretender to the title.

Fraga Neto began by declaring himself to be a materialist; worse still, a dialectical materialist, a disciple of Karl Marx and Friedrich Engels, "the two great modern philosophers, the geniuses who led the way to a new era for humanity." Basing his stand on the precepts of the masters, he demanded urgent and profound changes in the economic, social, and political structure of Brazil; only then could tropical diseases be completely eradicated. "As long as we're a semi-feudal country with an agrarian economy based on latifundium and one-crop agriculture, we cannot talk seriously about combatting tropical diseases. The principal disease we suffer from is our backwardness, and all the others are a consequence of that one." Consternation ensued among the professors, many of whom were also prosperous landholders and ranchers.

Here the debate took on unaccustomed virulence and almost

reached the stage of insults. One member of the board of examiners, Montenegro of the neologisms, was on the point of hysteria. "Absurd!" he cried out in panic.

Naturally the students were unanimous in favor of the candidate, and a turbulent claque applauded each outrage: "Our obsolete economy bears the main responsibility for schistosomiasis, leprosy, Chagas's disease, malaria, smallpox, endemic disease, and epidemics in our unhappy native land. Without a radical structural change in our society, we cannot hope to eradicate disease or take preventive measures in a systematic, serious way against the sicknesses that afflict our people; we cannot even talk about public health. To promise such measures is folly, if not a cruel and deceptive mockery. Until we have transformed Brazil all our research, even what is most earnest and original, will remain nothing more than isolated skirmishes, the outcome of the devotion and talent of a few learned men who are capable of enormous self-sacrifice. All the rest is only a sterile academic debate. That is the truth, whether we like it or not."

The most sensational moment came during Fraga Neto's defense of his thesis. Not content with the hubbub caused by his militant ideas, he quoted a faculty runner as one of his scientific authorities. Calling him "a talented anthropologist of broad sociological vision," he read a passage taken from that brochure published by Archanjo, that high yellow who thought he was as good as anybody: "In Bahia the conditions in which the lower classes live are so terrible, the misery is so great, and all medical or sanitary assistance is so totally lacking, as is the slightest show of interest on the part of the state or other public authorities, that merely staying alive in such conditions constitutes extraordinary proof of strength and vitality. For this reason, the preservation of custom and tradition, the organizing of societies, samba schools, parades, carnival parades, bands, and *afoxés,* and the creation of new dance rhythms and songs—all that signifies cultural enrichment—takes on the character of a veritable miracle which can only be explained by miscegenation. The mixture of races has given birth to a new race of so much talent and endurance, of such power, that it is able to rise above misery and despair in a daily creation of beauty and of life itself." There rose a bellow from the chairs reserved for the faculty: "I protest!" It was Professor Nilo Argolo, apoplectic and rising to his feet to shout:

"That quotation is an insult to this venerable faculty!"

Professor Argolo did not limit himself to those brief words, but pronounced many more in a speech which was doubtless an impeccable and annihilating refutation. Unfortunately, no one could hear it. The students were shouting *"Viva! Viva!"* at Fraga Neto, and various professors tried to intervene at the same time; asides, insults, boos, and whistles flew thick and fast, and pandemonium ensued. At the end of the examination, which he passed unanimously although two or three professors lowered his grade, Fraga Neto was borne off in triumph on the students' shoulders.

As for the invitation to be a witness for Tadeu at the civil ceremony, Professor Silva Virajá accepted it as a matter of course. He had known the engineer when, still a boy, he had waited at the parasitology lab for his godfather Archanjo, and he was aware of the difficulties he had had to overcome to get his degree. On several occasions he had given the boy a little money for the streetcar, an ice cream cone or a movie. He knew the Gomeses, too: rude backlands ranchers, choleric and backward people, far below Tadeu's intellectual level. But if the young man and the girl loved each other, why none of the rest mattered in the least. The thing for them to do was to get married and start having children.

17

It was a huge scandal, the only thing talked about in Bahia for weeks; only the Independence Centennial and the great July 2 holidays pushed it into oblivion. It was the cause of sharp discussions and even exchanges of insults. One would have thought it was the first time a mulatto and a white girl were being married. A white girl from Bahia, that is, one with a touch of the tar-brush, in the well-founded solidly based opinion of Countess Isabel Tereza, familiarly known to the future bride and groom as Zabela. The bridegroom was a mulatto with "a very dark complexion," to use Dona Emília's conciliatory phrase.

At that time such marriages were becoming fairly common. As they went into the church on their fathers' arms, Negro-white or white-Negro couples no longer aroused much excitement, only the natural sentimentality attendant on all matrimonial unions. This time, however, the bride was not entering the church on her father's arm, nor were lamps lit in nave and on altar. Both civil and religious ceremonies took place in the house of a friend. There was only a small number of guests and the atmosphere was full of menace. The chorus of arguments which constituted Tadeu's and Lu's wedding march had struck a spark in Bahia.

The powerful Gomes family, who owned a good part of the Sertão and were pre-eminent in upper-class society, had considered the marriage proposal an insult and sent the poor black suitor packing with a round, categorical no. When they closed the doors of the house where he had formerly been welcome and for-bade him ever to aspire to their daughter's hand, they failed to take into consideration the boy's real fortune: talent, a strong will, a rhyming examination at the Polytechnical School, the ability to solve extremely difficult problems in mathematics, honors in all of his subjects, and a brilliant career in Rio, where he was Paulo de Frontin's right-hand man.

Let's have a hand for the Gomes family! It was about time the honorable head of a family put an end to the criminal traffic of blood, the growing bastardization of the white race in Brazil; time to show the niggers where to draw the line—thus Nilo Argolo, Oswaldo Fontes, and the rest of his bellicose train praised the colonel's stand.

A useless, pathetic gesture, replied the Silva Virajás, the Fraga Netos, and the Bernards. Race hatred cannot flourish in Brazilian soil, and no wall of prejudice can long resist the momentum of the people.

All this, plus the beauty of the bride, the notable intelligence of the groom, and the steadfastness of their forbidden love, surrounded the marriage with an aura of romance and excitement. For a time it was at the center of the life of the city.

Tadeu had arrived by ship several days before. He had come almost incognito, and only a few friends knew of his presence in Bahia. He met Lu at Zabela's house and they settled the last details "in a hug you would have loved to see," as the ever more lame and more loquacious old woman announced to Master Archanjo.

Lu informed Tadeu of Dr. Passarinho's persistent courtship, his constant visits, his companionship with the colonel. The attorney, attentive and discreet, had acted with tact and good breeding. He did not try to impose his will, he had not even proposed; he contented himself with hints and speaking glances. He entrusted his cause to Dona Emília, who could not praise the suitor enough. He's so much in love, my dear, just waiting for a word from you, a mere gesture, a nod of assent, so that he can propose. After all, you'll soon be twenty-one. All your classmates at the Colégio das Mercês are married and some already have children; Maricota's even thrown her husband over, just think how awful! A better husband than Dr. Passarinho you'll never find, and your father likes him, and so do I. Soon you won't be able to get a husband. Be sensible. Don't be stubborn. Day and night that singsong in her ears and the question in the barrister's eyes.

The day before Lu's coming of age, Dr. Passarinho came to the house after dinner, and instead of remaining in the sitting room with the colonel to talk about politics or finance, he asked the girl if she would consent to listen to him for two minutes. They sat down under the big mango tree in the garden. Above them was a starry sky and a moon, and below them the waters of the gulf, the sea fort, and the silent shadows of ships—a night for lovers. Completely inexperienced at making avowals of love and feeling very foolish, the lawyer, after a long, embarrassing silence, finally overcame his bashfulness:

"I don't know if Dona Emília has already spoken to you—I

asked her permission to speak to you . . . I'm not a boy, you
know . . ."

"Dr. Rui, Mamma has spoken to me. I feel honored, because you
deserve all my respect and you've behaved beautifully. That's
why I can't let you go on. You see, I'm already engaged, and I'm
going to be married soon, very soon."

"Engaged? Married? Dona Emília didn't tell me that!" Really
startled, the lawyer was finally able to look into the girl's large
eyes, which were as clear as water.

"Hasn't anyone told you? I don't mean Daddy or Mother, because they never speak of it. But there was a lot of gossip about
the proposal."

"I don't know a thing about it. I live very much to myself,
and I don't much care for gossip."

"Then I'll tell you the whole story. That's the best way of
proving how much I respect you. Part of what I'm going to say
is a secret."

"I'm a gentleman, *senhorita*, and a lawyer. I've been entrusted
with many secrets."

"Almost a year ago, eight months to be exact, I was asked for
in marriage by Dr. Tadeu Canhoto, an engineer who graduated
in the same class as my brother Astério. We've loved each other
since we were children."

"Tadeu Canhoto . . . I recognize the name."

"My father wouldn't consent because Tadeu's a mulatto. A
poor mulatto. He started at the bottom and had to make sacrifices
in order to study. It was my parents who refused him. I love
Tadeu and consider myself his fiancée"—she would not let him
interrupt her. "I want you to hear the rest: tomorrow I'll be
twenty-one years old, and that very day I'm leaving this house
by that door to be married. I hope that by telling you the truth I
am reciprocating the honor you have paid me in thinking of having me for your wife. I know I needn't ask you to keep my
secret."

The barrister looked out at the sea covered with moonglow.
From somewhere there came the drumming of a samba, a *capoeira*
ballad:

Set the orange on the ground,
My massa went away, I won't stay
My towel is made of lace, tico-tico
Set the orange on the ground.

"Tadeu Canhoto? Wasn't he the student who wrote the answers to a math test in decasyllabic verse?"

"Yes, he's the one."

"I've heard a lot about him. They say he's a very talented young man. Just the other day a friend who has just arrived from Rio told me that Engineer Canhoto enjoys Dr. Paulo de Frontin's greatest confidence"—he stopped, listening to the distant song: *my love went away, I won't stay*—"I can't tell you I'm happy about it, for I thought I might have the honor of asking for your hand and of some day having you for my wife and companion. Well, I'll go back to my books and papers. After all, I do have the tastes of a bachelor, and I don't know whether I would have been a good husband. Allow me to congratulate you on your marriage. On your marriage, and on your courage. I don't know whether I can be of any use to you and to Dr. Tadeu, but if you have need of me in any way I am at your service."

"Thank you. I expected nothing less from you."

"Is everything all right, Doctor?" asked Dona Emília when the barrister, as always amiable and correct, a true gentleman, kissed her hand in taking his leave.

"Everything is quite all right, Dona Emília." Although he was disappointed, the lawyer felt a certain sense of relief; maybe he was born to be an old bachelor, after all.

"We'll see you tomorrow, Doctor. Come and dine with Lu."

"Thank you, Dona Emília, and good night."

Bombarded with questions, Lu parried them, smiling but nervous. Dona Emília informed the colonel about the march of events: everything's going well, tomorrow we'll have great news.

So they did, great and unexpected news. That morning Lu, who was now of age and could go and come as she liked, left the house very early and did not come back. She had left her parents a dramatic and laconic note: *Forgive me, I'm going to marry the man I love, good-bye.* Colonel Gomes ran to Dr. Passarinho's house, determined to stop the marriage by any means; to get his daughter back and have Tadeu thrown in jail.

No legal steps were possible, the attorney explained. The girl was of age, mistress of her own acts, and competent to marry anyone she wished. The suitor was not to her parents' taste? That was unfortunate, no doubt, but there was nothing they could do but make their peace with the bridegroom and forget their small differences.

Never! The colonel strode across the room. The black bounder! Astério's schoolmate, welcomed into their home by himself and by Dona Emília, who had often given him his only meal of the day! And he had repaid their kindness by turning their daughter's head. She was nothing but a child. That mulatto with no father and no mother, who had practically lived on charity until the day he graduated, a nobody, one Tadeu Canhoto.

"Excuse me, Colonel, but Dr. Tadeu Canhoto is not a nobody. We are speaking of an engineer with a fine reputation who undoubtedly has a great future before him. As for Lu, she is no longer a child. She is twenty-one years old, and if she has left her paternal home to marry Dr. Tadeu it must be because she really loves him."

"A mestizo!"

"Forgive me, Colonel. Only yesterday I myself was an aspirant to Lu's hand and when I informed you and Dona Emília of my intention I received the approval of both of you, a fact of which I am very proud. Nevertheless, Colonel, I too am a mestizo, so that is no reason . . ."

"You, sir? A mestizo?"

"What appears to weigh most with you, my dear Colonel, is color, not race. My paternal grandmother was a very dark mulatto. I turned out to be white, but I have a brother, a doctor in São Paulo, who is a handsome, dark-complexioned man. He took after our black grandmother. He is married, incidentally, to the daughter of a very wealthy Italian. In Bahia, Colonel, it would be hard to say who is not a mestizo."

"My family—"

"Colonel, if your daughter loves Dr. Tadeu, forget your prejudices and give her your blessing."

"Never! As far as I'm concerned, the day she marries that nigger she's dead and buried."

"When the grandchildren start coming . . ."

"Doctor, I forbid you to speak of such a disgraceful subject. I intend to stop this marriage by any means necessary. I came here to appoint you as my lawyer, to help me throw the scoundrel in jail and pack Lu off to a convent."

"I've already told you there's nothing that can be done, Colonel. The law . . ."

"What do I care about the law! You're a lawyer and you ought to know the law isn't made to be obeyed by everybody. When you're rich you're above the law. You have my authorization to spend whatever it takes."

"Impossible, Colonel. Not only is the law very clear, but there is one other detail you are not aware of: as of yesterday I am your daughter Lu's attorney. She has engaged me to see that her rights are guaranteed, to defend her, as a citizen in full possession of all her faculties, against any maneuver to impede her marriage to Dr. Tadeu Canhoto. That being the case . . ."

The colonel sought out his influential friends, raised his voice threateningly, and laid himself under obligation to the authorities. Police detectives were given orders to find Tadeu and take him to headquarters. They found him at the Tent of Miracles with lawyer Passarinho, who had searched all over Bahia to warn him of the *fazendeiro's* intentions.

"So you're my rival?" Tadeu smiled as they shook hands.

"I think I'm your lawyer now. I had a hard time getting hold of you, Dr. Canhoto."

They were deep in conversation when the secret police arrived. Tadeu refused to accompany them: "I've committed no crime and I have no reason to go to the police station."

"If you won't come along we'll drag you there."

The lawyer got around the impasse by offering to go to the chief of police himself. "I know him quite well, we were in the same class in the university, and our relations are excellent."

In the office of the chief of police, Dr. Rui demanded to know

whether the police apparatus existed in order to see that the law
was enforced or in order to violate it and connive in the practice
of abusive illegal acts.

"My dear fellow, don't be upset. I've had more than ten requests from Colonel Gomes demanding that Tadeu Canhoto be
arrested and given a beating. All I did was invite the said individual to appear at police headquarters and explain himself.
After all, it is a case of a minor's being carried off, and the daughter of one of our best families, at that."

"Minor? Carried off? Today is Lu's twenty-first birthday and
legally she is as much of age as you or I. She left home on her
own two feet and she left a letter of explanation. Now that those
details have been cleared up, I would like to inquire whether you
know who your 'said individual' is. If you don't, I'll tell you. He
is Engineer Tadeu Canhoto, a member of Dr. Paulo de Frontin's
team and his right-hand man. Professor Bernard of the Polytechnical School has in his pocket a power of attorney from Paulo
de Frontin to represent him as a sponsor of Dr. Tadeu's marriage
to Colonel Gomes's daughter."

"You don't say. I thought he was some cheap Don Juan."

The lawyer continued his interrogation: Do you know where
the girl is now? In Professor Silva Virajá's house. How are you
going to get her out? Didn't the chief of police have enough
problems with all the criticism stirred up by the excesses of Assistant Police Chief Pedrito Gordo? Was he asking for new
headaches? It was he, Passarinho, the engineer's lawyer, who had
stopped him from cabling Paulo de Frontin to inform him of the
threats of the police.

"I haven't threatened anyone. I asked him to come."

"You sent two gangsters with orders to bring him here. If I
hadn't been there they would have dragged Dr. Tadeu here by
force. Can you imagine what the consequences would have been?
What you're doing, whether you know it or not, is throwing
away your career to pander to the whims of a backwoods colonel. If Frontin so much as raises a finger the governor will just
have to fire you. Give it up, my dear fellow."

The chief of police called off his detectives, informing the
colonel that he was sorry he couldn't do anything but the case

was completely outside his jurisdiction. He loved his job. With the rake-off on the animal game alone, he had already been able to buy himself a house in Graça.

In desperation, the colonel threatened to impose his will by stopping the wedding at gunpoint and "slashing the black scoundrel across the face with a whip." He did nothing of the sort, however, but went off to his fazenda in a huff when the proclamation was posted in the Forum and the bans read in the Church of São Francisco. The comments, the gossip, the old wives' smothered laughter and questions did not echo as far as the plantation and the grazing fields. Word got around and no one in Bahia talked of anything else. Lu's grandmother, old Eufrásia, Dona Emília's mother, who was nearly senile, refused to join her daughter and son-in-law in their rural retreat. She couldn't stand the fazenda and enjoyed nothing so much as a good bit of gossip, the last remaining pleasure of old age. No, I'll stay here with the maids and the chauffeur; you couldn't drag me to that fazenda.

Several days later the marriage took place in strictest privacy. Not in Zabela's house, though, as had been previously arranged. Having invited Lu, at Archanjo's request, to stay in their home, the Silva Virajás also offered their mansion and champagne for the solemnities. Lu hesitated, fearing that the old lady would be hurt, but Tadeu accepted. "It's much more proper this way, darling." To make up for it, Zabela dressed up in all her finery; she looked as if she had stepped straight out of the pages of a nineteenth-century book of ladies' fashions. Frei Timóteo officiated and Judge Santos Cruz, acting on this occasion as head of the family, legalized the marriage. Both made speeches.

The friar, in German-accented Portuguese hard enough to break a stone, praised that union of loving hearts, that blessed union of different races, bloods, and cultures. The judge could do no less. A brilliant orator whose sonnets were published in the newspapers, he exalted in lyrical periods the love which rises above all differences of race and class to create new worlds of beauty. As Zabela said through her tears, the judge's oration was "a hymn to love, a poem, *une merveille*."

In doorways and on street corners in the neighborhood of the scientist's house were the most famous *capoeira* wrestlers in Bahia,

alert and ready for anything. The two masters, Budião and
Valdeloir, guarded the door to the street. In spite of the fact that
the colonel had left for the interior, Pedro Archanjo had not called
off his precautionary measures. He didn't want to take any
chances.

The only busybody at the wedding was Lu's grandmother.
Longing for a good gossip about her granddaughter's folly—
what a stubborn, ungrateful girl to leave her family for a penniless darkey—she had gone to visit Zabela, her girlhood friend.
And what a friend!

"Oh, Dona Eufrásia, Madame has gone to the wedding. Oh, I
wish I could have gone too!" The maid was aflutter with excitement.

"What wedding? My granddaughter's wedding? Lu's? Is it
today? Where is it?"

At Dr. Silva Virajá's house? Hurry, driver! Maybe I'll get
there in time to see something interesting. She arrived just as Frei
Timóteo was pronouncing his blessing on the couple and it was
time for the kiss.

Zabela saw a figure approach from the other room: *Nom de
Dieu*, it looks like Eufrásia.

"My friends, *chers amis*, the family is now represented. *La
grand-mère* has come to bless her granddaughter. *Entrez*, Eufrásia,
entrez!"

The old lady hesitated for a fraction of a second. Then she
smiled at Mrs. Silva Virajá, took a step forward, and contemplated her granddaughter. She looked lovely in her bridal gown
with the veil and wreath on her blond curls, smiling with her lips
and her great eyes there beside her husband, looking so distinguished in his well-cut frock coat and serious face, a handsome
dark boy and then some. She went over to Lu and Tadeu. Her
silly son-in-law could go jump in the lake! After all, this wasn't
the first time a mulatto had rolled around in the family beds. I
should know, shouldn't I, Zabela?

From their place behind the other guests, Pedro Archanjo
and Lídio Corró saw Tadeu in the embrace of Grandmother
Eufrásia Maria Leal da Paiva Mendes.

18

Pedrito Gordo's holy war went on for years, and little by little the tenacious resistance of the *mães* and *pais-de-santo* began to weaken. The people recorded the successive stages of the persecution in sambas and *capoeira* songs:

> *Ain't got no use for* candomblé
> *Where the witch doctor dances around*
> *But when I get an ache or a pain*
> *I'm the first one to be found.*

Many *babalorixás* and *iyalorixás* carried the sacred *axé* and their saints a long way off, banished from the city and its suburbs to open country, distant places that were difficult to reach. Others packed up their *orixás*, instruments, vestments, the special stones, their chants, their dances, their drummings and their rhythms, and moved bag and baggage to Rio de Janeiro. That is how the samba came to what was then the country's capital, came with the caravans of fleeing Bahianos. Some of the smaller *terreiros* could not hope to hold out against such persecution and succumbed once and for all. Others reduced their calendar of festivals to the indispensable obligations and held even those surreptitiously.

A very few persisted in a struggle to the death, the great houses with ancient traditions and dozens of adepts. On holy days when the drums called the saints, the people of these *terreiros* defied the police and the threats of jail and beatings:

> *Hide this saint*
> *Pedrito's here*
> *Here he comes singing* ô cabiecí
> *Here he comes singing* ô cabiecí.

The secret police, occasionally under the personal command of Pedrito himself, infested Bahia at night in search of *candomblés* and drumming; there was no one to stand up to the cudgels:

> *Shake the rattle*
> *Beat the tambourine*
> *Hurry, hurry, hurry*
> *Pedrito's coming in.*

From 1920 to 1926, during the reign of the all-powerful assistant chief of police, all customs of Negro origin without exception, from the women who sold food to the *orixás* themselves, were the target of constant and growing violence. The police chief never flagged in his resolve to put an end to popular tradition, with knives and cudgels if he could, with bullets if he had to.

The circle samba was exiled to the ends of the earth, or at least to lost lanes and tumble-down houses. Almost all the *capoeira* schools had to close their doors. Budião himself went underground for a while, and Valdeloir had a very tough time of it. With the *capoeira* wrestlers the persecution was not quite so blatant; the police were afraid to challenge them openly. It was safer to do it at a distance, behind their backs. Every so often the body of a *capoeirista* would be found at dawn riddled with bullets, shot from ambush, the work of a pack of criminals. That was the way Neco Dendê, Porcupine, João Grauçá, and Cassiano do Boné all died.

Among the victims of outrages and brutality in those days of unbridled vengeance was a certain *pai-de-santo*, Procópio Xavier de Souza, *babalorixá* of Ilé Ogunjá, one of the great *candomblés* of Bahia. He defied Pedrito, and in return suffered persecution and punishment without respite. He was constantly being arrested, and his back was crisscrossed with the bloody slashes made by rawhide whips. Nothing could discourage him; he refused to admit defeat. People sang of him in the streets:

> *Procópio was there in the tent*
> *Waiting for the saint to come down*
> *When Pedrito came instead*

Said, 'Procópio, you come along.'
The strength of a hen's in her wing
And a rooster's strong in the spur
Procópio's got his candomblé
And Pedrito's got his great big knife.

Procópio refused to muffle the drums; he would not flee from his house to the forest or to Rio de Janeiro. The circle of adepts shrank from a multitude to a handful, the *ogans* retired to wait for better days, but Procópio went on:

"Nobody's going to stop me from honoring my saint."

Bathed in blood, his clothes torn to ribbons, he repeated his challenge to Pedrito Gordo in the assistant police chief's office: I'm a *babalorixá* and I'm going to honor my saint, my father Oxóssi.

"Why are you so stubborn, you fool? Don't you see your saints aren't worth a nickel? Do you want to go on being beaten until you die?"

"I have to worship my *orixás* and drum for them on the holy days. It's my duty, even if you do kill me."

"Listen, you dumb animal: I'm going to turn you loose this time, but if you dare hold one more *candomblé*—pay attention, now—it'll be the last. The last, do you hear?"

"I won't die before the day set by God. Oxóssi will take care of me."

"Oh, you won't? Those saints of yours are worthless; if they had any power they would have killed me by now. I'm whipping them all to death and here I am, alive and well. What's happened to the spell that was going to kill me?"

"I work only for good. I never cast an evil spell."

"Listen, you dumb ox: the saints of the Church do miracles, that's why they're saints. All those saints of yours do is make noise, they're full of shit and that's all. The day I see one of those male whores work a miracle, that's the day I'll resign." He laughed and touched the Negro's torn chest with the tip of his cane. "In a few days it'll be six years since I lowered the boom on the *candomblés*. I've put a stop to almost all of them, and soon I'll finish off the rest. In all that time I never saw an *orixá* do a single miracle. Just a lot of gab, that's all."

The secret police echoed his laughter. The boss was very funny; the boss wasn't afraid of anything. Procópio listened to his final threat:

"Let me give you a piece of advice: close down the *terreiro*, throw away those drums, tell your saint to go to hell and I'll give you a job on the police force. It's a soft life, just ask those guys over there. Because I'm telling you, if you hold one more *candomblé* it'll be your last. I tell you no lies."

"Nobody's going to stop me from honoring my saint."

"Do it and you'll find out. I've warned you for the last time."

That fellow was a bad example to the others; he kept resistance alive, he was a flame lighting up the dark and perilous night. Unyielding Procópio was no liana to be bent any which way. Pedrito ran his eyes over his men, one by one, the "pack of gangsters and murderers who serve the assistant chief of police." Six years of command had taught him how to gauge the courage and loyalty of each member of the notorious band, the knights of the holy war. There was only one real man, one absolutely trustworthy, fearless heart, implacable arm, faithful submissive dog among them, and that was Bighearted Zé.

19

In Ilé Ogunjá's *terreiro* the great feasts of old had shrunk to a little group of adepts, fatalistic old aunts, and a few *ogans*. There were not even enough *alabês* to beat the drums at Oxóssi's festival. If Ojuobá and the *pai-de-santo* Procópio had not been there, there would have been no one to lead the orchestra. The rumor had spread that if Procópio dared hold a ceremony in the tent, Chief

Pedrito would come in person, and woe to anyone he found there. He had told the *pai-de-santo* himself: if you beat the drums this time, you'll never do it again.

In the alleys and along the country roads Procópio had already been given up for dead. The secret police would not stop with arrests and beatings and desecration of shrines. Their orders were to get the *babalorixá*. Scorning all advice and warnings, Procópio made up his mind to open the tent on the feast of Corpus Christi, Oxóssi's day, and be there to greet the *orixá*. "How can I not celebrate my saint's feast day?" he said to Pedro Archanjo in the Tent of Miracles. "Even if they kill me, I have to do my duty; that's why I was given the *deká*, the gift of the spirit."

Pedro Archanjo suggested that a brigade of *capoeira* wrestlers be organized to guard the *terreiro* and give the police chief's bullies a fight. The police had already killed many brave men in that war without quarter, beginning with Manuel de Praxedes, the first to go. Some people had been frightened into leaving, others had changed their way of life and laid down their *berimbaus*. A few fearless comrades were still left, nonetheless, and Pedro Archanjo knew where to find them. Procópio refused. If the police chief came it was better for him to find no one but the *pai-de-santo*, the adepts, and the *alabês*. The fewer people, the better.

The crowd was skimpy but enthusiasm ran high. The saints descended early and all at once, with a clamorous roar. Xangô and Yansan, Oxalá and Nanan Burokô, Euá and Roko, Yemanjá of the Waters, and Oxumarê, the huge serpent writhing on the ground. In the middle of the room was Oxóssi, King of Ketú, hunter of wild beasts, bow and arrow in his right hand, *erukerê* in his left. *Okê, arô!* Pedro Archanjo Ojuobá hailed him. Dancing in Procópio's body, Oxóssi went to the door of the *terreiro* and let out his challenging shout. Ojuobá and the *iyakêkêrê* led the singing and disposed the dancers, all in peace and joy, *Okê arô*, Oxóssi!

The sound of automobiles signaled the hour of death. For certain jobs Pedrito Gordo trusted no one but Bighearted Zé, he of the mouth without questions and the heart without doubts.

Fear and remorse found no room in the giant body. There was no one like him to stop a rebellious tongue forever.

As a rule Pedrito did not use Bighearted Zé against unarmed people or for easy tasks like raids on *candomblés,* samba circles, carnival groups, and drum fests. He was a bloodhound, a man on whom he could rely, a killer to be sent on dangerous missions. He was always there when there was real danger to be faced, mortal enemies, unregenerate assassins, political adversaries who were quick on the trigger. That was how it had been when Zigomar had been arrested: one cuff from Bighearted Zé had put the malefactor *hors de combat.* And that time at the Businessmen's Club when Américo Monteiro shot at the police chief almost point-blank, it was Bighearted Zé who deflected the aim of the revolver. The only reason he did not strangle the journalist then and there was because Pedrito wanted to give his foe a whipping with his cane: "Turn him loose, Zé, I want to see if he's so brave without his gun."

It was also Bighearted Zé's task to guard the door of Vicenza's castle in Amaralina, where the chief sometimes whiled away an afternoon seducing some married woman: cuckolds were sometimes brave, and Pedrito carried the proof of it in a slash across his belly.

And then there were the secret errands, responsible, well-paid jobs. Dead men turned up in the gutter with their heads split open by a powerful fist or the marks of fingers on their necks. When Bighearted Zé raised those enormous hands of his, even the bravest men turned into cowards. Guga Maroto was a lion, a he-man, a rough, tough bully. But when he felt Bighearted Zé's iron claws around his throat, he fell on his knees and begged for mercy.

Now the assistant chief of police was taking Bighearted Zé on a *candomblé* errand for the first time. On the off chance that there would be resistance, he rounded out the caravan with Sam Coralsnake and Zacarias da Gomeia, both of whom had personal grudges against *terreiros* and *orixás.* Standing in the doorway, impeccable in his English linen suit, cane in hand, Panama hat on his head, a dandy even to the long cigarette holder, Pedrito addressed the *pai-de-santo:*

"I warned you, Procópio!"

Pedro Archanjo heard the death sentence in his voice. The secret agents grouped themselves around their chief, and Master Archanjo recognized Ogun's Zé. He had not seen him for many years, not since Majé Bassan had banished the renegade from Xangô's *terreiro* and taken away his right to sing and dance because he had killed a *iaô*. When the saint entered into him his strength doubled. One night at the feast of Conceição da Praia he was already furious at the caprices of a headstrong girl, and when he received the saint it stopped the ceremony and put a whole patrol of soldiers to flight. They couldn't arrest him until the next day when he was found snoring the sleep of the innocent on the Market Ramp. That was when Pedrito recruited him, taking him out of jail and putting him on his bodyguard. The other agents nicknamed him Bighearted Zé because of his blunt speech and the composed way in which he did his killing. Pedro Archanjo Ojuobá recognized Ogun's Zé: anything might happen.

"Stop it, Procópio! Stop that!" ordered the police chief. "Give yourself up and I'll let the others go."

"I am Oxóssi and no one can stop me."

"I'm going to stop you right this minute, you and your shitty saint both!" Pedrito pointed Procópio out to Zé. "That one. Go get him. Dead or alive."

The black man advanced, taller than a house, but Ojuobá perceived with Xangô's eyes the slightest falter in his steps as he entered the sacred precincts of the *terreiro*. Sam Coralsnake and Zacarias da Gomeia took up their positions, on the alert to cut short any protest. Procópio went on with his dance; he was Oxóssi the hunter, lord of the jungle, King of Ketú.

They say that just at that moment Exú returned from the edge of the earth and entered the room. Ojuobá said: *Laroiê, Exú!* It all happened very quickly. As Bighearted Zé took the next step toward Oxóssi, he found Pedro Archanjo standing in his way. Pedro Archanjo, Ojuobá, or Exú himself, as many people had it. His voice soared imperiously in the terrible anathema, the fatal curse:

"Ogun kapê dan meji, dan pelú oniban!"

Bighearted Zé, big as a house, with his assassin's eyes, his arm like a winch and his deadly hands, stood stock still when he heard the incantation. Ogun's Zé gave a leap and a bellow, flung off his shoes, whirled around the room, and became an *orixá*. Possessed by the saint his strength doubled. *Ogunhê!* he cried, and all those present replied: *Ogunhê,* my father Ogun!

"*Ogun kapê dan meji, dan pelú oniban!*" repeated Archanjo. "Ogun called the two cobras, and they rose up against the soldiers!"

The *orixá* raised his arms like pincers. They were two cobras: Bighearted Zé, Ogun in his wrath, lunged at Pedrito.

"Zé, have you gone crazy, Zé?"

Sam Coralsnake and Zacarias da Gomeia had no choice but to stand between the devil and the police chief. With his right hand Zé seized Sam Coralsnake, killer of Manuel de Praxedes, the good giant of the boats and lighters. He lifted him up in the air and whirled him around as if he were a child's toy. Then he flung him to the ground headfirst with all his strength. Sam's head was pushed up into his neck, his spine broken, the base of his skull fractured; he lay dead at the police chief's feet. Zacarias da Gomeia was about to shoot but was not given time. He took a kick in the groin, lost consciousness in the middle of his bellow, and was never any good in a fight again.

Only twice in his whole life had Pedrito Gordo been afraid, and no one had ever known about those two occasions.

The first time he was an adolescent, a freshman in law school, and a gigolo for old whores. He made one of them miserable, a poor skinny tubercular wretch; and one night he woke up with a razor at his carotid artery. She was just beginning the job, but the skin was already broken and bleeding; Pedro still carried the scar. However, she was so drunk that after a moment of frozen terror the boy was able to wrest the razor away from her and artistically carve her face with it. There were no witnesses to his fear when he awakened and felt the razor at his throat.

The second time he was a grown man and had just graduated from the university. On his father's fazenda he made love to the wife of one of the farmhands. One afternoon when the man was out working, Pedrito was on top of the shameless woman when he felt a knife jabbed in his ribs and heard an angry voice saying:

"I'm gonna kill you, you son-of-a-bitch." Terror made him go limp on top of the woman. He was saved by someone calling the farmhand from outside. In that second when the outraged husband's attention was diverted, Pedrito pulled himself together, grabbed the poor devil's knife, and gave him a beating. No one knew about that fear, either—unless the woman had noticed her lover's heart skip a beat. The people who ran up to see the fight were witnesses to Pedrito's bravery in giving the farmhand a salutary lesson.

Now was the third time, and this time everyone in the room saw it and could bear witness; it was a public fear, mindless terror. When Bighearted Zé, the bloodhound, the murderer at his beck and call, his right-hand man, became Ogun the warrior and started after him, Pedrito needed every shred of pride he could muster to raise his cane in one last attempt at command. It was no use. The malacca cane snapped in the hands of the spellbound man, those serpent-heads raised against the commander of the blessed crusade, the holy war. Pedrito Gordo had no recourse but to flee in shameful panic, crying out for help, running toward the fast machine that would carry him away from that inferno of miracle-working *orixás*. But alas, the *macumbeiros* had let the air out of all four tires.

Everyone in the crowded streets saw Assistant Police Chief Pedrito Gordo, the scourge of the police, the sinister leader of a pack of gangsters, the bully-boy, the perverse devil without a soul, the terror of the people, in ignominious flight, pursued by an *orixá* from a *candomblé*, by the warrior Ogun blazing with cobras. It was the joke of the town, the funny story of the year, satirized comically in the opposition newspapers, in verse by Lulu Parola and as a street ballad:

> *Master Archanjo said "Enough"*
> *To Pedrito Gordo's brag and bluff.*

20

The chief of police accepted Pedrito Gordo's resignation with undisguised relief. An embarrassing legacy from the previous government with unlimited authority who did exactly as he pleased, neither asking for instructions nor giving an account of himself, commanding a troop of thugs—of ferocious murderers, indeed—the assistant chief had become an acute problem, and only fear had kept the chief of police from dismissing him in the name of the public good.

No one laid eyes on Pedrito for months, at least not in the streets of Bahia. He had gone off to Europe on a "study trip." As for Bighearted Zé, the police combed the city for him; it was the last mission of Pedrito's pack of gangsters. They found him wandering in the forest beyond the Cabula fields and shot him without pity. Mortally wounded, Bighearted Zé managed to seize Inocêncio Seven Deaths around the windpipe and took him along to murderers' heaven.

At last the *candomblés* could open their doors again; the *afoxés* returned to the streets, the sambas multiplied in carnival season, *ranchos* and *ternos* were organized again, and *bumba-meu-bois* and other popular pageants. The *capoeiras* went back to their *berimbaus*, and their ballads:

> *This snake's gonna bite you*
> Sinhô São Bento
> Ói, *watch out for the cobra*
> Sinhô São Bento
> Ei, compadre!

Ei, Compadre Archanjo, what a long fight we had! Master Lídio Corró reminisced in the Tent of Miracles, as he read in the paper that the assistant chief of police had resigned. It had been twenty-five years before, the end of the century, when they had begun their fight against the police, against the government, against blind bigotry; when they had thought up, organized, and taken into the streets the very first carnival *afoxé*, the African Embassy. The theme had been Oxalá's court, with Master Lídio as Ambassador and Valdeloir as the Dancer.

Then, when they were just beginning, they had vanquished and tumbled from his post the chief of police himself, Dr. Francisco Antônio de Castro Loureiro, the man who had forbidden the *rancho* parades and *afoxés*, the drumming, the sambas. Those were the good old days, eh, *compadre!* when we were young and bold. That time when we went out with the Sons of Bahia, up your ass for the police, long live the people and long live their carnival! You remember, *compadre?* It's been a long, long fight and it looks as if it may never end. And Major Damião de Souza, when he was just a kid, grabbing that soldier's cap right off his head when Manuel de Praxedes was Zumbí. After that we never stopped fighting, *compadre:* in the streets, on the *terreiro*, in books and newspapers, with ink and with rocks, with parties and with fist fights. What a long struggle we've had! Do you think it will ever end, old *compadre?*

It will end some day, *meu bom*, but we won't live to see it, *camarado*. We're going to die fighting while we're still enjoying the fight. Old Pedrito pounding away with Ogun right behind him with his hands like cobras! Let me get my laugh out, *compadre*, I never saw anything so funny. We're going to go down fighting. Young and bold, *meu bom*. Fuck the police and long live the people of Bahia!

One night, quite a long time after the incident of Procópio's *candomblé,* some men were coming back in a car from a festival at the White House, the Old Sugarmill Terreiro, now restored to its former grandeur. The car belonged to Professor Fraga Neto, acting professor of Parasitology, and with him were Frei Timóteo (dressed as he was in civilian clothes he looked like a Russian pedlar, with his jacket and long beard and rosy Dutch face), the saint-carver Miguel, and Pedro Archanjo. They left the friar at the monastery and the saint-carver got out too, since he lived in a little room in the same Rua do Liceu where he had set up his shop full of statues.

But Professor Fraga Neto had come back from Germany with nocturnal habits and a taste for beer:

"What do you say we wet our whistles, *Seu* Pedro? My mouth is dry. That oily food's awfully good, but it makes me thirsty."

"Some beer would taste good."

When they were seated in Pérez's Bar on the corner of the Terreiro, the cathedral on one side and the School of Medicine facing them across the square, they sipped their first drink as Professor Fraga Neto picked up the thread of the conversation:

"We're not a professor and a runner from the Parasitology Department here, we're two men of science and two friends. Let's talk frankly and you can call me '*meu bom*' the way you do everyone else if you like. Tonight I wish you'd explain a few things to me."

Friends? thought Archanjo. It was true that a strong mutual respect linked the runner and the professor. Fraga Neto, an impetuous and a generous man whose easily aroused enthusiasm and explosive temperament led him to make categorical statements and enter into fiery debates, had found in Archanjo a maturity and assurance whose passionate spirit of rebellion was clothed in gentleness and *joie de vivre*. Could a runner have a professor for a friend? Archanjo did consider himself a friend of Silva Virajá. For many years, more than fifteen in fact, he had enjoyed the warmth of the scientist's affection, which was almost paternal though the difference in their ages was not very great. During all that time the teacher's hand had pointed out pathways to him and Silva Virajá had given him refuge and support, an aid that was constant and unobtrusive. Yes, and he was also a friend of Fraga Neto, ever since the latter had quoted from *African Influence on the Customs of Bahia* in his examination thesis, and also because he constantly sought out Archanjo's company. He had gone to the Tent of Miracles several times. He had not seen it in the days when it had been a noisy, bohemian song- and dance-hall, and now it was only a modest, bustling printing shop where proprietors and customers met to discuss a little of everything. Yes, certainly they were friends; but it was a different kind of friendship from that he felt for Lídio, Budião, Valdeloir, Aussá, Mané Lima, and Miguel. These were friends and equals, while Silva Virajá and Fraga Neto were a few steps higher on the ladder Master Archanjo had not wished to climb, not even when friendly hands were outstretched to help him up. Major Damião had one foot on the bottom and another farther up, but he was the only one who could perform a balancing act like that. And Tadeu? There had been no news of him for a long time. Master Pedro Archanjo took a sip of his beer. Professor Fraga Neto scrutinized the runner's face: what lay hidden in the shadow of those eyes, in that bronze gentleness? What did he think about, what creed did he live by?

Fraga Neto had begun going to the Tent because he wanted contact with the people, with "the working masses," as he put it. Sometimes, hearing him talk about life in Europe, his studies and the political movements and labor agitation he had witnessed, listening to the generous prophet's news of a world where not even the subtle differences that separated Archanjo and Fraga Neto would persist, Pedro Archanjo felt antediluvian, like a vestige of another age.

"Well, *meu bom*," said the professor, imitating Archanjo and interrupting his train of thought, "there's one thing about you I can't make out, and it piques my curiosity. I've been wanting to talk to you about it for a long time."

"What is it? Ask me and I'll answer if I can."

"I've been wondering how it's possible for you, a man of science—yes, a man of science, and why not? Because you didn't graduate from a university? Let's stop this nonsense and call a spade a spade—I wonder how it's possible for you to have any belief in *candomblé*."

He drained his glass of beer and filled it again.

"Because you do believe in it, don't you? If you didn't, you surely wouldn't lend yourself to that performance of singing, dancing, and all those other capers, letting people kiss your hand and all that. Oh, it's a very good show you put on, I'll grant you that. The friar practically drools over it. But you'll have to agree, Master Pedro, that's it's all very primitive. Superstitious barbarism, fetishism, barely the initial stage of civilization. How can you do it?"

Pedro Archanjo remained silent for a time. Then he pushed away his empty glass and asked the Spaniard for a glass of *cachaça:* the kind you know I like, not the other.

"I could say it's because I like to sing and dance. Frei Timóteo likes to watch it and I like to do it. That would be enough."

"No sir, it wouldn't. What I want to know is how you manage to reconcile your scientific knowledge with your *candomblé* obligations. That's what I want to know. I'm an empiricist, as you know, and sometimes I'm flabbergasted by the contradictions in human beings. In you, for instance. There seem to be two men inside you: the one who writes those books and the one who dances in the *terreiro*."

The rum had arrived and Pedro Archanjo emptied his glass in turn; that meddler wanted the key to the hardest riddle of all, the most painful enigma.

"Pedro Archanjo Ojuobá, the conversationalist and the book-worm, the man who talks and argues with Professor Fraga Neto and the one who kisses the hand of Pulquéria the *iyalorixá*—are they two different people, the white man and the black, perhaps? You're mistaken, Professor, if that's what you think. There is only one, a mixture of the two. Just one mulatto."

His voice was slow, severe, and full of unaccustomed gravity. Every word seemed to have been dragged out of his breast.

"But Master Pedro, how can you possibly reconcile such enormous differences, be no and yes at one and the same time?"

"Because I'm a mestizo, part black and part white, and so I'm white and black at the same time. I was born to *candomblé*, I grew up with the *orixás*, and when I was still a boy I assumed a high position in the *terreiro*. Do you know what *Ojuobá* means? I, my distinguished professor, am the eyes of Xangô. I took on a commitment and a responsibility."

He rapped on the table to call the waiter. More beer for the professor, and *cachaça* for me.

"You want to know whether I believe in it or not? I'm going to tell you something I've never told anyone except myself, and if you tell anybody I'll have to say you are lying."

"Don't worry, I won't."

"For years and years I believed in my *orixás* just as much as Frei Timóteo believes in his saints, in Christ, and in the Virgin. At that time all I knew was what I had learned in the streets. Later I went in search of other sources of knowledge, and though I learned many things that were good, I lost my faith. You, professor, are a materialist, you say. I haven't read the authors you like to quote, but I'm just as much a materialist as you are. Maybe more, who knows?"

"Maybe more? Why do you say that?"

"Because I know, just as you do, that there is nothing except matter, but I also know that sometimes, even so, fear fills my days and I am disconcerted. I am not limited by what I know, Professor."

"Please explain what you just said."

"Everything that was my ballast, the earth where my feet were firmly rooted, all that has turned into a childish game of riddlemeree. What was once the miraculous descent of the saints is reduced to a state of trance that any college freshman could analyze and expose. As far as I'm concerned, Professor, all that exists is matter. But that is no reason for me to stop going to the *terreiro* and carrying out the duties of my position as Ojuobá, of fulfilling my commitment. I refuse to limit myself, as you do. You're afraid of what other people may think; you're afraid to cut your materialism down to size."

"At least I'm consistent, and you're not!" exploded Fraga Neto. "If you don't believe in it any more, don't you think it's dishonest to take part in a farce as if you did believe in it?"

"No. First of all, as I've already told you, I like to dance and sing. I love parties, especially *candomblé* parties. Besides, there's this: we're engaged in a hard, cruel struggle. Look at how violently they try to destroy everything that belongs to us Negroes and mulattoes, our goods and even our very features. Just a short time ago, when Chief Pedrito was still around, anyone who went to a *candomblé* was taking his life in his hands. You know that; we've talked about it before. But do you know how many people were killed? And do you know, incidentally, why that violence let up? It hasn't stopped, only diminished. Do you know why the assistant police chief was fired? Do you know how it happened?"

"I've heard about it once or twice. A crazy story with your name mixed up in it."

"Do you think if I had gone and argued with Chief Pedrito, as I'm arguing with you here, that any good would have come of it? If I had proclaimed my materialist philosophy, washed my hands of *candomblé*, said that all that stuff was just a game for children, a product of primitive fear, ignorance, and misery, who would I have been helping? I would have been helping Pedrito and his pack of gangsters, Professor. I would have helped destroy that festival of the people. I'd rather go on taking part in the *candomblé*. Besides, I like to go. I love to lead the singing and dancing in front of the drums."

"Well, Master Pedro, you'll never change society or transform the world that way."

"Won't I? I think the *orixás* are a blessing to the people. *Capoeira* fighting, circle sambas, *afoxés*, *atabaques*, *berimbaus* are all blessings for the people. All those things and many others that

you, with your narrow way of thinking, would like to do away
with, just like Chief Pedrito, if you'll pardon my saying so. My
materialism does not limit me. As for change and transformation,
Professor, I believe in it. Do you think I've done nothing to help
it along?"

His gaze was lost in the Terreiro de Jesus.

"Terreiro de Jesus. Everything in Bahia is a mixture, Professor.
The churchyard of Jesus Christ, the Terreiro of Oxalá, Terreiro
de Jesus. I'm a mixture of men and races; I'm a mulatto, a Brazilian. Tomorrow things will be the way you say and hope they
will, I'm sure of that; humanity is marching forward. When that·
day comes, everything will be a part of the total mixture, and
what today is a mystery that poor folk have to fight for—meetings of Negroes and mestizos, forbidden music, illegal dances, *candomblé*, samba, and *capoeira*—why all that will be the treasured
joy of the Brazilian people. Our music and ballet, our color, our
laughter. Do you understand?"

"I don't know. Maybe you're right. I'll have to think about it."

"Let me tell you something else, Professor. I know for a fact
that nothing supernatural exists, that it is a result of emotion, not
reason, and is almost always born of fear. Still and all, when my
godson Tadeu told me he wanted to marry a rich white girl,
I thought, unconsciously and without meaning to, of the shells
cast by the *mãe-de-santo* on his graduation day. All that is in my
blood, Professor. Primitive man is still alive in me, somewhere
beyond the reach of my will, because he and I were the same
person for so long. Now let me ask you this, Professor: is it easy
or is it hard to reconcile life and theory, the things we learn from
books and life as we live it?"

"When we try to apply our theories with fire and sword they
burn our hands. That's what you mean, isn't it?"

"If I proclaimed my own truth to the four winds and said all
this is nothing but a game, I'd be siding with the police and would
surely rise to a higher station in life, as they say. Listen, *meu
bom:* one day the *orixás* will be dancing on the stage. I don't want
to rise, I just want to be in the forward march, *camarado*."

22

"This time that fool Nilo Argolo has gone too far. Just think, he's sending this essay to Parliament hoping they'll pass a bill! And not just one law, a whole body of laws; he's set his sights pretty high." Professor Fraga Neto, steaming with indignation, waved the leaflet in the air. "No legislation as brutal as this has ever been considered, even in North America. Argolo the monster has outdone even the worst, the most odious laws of any Southern state, the most racist in the United States. Oh, this is really a gem! You've got to read it."

Fraga Neto was easily aroused. Enthusiasm and repugnance continually led him into impromptu rallies about the most varied subjects, in the halls of the School of Medicine or under the trees in the Terreiro. In little more than five years he had become extremely popular with the students, who sought him out on any pretext and who had made him a sort of unofficial advocate of all good causes.

"That Argolo is a raving lunatic. It's time someone taught him a lesson!"

Pedro Archanjo took the brochure and read it. It was a little leaflet in which the professor of Forensic Medicine had set out an orderly résumé of his well-known ideas and theories about the race problem in Brazil. The superiority of the Aryan race. The inferiority of all the others, particularly the Negro race, which was still in a primitive, subhuman state. Miscegenation was the greatest peril, a sword hanging over Brazil, a monstrous assault, the creation of a subrace out of the heat of the tropics, a degenerate, incompetent, indolent subrace, predisposed to crime. All our backwardness was due to miscegenation. The Negroes could at least be of some use for heavy work; they had the brute strength of beasts of burden. But the mestizos, being so lazy and treacherous, were good for nothing. They were a blot on the Brazilian landscape, they eroded the character of its people, they were a stumbling block to any serious effort in the way of progress, or "progressiveness." In a tangle of quotations in euphuistic fifteenth-century Portuguese full of words like "altiloquence," "quincunx," and "magniloquent perfectivism," Professor Argolo diagnosed the disease, exposed its extent and gravity, and placed in the hands of the national legislature the prescription, the scalpel, and the necessary instructions for a drastic surgical intervention. If out of the patriotism of the members of Parliament came a body of laws imposing racial segregation, then Brazil might even yet be snatched from the abyss into which it was in danger of being thrust by "debased and debasing miscegenation."

Such a body of legislation, which would cover everything that pertained to Negroes and mestizos, would pivot about two basic plans.

The first would relocate and isolate all Negroes and mestizos in certain geographically prescribed reserves, which Professor Nilo Argolo had already chosen: specific sections of Amazônia, Mato Grosso, and Goiás. Photographs of maps drawn by the professor and reproduced in his pamphlet left no doubt as to the inhospitable nature of these areas. The confinement was not meant to be definitive, however; it was simply meant to keep the "inferior race" and the "debased subrace" apart from the rest of the Brazilian population until their final disposition could be determined. The professor foresaw the acquisition by the government of some African territory large enough to contain Brazil's entire Negro and mestizo population. It would be a sort of Liberia, of course free of the errors made in that North American experiment. In the case of Brazil, every Negro and mestizo would, if humanly possible, be deported—sent away at once and for all time.

The second project, which was clearly even more imperative than the first, was nothing less than a law, or rather decree, of national salvation through the prohibition of marriage between whites and blacks. It was understood that all carriers of "Afro blood" would be classified as blacks. The prohibition would be ironclad. That was the only way to put a stop to miscegenation.

Epitomized in this way and stripped of the noble language, "immeritedly fallen into desuetude," in which they were couched, such projects and theories may seem merely absurd. Nevertheless, they were taken quite seriously by essayists and members of Parliament, and on the occasion of the Constitutional Assembly of 1934 there were those who pulled out of the depths of the Chamber's archives the proposals contained in Professor Nilo Argolo's leaflet: *An Introduction to the Study of a Code of Laws for National Salvation.*

It had been a long time since Pedro Archanjo had let anger take possession of him. Since Colonel Gomes's refusal of Tadeu's proposal of marriage to Lu, nothing had produced so violent a reaction in Master Archanjo. Even in the struggle against Chief Pedrito's outrages, when his heart ached at the floggings, the raids, the arrests, and the murders, Pedro Archanjo had not lost the apparent placidity and restraint of gesture that were a sign of his maturity and the onset of old age. He was self-contained, agile, ready and quick to act when action was called for, but peaceful and gentle in his day-to-day relationships, a gay, understanding good comrade. But when he read Nilo Argolo's pamphlet he was beside himself and cursed as he gave vent to his rage: "Old he-goat, cretin, dunce, scrotum!"

Still in the first flush of anger he went to see Zabela, who was now completely unable to get about by her own efforts. She was chained to a rocking chair and looked very old. Pedro Archanjo had never been able to ascertain how old the countess really was. When he had met her twenty years before, "an old broken-down wreck," she had struck him as an old woman nearing the end of an ardent, intense, and wearing life. But for more than a decade Zabela had stayed exactly as she was that afternoon at the Tent of Miracles, incessantly on the go, curious and indefatigable as ever. Sometimes she was like an adolescent, such was the vitality and enthusiasm of the ex-Princess of the Recôncavo and former Toast of Paris.

At last rheumatism put a stop to her comings and goings. Full of pain and riddled with injections, she argued with the doctors and was often cantankerous. She did not give in all at once but resisted as long as she could, going up and down the streets until her legs gave out and refused to go any more. Then she did have to give in and use the wheelchair sent from São Paulo by Silva Virajá, who had heard of his old friend's infirmities through one of Archanjo's letters. She did not give in to ill humor, however. Her peevishness was coquettish, not whining, an old woman's charm; and she kept her lucidity and presence of mind up until the last. She loved life but could not bear the thought of becoming senile, of being "soft in the head" or demented, a target of scorn and laughter. "If I do start babbling like a fool," she told Archanjo, "you be sure and get hold of some poison or other at the Medical School, the kind that kills in the twinkling of an eye, and give it to me without my knowing it." How old was she, really? Almost ninety, at least.

Any friend's visit was a festive occasion, and a visit from Archanjo was extra special. They would talk for hours. The old lady asked for news of Tadeu and Lu, who were terrible correspondents. Was it true that the Gomeses had made up with them? Zabela had been well informed as long as Eufrásia was alive. But Lu's grandmother had kicked the bucket and she had only heard the sensational news by chance: a distant cousin who lived in Rio had come to Bahia and remembered to pay her a visit, what praiseworthy charity! Well, this cousin, Juvêncio Araújo, an insurance broker, had run into the Gomes family in the capital: Emília and the colonel, Lu and Tadeu, all strolling through Copacabana together in the greatest harmony. It was the intransigent colonel who had introduced Tadeu to the insurance broker: "My son-in-law, Dr. Tadeu Canhoto, one of the engineers who are urbanizing Rio de Janeiro." Beaming with pride in his clever son-in-law, with whom he was walking arm in arm. Archanjo confirmed the news. He had not heard it from Tadeu or Lu; they had not written in ages. But he had run into Astério, the girl's brother, who was back from the United States. The boy had been very friendly and had given him news of the couple and the end of Colonel Gomes's resistance. When he heard that his daughter was pregnant he had rushed off to Rio. Unfortunately Lu had lost the child by miscarriage, but everything else was just fine; they

were all very happy. Tadeu—I'm sure you know this as well as
I do—is making an extraordinary career for himself. He's considered to be an exceptionally good urban planner and he has
Colonel Gomes completely under his thumb. That nice boy had
winked and grinned, an easygoing fellow totally uninterested in
work of any kind.

Doesn't Tadeu strike you as rather ungrateful? demanded
Zabela. Ungrateful? Because he doesn't write? He's got too much
work to do, too many responsibilities, too little time. He, Archanjo, was a flop himself when it came to writing letters. Zabela
looked him in the eye: that mulatto was full of mysterious notions.

Pedro Archanjo read aloud to her; Zabela remembered poems
she was fond of and asked for more news; they sipped liqueurs.
The old woman paid no attention to the doctors' strict prohibition of alcohol. What harm could a wee drop do?

On the visit in question Pedro Archanjo went to ask Zabela's
permission to make use, in a book he was planning to write, of the
information she had given him during those twenty years about
the aristocracy of Bahia, the great noble families who were so
jealously proud of their grandmothers, the "de's" in their names,
and their pure white blood. He showed her Professor Nilo
Argolo's pamphlet: all the Negroes and mestizos were to be
shipped off to the swamps of Mato Grosso or the Amazon jungle,
with its mosquitoes, its malaria and other fevers lurking in the
meandering coils of its rivers.

"There won't be a single one left to tell about it," Zabela
laughed and then grimaced; laughter was painful.

Pedro Archanjo laughed too; the old lady had restored his
good humor.

"Nilo Argolo is a worm, a microbe, *un sal individu*, a pig, not
a man. Go ahead, my boy, tell it all just the way it is, every jot
and tittle, and hurry up and get it all down on paper so I can have
the last laugh on *ces emmerdeurs* before I die."

Pedro Archanjo went back to working under discipline and
wrote as fast as he could, as Zabela had asked him to do: "I want
to see that book of yours published, I want to send a copy to Nilo
d'Ávila Argolo de Araújo *avec une dédicace*."

There wasn't time, though; she died before it was finished. Completely lucid the night before her death, she had laughed ferociously and couldn't stop, *un fou rire, mon cher*, when Archanjo told her of his most recent discovery: a certain Negro called Bomboxê was one of his, Archanjo's, ancestors, and do you know who else's? Professor Nilo Argolo de Araújo's. *Ooh la la!*

In the morning the maid found Zabela dead in her rococo bed. She had died in her sleep, the only quiet, discreet act of all her long, rich, festive, passionate life. On that gloomy wet gray day only a few people had gathered around the skinny corpse: some from mansions in Vitória, some from the steep streets of Pelourinho and Tabuão. When it came time to take the coffin to the mausoleum of the Araújo e Pinhos, Archanjo and Lídio were pallbearers along with Ávilas, Argolos, Gonçalveses, Martins, and Araújos, each taking hold of a handle of the casket.

Pedro Archanjo went straight back to work from the cemetery, keeping up the same urgent rhythm as if Zabela were still alive. About a year after the publication of Professor Nilo Argolo's proposed legislation, Lídio Corró managed to print and bind 142 copies of the *Notes on Miscegenation among the Families of Bahia*, an ungainly volume on paper of the worst quality. There hadn't been enough money to do the job properly; it had cost a fortune to get the press in working order again, and they had had to be satisfied with a few reams of newsprint obtained as a special favor and paid for by dint of much sacrifice.

In his third book Pedro Archanjo analyzed the sources of miscegenation and proved how extensive it was, far more extensive than he himself had imagined. Except for a few recently arrived gringos, who didn't count, there was not a single family of unmixed blood. A pure-blooded white was a thing that did not exist in Bahia. All its white blood had been enriched with that of Indians or Negroes, and usually both. The mixture which began with the shipwrecked Caramurú had never stopped its swift and irresistible flow; it was the very foundation of Brazil.

The chapter dedicated to proving the intellectual capacity of mestizos included an imposing list of writers, politicians, artists, engineers, journalists, and even imperial barons, diplomats, and bishops. All were mulattoes, and they were the cream of the country's intelligentsia.

The volume closed with a long list, the basis for all the shouting and scandal and persecution of its author. Pedro Archanjo listed the noble families of Bahia and filled in their family trees, which had heretofore gracefully bypassed certain grandmothers, legitimate marriages, and bastard children. There the genealogies were, based on irrefutable proof from the trunk to the twigs; whites, blacks, and Indians, colonists, slaves, and freedmen, soldiers and men of letters, priests and witch doctors, the good old Brazilian mixture. At the head of the grand parade were the Ávilas, the Argolos, and the Araújos, the ancestors of the professor of Forensic Medicine, the pure-blooded Aryan who wanted to practice the strictest discrimination and deport those born criminals, Negroes and mestizos.

The book was dedicated to that gentleman, in fact: "To the distinguished Herr Professor and man of letters, Dr. Nilo d'Ávila Oubitikô Argolo de Araújo, as a contribution to his study of the question of race in Brazil, the modest pages which follow are offered by his cousin Pedro Archanjo Oubitikô Ojuobá." Archanjo had refused to weigh the consequences.

He addressed the professor of Forensic Medicine as a relative and cousin throughout the book's 180 pages. My cousin this, my relative that, my illustrious blood relation. They were cousins on their common great-grandfather's side: Bomboxè Oubitikô, whose blood ran in the veins of both professor and runner. There was abundant proof: dates, names, certificates, love letters—oh, more than enough. This Oubitikô was linked to the first great *candomblés* in Bahia, and being a fine-looking Negro, he had lain with a certain Missy Yayá Ávila, my dear cousin, and produced green-eyed mulatto children.

And what about the Araújos? He repeated Zabela's question: Why did the professor talk so much about the Argolos and keep so mum about the Araújos? Was it possible that he wanted to hide Black Araújo in the background? That magnificent Colonel Fortunato de Araújo, hero of the War of Independence, mulatto of the Recôncavo, without a doubt the most aristocratic of all the sugar aristocracy when it came to intelligence, courage, and enlightened attitudes?

In his *Notes* Master Archanjo set down the whole truth. Now those families could see where they came from, could look at the whole face, both wheat and coal, instead of at only one side; now they could know just who had gone to bed with whom.

The world came to an end.

23

The students came out in support of Pedro Archanjo in fiery speeches against discrimination and racism in the Terreiro de Jesus. Law and engineering students joined their colleagues at the School of Medicine in holding a mock funeral for Professor Nilo d'Ávila Argolo de Araújo, Nilo Oubitikô, with a coffin, streamers, and placards. On every street corner in town, in harangues, slogans, and jests, the students protested against the persecution of Pedro Archanjo. The police broke up the funeral in Campo Grande and the coffin had to be abandoned before it could be burned in the Terreiro de Jesus in a symbolic bonfire "kindled by the fanatical hatred of Professor Argolo himself, that king of bigots," to use the phrase of a senior, Paulo Tavares, who had been confined to a wheelchair by infantile paralysis since his boyhood but was not one whit less effective as an agitator, revolutionary leader, and orator for all that.

Students surrounded the runner and applauded him when, smiling, he calmly left the school on the afternoon when the faculty voted in plenary session that he be dismissed from the humble post he had filled honorably for almost thirty years, and forbidden ever to enter the School of Medicine again.

A tremendous chorus of boos greeted Professor Nilo Argolo when the meeting ended. He crossed the plaza to cries of "Monster!" "Nilo Oubitikô!" "Hangman!" He called for a police guard. Oswaldo Fontes, Montenegro, and a few others who were implicated in the wretched enterprise were also excoriated. Fraga Neto, on the other hand, won acclaim when he mounted an improvised podium "to protest once more against this unjust and small-minded act of vengeance against an exemplary employee and a superb scholar. I wish to protest here in the public square as I did at the faculty meeting, protest in indignation and disgust!"

A few details of the meeting became public knowledge. Turning to Argolo, Professor Isaías Luna had asked: "I see you intend to prove beyond a shadow of a doubt that the student in one of your classes who called you Savonarola was right. So you're going to set up another Inquisition in the Bahia School of Medicine!" Professor Argolo went into hysterics and tried to attack the instructor. Before the vote was taken at the end of the meeting, a letter from Silva Virajá was read aloud. He had written from São Paulo as soon as he had heard of the measure proposed by the faculty committee "to vindicate Professor Nilo Argolo, whose honor has been impugned by the runner Pedro Archanjo."

"Dismiss the runner if that seems good to you," wrote Silva Virajá. "Commit this injustice, this violation of human rights. However, you will never succeed in erasing from the annals of the School of Medicine the name of the man who, by dint of humility and assiduous labor, has created a work which has redeemed the name of our school, dragged in the mire by those who preach race hatred, by pseudoscientists, by petty little men."

Pedro Archanjo, dismissed but applauded, walked down Pelourinho. At the Tent of Miracles he found Lídio Corró and two policemen waiting for him.

"You're under arrest!" one of them said.

"Under arrest? But why, *meu bom?*"

"It's all written down here: disorderly, tricky rascal, a bad character. Come on, let's go."

"I wasn't able to warn you, *compadre*, they wouldn't let me leave," Lídio explained.

Pedro Archanjo Ojuobá was escorted to headquarters between

two police detectives to be put behind bars. When they reached the square they had met a squad of soldiers heading for Tabuão Street.

As soon as the detectives had taken Archanjo away, Lídio Corró ran out to look for Dr. Passarinho. He couldn't find him at his office, at the Forum, at his house, or anywhere else. He managed to leave a message for Dr. Fraga Neto, then rushed back to the lawyer's house and got him up from the table. Dr. Passarinho promised to go to the police as soon as he had finished his dinner: it was absurd that he should have been arrested, Lídio was not to worry, he would see to it that Archanjo was released in short order. He kept his promise, at least in part. When he got to the police station he found Professor Fraga Neto already there. The orders, however, were strict: that mulatto had been needing a lesson for a long time. Look at his police record.

The news spread and although nothing had been arranged, people began to converge from all directions to police headquarters in the plaza. Men and women, black men, white men, and mulattoes, old men and youths, Terência and Budião, Miguel the saint-carver and Valdeloir, Mané Lima and Fat Fernanda, old Aussá. Poor people from everywhere, more and more of them, a growing procession. Alone or in groups of three or four, sometimes a whole family, mothers with children on their hips, all streaming toward the plaza.

They gathered in front of police headquarters, a few dozen people at first, and then hundreds, and then hundreds more. Wherever the news was told it set people to marching. They came from the alleys and stinking lanes, from workshops, stores, bars, houses of prostitution; they poured into the square from every direction. At their head was Major Damião de Souza in a white suit, because he was a son of Oxalá, and a shirt with a turn-down collar; a cigar was in his mouth and angry words were on his tongue.

Mounted on a gasoline drum, hand upraised, he let the fiery words flow in an unending stream. He would get down, go through the door of police headquarters, disappear into the corridor, and come back more excited than before. Again he would mount the drum and go on with his harangue. When he began to speak it was just getting dark, and he kept it up until far into the night: What crime had Ojuobá committed, of what do they accuse Pedro Archanjo? Whom did he kill? Whom did he rob? What was his crime?

"What was his crime?" asked the people.

Inside the police station there was a long and heated argument between the detectives, attorney Passarinho, the chief of police, and Professor Fraga Neto. "I can't do anything until the governor okays it," the police chief kept saying. "He was the one who gave the order to arrest him and he's the only one who has the authority to let him go." No one knew the governor's whereabouts; he had gone out after dinner without leaving any message.

Early in the evening Lídio Corró heard some bad news. He ran back to the Tent of Miracles, but when he got there and saw the wreckage, the soldiers had already left.

From atop the gasoline drum, his coarse voice raised against the outrage, Major Damião de Souza reached his peroration and started in all over again: free the good man who never lied, who never used his knowledge to do evil; free the man who knows and teaches freedom.

Now it was very late, but people were still coming through the streets; the plaza was full. They had come by almost impassable roads, bringing lanterns and oil lamps. Dim lights pierced the Plaza of the Police, now occupied by the people. Ojuobá! a voice sang out; another answered, and then another and another; the song passed from mouth to mouth and up to the empyrean. It echoed inside the jail: many voices raised as one, the loving song of his friends. Archanjo was happy; it had been an interesting day. He was tired; it had been a hard day. He heard that voice of many voices, that sweet loving chant, and was rocked to sleep by that caressing lullaby.

Philosophizing on the theme

of talent and success,

Fausto Pena

takes his leave.

And about time.

Obviously talent and erudition are not enough to ensure success in this world, whether it be in letters, science, or the arts. A young man's struggle for fame and fortune is never easy; his path is arduous. A commonplace? Of course. My heart is heavy, and all I am trying to do is give expression to my thoughts, without worrying about stylistic pomp and frills.

To earn a smattering of applause and to get one's name in the newspapers; to be quoted by columnists in magazines; in fact, for any slightest puff of success, one pays a high price in entangling commitments, hypocrisy, silences, omissions—in vileness, let's call a spade a spade. And who among us scorns to pay the price? Among all my colleagues in the fields of sociology and art, anthropology and fiction, ethnology and criticism, I know of none who has even tried to drive a hard bargain. On the contrary, those who have stooped to the dirtiest tricks are the very ones who insist on the highest standards of decency and integrity—in others, of course. They pose as incorruptible and proclaim their own spotless virtue; their mouths are always full of words like "dignity" and "conscience," and they are fierce, implacable judges of other people's conduct. What bare-faced impudence! But it gets results; at least there are those who think so.

In this industrial and electronic age of races to the stars and urban guerrillas, anyone who isn't pretty smart and pretty hard-nosed, anyone who doesn't have plenty of nerve and who doesn't go in there pitching, is absolutely nowhere. And I mean nowhere. With no place else to go.

And yet, just the other day I heard a square old author come out with the weirdest idea, as if he wanted to get it off his chest: he said that young people today find themselves in a world of limitless, glowing opportunity and every conceivable option. That the world is ours and Youth Power is the proof.

Well, there is such a thing as Youth Power, no doubt at all about that, and I'd be the last to deny it; in fact, I think of myself as part of the movement. In the depths of my ego there is a rebel, an outlaw, a radical, a guerrilla; and I don't hesitate to say so on suitable occasions (there aren't too many of those just now; it's hardly necessary to explain why not, the reason is staring us in the face, you might say). Yes, young people are imposing their revolution on everybody else, they're in command, all right; but youth doesn't last forever, and when it's over you've got to make a living. To say that there are *too many* opportunities and that victory is within the reach of anyone—now that's going a little too far! When I think of what I've had to do to get a little bitty corner of a place in the sun, my neck hurts from all the bowing and scraping. With all my stumbling and falling down and getting up and going on again, paying the price I've had to pay, where did it get me? It's a pretty gloomy balance sheet. The only really big thing was my research on Pedro Archanjo commissioned by James D. Levenson, the genius; that's my visiting card. The rest is all crumbs and trifles. There's the Young Poets' Column, the flattering phrases about my poetic talent in exchange for my flattering phrases about other poets—a mutual back-patting society —and the promise of an evening TV show, not on prime time, called *Bossa Nova*. What else? Three poems in the *Anthology of Young Bahian Poets* edited by Ildásio Taveira and published by a government outfit in Rio. Three of my poems and *five* of Ana Mercedes's—can you imagine?

And that, in a nutshell, is all that I have to my credit after facing stiff competition and putting in a hell of a lot of hard work. I don't include my fornications with a number of lady poets, who were not all as sincere or even as clean as they might have been. The truth is that I am vegetating, poor and unpublished. The only great and beautiful thing life has ever given me, the only pure gold coin, was Ana Mercedes; and I threw it away out of jealousy.

I could mention one more thing on the credit side: the contract I finally signed with Mr. Dmeval Chaves, bookstore owner and publisher, an influential man in commerce and industry. He is committed to publishing two thousand copies of my essay on Pedro Archanjo, plus royalties: ten per cent of the cover price on all copies sold and a settling of accounts every six months. It sounds okay, if the accounts really do get settled.

On the historic day the contract was signed in Mr. Chaves's office on the Rua da Ajuda, on the second floor above his bookstore where he sat surrounded by secretaries and telephones, the good Maecenas was cordial and, I thought, generous. While I was there he acquired an original engraving by Emanoel Araújo and paid cash on the spot, without blinking at the price asked by the snobbish artist laureate, a true protégé of Lady Luck. The publisher explained to me that he was making a collection of paintings, engravings, carvings, and drawings for the walls of his new house on the Morro do Ipiranga—Millionaires' Hill—to which he had recently added a third floor. (He already has eight children and fully intends to have fifteen if God gives him the strength and the will.) Such prodigality encouraged me to make two requests.

First I asked for a modest advance on the royalties. I never saw such a rapid change of expression on a human face. The publisher's sleek, jovial countenance, which had been until that moment one broad smile of euphoria, turned sad and disillusioned the second he heard the word "advance." He told me that it was not up to him at all; that it was a question of principle. After all, he said, we had signed a contract with explicit clauses, duties, and rights spelled out for both sides. And now that we had just finished signing it, were we going to tear it up and flout the letter of those clauses? If we broke a single clause, the contract would become worthless as a serious legal document. It was a question of principles. What those principles were I never learned. They must have been very solid, though, for no argument could budge the publisher out of his categorical refusal. I could ask him for anything else I liked, but not that he abandon his principles.

When the incident was closed, his color back and his affable face once again wreathed in smiles, he welcomed two more visitors, the engraver Calazans Neto and his wife Auta Rosa, and asked my opinion of the work the famous artist had brought with him. He hesitated over two or three of the engravings, unable to make up his mind. This was obviously a good day for engravings. After pondering for some time he made his choice and paid for it—those fashionable artists can set their own price, or rather, it's the wives who set the prices and get the money: they have sense enough to charge as much as the market will bear. When the couple had gone I returned to the attack a second time: I am persevering, as you know.

I told Mr. Chaves candidly that my sole ambition was to see, in bookstore display cases and on counters, a small volume containing my selected poems, with the name of the long-suffering bard on the cover. The poems certainly deserve to be published, with a cocktail party to celebrate the event, an afternoon for autographing copies, and plenty of readers. It is not I who say so, but the most important young critics in Rio and São Paulo.

I have quite a respectable assortment of critical opinion, some printed in literary columns, some unpublished, some scrawled in restaurants and bars on that occasion when I went to Rio with Ana Mercedes. Ah! Those were the days of feasting and rejoicing. With all that praise to back me up I could probably have the book published somewhere in the South; but since Mr. Dmeval Chaves has signed a contract to publish my book about Archanjo I have decided to prove my friendship by putting in his hands the MS of "these poems of ubiquitous supra-social connotations," to quote Henriquinho Pereira, the acme of unarguable Carioca literary opinion. The book was bound to be a success, both critically and financially. He could be absolutely certain it would sell. But Mr. Dmeval Chaves is a skeptic. He had doubts about the sales, certain or uncertain. He thanked me all the same for giving him first chance, and said he was touched by my confidence in him. It was odd: he seemed to be the poets' favorite publisher. As soon as they had written enough poems to fill a volume they came running to him to lay their first-born in his hands.

I offered to waive the royalties and let him have my poems for nothing, but he declined. He did leave the door open a crack: he was willing to think it over if I, who had so many contacts in Rio, would bring him a written promise, or rather, a pledge of funds from the National Book Institute for the purchase of five hundred copies of the compilation, or three hundred at the very least. The size of the edition would vary from six hundred to eight hundred copies depending on how many the Institute promised to buy.

It isn't a bad idea; at least it's worth a try. I did make some good contacts in Rio with all those dollars I spent on lunches, dinners, whiskey, and nightclubs; now we'll see whether I get any of it back with interest. Who knows? My readers may see me next, not in the role of a dry sociologist but as the libertarian bard of a new era, a master of Youth Poetry. And when Ana Mercedes sees me as the triumphant author of published books, a poet on a national scale, perhaps she will be touched and the flame of love will spring up again in her ardent breast. Even if I have to divide her with composers of popular music and with other young poets, even if I have to stagger under the burden of all the horns in the universe, I don't care, I want her; far from her body, poetry languishes.

As for Master Pedro Archanjo, I'll leave him in prison and not accompany him any farther; it isn't worth the trouble. Except for the cookbook, what positive achievements do his last fifteen years have to offer? A labor strike, decadence, and poverty. Dr. Zèzinho Pinto has persuaded me that it is best to respect the moral integrity of great men by representing them as free from defects, vices, tics, and pettiness, even if their characters did contain such imperfections. I see no reason to call to mind those bad, sad times, now that glory mantles the face of the great Bahian. Which face? Well, to be truthful, I don't know myself. In this grand centennial the noise is so strident, the catherine wheels of official praise are exploding with such blinding light, that it is not easy to make out the exact features of his face. His own face, or that of his statue?

Only yesterday our dynamic mayor gave Archanjo's name to a new street, and once again the author of *Daily Life in Bahia* has been promoted to patron saint of entrepreneurs, this time in a speech by a rather ignorant alderman. Not even the mayor with all his authority has been able to put things in their proper perspective; not even he has been able to restore Archanjo to his own time and poverty. Articles and speeches, ads and billboards use the glory of his name and fame to praise third persons: politicians, industrialists, and high-ranking Army officers.

I was told that in a recent memorial ceremony—the dedication of the Pedro Archanjo High School in the working-class section of Liberdade—in the presence of civil, military, and religious authorities, the official orator, Dr. Saul Novais, the municipal functionary responsible for cultural affairs (forewarned that references to racial equality, miscegenation, etc. and so forth —everything the man who was being honored had stood for— might possibly be inopportune), resolved the problem in a most radical and ingenious way: he left Pedro Archanjo out of his speech entirely. His magnificent oration, a hymn to the noblest sentiments of Brazilian patriotism, had the other Archanjo as its subject: the elder Archanjo, "who went as a volunteer to defend the honor and greatness of Brazil on the battlefields of Paraguay." He spoke of the heroism, the courage, the blind obedience to superior orders, all the splendid qualities which won him stripes and citations before he died at his post, an example to his son and all future generations. In this way he managed to mention Pedro Archanjo, son of the immortal soldier, but only briefly and discreetly, in passing. He took his gloves off but never dirtied his hands, a real artful dodger.

Who am I to aspire to jump through such tricky hoops as that? Why should I show Master Pedro Archanjo, old and shabby, shuffling down Pelourinho toward that miserable castle? The monument takes shape in the glow of all the homage: the statue, bleached almost to pure white, reveals a wise functionary of the School of Medicine, castrated and mute, clothed in a military tunic—Pedro Archanjo, pride of Brazil.

And here, ladies and gentlemen, I take my leave of you and bow out, leaving Pedro Archanjo in jail.

The question

and

the answer

I

"Well, we're back where we started. Back to the barber's chair," said Mr. Lídio Corró.

Could he still shave a customer if he had to? He no longer had the cunning wrist and light hand of old, but his hand was firm and clever enough when it came to drawing miracles. Miracles were his real profession, and although he had exchanged it for the much more lucrative printing shop, he had never completely abandoned his old art. He had to refuse most orders for lack of time, but he was severely tempted whenever a miracle challenged his imagination because of its rarity or its magnitude. "The Miracle of our glorious Lord of Bonfim, who saved all six hundred passengers aboard the transatlantic liner *King of England,* victim of a fearful conflagration when passing the bar in Bahia Harbor." Six hundred passengers, every one of them Protestant except for one Bahiano, who had cried out in the hour of danger, his eyes fixed on the Holy Hill: "Save me, Lord of Bonfim!" He promised an ex-voto to the church and a calf and a goat to Oxalá. At that very instant a gigantic wave swept over the ship and put out the raging fire.

The day Pedro Archanjo was fired and taken captive ("The Negro's a prisoner now, *meu branco,*" the police detective had informed Professor Argolo at the bidding of the chief of police), the soldiers passed through the Tent of Miracles and nothing was left of the shop. The apprentice had run to the police with the news stamped on his face: the soldiers had invaded the shop, destroying the presses, the type trays, and the reams of paper bought on credit to complete the edition of the *Notes.* ("We'll need to print at least five hundred copies, everybody's going to want it," Lídio had said.) They had thrown the type into burlap bags along with the books. Their orders were to seize every copy of the *Notes* they could find, and they had taken Archanjo's library too, all except the books he kept in his attic room, the ones he liked to browse through and kept beside his bed. But many others were bundled off to jail: Hovelacque and Oliveira Martins, Frazer, Ellis, Alexandre Dumas, Couto de Magalhães, Franz Boas, Nina Rodrigues, Nietzsche, Lombroso, Castro Alves, and many others, a long list of philosophers, essayists, novelists, and poets; dozens of volumes, including a cheap abridged Spanish edition of *Das Kapital* published in Buenos Aires, and *The Book of St. Cyprian.*

Detectives and policemen sold the books one at a time and most of them ended up in secondhand bookstores. Archanjo managed to buy back a few from Bonfanti: "I'm selling them to you for the price I paid myself, *figlio mio,* I'm not making a penny on the deal." Forty-nine copies of the *Notes* were seized. Lídio had sent the rest to universities and professional schools, critics, professors, newspaper offices, bookstores, or had sold them directly—not all were "burned in the bonfire of the Inquisition, kindled at police headquarters at the request of Savonarola Argolo de Araújo," as Professor Fraga Neto informed Silva Virajá in a letter. Some were sold on the sly for high prices by the secret police, and there was not a single police officer or inspector who did not take a copy home with him, just to have a look at the famous list of Bahia mulattodom. "And don't forget to save one for the governor!"

Up to his eyes in debt, with no prospect of putting the shop back on its feet and in urgent need of money, Lídio sold the presses and what was left of the type at virtually the price of scrap iron. Once free of his most insistent creditors, he considered himself well repaid for all the damage. Compadre Archanjo had torn off the plumes, the spangles, and the paste jewelry that had adorned those half-assed professors, that gang of braying idiots, horses on two legs, intolerant dolts, simpletons, oxen. They had been stripped naked, tarred and feathered in the public square. They had had to resort to the whips of the police, the detectives, and the soldiers. For the rest, they were being laughed at all over town.

Two strong mulattoes, two laughing compadres. Master Lídio Corró painted miracles and Master Pedro Archanjo taught grammar and arithmetic to children, and French to three or four older pupils.

True, Lídio was not in the best of health. He had just passed his sixty-ninth birthday; his circulation was not good, and if he walked a little too far his legs swelled. Dr. David Araújo prescribed a quiet life and a strict diet: sensible food with no palm oil, coconut, or pepper, and not a drop of alcohol. The only thing he did not prohibit was women. Perhaps he assumed that Lídio had put his knife back in its sheath and no longer thought of such things. Doctor, you can't forbid a man palm oil and *cachaça* when he has just lost what little he had, smashed by revolver butts and trampled underfoot by soldiers, and has to begin all over again. As for women, they still preferred him to many a younger man. If you want to know, Doctor, just ask anybody in the neighborhood.

Eight years younger than Lídio, Pedro Archanjo had no complaints as to health. Still a vigorous, fine-looking man, fond of eating and drinking, he always had a new girl and sometimes more

than one. However, he could not hide his dissatisfaction at having
to teach children. He no longer had as much patience as he used
to, and his time was too short, too precious, to waste giving lessons
in grammar.

What he really enjoyed was a good long talk. He liked to go
from door to door, from shop to shop, house to house, party to
party; and he loved to go to Miguel the saint-carver's shop to
watch the procession of the needy and afflicted who went to consult Major Damião de Souza. Sometimes he spent whole mornings
there, scribbling in his little black notebook. People thought he
was the major's secretary.

He liked to hear old stories about the *orixás* from Pulquéria or
Aninha, tales of the slave days told by old uncles with woolly
white pates; to watch the rehearsals of the African Merrymakers,
on whose board of directors he had been invited to serve by
Mother Aninha when Bibiano Cupim, leader of the Gantois *candomblé*, picked up the glorious banner again and paraded it
through the streets; or to sit with the orchestra at Master Budião's
or Valdeloir's *capoeira* academy, pick up the *berimbau*, and strike
up a song:

> *How are you how are you today*
> Comunjerê
> *How's your health this fine day*
> Comunjerê
> *I came here to see you today*
> Comunjerê
> *It's a pleasure to see you*
> *How are you how are you today*
> Comunjerê.

What he loved best of all was to lead the singing in the *terreiro*, giving his blessing to adepts and *iaôs*, sitting next to the
mãe-de-santo:

> *Kukuru, Kukuru,*
> *Tibitiré la wodi la tibitiré.*

Whether you eat well or badly, you want to go on living.
Isn't that right, Father Ojuobá? Give me your blessing, I'm going
now; the last one to follow me out, close the gates.

While Master Lídio sought out customers and announced his return to miracle painting—there never was a painter of miracles to equal him and there never will be again—Master Archanjo cut down on the number of his students and classes and spent all day in the streets, chatting with this one and that one, laughing, asking questions: spit it out, *camarado*, let's hear the gist of it, let's see what you're getting at. He would listen to a story and then retell it. No one could thread his way through the maze of a story so instructively and entertainingly, never giving away the secret until the very end.

He had not felt such eagerness, such lust for life since his adolescence, when he came back from Rio and plunged into the life of Bahia. Time was growing short: the days were getting smaller, and the weeks and months rushed by. He never had as much time as he needed, and here he was wasting it teaching children. When Bonfanti asked him to write the cookbook, he took advantage of the excuse to send away the rest of his pupils. Now he felt completely free of any commitments by the clock and unhampered by restrictions. Now he was master of his own time, restored to the streets and to his people.

He watched Master Lídio's hand carefully drawing a miracle, choosing colors for the animated scene. Dona Violeta, fat and forty, was lying in front of the streetcar with a broken leg, her dress torn and blood running down her thigh; Dona Violeta gazed imploringly at the image of Our Lord of Bonfim. The dramatic accident—dangerous fall, murderous streetcar, pious gaze—all this occupied but a small space in the picture. The remaining two-thirds was taken up by the streetcar, a festive drawing room where passengers, motorman, conductor, inspectors, a guard, and a dog were discussing the event. The artist worked lovingly on each separate figure: a man with big mustachios, an old Negro holding a white child by the hand, a yellow woman, a bright red dog.

Suddenly he lifted his head and looked at Archanjo:

"*Compadre*, did you know Tadeu was here in Bahia?"

"Tadeu? When did he get here?"

"I don't know. Several days ago. I heard the news early this morning at Terência's. Damião ran into him in the street. He said he was going to Europe. He's staying with Lu's family . . ."

"*His* family, *meu bom*. Isn't he the colonel's son-in-law?"

"He hasn't even come to say hello . . ."

"I'm sure he will. He just got here; he has things to do, places to go, relatives to visit."

"Relatives? What about us?"

"Are you his relative, *meu bom?* Since when? Because he called you uncle? That was when he was an apprentice, *meu camarado.*"

"And you aren't his relative either, I suppose?"

"I'm everybody's relative and nobody's. I made lots of sons but I don't have any now. I didn't keep a one, *meu bom*. Don't be upset. Tadeu will come around, when he has time. To tell us good-bye."

Lídio lowered his eyes to the painting. Archanjo's voice was neutral, it sounded almost indifferent. Where was that deep love, that affection bigger than the whole world?

"Speaking of the devil, here he is," chuckled Pedro Archanjo. Lídio raised his eyes.

There at the door of the Tent, in trim and sober elegance, straw hat on his head, well-clipped mustache, manicured hands, high collar, gaiters, and a walking cane with a mother-of-pearl knob—a prince, in a word—Tadeu Canhoto said:

"I didn't hear about what happened until today. I was going to come and see you two anyway, but I came as soon as they told me. Is it true? Couldn't you even salvage the presses?"

"No, but we had our fun," said Archanjo. "*Compadre* Lídio and I both think it was worth it."

Tadeu went up to them and kissed his godfather's hand. Lídio, touched, took him in his arms:

"You look like a lord!"

"Well, in my position I have to be well dressed."

With friendly eyes Pedro Archanjo examined the important gentleman standing before him. Tadeu must be about thirty-five years old. He was fourteen when Dorotéia took him to the *terreiro* and handed him over to Archanjo: all he talks about is reading and doing sums; he's no good to me but I can't alter his fate, change his road, stop time, keep him from rising, *Compadre* Lídio, *meu bom*. Tadeu Canhoto is following his own true path. He'll get all the way to the top of the ladder; that's what he studied for, and we helped him do it, *meu camarado*. Look, Dorotéia, your little boy's gone a mighty long way and he won't stop now.

"What can I do to help? I have some money set aside that I was saving for a problem I can't settle except in Europe. You knew I was going, didn't you? The government's given me a scholarship to take a course in urban planning in France. Lu's going with me. We'll be traveling for a year in all. When I come back I'll take the chief's place; he's going to retire. At least I think he is, it's almost certain."

"How could we know if you never write?" complained Lídio.

"Where would I get the time to write? I'm always rushing around from one thing to another. I've got two teams of engineers to worry about, and engagements every night; Lu and I go out quite a bit. It's a hell of a life"—from his tone of voice it was easy to see how much hell suited him. "But as I was saying, I've got a little money stashed away. I was thinking of spending it on a treatment to see if Lu can manage to get through a pregnancy without a miscarriage. She's already lost three babies."

"Keep your money, Tadeu. Get the treatment for Lu, we don't need a thing. We've decided not to go on with the printing; it was too much work and there's too little profit in it. Lídio was killing himself working day and night. It's better for both of us this way: my *compadre* draws his miracles—look what a beautiful picture he's painting. And I teach when I have the time. I've taught all my life. And the Italian asked me to do a book and I'm working on that. So we don't need money. You need it more; a trip like that is no joke."

Tadeu was still standing, the point of his walking stick thrust into the rotten floorboards. Suddenly the three seemed to have nothing to say to one another. Finally Tadeu said:

"I was awfully sorry to hear about Zabela. Colonel Gomes told me she suffered a great deal."

"The colonel's mistaken. Zabela was in pain, she was very lame, and she loved to complain. But she was happy and making jokes until the very last day of her life."

"I'm glad. Now I really do have to go. You can't imagine how many people we still have to say good-bye to. Lu said to tell you how sorry she was she couldn't come. We have to divide up, it's the only way we can manage. She asked me to give you her regards."

After the abrazos and good wishes for the journey, Archanjo started after Tadeu as he was crossing the threshold and caught up with him in the street:

"Tell me something! Will you be passing through Finland in your wanderings?"

"Finland? No, I'm sure we won't. I have no reason to go there. We'll have nine months in France for the course, and then just quick stops in England, Italy, Germany, Spain, and Portugal, '*à vol d'oiseau*,' as Zabela would say." He smiled and was about to go his way, then stopped. "Why Finland?"

"Oh, nothing."

"Well then, until next time."

"Good-bye, Tadeu Canhoto."

From the doorway Archanjo and Lídio watched him go up the street with a firm step, twirling his cane in his hand; an important, well-dressed gentleman with a ring on his finger, distant, circumspect, Dr. Tadeu Canhoto. This time the good-bye was forever. Troubled, Lídio Corró went back to his painting:

"You'd never know he was the same person."

Why did we scrimp and save and struggle so, *Compadre* Lídio, *meu bom, meu camarado?* What are we doing here, two old men without a penny in our pockets? Why did they put me in jail, why did they destroy the printing plant? Why? Because we said that everybody ought to have the right to study and get ahead. Do you remember Professor Oswaldo Fontes, *compadre,* and that article in the gazette? The Negro and mulatto scum are taking over the professional schools and filling all the vacancies; we've got to apply the brakes and put a stop to this disgraceful situation. Do you remember the letter we wrote to the editors? They turned it into a feature story and the pages of the newspaper were pasted on the walls of the Terreiro. This is where Tadeu got his start, this is where he began to go up in the world. He went up and he doesn't belong here any more, he lives in the Corredor da Vitória with the Gomes family; he's Dr. Tadeu Canhoto.

At Budião's Academy the *capoeira* wrestlers sang an old song from slavery times:

> *When I had money*
> *I ate with* ioiô
> *I lay with* iaiá
> Camaradinho, eh
> Camarado!

Dr. Fraga Neto says there aren't any white men or Negroes, just rich and poor. You can't have it both ways, *compadre*. Do you want the boy to study and then stay here on Tabuão Street and be poor all his life? Was that what he studied for? Dr. Tadeu Canhoto, the colonel's son-in-law, heir to land and cattle, with his scholarships in France and his trips to Europe? There's no white or black about it. In the Corredor da Vitória money makes you white, and here in Tabuão Street poverty makes you black.

Everyone has his destiny, *meu bom*. The boys on this street, *camarado*, are bound to go their different ways. Some will wear shoes and ties and have Ph.D.'s, and some will stay here with the hammer and anvil. The dividing line between white and black, *meu bom*, will end when the mixing is complete; and we've done our part, *compadre*. Now there's another kind of dividing line, and whoever comes behind has to close the gates.

Good-bye, Tadeu Canhoto, man on the make. If you stop off in Finland, ask for the King of Scandinavia, Ojú Kekkonen. He's your brother. Give him my love and tell him his father, Pedro Archanjo Ojuobá, is just fine and doesn't need a thing.

"Dr. Tadeu Canhoto is a rich, distinguished gentleman, *compadre*. Life goes on and the wheel keeps turning. Let's go out for a little while, *meu bom*. Who's having a party tonight, *camarado*?"

Several days later, late one afternoon when he had come back from Bonfanti's secondhand bookstore where he had gone to get the proofs of his cookbook, Pedro Archanjo found Lídio Corró, *compadre*, friend, brother, twin, dead in the Tent of Miracles on top of the unfinished miracle of the streetcar, real blood flowing over the rails.

The painter's brush paints out the letters over the door: the Tent of Miracles is no more. An old man walks slowly down the street.

The strike, which was restricted at the start to streetcar motormen, conductors, inspectors, and other employees of the Circular Transportation Company of Bahia but later spread to its subsidiaries, the Electric Power Company and the Telephone Company, found Master Pedro Archanjo going up and down Pelourinho, Carmo, Passo, and Tabuão and delivering light bills all over Shoemakers' Hollow. He had obtained the job through Dr. Passarinho, who was a consulting lawyer for the company. It was tiring work and paid very little, but he preferred it to the sedentary work of teaching children. He could go from house to house and store to store delivering bills and so have a chance to gossip, to hear one story and tell another, to talk about the news of the day and accept an occasional swig of *cachaça*. A Turk had opened a notions store, a little bazaar, in the shop where the Tent of Miracles used to be.

Although the employees of the Electric Power Company had waited for several days before joining the strike, from the day the motormen and conductors stopped work Pedro Archanjo never missed a union meeting. His energy and enthusiasm were infectious; few of the younger men were able to match that old fellow in vigor and initiative. He did not act out of any sense of duty, or simply to follow orders or carry out a task at the bidding of some group or party. He did it because he thought it was right and because he enjoyed doing it.

For the first time in six years he stopped at the gate of the Medical School. The students of his time had already graduated, so he did not recognize the faces of the young people, nor did they recognize him. The professors did know him, however, and some of them stopped to greet him. Pedro Archanjo was waiting for Professor Fraga Neto and went over to him as soon as he appeared, carrying on a heated discussion with some students.

"Professor . . ."

"Archanjo! It's been such a long time—! Did you come to see me? Do you know who this is?" he asked the students.

The young men turned to look at the poor mulatto in his clean but threadbare clothes, his old shoes polished to a shine. The habit of cleanliness was still proof against old age and increasing poverty.

"This is the famous Pedro Archanjo. He was a runner here at the school for thirty years, and he knows all about the life and folkways of Bahia. He's an anthropologist who has published books, important books. He was dismissed from the Medical School because he wrote a book in rebuttal to a racist pamphlet by Professor Nilo Argolo. Archanjo proved in his book that all of us in Bahia are mulattoes. It stirred up a scandal—"

"I heard about that. That was why Argolo the monster retired, wasn't it?"

"That's right. The students never forgave him his bigotry. They always called him by the name of . . . what was it, Archanjo?"

"Oubitikô."

"Why did they call him that?"

"It's one of the professor's surnames, one he never used. A name inherited from Bomboxê, a Negro, the professor's great-grandfather. Mine too, as it happens . . ."

" 'My cousin, Professor Argolo . . .' " Fraga Neto reminisced. "Excuse me, *senhores*, but I'm going with Archanjo. It's been much too long since I've seen him."

The professor and the ex-runner sat down in Pérez's Bar, as in olden times.

"What will you have?" asked Fraga Neto.

"I won't say no to a little *cachaça*, if you'll have some too."

"I can't. No alcohol for me, not even beer, unfortunately. Liver complications. But I'll have plain tonic."

He looked at Archanjo out of the corner of his eye; he had gone down a lot. He had not only aged; he no longer had his old pride, a kind of majesty. How much longer could he still make the effort of keeping his clothes clean and his shoes shined? He had not seen Archanjo for years, not since Frei Timóteo's death, when they had both gone to the cloister to sit with the body of the Dutch friar. On another occasion he had gone to look for him to try to get a copy of the *Notes* but had found the Tent of Miracles gone. In the place where it had been was a little shop run by a Turk. Pedro Archanjo? He had no fixed address, sometimes he was seen in the neighborhood, if he wanted to leave a message . . . Fraga Neto had let it go. And now, sitting at the table in the bar he verified his first impression and saw that old Archanjo had gone down a great deal.

"Professor, I came to talk to you about the transportation strike."

"About the strike? It's a general strike, isn't it? Has everything stopped? Streetcars, tramways, the Lacerda Elevator, the

Xarriô, nothing's running at all? That's splendid, isn't it!"

"Yes, it's splendid! It's a just strike, Professor; the salaries they pay are miserable. If the Telephone and Power Companies will join us we're sure to win."

"We? What have you got to do with it?"

"That's right, you don't know. I'm an employee—"

"Of the Transportation Company?"

"The Electric Company, but it amounts to the same thing. It's all part of the trust, as you call it, Professor."

"That's right, the imperialist trusts," chuckled Fraga Neto.

"The thing is, Professor, I'm on the solidarity committee that's supporting the strikers. And the reason I wanted to see you . . ."

"Is it money?"

"No, sir. That is, money would help, of course, but there's another committee for that, the finance committee. If you want to help out with money, I'll talk to someone from finance and they'll come and talk to you. No, what I'm after is something else: I want you to come to the union. We're holding permanent meetings, day and night, and a lot of people come to give us their support and the newspapers write it up. It means a lot to us. Lots of people come: law professors, state deputies, reporters, writers, lots of fine people, lots of students. I thought that you, Professor, with your ideas . . ."

"With my ideas . . . You were right to think of me. I still have the same ideas; they haven't changed. There's nothing more just than for workers to go on strike; it's their only weapon. But the thing is, I can't go. I don't know whether you knew it, but I'm about to compete for the lifetime professorship."

"But what about Professor Virajá? I know he's still alive, I saw something about him the other day in the newspaper."

"Professor Silva Virajá is retiring. He doesn't think it's right to occupy the chair since he isn't teaching and doesn't intend to come back. I tried to keep him from doing it, but he insisted. I have two competitors, Archanjo. One is quite a capable man, an instructor in this same subject in Recife. The other's an idiot from here in Bahia who's got friends in all the right places. It's going to be one of those knock-down, drag-out fights you and I know so well, Archanjo. I hope I'll win, but they've started a smear campaign against me. They're using every kind of ammunition they can find, especially those ideas that you mentioned. If I go to the union I can kiss the professorship good-bye, my dear fellow . . . Do you understand, Archanjo?"

Archanjo nodded. The professor went on:

"I'm not in politics. I have my convictions but I'm not a political activist. Maybe I should be; that might be the right thing to do. But my dear Archanjo, not everyone in this world has the courage to throw away jobs and titles for the sake of his ideas, like you. Try not to judge me too harshly."

"A runner's title? That doesn't amount to much, compared to a professor's. Everything has its price and its value. Who am I to judge you, Professor? I'll tell the people on the finance committee to visit you."

"The best thing would be for them to come to my house in the evening."

Archanjo stood up and Fraga Neto rose also, drawing out his wallet to pay for their drinks.

"What's your job at the Power Company?"

"I deliver light bills."

The professor was moved; he lowered his voice:

"Archanjo, can I help you in some way? Would you be willing . . ." He took a bill out of his billfold.

"Please don't insult me, Professor. Keep your money, or add it to what you were going to contribute to the strike. I wish you luck on the examination. If I hadn't been told not to set foot in the Medical School I'd go there to root for you."

Fraga Neto followed him with his eyes: confounded stubborn old man. Not quite easy in his mind, he left the bar and reluctantly started toward his car. Confounded old man, no common sense at all. Delivering light bills! An examination's an examination, a professorship's a professorship. A young professorial candidate just back from Europe had the right to breathe fire and go around saying he was a Marxist. But a professor in the School of Medicine on the eve of disputing a lifetime title with two competitors, one a competent man, the other a protégé of several ministers, would only visit a labor union on strike if he wanted to forfeit the contest and write finis to his career. I might as well throw that professorship out the window and be done with it, Archanjo. A runner's title is one thing, a professor's title another; there's no comparison, you said so yourself. Poor runner = poverty and pride. Rich professor—where's the pride and self-respect? Were pride and self-respect only for runners? He began to run after the old man:

"Archanjo! Archanjo! Wait!"

"Professor?"

"The union . . . What time? Tell me what time I ought to be there."

"Right now if you'll go, Professor. Come with me, *meu bom.*"

Professor Fraga Neto did not lose the professorship. He carried everything before him brilliantly in the examination, scored highest honors, and defeated both the competent man and the protégé. It was Pedro Archanjo who lost his job. The confounded old man, not satisfied with shepherding sympathizers to the union, tried his hand as an agitator—talked, persuaded others, and was one of those responsible for setting off the strike at the Electric Power Company. The spark soon jumped to the Telephone Company. It was a general strike and a successful one; no one was fired just then. The dismissals began a month after it was over, and Pedro Archanjo was one of the first on the list.

He went down Pelourinho laughing to himself. Unemployed again. Yes, Zabela, *chômeur.*

Then followed a long and sorry history of one job after another, all badly paid, none lasting long. It was hard enough for an old man to find a job, and this confounded old man wouldn't stick to schedules, left jobs half done, showed up late, left early, and sometimes failed to appear at all, forgetting everything in street-corner conversations. With the best will in the world it was impossible to keep him on.

First he was hired as a stand-in proofreader in the composing room of a morning paper. He would go every evening to see whether his services were needed, and often they were: today this man hadn't come, tomorrow it would be someone else, and the old man had some experience and was good at grammar and knew where to put the accents. At his early morning meal of bloodpudding and *cachaça* he imparted the news of the world and Brazil to his friends Miguel, the major, Budião, and Mané Lima. They were always the first to know everything. Things were not going well; the world was stumbling from one mess to another. The Fascists were killing blacks in Abyssinia and overthrowing Sheba's throne. Oh, Sheba, Sabina dos Anjos, your king has been put in a concentration camp! One pogrom followed another, and then there was the official proclamation of Aryanism; world war approached to the tattoo of drums. And in Brazil —well, we know what things were like in Brazil: the Estado Novo, with its closed mouths and full jails. It was not long before the old man was not only fired but managed to get his name on the newspapers' black list.

There is very little doubt that Pedro Archanjo deliberately pied an article deifying Hitler which was signed by a high government official, a Colonel Carvalho, and distributed to the newspapers by the Press and Propaganda Bureau, with strict injunctions to give it a prominent place. When it came out the whole article was studded with typos and jumbled letters. Just conceivably, the chief of the State Board of Censors told the publisher of the paper (the two men were friends), just conceivably one might give you the benefit of the doubt and swallow "Hitler, blight of the world" instead of "Hitler, light of the world" as a linotyper's error. That extra letter might have crept in by mistake. But it was a good deal harder to swallow "scourge of humanity" instead of "savior of humanity," which was what the original said. And that word *chibungo*, repeated twice next to the Fuehrer's name, was absolutely beyond the pale. It was lucky no one in Rio knew that *chibungo* meant a male prostitute. Even so, devastating orders had come from the capital, and the censor was putting his own job in jeopardy by reducing the punishment (and the scandal), merely confiscating the offending edition and suspending circulation for eight days—eight working days—besides ordering the paper's own censors to hold an immediate investigation to fix the responsibility.

The censors never did get to the bottom of the affair; the revised proofs had vanished from the face of the earth. The unanimity was overwhelming: no one knew anything, they were all blind and mute. Since the old man was only an occasional substitute his name was not even mentioned. Even the newspaper's owner, enraged by the suspension and his subsequent losses but even more enraged by the dictatorship, did not give away the name of the crackpot, though he did add Archanjo's name to the black list kept by the press: "If he goes on reading proofs, we'll all of us end up in jail." "Well, the old son-of-a-gun!" said the linotypers. The edition was sold under the counter at good prices.

As a copier of transcripts in a notary public's office in the Forum, he would have got on all right even though he didn't work himself, as one of the clerks, Cazuza Pivede, explained to Major Damião de Souza. What was bad was that he not only did no work himself, he would not let anyone else work either. No sooner did he arrive than all activity stopped; the confounded old man could spin a yarn like nobody's business, every one of his tales more complicated and exciting than the one before, *Seu* Major. Why, I even drop what I'm doing and listen to them myself.

A job as proctor in a private school lasted just one day: the boys who were interned there seemed like prisoners to Archanjo, torn from their homes and the streets, subjected to intolerable discipline, constantly hungry for food and freedom. On his first and only night of supervision he put on a literary-musical evening for the boys, with poems and *cavaquinho*. They would have gone on singing until dawn if the director, called in a hurry, had not imposed his authority and put a stop to that "indescribable bedlam." As a hotel doorman, he left the door unguarded on the slightest pretext. As doorman at the Olímpio movie theater in Shoemakers' Hollow, he let kids slip into the Sunday matinees free. As timekeeper on a construction job, rain or shine, he struck up conversations with the workers and the rate of work fell drastically; telling other people what to do was not the old fellow's long suit, much less the role of Simon Legree. After all, why should those ill-paid, exploited masons, carpenters, handy men, and skilled workmen of every sort kill themselves working so that other men could make easy money? The old man had never followed a schedule in his life: even in his studies he had obeyed an inner discipline, not subject to the hands of a clock; he was not one to live by clocks or calendars.

His clothes were worn out, his shirts were threadbare, his shoes were shabby. He had one suit, three shirts, two pairs of shorts, and two pairs of socks: not enough to keep up appearances. Even so, he had such a horror of dirt that he washed those few clothes himself; and Cardeal, a bootblack in the Terreiro for more than twenty years, brushed and shined his shoes for nothing:

"Come on, Father, let's put some shine on those boots."

His good humor never flagged, and he was always on the go. At the Dante Alighieri Bookstore he called Bonfanti a thief: "Where's my cookbook money, you Calabrese?" "Call me a thief but don't ever call me a Calabrese, *io sono toscano, Dio merda!*" He spent whole mornings and afternoons talking in Miguel's shop or some other workshop on Pelourinho, or at the foodstands of the Golden Market, the Model Market, and St. Barbara's Market. He ate here and there, always a welcome guest. He was constantly at Terência's table, but now he was served by her niece Nair, a young woman of twenty-five summers and six small children. The first was Terência's own grandchild, for Cousin Damião was not fool enough to leave that tempting family morsel for an outsider. Each of the other five had a different father; the children formed a living color scale from blond to black. Nair had no color prejudice and she wasted no time.

"I never saw anything like it! She chases after every pair of pants she sees," white-haired Terência complained, her eyes on her *compadre*. "She's not as proud as you are, *compadre*."

"Proud, *comadre?* What makes you say that?"

He read the answer in her doleful eyes: she had waited so many years for a word, a request, a plea. It wasn't pride, *comadre*, it was respect. You talked about Crooked Souza all the time, and your voice was angry but your heart was yearning for him. I ate your bread, I taught your boy to read, but I respected that empty bed, thinking that . . . Oh, *compadre*, you're so smart, oh, *compadre*, you're Xangô's eyes, oh, *compadre!* why didn't you have eyes to see what was right in front of your nose? Now it's too late; we're old folks now and there's not a thing we can do about it. Isn't there, *camadre?* Who do you think is the father of Nair's next-to-last child, that naughty little devil? He's less than two years old, and his father, *comadre*—I'm telling you now in case you didn't know—is your humble servant, at your feet.

At the *capoeira* schools he discussed and argued with Budião and Valdeloir. At street plays, at the meeting place of the African Merrymakers, in the *terreiros*, at dawn by the Seven Gates or Água dos Meninos, darting from one conversation to the next, taking notes in his little black notebook, making people laugh and cry with his stories and accounts of everyday happenings, always on the go, Pedro Archanjo lived out the last years of his life. With all the coming and going, all the people around him, he was very much alone.

He had been lonely ever since Lídio Corró died. It had taken him a long time to get over it; it had drained him of all his energy and thirst for life. Little by little his *compadre* was resurrected as the hero of a thousand stories. Everything the old man had seen and done had been done in Lídio's company. Brothers, twins, Siamese twins. "Once years ago, *Compadre* Lídio and I went to a festival for Yansan a long way off, out Gomeia way, when Commissioner Pedrito's club was coming down hot and heavy on our backs. *Compadre* Lídio . . ."

Seeing him so poor and in such need, Mother Pulquéria, whom he had often helped in solving problems in the *terreiro*, offered him a paid job. She needed someone to take care of collecting the monthly dues from the members of the *axé*, and the rents and payments for the squatters' shacks, the dwellings of relatives and followers of *candomblé* devotees. It would have to be someone she could trust to keep the accounts; she didn't have the time to do it herself. She couldn't pay him much but at least it would be something, a little small change for streetcar fare. But he had not had to pay to ride in a streetcar since the strike, and he had plenty to

eat at a wide choice of tables. I'll take on the job, Mother Pulquéria, as a duty for Ojuobá and a pleasure for a friend, but only
on one condition: I won't let you pay me anything. Don't insult
me, Mother. He thought to himself: if I still believed in the
mysteries, if I had not penetrated to the heart of the riddle, if I
were a true believer, then perhaps I could take money from the
saints. But now, Mother Pulquéria, I'm just a devoted friend
doing a job for you. You can pay a fellow believer but you can't
pay a friend. Friendship can't be bought or rented; it's paid for in
a different kind of coin. I ought to know! And so until the end
of his life Pedro Archanjo busied himself with the dues of the
members of the sect, the sons and daughters of Pulquéria's
terreiro, and the rents and leases of the tenants and lessees. He
kept the accounts in perfect order, and when he could afford it he
put nickels from his own pocket in the gourd of the orixá there
at Xangô's shrine, in Exú's dwelling place.

Once he disappeared for several days and when his friends
realized it there was an uproar. They searched and searched,
everywhere they could think of, but couldn't find a trace of him.
Where was he living? After he had to leave the attic facing the
ocean, his home for thirty years, he never again had a fixed dwelling but moved haphazardly from one room and bed to another
every month. He was finally tracked down by Ester, the madam
of a whorehouse in Upper Maciel, a respected chatelaine and
Pedro Archanjo's godchild in the terreiro. She had entered the
orixá's service when she was a young girl working as a waitress in
a café. At that time old Majé Bassan could hardly get around, and
Ojuobá had been a great help to her in leading the boat full of
iaôs to the safe port of the ôrunkó, the day of the naming. When
it was time for Ester's head to be shaved, Majé Bassan was so
weak that she borrowed Ojuobá's hand and let him wield the
razor.

In a filthy pigsty of a room, without a bed, without a mattress, with nothing but a torn rag of a blanket and his crate of
books—Ester had never seen such misery—Archanjo lay burning
with fever and insisted it was nothing, just a cold. The doctor
diagnosed the beginnings of pneumonia and prescribed pills, injections, and the immediate removal of the patient. Archanjo

dug his heels in. Not to a hospital—he refused to set foot in one. A poor man in a hospital is the nearest thing to a corpse. The doctor shrugged his shoulders: take him any place fit for a Christian to live in, then. He certainly can't stay in this damp hole where even rats couldn't survive.

Ester had a little back room at her castle for the boy who served beer, vermouth, and brandy to the customers, besides acting as bouncer and protecting the girls. All of these varied and responsible duties were entrusted to one Mário Formigão. A robust, freckle-faced mulatto and an exemplary family man, he lived with his own wife and children, and so the little room was vacant. A whorehouse wasn't the proper place for Father Ojuobá, but Ester could see no help for it since the stubborn old man would not hear of going to a hospital.

In that back room in Ester's castle, that narrow little cubicle, Pedro Archanjo lived out his last days; and they were happy ones. Going from one job to another—not real work, just odd jobs—he passed his seventieth birthday without celebration. Before he was seventy-one the war broke out and became his only job. It took up every second and hour of his days.

In every corner of the city, from the castles to the markets, from the markets to the shops, from the workshops to the terreiros, indoors and out, he argued excitedly. All that he had done and believed in was at stake. His ideals were in danger, mortal danger.

Pedro Archanjo, the most civil of civilians, became a soldier and a general overnight. Both tactician and strategist, he traced routes and laid battle plans. When everyone else lost heart and thought all was lost, he assumed command of an army of mulattoes, Jews, Negroes, Arabs, and Chinese and went forth to defy the hordes of Nazidom. Come on, meu bom, we'll fight this raging, unspeakable death and we'll win!

5

An inveterate walker, the old man followed the parade from its starting point in Campo Grande to Cathedral Square, where the impressive demonstration marking the fourth anniversary of the beginning of the Second World War was closing with a monster rally. To make the walking a little easier he had lined his battered old shoes, which were full of holes, with bits of paper. He no longer tried to repair the stains on his jacket or his tattered trousers.

The anti-Fascist forces had gathered thousands strong. One newspaper said there were 25,000 people at the rally, another said 30,000. Students, intellectuals, workers, statesmen, people of every social class had come to demonstrate. By the light of torches lit with the forbidden Brazilian oil whose existence was officially denied—not a few people were tried and sent to prison because they said the oil was there—the mass moved slowly forward in a huge procession, shouting slogans and crying *Viva!* and *Morra!*

There were the flags of the Allies, placards, streamers, and huge portraits of the leaders of the war against National Socialism. At the head of the procession, members of the board of the Medical Front carried on their shoulders a large portrait of Franklin Delano Roosevelt. Old Archanjo recognized one of the men supporting a pole of that saint's litter: it was Professor Fraga Neto, head held high, Mephistophelian red mustache and jutting, argumentative goatee. He had been one of the first to defy the police and call publicly for the dispatch of Brazilian troops to the field of battle.

There followed portraits of Churchill, Stalin—delirious applause—de Gaulle, and Getúlio Vargas. Two demands dominated the demonstration. The first called for the immediate formation of an Expeditionary Force which would transform Brazil's purely symbolic declaration of war on the Axis to one of real participation. The other called for effective measures to drill for Brazilian oil, which the speakers knew beyond a doubt had been discovered in the Recôncavo. The first appeals of amnesty for political prisoners were also heard. As for freedom, the people were trying to fight for it in earnest through their protest parades and rallies. The shabby, slow-moving old man never missed a rally. He had his preferences among the speakers and was able to distinguish the political coloration of every one of them in that united front for victory in the war.

The parade stopped briefly in front of the Polytechnical School in São Pedro, and from a second-story window a fiery voice was raised denouncing the crimes of racist, totalitarian Naziism and praising the soldiers of democracy and socialism. Every word drew applause. With an effort, the old man climbed up on a bench to have a better view of the speaker, one of his favorites: Fernando de Sant'Ana, an engineering student and unchallenged student leader. He had a resonant voice and well-rounded periods and was thin and dark-skinned, the same color as Tadeu. Many years before, during World War I, the old man had heard another student, Tadeu Canhoto, demand from that same window that Brazil take part in the fight against German militarism. The first great war had not affected him much one way or the other, although of course he had used up a lot of breath and saliva in arguing for France and England. He had been deeply moved, though, by Tadeu's speeches, by the boy's captivating intelligence, his knack for just the right phrase, his cogent reasoning. He had read in the paper a few days before the news of engineer Tadeu Canhoto's appointment as Secretary of Municipal Public Works for the Federal District, among other tributes to "the talent of the well-known urban planner from Bahia." The Gomeses had moved to Rio de Janeiro to be nearer the grandchildren who had finally come. Was it because of the treatment Lu had had in France, or due rather to Dona Emília's promise to Our Lord of Bonfim in Bahia?

Now the case was very different: the old man eagerly drank

in every word the young student spoke, that ardent mestizo who argued so vehemently against racism, an impetuous youth who had caught a glimpse of the future. Pedro Archanjo got down off his bench. He was a veteran of that war, he had been fighting it for years and years. His life had been burned away in those trenches.

The procession stopped again in Castro Alves Square and the crowd spilled over into Barroquinha, Montanha, and São Bento Hill. From the middle of that steep street the shuffling old man saw the major on the pedestal of the poet's monument, finger upraised like a lance. Archanjo could hear nothing but the clapping. The orator's words did not reach him, but it made no difference, he knew them all: all the terms and phrases, the grandiloquent adjectives, the apostrophes:—Oh, People! People of Bahia! Parceled out among the entire city, he was Justice to the poor, Hope for prisoners, Providence to the needy, Learning to the illiterate, Attorney of the People. There was his boy Damião with his foot on the first rung of the ladder. Though already slightly under the influence, with a goodly quantity of *cachaça* under his belt even at that hour, he was as lucid and brilliant as ever. No one had ever caught him drunk. All of the other speakers represented this or that organization, front, syndicate, class, union, persecuted or clandestine party. Only the major spoke for the people—almost at street level, standing on that first little rung of the pedestal.

Like a huge serpent the procession wound its way up the Rua Chile, and the provisional governor waved to the multitude from the balcony of the palace. At city hall Professor Luis Rogério shouted to the crowd: Victory! We're going to win! The old man remembered him as a boy, a medical student who had taken part in the symbolic funeral of the racist professor and had made a speech in the Terreiro de Jesus protesting the dismissal of the runner.

In the Praça da Sé the closing speeches were made from a scaffold gaily festooned with flags. The old man insinuated himself into the pressing crowd, saying excuse me, excuse me, and when he was recognized people made way for him. He was finally able to get close to the platform. A tall, handsome young mulatto from Cabo Verde with a bass voice was speaking in the name of the anti-Fascist Medical Front: it was Dr. Divaldo Miranda. A recent graduate, he was not known to the old man, but lo and behold, on that first day of September, 1943, the young man evoked long-forgotten events and disinterred shadowy shapes and ghosts. He referred to an essay by a certain professor of the School of Medicine, Nilo Argolo de Araújo, in which he proposed that Brazilian mestizos should be put on reservations in the most inhospitable regions of the country and that whoever survived the climate and disease should be deported to Africa. The proposal was not carried out, of course; it had provoked laughter and indignation. When Hitler rose to power in Germany and announced the beginning of the Aryan millennium, the professor was still alive and had greeted the Fuehrer in tones of delirious joy: *Sent by God!* Sent by God to exterminate Negroes and Jews, Arabs and mestizos, the whole sordid mulatto rabble, and to turn his own genocidal bill into law at last.

In the plaza, admiring that so handsome and ardent young man, Pedro Archanjo remembered a conversation that had taken place more than thirty-five years before. He had just published his first book, and Professor Argolo had intercepted him in the school corridor. "We're dealing with a cancer," the lecturer had said, referring to the mestizos, "which must be extirpated. Surgery may seem a cruel form of medicine, but it is actually beneficial and necessary." Archanjo, a young man quite as sincere as the boy on the platform, had held in his laughter and asked: "You mean kill us all, Professor, one by one?" A yellow glint of fanaticism had kindled in the professor's eyes and he pronounced the pitiless, implacable curse: "Yes, extirpate you every one and leave a world of Aryans, of superior beings, conserving only what few slaves are needed for the roughest tasks." A genius, a leader, a messenger straight from God had taken up the abominable idea, an unvanquished warlord on a supreme mission: to cleanse the world of Jews, Arabs, and yellow-skinned people, to sweep from Brazil "that African scum that befouls our shores."

All that the professor had called for and foreseen had become reality. All that the old man had preached and defended was in peril. Their theories and ideas were at sword's point, confronting one another again. But it was no longer an academic debate; now it was a real fight with real weapons. Blood ran and legions of soldiers bore death in their hands.

If Hitler did win, Hitler or some other fanatical racist, could he kill them all off, or sell them into slavery? The professor said he could and clamored for a leader who would make it happen, and from the mists of Germany Hitler answered: Here I am! If he won the war, would he make dead men or slaves of them all? The old man searched for an answer in the speakers' words.

Giocondo Dias, a revolutionary whose steel had been tempered in action, saluted the combatants of the free world in the name of the Brazilian workers and said the word "amnesty," repeated by the crowd in a long, clamorous shout that was not to be extinguished until the prison doors were thrown open on the eve of victory. Nestor Duarte, a writer and law professor, with hoarse voice and fiery words attacked the restrictions on freedom that dictatorship had brought with it and called for democracy: "Soldiers are bearing arms against Naziism to defend democracy." Professor Tzalie Jucht, with his drawn, long-suffering, passionate face and all the sorrow of the ghettoes and the pogroms in his voice, spoke for the Jews. Edgard Mata, a popular and beloved figure and high-flown orator, closed the rally with a Gongoresque prophecy: "Hitler, the Scourge of Satan and the Beast of the Apocalypse, will writhe in the slime of defeat!"

The crowd responded with enthusiastic shouts and applause. The colossal mass began to move, to crowd closer together, and started to vacate the plaza. Shoving and pushing, the old man tried to get through. He would have to leave with his question unanswered: could anyone really kill off all of them? Hitler or someone else, today or tomorrow? Almost crushed to death, he followed in the wake of a burly sailor and finally escaped from the crowd. He was finding it hard to breathe.

As he began to walk toward the Terreiro de Jesus a sharp pain pierced him. It was not the first time. He tried to support himself against the wall of the episcopal palace but could not quite reach it. As he was about to fall a girl ran up to him and caught him. The old man got his breath back and his heart in working order again, and the pain receded. Now it was the thin stab of a knife, at a distance.

"Thank you."

"What is it that's hurting you? Try to tell me, I'm a medical student. Do you want me to take you to a hospital?"

He had a horror of hospitals; a poor man in a hospital might as well order his coffin and be done with it. No, it was nothing, just that I couldn't get enough air in that crowd and I thought I was suffocating. Nothing serious, thanks.

His worn eyes gazed at the dark-haired girl who was holding him. He knew that beauty; it was familiar to him. Ah! She couldn't be anyone but Rosa's granddaughter! That sweetness, that allure, that eagerness, that charm, that extreme beauty—he knew it all.

"Are you Rosa's granddaughter? Miminha's girl?" His voice was infinitely tired, but happy.

"How did you know?"

So like her and so different. How many kinds of blood had gone into the mixture to make her perfection? That long silky hair, that fine skin, those blue eyes, and the dense mystery of her firm, slender body.

"I was a friend of your grandmother, I went to your mother's wedding. What's your name?"

"Rosa, the same as hers. Rosa Alcântara Lavigne."

"Are you studying medicine?"

"Yes, I'm in my third year."

"I thought I'd never live to see another woman as beautiful as your grandmother. Rosa Alcântara Lavigne . . ." He gazed into the girl's frank, curious blue eyes, inherited from the Lavignes. Or from the Alcântaras. Blue eyes, brown skin: "Rosa de Oxalá Alcântara Lavigne."

"Oxalá? Whose name is that?"

"Your grandmother's."

"Rosa de Oxalá . . . That's lovely, I think I'll use it myself."

A group of students was calling her: Rosa! Rosa! Come on, Rosa! Just a minute, answered Rosa granddaughter of Rosa so like so different.

The rally was breaking up and people were pouring into the streetcars. Twilight was falling on the lampposts where no lights burned. The old man smiled, tired and happy. The girl somehow understood that that stumbling, probably sick old man in the wrinkled jacket and patched trousers, with holes in his shoes and a leaky heart, was close to her, perhaps a near relation. She had never been told very much about her grandmother's family. The lost thread, the silent mystery, the family of Oxalá.

"Good-bye, my dear. Seeing you was just like seeing Rosa again."

Suddenly, impelled by she knew not what strange power or sentiment, the girl took the dark, poor hand in hers and kissed it. Then she ran back toward the merry band of students and they went off singing down the shadowy street.

Slowly old Archanjo crossed the Terreiro de Jesus toward Maciel de Cima. It was time for supper in Ester's castle. Could any leader, however many armies he had at his command, kill off all the people and make slaves of them? Kill Rosa and her granddaughter, kill perfection?

After the news came the war bulletins. "Those Russians are great!" Maluf passed around the rum and they talked about the parade and the rally, the courage of the indomitable British, the epic of the Americans on those lost islands in the Pacific, the feats of the Soviet Army. Ataulfo, who was a pessimist, did not think that victory was a sure thing at all. Far from it. Hitler still had a lot of tricks up his sleeve—secret weapons that could destroy the world.

Destroy the world? If Hitler won the war could he kill and

enslave everyone who was not pure white, an authentic Aryan? Put an end to life and liberty, so that we'll all die, or worse still, be slaves? All of us, every single one?

The argument grew heated: yes, no, why not, bet your life it could happen! Finally the blacksmith had heard all he could stand:

"Not even God who made us all can kill everybody at once. He kills people one by one, and the more he kills the more people are gonna be born and grow up and go on being born and growing up and mixing, and no son-of-a-bitch is gonna stop 'em!"

Slamming his huge hand, as big as Manuel de Praxedes's or Bighearted Zé's, on the counter, he turned over a glass and spilled all the *cachaça*. Maluf the Turk, a good bartender and a good host, served another round on the house.

Old Pedro Archanjo repeated the answer he had finally been given:

". . . they'll keep on being born and growing up and mixing, and no one can do a thing about it. You're right, *camarado*, you've hit the nail on the head. Nobody can kill us off, ever. Nobody, *meu bom*."

It was late now and he still felt the numbness in his arm and the pain, deep down, lying in wait for him. He bade them all a cheerful good night: see you tomorrow, *meus bons*, friends make life worth living, and so do a swig of *cachaça* and a certainty that's very sure. I'm going now; whoever comes behind me, be sure to close the gates.

On the dark steep street, making one last painful effort, Master Pedro Archanjo climbs the hill and walks forward. Then the pain cuts him in two. He staggers against a wall and rolls over on the ground. Ah, Rosa de Oxalá!

Of the glory

of Brazil

The eminent Dr. Zèzinho Pinto had predicted correctly and chosen the right place for the closing ceremony: the impressive Great Hall of the Historical and Geographical Institute of Bahia was filled to capacity. When he saw such a distinguished audience assembled, the Dean of the School of Medicine told His Excellency the Governor that if a bomb had fallen on the institute just then, Bahia would lose at a stroke the best of its intelligence, its capital, and its resources. It was true: all the ablest men, all the great men of the city, were there to celebrate the centenary of

Pedro Archanjo's birth. They were unanimously obeying the most pleasant of civic duties: honoring one of the authentic glories of Brazil.

As he declared the session officially opened and in a brief and graceful address invited the governor to preside, the president of the institute could not refrain from the pleasure of thrusting a barb into the pretensions of certain hypocrites: "We are met here this evening to celebrate the grand centennial birthdate of the man who taught us our ancestors' full names." In spite of his advanced age and his weighty historical works, President Magalhães Neto was fond of a good epigram and sometimes even rhymed them in the best Bahian tradition.

When the dignitaries had taken their places at the front of the room, the governor invited Dr. Zèzinho Pinto, owner of the *City News* and master of ceremonies, to say his piece. "In sponsoring these grand festivities, the *City News* is effecting one of the most important items on its agenda: that of honoring and publicizing the names of those outstanding men whose example lights the way for future generations. Alerted by the bugles of the *City News*, the city of Bahia, at last moving swiftly along the rails of industrial development, is paying off the debt of gratitude it owes to Pedro Archanjo, from whom Brazil is reaping glorious profits, a rich dividend in international renown."

The next speaker was Professor Calazans, who, thankful that he was still alive and at liberty at the end of the marathon, read the translation of a letter from the great James D. Levenson to the Memorial Committee. After praising the whole undertaking in a general way, the Nobel Prize winner recounted the critical and popular success achieved by the Bahian's works in translation, not only in the United States but in the whole civilized world. "With the dissemination of Pedro Archanjo's work, Brazil's original and noteworthy contribution to a solution of the race problem, a lofty and hitherto ignored expression of humanism, has become the object of interest and close study in the most diverse and prestigious centers of scientific research."

Dr. Benito Mariz, speaking for the Society of Medical Writers, praised above all Pedro Archanjo the stylist, the man of "lusty, healthy language," who "in his long intimacy with doctors of medicine, learned to handle both science and *belles lettres*." The dean of the School of Medicine put great weight on the old theme: "Pedro Archanjo belongs to the School of Medicine, he is part of the patrimony of the great school, for he worked and built the edifice of his thought there, and it was the School of Medicine which provided him with an atmosphere conducive to scholarship."

No one represented the School of Philosophy, since Professor Azevedo was still furious about the forbidden seminar on miscegenation and apartheid and had angrily refused the invitation: his overt tribute to Archanjo was the book he had written, which was now on the presses. He explained his reasons to Calazans:

"They're quite capable of asking for a copy of my speech beforehand so they can censor it."

"Who?" asked the secretary of the Center for the Study of Folklore, Edelweiss Vieira, whose inability to handle the subtle nuances of language so indispensable at times of political upheaval and intervention in the field of culture had become increasingly obvious. "Who's intervening?" "Please, Dona Edelweiss, don't ask any more questions, just get up there and make your speech."

At the rostrum Edelweiss Vieira gave a touching little speech of thanks to "the father of the study of Bahian folklore," for the vast treasure preserved from oblivion and neglect in the pages of his books. A light creamy-white mulatta with a round face, a soft voice, and a modest smile—a very charming person—she concluded her words of gratitude and affection by addressing the deceased: "Your blessing, Father Archanjo." Delving as she had in fields which he had cleared, wandering down lanes and short cuts opened up by the author of *Daily Life in Bahia*, the folklorist, amid all that formality and all those eloquent and empty words, seemed a reverent daughter of the *terreiro* kneeling before her little father. At that instant, the figure of Archanjo was strongly present in the room. Only for a brief moment, though, for the next to take the floor was Batista, the famous academician and principal speaker of the evening. Professor Ramos had not come from Rio after all, for the same reasons as those advanced by Professor Azevedo. "Maidenly sensibility," snorted Dr. Zèzinho. He was an old whore in politics and had no choice but to swallow cheerfully every insult and affront (all the toads and snakes, as the saying goes).

So far all of the speeches had been reasonably short; none had lasted more than half an hour. The speakers had followed Secretary Calazans's advice: "Half an hour for each one adds up to three hours of oratory, and that's about as much as the public can stand." However, when our acquaintance Batista mounted the platform, gloom settled on every face, and if there was no general rush for the exit it was only out of consideration for the *City News*, Dr. Zèzinho, the governor there in his own person, and, to be truthful, a certain degree of fear. Professor Batista was one of those in command of the present situation and had been responsible, so people said, for many accusations and not a few trials of subversives. In these circumstances, there was little room for hope: he was free to take advantage of the situation as much as he liked and drone on and on for as many hours as he chose.

Part of his voluminous oration had been written some time ago, in fact, during Levenson's visit to Bahia. It had been intended for the dinner in his honor which the eccentric Nobel Prize winner had refused to attend because he was more interested in the life of the common people and the charms of Ana Mercedes than in making the acquaintance of eminent persons. To this old beginning the prolix Batista had added some chapters concerning Archanjo and related problems of general and immediate interest. He had thus composed what the *City News* reporter described as "a masterly piece of erudition and patriotism." Masterly and interminable.

And rather polemical, as well. In the first place, Batista had a bone to pick with James D. Levenson, arguing that science and culture were not the gringo's exclusive prerogative: he himself, although recognizing the North American's merit, was not afraid to cross swords with him. He lauded Levenson above all for his titles, his professorship, his Nobel Prize, and his nationality, worthy of every encomium. What he criticized was Levenson's continual attitude of scientific heresy, his lack of respect for those on whom honor had already been bestowed, the nonchalance with which he broke taboos and called august celebrities "sanctimonious charlatans." Then he picked a quarrel with Archanjo. To Batista's way of thinking, the man who was being so much honored that night, the object of the generous approbation of those present, should never have gone beyond the limits of his research into folklore, "which, though riddled with all kinds of defects, does represent a promising attempt and deserves for this reason to be studied by scholars." By aspiring, however, to glean a harvest from ground already tilled by scholars of the stature of Nilo Argolo and Oswaldo Fontes, "he wrote outlandish absurdities without the slightest, most fragile leg to stand on." Batista did not dwell for very long on the subject of Pedro Archanjo, however. Most of his speech was a hymn of praise to "the true tradition, the only tradition truly worthy of eulogy, the tradition of the Christian Brazilian Family." Professor Batista had recently assumed the presidency of the worthy Association in Defense of Tradition, the Family, and Private Property, and he felt a personal responsibility for the national security. He was an Argus-eyed secret agent who saw enemies of Brazil and the régime everywhere. He even suspected certain individuals in the highest ranks of state government of being in collusion with subversives and he was known to have denounced a few of them—please don't ask who or to whom, Dona Edelweiss.

All things come to an end, and Batista's dire oration ended at about 11:30 that night, in an atmosphere of heavy silence from the unanimously discomfited audience. Judging by what they had seen and heard, if Archanjo had dared to show his face there the speaker would probably have called the police.

With a sigh of relief, the governor prepared to adjourn the meeting.

"If no one else wants the floor . . ."

"I want the floor!"

It was Major Damião de Souza. Late as usual, his eyes bloodshot because by then he had absorbed a fair amount of the alcoholic resources of Bahia, he had entered the room just as the virtuous Batista began his deadly harangue. With him was a ragged *mulata* in an advanced state of pregnancy, not at all at ease in such splendid surroundings. The major addressed the poet and sociologist Pena:

"Bard! Give your seat to this poor gal. She's in the family way and she can't stay on her feet for very long."

Fausto Pena obediently got up. With him, all solidarity and melting glances, rose a fragile authoress, the newest chicken in the poet's brood, who had recently made her debut in the Young Poets' Column.

"Sit down, my dear," the major said to the *mulata*.

He seated himself in the other empty chair, fixed his gaze on the speaker, and immediately fell asleep. The clapping woke him in time to ask for the floor.

On the podium, after directing a melancholy glance at the glass of mineral water—"Why don't they have the sense to offer speakers beer?"—he saluted the dignitaries and that "nosegay of talent" gathered to pay tribute to Pedro Archanjo, teacher of the people, the man who had taught the major himself his ABC's; a learned man who had attained greatness through his own efforts, a name to be conjured with in Bahia, one who, with Ruy Barbosa and Castro Alves, made up the "Sublime Trinity of Genius." After Batista's murky, oppressive speech, punctuated with innuendo and veiled threats, the major's words, grandiloquent, baroque, and quintessentially Bahian, made the air fit to breathe again and earned him a cheerful round of applause. The major spread his arms dramatically: "Very good, ladies and gentlemen! All of these tributes made to Master Archanjo during this month of December by the cream of the Bahian intelligentsia, all are very just and very wonderful, but . . ."

"If you lit a match in front of his mouth you'd set him on fire," murmured the president of the institute to the governor, but his words were full of fond indulgence. Major Damião de Souza's hoarse voice and *cachaça*-laden breath were a thousand times better than the abstemious Batista's well-pitched voice and sinister gaze.

With outstretched arms and a sob in his voice, the major reached his peroration: so many parties, so many speeches, so much praise of Archanjo, who deserved all of this and much besides—but let's look at the other side of the coin! Archanjo's family, Archanjo's descendants, Archanjo's relatives, are wasting away in the greatest misery, suffering hunger and cold. And right here in this room in which such a great celebration is taking place, right before your eyes is one of Archanjo's close relatives, mother of seven children and about to give birth to her eighth—a poor widow, still mourning the death of her beloved husband, a poor widow in need of a doctor, a hospital, medicine, money to buy food for the children . . . Here in this very room where praises have been heaped on Pedro Archanjo, right here before us. . . .

He pointed to the *mulata* sitting in the chair:

"Stand up, my dear, stand up so that all these people can see the condition of a descendant, a close relative of the immortal Pedro Archanjo, glory of Bahia and Brazil, glory of our native land!"

She stood up with her head bowed, not knowing what to do with her hands or where to look, with her stuffed belly, run-over shoes, and worn-out dress, a symbol of rock-bottom poverty. A few people craned their necks to see better.

"Ladies and gentlemen, instead of adjectives and fine words, I beg you to give a mite to this poor widow in whose veins runs the blood of Pedro Archanjo!"

He finished speaking and got down from the podium with his hat in his hand. Beginning at the chairman's table, he collected money from every one of those present. When he reached the back of the room the governor pronounced the session closed "with this meritorious exercise of Christian charity," and the major emptied the notes of different values, the whole pile of money, into the lap of the embarrassed beneficiary. When his hat was empty he took Arno Melo by the arm and said:

"*Meu negro*, come treat me to a glass of beer. My mouth is dry and I'm stiff as a board."

And so the two men went off to the Bizarria Bar with Ana Mercedes on Arno's arm, anchored at last in the safe port of advertising and publicity. She proved to be a marvel at making contracts; no client could resist her powers of persuasion. Once outside the hall Arno said to the major: "Do you mind if I kiss her? It's been three hours since I tasted her lips, and I heard so much garbage in there, it made me so hungry I may die if I don't kiss her." "Go ahead, old man, get rid of what's ailing you, but don't take too long; don't forget you've got some nice cold beer waiting for you. Afterward, if you want to, I'll show you where there's a nice little castle from Archanjo's time."

As the room emptied Professor Fraga Neto, whose goatee and mustache were now quite white but who was still as lively and argumentative as ever, went up to Pedro Archanjo's poor relation:

"Archanjo was a friend of mine, my dear, but I didn't know he had any family or that he had left descendants. Whose daughter are you? What relation are you to him?"

The *mulata*, who had still not recovered from her bashfulness, tightly clutched the cheap purse into which she had thrust the bills—she had never seen so much money before in her life!— and looked up at the inquiring old gentleman before her:

"*Meu senhor*, I don't know anything about that, sir. I didn't know that Archanjo they were talking about, I don't even know who he was, today's the first time I ever heard of him. But the rest of it's all true. I need everything, I've got little children, I don't have seven but I do have four, yes sir, my man didn't die but he did go off and leave me without a nickel in the house . . . So I went to look for the major to see if he could help me. I found him there in the Triunfo Bar, he told me he didn't have any money but he said to come with him to a place where he'd get me some. So he brought me here . . ." She smiled and walked out the door. In spite of her pregnant state she swayed her hips and walked with a rolling gait just like Archanjo's.

Professor Fraga Neto smiled, too, and shook his head. From Zèzinho Pinto's initial inspiration to the closing words of that speech by Batista on Tradition and Property—the dangerous fool! —everything about this centennial had been a farce and a lie, a string of absurdities. Maybe the only honest thing about it, after all, was the major's clever ruse, the pregnant, hungry *mulata* jade, false descendant, true relation, Archanjo's people, Archanjo's world. He repeated the words he knew by heart: "The shrewdness and ingenuity of the people is the only truth; no power will ever succeed in denying or corrupting it."

Of the land

of magic

and reality

In the Carnival of 1969, the Sons of Tororó took to the streets with a theme of "Pedro Archanjo in Four Movements" which was highly successful and won several prizes. The samba school paraded through the city singing the theme song by Waldir Lima, who won the composer's award by defeating five strong competitors:

Thrilling author
Sensational realist

He dazzled the world
Oh! Pedro Archanjo the genius
Whose life in four movements
We'll show you in this carnival.

Finally Ana Mercedes had her chance to be Rosa de Oxalá,
and she was not outdone by the original in voluptuous coquetry.
The crowd went wild at her revolving behind, breasts bobbing
under her lace and cambric shift, ardent eyes demanding a bed
and an engine in high gear—oh, that *mulata* wasn't born for any
pipsqueak to pee on, oh no! Was there a man in the crowd who
didn't dream of her long thighs, her smooth belly, her proffered
navel? Drunks and masked revelers threw themselves at her dancing feet.

Ana Mercedes did her dance among the highest steppers from
the popular samba clubs, each of whom represented a character in
the story: Lídio Corró, Budião, Valdeloir, Manuel de Praxedes,
Aussá, and Paco Muñoz. In the float rode the *Afoxé* of the Sons
of Bahia: the Ambassador, the Dancer, Zumbí and Domingos
Jorge Velho, the Negroes of Palmares, the imperial soldiers, the
beginning of the struggle for freedom. They sang their hearts out:

> *From the land of magic and reality*
> *The grandeur of our nation's mind*
> *He drew from people and from things*
> *A lyrical spontaneity.*

Kirsi made of snow and wheat, dressed as the Morning Star,
came at the head of the folk play of the shepherds, so blond, so
white, a lovely *sarará* from Scandinavia. The float which doubtless made the greatest impact was one on which a good part of
the feminine contingent, dozens and dozens of women including
famous beauties, actresses, princesses, and domestics of the highest quality, reclined in sensual poses on the colossal bed which
took up the whole float. Preceding it on a raised platform, the
master of ceremonies displayed a placard bearing the title of that
allegory of so many women sharing one infinite bed: *PEDRO
ARCHANJO'S SWEET LABOR.* There they all were, talking
and laughing: concubines, *comadres*, prostitutes, married women,

virgins, black women, white women, *mulatas,* Sabina dos Anjos, Rosenda, Rosália, Risoleta, pensive Terência, Quelé, Dedé, each in her turn, jumping out of the bed half-naked to join the samba circle:

> Glória glória
> *Brazilian mulatto*
> *Of our time*
> Glória glória.

Then the *candomblé* with its adepts, *iaôs,* and *orixás* dancing to the sound of *atabaque* drums and *agogôs,* iron bells, gourds, and rattles. Procópio being flogged in a sinister ballet by the secret police. Ogun, the huge Negro as big as a house, making Assistant Police Chief Pedrito Gordo run for his life as he peed in his pants. The invincible dance went on.

The *capoeira* wrestlers traded impossible blows. Mané Lima and his Fat Lady danced the maxixe and the tango. The old lady with an open parasol, a ruffled skirt, and cancan rhythm was the Countess Isabel Tereza Martins de Araújo e Pinho, Zabela to her friends, Princess of the Recôncavo, gay *parisienne.*

Wrapped in red-tissue-paper flames and with devil's horns on her head, Dorotéia announced the end of the procession and disappeared in a blaze of sulphur.

> *Let us now praise his glory*
> *And his great works*
> *As this is God's own world*
> *Everything we've shown on the avenue*
> *Are stories lived and stories true*
> *You can read them in his books.*

Capoeira wrestlers, *filhas-de-santo, iaôs,* shepherdesses, *orixás,* pageant of the Three Kings and the *afoxé,* high-stepping dancers, luscious beauties, sing, dance, and make way: Master Pedro Archanjo Ojuobá is coming through:

> *Glória glória*
> *Glória glória.*

Pedro Archanjo Ojuobá's dancing by, not one but several, many, multiple: old, middle-aged, young, adolescent; vagabond, dancer, fine talker, hard drinker, rebel, radical, striker, street fighter, guitar and *cavaquinho* player, wooer, tender lover, studhorse, writer, sage, sorcerer.

And every one of them mulatto, indigent, native of Bahia.

Vila Aroeira, in the fraternal house of Nair and Genaro de Carvalho, Bahia, March to July, 1969.

GLOSSARY

adê—Emblem of African divinity Dadá (elder brother of Xangô).

afoxé—Afro-Brazilian Carnival group.

agogô—Double metal bell played in Carnival and *candomblé* rites.

alabê—Drummer at *candomblé* ceremonies.

amalá—See *carurú:* a similar dish, but thicker in consistency.

atabaque—Tall drum played in *candomblé* rites.

axé—*Candomblé* spell.

axexê—West African funeral ritual.

axogun—Member of *candomblé* sect charged with performing ritual sacrifices.

babalaô—*Candomblé* priest and soothsayer.

babalorixá—Pai-de-santo, priest in *candomblé* rites.

balangandan—Gold or silver brooch hung with charms and amulets, worn by Negro women in Bahia.

bandeirante—Early Brazilian pioneer (lit. "flag-bearer").

batucada—*Batuque* rhythm or dance.

batuque—Any Afro-Brazilian dance or Carnival march accompanied by percussion instruments.

berimbau—Word of unknown origin (also spelled *berimbão, birimbão*) used in Brazil for two musical instruments: a musical bow whose string passes through a gourd resonator held against the player's chest or stomach and is tapped with a small stick; and a form of jew's-harp.

bumba-meu-boi—Traditional popular dance and pageant of Northeast Brazil.

caboclo—Person of mixed white and Indian blood. At times, term is loosely applied to inhabitants of backlands of whatever race.

cachaça—White rum, firewater.

camará—Short for *camarada*, comrade, or Whitmanesque form "*camarado*."

camaradinho—Little pal.

candomblé—The great annual celebration of the Afro-Brazilian cult. Term is also applied to voodoo ceremonies in general.

cangaceiro—Brazilian bandit of the backlands.

capoeira—Style of fighting brought from Africa by Negroes of Angola in the sixteenth century, in which they use hands and feet and head-butting, although in the past they at times also resorted to razors and daggers. As graceful as a ballet.

capoeirista—*Capoeira* wrestler.

caruru—Okra or other greens cooked with fish, pepper, and palm oil.

catedrático—University professor, usually with lifetime tenure.

cavaquinho—Four-stringed guitar; ukulele.

caxixi—Stringed gourd (musical instrument).

comadre, compadre—Godmother, godfather, in relation to godchild's parents. By extension, intimate friend, crony, gossip.

cruzeiro—The Brazilian monetary unit. Replaced the milreis in 1942.

cucumbí—Afro-Brazilian secret ceremony.

dendê—Palm oil, a staple in West African and Bahian cooking.

ebiri—Emblem of the venerable African water divinity Nãnã.

efó—Afro-Brazilian dish of shrimp, greens, red pepper, and *dendê*.

egun—Spirit of the dead.

Eparrei—Greeting by devotees to *candomblé* divinity Yansan.

eruexim—Horsetail whip, emblem of Yansan.

erukerê—Oxtail fan, emblem of Oxossi.

Euá—African divinity of pools and fountains.

Exú—Mischievous, restless divinity, messenger of the other gods. Sometimes erroneously identified with the Devil.

fazenda—Large farm or ranch.

fazendeiro—Rancher, landowner.

feijoada—Typical Brazilian dish made of black beans cooked with pork sausage, dried beef, and peppers and served with rice and manioc meal.

figa—Fertility symbol and good-luck charm in the shape of a clenched fist with the thumb clasped between the forefinger and middle finger.

gafieira—Low-class samba dive; shindig.

ganzá—Rattlebox (musical instrument).

iaba—Female devil.

iaô—Votary of an *orixá* (African divinity) who dances, is possessed by that spirit, and goes into trance during *candomblé* rituals.

igualita—"Just like" (Spanish).

ilú—Round drum of the Ijexá nation, smaller than an *atabaque*.

itá—Fetishistic emblem of an *orixá*.

iyá—Mother (Yoruba).

iyakêkêrê—Singer in *candomblé* ceremonies.

iyalorixá—*Mãe-de-santo*, *candomblé* priestess.

lundu—Sensual African dance.

macumba—Brazilian version of voodoo or fetishism. Cf. *candomblé*.

mãe-de-santo—*Candomblé* priestess (lit. "saint-mother"), interpreter of instructions of *orixá*'s.

malagueta—Red pepper.

milreis—Former Brazilian monetary unit. Replaced in 1942 by cruzeiro.

obá—King (Yoruba); male dignitary in *candomblé*.

ogan—Dignitary of the *candomblé*. It is the duty of *ogan*'s to look after the ceremonial site.

Ogun—African divinity, patron of warriors, farmers, all who use iron tools or weapons. Syncretized with St. Anthony.

ojuobá—Eyes of the King (Yoruba).

Omolú—African divinity of disease and pestilence.

orixá—West African divinity, half saint, half animistic spirit. When the *candomblé* was forbidden in Brazil, the *orixá*'s were syncretized with Christian saints.

Ossain—Lord of medicinal herbs and liturgical rites.

Oxalá—Lord of Creation; greatest of *orixá*'s. Syncretized with Our Lord of Bonfim.

Oxalufan—Old Oxalá.

Oxossi—God of hunters and the forest. Syncretized with St. George.

Oxumarê—Hermaphrodite god of the rainbow, symbolized by a cobra. Syncretized with St. Bartholomew.

Oxun—River goddess; second wife of Xangô.

pai-de-santo—*Candomblé* priest (lit. "saint-father").

paxorô—Ornate staff surmounted by a bird, carried by Oxalufan or Xangô.

pejí—Fetishistic altar.

pinga—Rum; booze.

rancho—Carnival march, usually slow and majestic. Not "ranch," except in southern Brazil.

Recôncavo—A large and fertile region on the coast of Bahia.

sarará—Light-skinned, freckled mulatto with blue or green eyes and red hair.

Sinhá—Missy; missus.

terreiro—Fetishistic temple or sacred ground.

tostões—Brazilian coins. A *tostão* is ten centavos.

vatapá—Chicken stewed in coconut milk and seasoned with sliced shrimp, onions, *malagueta*, and olive oil.

Xangô—African thunder-god. Syncretized with St. Jerome.

xaréu—Jackfish.

xaxará—Emblem of Omolú.

xinxim—Chicken stewed with shrimp, onions, and crushed squash or watermelon seeds.

Yansan—Goddess of winds, storms, and waterfalls; principal wife of Xangô. Syncretized with St. Barbara.

Yemanjá—Water goddess; mother of the gods. Syncretized with Our Lady of the Immaculate Conception.